A BOOK-OF-THE-MONTH CLUB
Alternate Selection
Benjamin Franklin Awards
"Best Career Title"

What Others Are Saying...

"Dennis Damp's book is simply the best. He covers all aspects of applying, interviewing and then getting a job with the federal government and provides many useful tips and references... Damp's book is by far the top of the class. I highly recommend this book for anyone interested in getting a job with the federal government and jobs counselors as a useful resource in your reference library. This book is the A to Z on the federal job search process and a must read for federal job seekers."

— Mark S., OH, Ebook Reviews

"If ever a book's tittle described its content, this one does...this valuable reference tool continues to provide essential information and advice for those seeking to obtain secure, high-paying federal government jobs. A useful and popular source on the process of finding government employment, this is recommended."

— LIBRARY JOURNAL

"The Book of U.S. Government Jobs is a no-nonsense career resource that explains in plain terms where available American government jobs are and how to get one... Point-by-point requirements, recommendations, and contact information for each institution from which one can seek employment form the heart of this handy and easy-to-use resource."

— BOOKWATCH

"Updated guide to the federal employment process provides information that can improve a person's chances of government employment..."

— JOURNAL OF ECONOMIC LITERATURE

"The Book of U.S. Government Jobs is an easy-to-read book with plenty of graphics and well-written text. It clearly introduces students to Uncle Sam's world."

— CAREER OPPORTUNITIES NEWS

"A year ago you gave me pointers on finding a federal job. Well, it all worked out and I'm a paralegal specialist in Oklahoma. I just wanted to say thanks."

— J.G., Tulsa, OK

Books by Dennis V. Damp

The Book of U.S. Government Jobs (1st through 10th editions)
Health Care Job Explosion! (1th through 4th editions)
Post Office Jobs (1st through 4th editions)
Take Charge of Your Federal Career (1998)
Dollars & Sense (1989)

THE BOOK OF U.S.
GOVERNMENT JOBS

WHERE THEY ARE,
WHAT'S AVAILABLE
& HOW TO GET ONE

Dennis V. Damp

Tenth Edition
Completely Revised

Bookhaven Press LLC
McKees Rocks, Pennsylvania

The Book of
U.S. GOVERNMENT JOBS
Where They Are, What's Available, and How to Get One
By Dennis V. Damp

BOOKHAVEN PRESS LLC
249 Field Club Circle
McKees Rocks, PA 15136
Orders@BookhavenPress.com; http://BookhavenPress.com

Copyright © 1986 through 2008 by Dennis V. Damp

First Edition 1986. Tenth Edition/Twentieth Printing 2008, Completely Revised
Printed in the United States of America

Disclaimer of All Warranties and Liabilities

Library of Congress Catalog-in-Publication Data

Damp, Dennis V.
        The book of U.S. Government jobs: where they are, what's available, and how to get one / Dennis V. Damp. -- 10th ed., completely rev.
        p. cm.
    ISBN-13: 978-0-943641-26-3 (alk. paper)
    ISBN-10: 0-943641-26-8
    1. Civil service positions --United States. I. Title: II: Book of US government jobs.
    III. Title: Book of United States government jobs.
    JK716D36 2007
    331.12'4135173--dc22
                    2007016802

For information on distribution or quantity discount rates, telephone 412/494-6926 or write to: Sales Department, Bookhaven Press LLC, 249 Field Club Circle, McKees Rocks, PA 15136. Distributed to the trade by Midpoint Trade Books, 27 West 20th Street, Suite 1102, New York, NY 10011, Tel: 212-727-0190. Individuals can order this title with credit card toll free (ORDERS ONLY) at 1-800-782-7424.

Table of Contents

About the Author

DENNIS DAMP is the author of over 21 books and a recognized government employment expert. He retired in 2004 at age 55 with 35 years of federal government service. He can attest at first hand to how rewarding civil service employment can be – and was in his case. Dennis has been a guest on hundreds of radio talk shows, lectured at universities and colleges, and has written hundreds of articles for national magazines and newspapers. He is a contributing writer for Monster.com and other Web portals and his books have been featured in the Wall Street Journal, Washington Post, New York Times, and U.S. News & World Report.

His government career began when he was drafted in 1968. Dennis joined the Air Force prior to call-up and spent over three years on active duty and an additional seven years with the Air National Guard. He was hired by the Department of Defense (DOD) to maintain aircraft avionics systems after leaving the service and eventually landed an electronics technician position with the Federal Aviation Administration (FAA) in 1975. He spent the remainder of his career in various positions with the FAA.

During his time with the FAA, Dennis worked on staff in various positions including training instructor, project engineer, computer based instruction (CBI) administrator, training program manager and program support manager. The last 20 years included numerous supervisory and management positions where he was responsible for recruiting, rating and interviewing applicants, outreach, and hiring for his organization. His last position was technical operations manager at the Greater Pittsburgh International Airport's air traffic control tower.

Dennis based this book on his 35 years of personal government experience. This all-new 10th edition presents an insider's first-hand view of what it takes to go from job hunter to hired employee, and everything in between, to improve your chances of landing a high-paying government job.

Preface

This completely updated and expanded edition features the latest information available for finding and applying for federal government jobs. The author and editors have over 110 years of combined federal government service. Considering that federal employees earn an average annual compensation of $106,871, including pay and benefits, compared to $53,288 in the private sector — according to the United States Bureau of Economic Analysis — the federal sector is an attractive option for job seekers.

The federal government's new recruiting, outreach, and retention programs are attracting new applicants with lucrative incentives. Today federal agencies can pay off new hires' student loans, negotiate starting salaries, and offer relocation allowances for critical vacancies.

Readers will find an expanded application and résumé chapter that takes readers step-by-step through a typical job announcement and instructs readers on how to write effective federal style résumés and Knowledge, Skills, and Abilities (KSAs) statements. Résumé samples, compiled by the author and Kathryn Kraemer Troutman, the author of *Federal Résumé Guidebook,* are included to guide job seekers through the sometimes confusing application process.

Considerable improvements were implemented over the past few years to the archaic Civil Service examination process. Uncle Sam has finally dropped most general and administrative written entrance examinations and substituted an ***"Occupational Questionnaire"*** and/or ***"Self Certification"*** in most cases. New applicants for certain occupations may still be required to take written tests, but most agencies, other than the U.S. Postal Service, forgo testing and opt to use Occupational Questionnaires.

Agencies are still evolving since the September 11 attacks and the massive reorganization that established the Department of Homeland Security (DHS). DHS was established to consolidate law enforcement and security functions, and 22 agencies transferred significant operational functions and personnel to Homeland Security since its inception.

The impact of this reorganization and the increased security requirements in all agencies have changed government demographics. An entire chapter is devoted to law enforcement and DHS careers and the many job opportunities that are now available in the government's third largest agency. DHS employs more than 154,000 workers in hundreds of occupations.

Many changes were initiated since the previous edition was published. Agencies — across the board — have implemented *"pay for performance"* programs and placed workers in core compensation pay bands. Their pay is tied to performance rather than automatic General Schedule step increases. Lucrative recruitment incentives were authorized by Congress, programs such as the Veterans Recruitment Appointment (VRA) were revised, and the student hiring program was reorganized under the eScholar program. This edition also added information on the Senior Executive Service (SES), and all these changes expanded the new 10th edition to 352 pages.

Decentralization continues to evolve in the federal sector. The Office of Personnel Management (OPM) was originally the central human resource department for most agencies. Today, most agencies recruit and advertise vacancies in-house. Decentralization has created new challenges for those seeking federal employment. Job seekers may have to visit specific agency Web sites to locate all current job vacancies. This book's companion Web site offers hot links to 143 federal recruitment sites at http://federaljobs.net.

The federal government's total civilian workforce as of September 2006 was 2,700,392, a slight decrease in total employment since the last edition of this book. Approximately 50 percent of the federal workforce is currently eligible for either early or regular retirement. This is creating significant employment opportunities for anyone interested in working for Uncle Sam. Over 1.3 million jobs will need to be filled as the baby boomers opt to leave government service.

This Tenth Edition of *The Book of U.S. Government Jobs* will help job seekers land high-paying, benefit-loaded, and secure government jobs. Updates will be posted on http://federaljobs.net to complement the new Tenth Edition, including revised Web site addresses, job hotlines, resources, and program changes.

If you're looking for a position with good pay with excellent benefits, explore the high-paying and secure federal job market. The average annual salary for all full-time employees was $67,186 in December 2005, and you can work at thousands of stateside and overseas locations. Use this book's resources, including the Job Hunter's Checklist in Appendix A, to begin your personal job search.

Dennis V. Damp

Acknowledgments

I haven't cited all the sources and authorities that were consulted in the preparation of this guide. The list would include numerous federal departments and human resource specialists, system specialists, federal job seekers I've interviewed along the way, librarians, periodicals, thousands of federal directives and regulations, and hundreds of Internet Web sites.

I would like to thank my cover designer, Salvatori Concialdi, for his exceptional work, and guest editors Perry Barker, retired FAA manager with 35 years of service, and Chuck Jumpeter, a recent federal retiree with 40 years of service and a highly respected consultant, independent business owner, and our *Health Awareness Forum* contributing writer.

Kathryn Kraemer Troutman, noted author, consultant, and owner of The Résumé Place, contributed federal résumé samples for Chapter Six to help job hunters understand the significance of writing a professional federal style résumé. Dennis Damp Jr. edited and updated several of the appendices and our chief editor Robert A. Juran provided valuable insight and input.

Others include: Kate Bandos, KSB Promotions; Karen Church and Brenda Cook, Office of Personnel Management (OPM) specialists; James Rankin, Bureau of Economic Analysis; Tracy Graham, USPS HR specialist; and Eric Kampmann, Gail Kump, Chris Bell, and Margaret Queen, Midpoint Trade Books. Many of my former associates and friends in the Federal Aviation Administration inadvertently contributed over the years as I either relied on their succinct counsel and guidance or participated with them on various committees, rating panels, interviews, and selection panels. They include Richard Fisher, Conley Powell, Frank Cullen, Loretta Kusk, Abby Moserowitz, Thomas Simko, Charles Siebott, James Preston, Carl Didio, Carole Rossi Meyer, Edward Manges, Judy Torcivia, Dennis Hays, Linda Giordano, and many others.

I wish to sincerely thank all who contributed. Without their input, counsel, and guidance over the years this book could not have been written.

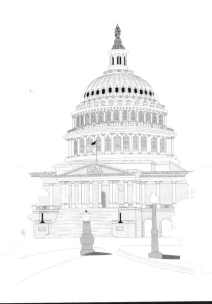

CHAPTER ONE
Introduction to
Government Employment

Why not consider working for Uncle Sam? There are over 2,700,000 federal civilian employees, of whom half are now eligible for regular or early retirement. Over a million jobs must be filled as baby boomers say so long to their federal careers. I was at the front end of the baby boomer exodus and retired in 2004 at the age of 55 with 35½ years of service. My last position was manager of technical operations for the Federal Aviation Administration at Pittsburgh's air traffic control tower. I know first-hand how rewarding a federal career can be, and was in my case. This book offers an insider's perspective of what it takes to go from job hunter to hired and everything in between.

The average annual salary now exceeds $67,186.

There are many reasons to consider federal employment. The average annual federal worker's compensation, pay plus benefits, is **$106,871** compared to **$53,288** for the private sector.[1] Student loan payoff, relocation, and cash incentives are now offered for hard-to-fill positions and the benefits package is exceptional.

Each chapter lists objectives, as noted below, to present the key elements included in the chapter. The image to the right is used throughout this book to highlight points of interest.

CHAPTER OBJECTIVES

- Understanding the opportunities
- Determining the nature of federal employment, working conditions, occupations, training, outlook, pay and benefits
- What benefits to expect including retirement
- How to develop your career and get promoted
- What education and qualifications are required

---

[1] Bureau of Economic Analysis, National Income & Product Account Tables 6.2D and 6.5D, 2005.

It is difficult to imagine just how large the federal job market is until you compare it to its closest private-sector rival. Wal-Mart is the largest company world-wide, with annual sales of $346.5 billion and 1.8 million workers. There are Wal-Marts and Sam's Clubs located in most metropolitan areas. Most people aren't aware that Uncle Sam employs **2,700,392** workers, almost a million more workers than Wal-Mart, and from 2001 through 2006 hired an average of **238,184** employees annually to replace workers who transferred to other jobs, retired, or stopped working for other reasons.[2] The **average annual salary for all pay plans was $67,186 in 2005.**[3] The U.S. government is the largest employer in the United States, hiring approximately 2 percent of the nation's civilian workforce.

Job hunters will find helpful information and resources in this book to re-search employment options, locate job vacancies, understand the federal job market, and apply for federal jobs. Numerous programs, options, and resources are reviewed and explained in detail, including:

- How to approach the federal sector and identify available recruit-ment incentives including the Student Loan Repayment Program that is now offered for hard-to-fill vacancies.

- How to complete and tailor federal-style résumés to the job an-nouncement to obtain the highest rating and attract the selecting official's attention.

- Learn an easy and effective way to evaluate job announcements and write effective Knowledge, Skills, Abilities, and Other Charac-teristics (KSAOs) statements that are required for certain jobs.

- Most non-Postal Service federal jobs, over 80 percent, don't require written exams. Determine whether your occupation requires a writ-ten entrance exam and if one is required how to prepare for it.

- Over a thousand resources are listed, including interactive employ-ment Web sites, contact numbers for personnel specialists, and 24-hour telephone job vacancy auto-response request lines.

- You will learn about the Student Educational Employment Program, veterans preference and the Veterans Recruitment Appointment (VRA) programs, hiring opportunities for the disabled, Post Office jobs, and much more.

- Prepare for interviews, learn about overseas job options, and law en-forcement opportunities, and use our comprehensive agency direc-tory and other resources to network and locate positions.

---

[2] The Fact Book, Federal Civilian Workforce Statistics, February 2005 and the new hire figures from OPM's Employment Cubes, for years 2005 and 2006, located at http://www.fedscope.opm.gov/index.asp.

[3] Congressional Budget Office, Characteristics and Pay of Federal Civilian Employees, March 2007

You need to know how to take
advantage of the federal hiring system
and recent changes to successfully land
the job you want in government.

Excellent job opportunities are available for those who know how to tap this lucrative job market. All government hiring is based on performance and qualifications regardless of your gender, race, color, creed, religion, disability, or national origin. Where else can you apply for a high-paying entry-level job that offers employment at thousands of locations internationally, excellent career advancement opportunities, and careers in hundreds of occupations?

From 1996 through 2004 the federal government has hired as many as 1,092,888 people in 2000 and as few as 199,463 in 1996 nationwide.[4] In the year 2000 over half of the new hires were temporary employees hired by the Census Bureau. Add another 40,000 Postal Service vacancies to that figure to see the total picture. Other vacancies exist in the legislative and judicial branches. Numerous job opportunities are available for those willing to seek them out.

> Many additional opportunities will be created as those who are at or beyond retirement age opt to retire. Approximately 50 percent of the total workforce is now eligible for regular or early retirement; that's **1,340,000** vacancies.

The following statistical analysis will help you focus on just where the greatest opportunities are. The largest agencies are featured and their employment trends analyzed. Large agencies hire a broad spectrum of workers in hundreds of occupations. It's best to expand your search to as many agencies as possible to improve your chances.

Seven agencies, including the Postal Service, employ approximately 80 percent of the workforce, or 2,147,363 employees. Of the 88,700 overseas jobs, 72 percent, or 67,804, are U.S. citizens. The remaining overseas employees are foreign nationals. The changes from the previous Ninth Edition in Table 1-1 show that one of the largest departments decreased in size and five increased.. The Department of Homeland Security increased by 19,576 employees. Overall, the total employment decreased slightly, by less than 1 percent, while the Judicial branch decreased by 0.1 percent and the Legislative branch by 1 percent. The largest change was in the Treasury Department – from 126,408 workers in 2004 to 106,623 in 2005, for a loss of 20,582. Many of the positions were transferred to the Department of Homeland Security over the last several years.

---

[4] The Fact Book – Federal Civilian Workforce Statistics, July 2006.

TABLE 1-1
The Six Largest Federal Departments

Total Workforce	**2,700,392**	**100 %**
Legislative branch	29,486	1.10 %
Judicial branch	33,760	1.30 %
USPS & PRC *	757,467	28.00 %
Executive (non-postal)	1,879,679	69.60 %
❶ Defense	677,744	
❷ Veterans Affairs	239,299	
❸ Homeland Security	154,100	
❹ Treasury	106,925	
❺ Justice	106,781	
❻ Agriculture	105,047	
All Other	389,783	

* The United States Postal Service (USPS) and the Postal Rate Commission (PRC).
Federal Civilian Workforce Statistics – September 2006

NATURE OF FEDERAL EMPLOYMENT

The federal government's essential duties include defending the United States from foreign aggression and terrorism, representing U.S. interests abroad, enforcing laws and regulations, and administering domestic programs and agencies.[5] U.S. citizens are particularly aware of the federal government when they pay their income taxes each year, but they usually do not consider the government's role when they watch a weather forecast, purchase fresh and uncontaminated groceries, travel by highway or air, or make a deposit at their bank. Workers employed by the federal government play a vital role in these and many other aspects of our daily lives.

This book describes federal government civilian career opportunities, including jobs with the Postal Service (an independent agency of the federal government). Armed forces career opportunities are described in the current edition of the Occupational Outlook Handbook

---

[5] The 2006-07 Career Guide to Industries, U.S. Department of Labor

Over 200 years ago, the founders of the United States gathered in Philadelphia to create a Constitution for a new national government and lay the foundation for self-governance. The Constitution of the United States, ratified by the last of the 13 original states in 1791, created the three branches of the federal government and granted certain powers and responsibilities to each. The legislative, judicial, and executive branches were created with equal powers but very different responsibilities that act to keep their powers in balance.

The legislative branch is responsible for forming and amending the legal structure of the nation. Its largest component is Congress, the primary U.S. legislative body, which is made up of the Senate and the House of Representatives. This body includes senators, representatives, their staffs, and various support workers. The legislative branch employs only about 2 percent of federal workers, nearly all of whom work in the Washington, D.C. area.

The judicial branch is responsible for interpreting the laws that the legislative branch enacts. The Supreme Court, the nation's definitive judicial body, makes the highest rulings. Its decisions usually follow the appeal of a decision made by the one of the regional Courts of Appeal, which hear cases appealed from U.S. District Courts, the Court of Appeals for the Federal Circuit, or state Supreme Courts. U.S. District Courts are located in each state and are the first to hear most cases under federal jurisdiction. The judicial branch employs about the same number of people as does the legislative branch, but its offices and employees are dispersed throughout the country.

Of the three branches, the executive branch — through the power vested by the Constitution in the office of the president — has the widest range of responsibilities. Consequently, it employed 96 percent of all federal civilian employees (excluding Postal Service workers) in 2006. The executive branch is composed of the Executive Office of the President, 15 executive Cabinet departments, including the newly created Department of Homeland Security, and nearly 90 independent agencies, each of which has clearly defined duties. The Executive Office of the President is composed of several offices and councils that aid the president in policy decisions. These include the Office of Management and Budget, which oversees the administration of the federal budget; the National Security Council, which advises the president on matters of national defense; and the Council of Economic Advisers, which makes economic policy recommendations.

Each of the 15 executive Cabinet departments administers programs that oversee an aspect of life in the United States. The highest departmental official of each Cabinet department, the secretary, is a member of the president's Cabinet. The 15 departments, listed by employment size, are listed below with a brief description and total employment.

Defense: (675,744) Manages the military forces that protect our country and its interests, including the Departments of the Army, Navy, and Air Force and a number of smaller agencies. The civilian workforce employed by the Department of Defense performs various support activities, such as payroll and public relations.

Veterans Affairs: (239,299) Administers programs to aid U.S. veterans and their families; runs the veterans hospital system, and operates our national cemeteries.

Homeland Security: (154,100) Works to prevent terrorist attacks within the United States; reduce vulnerability to terrorism; and minimize the damage from potential attacks and natural disasters. Conceived after the September 11, 2001 attacks and officially established in early 2003, the DHS includes new hires, as well as workers transferring from other agencies—mostly from within the Departments of Justice, Transportation, Agriculture, and the Treasury. Agencies are housed in one of four major directorates: Border and Transportation Security, Emergency Preparedness and Response, Science and Technology, and Information Analysis and Infrastructure Protection.

Treasury: (106,925) Regulates banks and other financial institutions, administers the public debt, prints currency, and collects federal income taxes.

Justice: (106,781) Enforces federal laws, prosecutes cases in federal courts, and runs federal prisons.

Agriculture: (105,047) Promotes U.S. agriculture domestically and internationally and sets standards governing quality, quantity, and labeling of food sold in the United States.

Interior: (72,274) Manages federal lands, including the national parks and forests; runs hydroelectric power systems; and promotes conservation of natural resources.

Health and Human Services: (61,163) Sponsors medical research; approves use of new drugs and medical devices; runs the Public Health Service; and administers Medicare.

Transportation: (53,865) Sets national transportation policy; plans and funds the construction of highways and mass transit systems; and regulates railroad, aviation, and maritime operations.

Commerce: (40,079) Forecasts the weather; charts the oceans; regulates patents and trademarks; conducts the Census; compiles statistics; and promotes U.S. economic growth by encouraging international trade.

State: (34,160) Oversees the nation's embassies and consulates; issues passports; monitors U.S. interests abroad; and represents the United States before international organizations.

Labor: (16,195) Enforces laws guaranteeing fair pay, workplace safety, and equal job opportunity; administers unemployment insurance; regulates pension funds; and collects and analyzes economic data through its Bureau of Labor Statistics.

Energy: (14,795) Coordinates the national use and provision of energy; oversees the production and disposal of nuclear weapons; and plans for future energy needs.

Housing and Urban Development: (9,935) Funds public housing projects; enforces equal housing laws; and insures and finances mortgages.

Education: (4,229) Provides scholarships, student loans, and aid to schools.

There are numerous independent agencies that perform tasks which fall between the jurisdictions of the executive departments, or that are more efficiently executed by an autonomous agency. Some smaller but well-known independent agencies include the Peace Corps, the Securities and Exchange Commission, and the Federal Communications Commission. Although the majority of these agencies are fairly small, employing fewer than 1,000 workers (many employ fewer than 100 workers), some are quite large. The largest independent agencies are:

- *Social Security Administration:* Operates various retirement and disability programs and Medicaid.

- *National Aeronautics and Space Administration:* Oversees aviation research and conducts exploration and research beyond the Earth's atmosphere.

- *Environmental Protection Agency:* Runs programs to control and reduce pollution of the nation's water, air, and lands.

- *Tennessee Valley Authority:* Operates the hydroelectric power system in the Tennessee River Valley.

- *General Services Administration:* Manages and protects federal government property and records.

- *Federal Deposit Insurance Corporation:* Maintains stability of and public confidence in the nation's financial system, by insuring deposits and promoting sound banking practices.

WORKING CONDITIONS

Due to the wide range of federal jobs, working conditions are equally variable. While most federal employees work in office buildings, hospitals, or laboratories, a large number also can be found at border crossings, airports, shipyards, military bases, construction sites, and national parks. Work environments vary from comfortable and relaxed to hazardous and stressful, such as those experienced by law enforcement officers, astronauts, and air traffic controllers.

The vast majority of federal employees work full time, often on flexible or "flexi-time" schedules that allow workers more control over their work schedules. Some agencies also offer telecommuting or "flexi-place" programs, which allow selected workers to perform some job duties at home or from regional centers.

Some federal workers spend much of their time away from the offices in which they are based. Inspectors or compliance officers, for example, often visit businesses and work sites to ensure that laws and regulations are obeyed. Some federal workers frequently travel long distances, spending days or weeks away from home. Auditors, for example, may spend weeks at a time in distant locations.

EMPLOYMENT

The federal government, including the U.S. Postal Service, employs about 2.7 million civilian workers, or about 2 percent of the nation's workforce. The federal government is the nation's single largest employer. Because data on employment in certain agencies cannot be released to the public for national security reasons, this total does not include employment for the Central Intelligence Agency, National Security Agency, Defense Intelligence Agency, and National Imagery and Mapping Agency.

The federal government makes an effort to have a workforce as diverse as the nation's civilian labor force. The federal government serves as a model for all employers in abiding by equal employment opportunity legislation, which protects current and potential employees from discrimination based on race, color, religion, gender, national origin, disability, or age. The federal government also makes an effort to recruit and accommodate persons with disabilities.

Even though most federal departments and agencies are based in the Washington, D.C., area, fewer than 15 percent of federal employees worked in the vicinity of the nation's capital in 2005. In addition to federal employees working throughout the United States, about 3 percent are assigned overseas, mostly in embassies or defense installations.

OCCUPATIONS

Although the federal government employs workers in every major occupational group, workers are not employed in the same proportions in which they are employed throughout the economy as a whole (Table 1-2). The analytical and technical nature of many government duties translates into a much higher proportion of professional, management, business, and financial occupations in the federal government, compared with most industries. Conversely, the government sells very little, so it employs relatively few sales workers.

Table 1-2

Percent distribution of employment in the federal government
and the private sector by major occupational group

Occupational Group	Federal Government	Private Sector
Total	**100**	**100**
Professional and related	32.8	19.9
Management, business, and financial	27.4	9.0
Office and administrative support	16.7	17.6
Service	10.6	19.3
Installation, maintenance, and repair	4.8	4.0
Transportation and materiel moving	3.1	7.2
Production	2.1	7.6
Construction and extraction	1.9	4.7
Sales and related	0.4	10.1
Farming, fishing and forestry	0.2	0.7

Professional and related occupations accounted for about one third of federal employment in 2006. The largest group of professional workers worked in life, physical, and social science occupations, such as biological scientists, conservation scientists and foresters, environmental scientists and geoscientists, and forest and conservation technicians. They do work such as determining the effects of drugs on living organisms, preventing fires in the national forests, and predicting earthquakes and hurricanes. The Department of Agriculture employed the vast majority of life scientists, but physical scientists were distributed throughout a variety of departments and agencies.

Many health professionals, such as licensed practical and licensed vocational nurses, registered nurses, and physicians and surgeons, were employed by the Department of Veterans Affairs (VA) in VA hospitals.

Large numbers of federal workers also held jobs as engineers, including aerospace, civil, computer hardware, electrical and electronics, industrial, mechanical, and nuclear engineers. Engineers were found in many departments of the executive branch, but they most commonly worked in the Department of Defense, the National Aeronautics and Space Administration, and the Department of Transportation. In general, they solve problems and provide advice on technical programs, such as building highway bridges or implementing agency-wide computer systems.

Computer specialists — primarily computer software engineers, network and computer systems analysts, and computer systems administrators — are employed throughout the federal government. They write computer programs, analyze problems related to data processing, and keep computer systems running smoothly. Many health professionals, such as registered nurses, physicians and surgeons, and licensed practical nurses are employed by the Department of Veterans Affairs (VA) in one of many VA hospitals.

Management, business, and financial workers made up about 27 percent of federal employment and were primarily responsible for overseeing operations. Managerial workers include a broad range of officials who, at the highest levels, may head federal agencies or programs. Middle managers, on the other hand, usually oversee one activity or aspect of a program. One management occupation — legislators — are responsible for passing and amending laws and overseeing the executive branch of the government. Within the federal government, legislators are entirely found in Congress.

Management, business, and financial workers made up about 27 percent of federal employment.

Others occupations in this category are accountants and auditors, who prepare and analyze financial reports, review and record revenues and expenditures, and investigate operations for fraud and inefficiency. Purchasing agents handle federal purchases of supplies. Management analysts study government operations and systems and suggest improvements. These employees aid management staff with administrative duties. Administrative support workers in the federal government include secretaries and general office clerks. Purchasing agents handle federal purchases of supplies, and tax examiners, collectors, and revenue agents determine and collect taxes.

Compared with the economy as a whole, workers in service occupations were relatively scarce in the federal government. About seven out of 10 federal workers in service occupations were protective service workers, such as detectives and criminal investigators, police and sheriff's patrol officers, and correctional officers and jailers. These workers protect the public from crime and oversee federal prisons.

Federally employed workers in installation, maintenance, and repair occupations include aircraft mechanics and service technicians who fix and maintain all types of aircraft. Also included are electrical and electronic equipment mechanics, installers, and repairers, who inspect, adjust, and repair electronic equipment such as industrial controls, transmitters, antennas, radar, radio, and navigation systems.

The federal government employed a relatively small number of workers in transportation; production; construction; sales and related; and farming, fishing, and forestry occupations. However, they employ almost all air traffic controllers in the country and a significant number of agricultural inspectors and bridge and lock tenders.

TRAINING AND ADVANCEMENT

In all but a few cases, applicants for federal jobs must be U.S. citizens. Applicants who are veterans of military service may also be able to claim veteran's preference status over other candidates with equal qualifications. For an increasing number of jobs requiring access to sensitive or classified materials, applicants must undergo a background investigation in order to obtain a security clearance. This investigation covers an individual's criminal, credit, and employment history, as well as other records. The scope of the investigation will vary, depending on the nature of the position in the government and the degree of harm that an individual in that position could cause. Generally, the higher the level of clearance needed, the greater the scope of the job.

In all but a few cases, applicants for federal jobs must be U.S. citizens.

The educational and training requirements for jobs in the federal government mirror those in the private sector for most major occupational groups. Many jobs in professional and related occupations, for example, require a four-year college degree. Some, such as engineers, physicians and surgeons, and biological and physical scientists, require a bachelor's or higher degree in a specific field of study. Because managers usually are promoted from professional occupations, most have at least a bachelor's degree. However, registered nurses and many technician occupations may be entered with two years of training after high school. Office and administrative support workers in the government usually need only a high school diploma, although any further training or experience, such as a junior college degree or a couple of years of relevant work experience, is an asset. Most federal jobs in other occupations require no more than a high school degree, although most departments and agencies prefer workers with vocational training or previous experience.

Once the person is employed, each federal department or agency determines its own training requirements and offers workers opportunities to improve job skills to advance to other jobs. These may include technical or skills training, tuition assistance or reimbursement, fellowship programs, and executive leadership and management training programs, seminars, and workshops. This training may be offered on the job, by another agency, or at local colleges and universities.

Advancement for most workers in the in the federal government is currently based on a system of occupational pay levels, or "grades," although more departments and agencies are being granted waivers to experiment with different pay and promotion strategies. Workers typically enter the federal civil service at the starting grade for an occupation and begin a "career ladder" of promotions until they reach the full-performance grade for that occupation. This system provides for a limited number of noncompetitive promotions, which usually are awarded at regular intervals, assuming job performance is satisfactory. The exact pay grades associated with a job's career track depend upon the occupation.

Typically, workers without a high school diploma who are hired as clerks start at grade 1, and high school graduates with no additional training hired at the same job start at grade 2 or 3. Entrants with some technical training or experience who are hired as technicians may start at grade 4. Those with a bachelor's degree generally are hired in professional occupations, such as economist, with a career ladder that starts at grade 5 or 7, depending on academic achievement. Entrants with a master's degree or Ph.D. may start at grade 9. Individuals with professional degrees may be hired at the grade 11 or 12 level. Those with a combination of education and substantive experience may be hired at higher grades than those with education alone.

New employees usually start at the first step of a grade; however, if the position in question is difficult to fill, entrants may receive somewhat higher pay or special rates. Almost all physician and engineer positions, for example, fall into this category.

Once non-supervisory federal workers reach the full-performance level of the career track, they usually receive periodic step increases within their grade if they are performing their job satisfactorily. They must compete for subsequent promotions, and advancement becomes more difficult. At this point, promotions occur as vacancies arise, and they are based solely on merit. In addition to within-grade longevity increases, federal workers are awarded bonuses for excellent job performance.

Workers who advance to managerial or supervisory positions may receive within-grade longevity increases, bonuses, and promotions to higher grades. The top managers in the federal civil service belong to the Senior Executive Service (SES), the highest positions that federal workers can reach without being specifically nominated by the president and confirmed by the U.S. Senate. Relatively few workers attain SES positions, and competition is intense. Bonus provisions for SES positions are even more performance-based than are those for lower-level positions. Because it is the headquarters for most federal agencies, the Washington, D.C. metropolitan area offers the best opportunities to advance to upper-level managerial and supervisory jobs.

OUTLOOK

Wage and salary employment in the federal government is projected to grow by 2.5 percent through the year 2014, while the salaried economy as a whole is expected to grow by 14 percent. Job growth generated by increased homeland security needs may be largely offset by projected slow growth or declines in other federal sectors due to governmental cost-cutting, the growing use of private contractors, and continuing devolution—the practice of turning over the development, implementation, and management of some programs of the federal government to state and local governments.

Staffing levels in government, while relatively stable in the short run, can be subject to change in the long run, due mainly to changes in public policies as legislated by Congress, which affect spending levels and hiring decisions for the various government departments and agencies. In general, over the coming decade, domestic programs are likely to see cuts in their budgets as Congress seeks to reduce the federal budget deficit, but the cuts will likely affect some agencies more than others. Any employment declines, however, generally will be carried out through attrition—simply not replacing workers who retire or leave the federal government for other reasons. Layoffs, called "reductions in force," have occurred in the past, but they are uncommon and usually affect relatively few workers. In spite of this, there still will be numerous employment opportunities in many agencies, due to the need to replace workers who leave the workforce, retire, or accept employment elsewhere.

While there will be job openings in all types of jobs over the coming decade, demand will continue to grow for specialized workers in areas related to border and transportation security, emergency preparedness, public health, and information analysis.

A study by the Partnership for Public Service, which surveyed federal department and agency hiring needs for the 2005-2006 period, found that most of the new hires in the federal government will come in five major areas. They are: security, enforcement, and compliance, which includes inspectors, investigators, police officers, airport screeners, and prison guards; medical and public health fields; engineering and the sciences, including microbiologists, botanists, physicists, chemists, and veterinarians; program management and administration; and accounting, budget, and business, which includes revenue agents and tax examiners needed mainly by the Internal Revenue Service. The Department of Health and Human Services will need health insurance specialists and claims and customer service representatives to implement the Medicare prescription drug benefit. Patent examiners, Foreign Service officers, and lawyers also are in high demand.

The distribution of federal employment will continue to shift toward a higher proportion of professional, business and financial operations, and protective service workers. Employment declines will be the greatest among office and administrative support occupations and production occupations, due to increasing office automation and contracting out of these jobs.

Competition is expected for some federal positions, especially during times of economic uncertainty, when workers seek the stability of federal employment. In general, federal employment is considered to be relatively stable because it is not affected by cyclical fluctuations in the economy, as are employment levels in many construction, manufacturing, and other private sector industries.

GETTING STARTED

The Book of U.S. Government Jobs walks you through the federal hiring process. This book steers readers to highly informative government and private sector Internet Web sites, self-service job information centers, and telephone job hotlines, and it explores all facets of the federal job market.

Readers will find up-to-date information on how the federal employment system works from an insider's perspective, how to locate job announcements through various methods, and guidance on how to complete a federal application package that will get the attention of rating officials. You'll learn about special hiring programs for the physically challenged, veterans, students, and scholars, thousands of job opportunities, Civil Service Exam requirements, overseas jobs, Postal Service jobs, how to complete your employment application, and much more. Appendix A provides a comprehensive checklist that will take you through the entire federal employment process. Use Appendix A throughout your job search and visit http://federaljobs.net, this book's companion Web site, for book updates, valuable links, résumé and KSA services, qualification standards for all occupations, and for links to federal personnel Web sites that list tens of thousands of job announcements.

The five appendices include an easy-to-use federal job check list, complete lists of federal occupations, comprehensive agency summaries, an agency skills index, and contact lists including employment office addresses and phone numbers.

This book will guide you step-by-step through the federal employment process, from filling out your first employment application to locating job announcements, networking resources, and hiring agencies. Follow the guidelines set forth in this book to dramatically improve your chances of landing a federal job.

PAY AND BENEFITS

Job security, good pay, and an excellent retirement system are just a few of the top reasons most people seek federal employment. Others consider government careers because of desirable travel opportunities, training availability, diverse occupations, and the ability to locate jobs nationwide and overseas.

In an effort to give agencies more flexibility in how they pay their workers, there are now several different pay systems in effect or planning to be implemented over the next few years within the federal government. The two largest departments that are experimenting with new pay systems are the Departments of Defense and Homeland Security. A number of agencies like the Federal Aviation Administration implemented core compensation pay band systems as early as 1995. The new systems incorporate fewer, but wider, pay "bands," instead of grade levels. Pay increases, under these new systems, are almost entirely based on performance, as opposed to length of service.

A number of agencies like the Federal Aviation Administration implemented core compensation pay band systems as early as 1995.

There are eight predominant pay systems. Approximately half of the workforce is under the General Schedule (GS) pay scale, 20 percent are paid under the Postal Service rates, and about 10 percent are paid under the Prevailing Rate Schedule (WG) Wage Grade classification. The remaining pay systems are for the Executive Schedule, Foreign Service, Special Salary Rates, and Nonappropriated Fund Instrumentalities pay scales, and Veterans Health Administration.

It is the case, however, that the majority of professional and administrative federal workers are still paid under the General Schedule (GS). The General Schedule, shown in Table 1-3, has 15 grades of pay for civilian white-collar and service workers, and smaller within-grade step increases that occur based on length of service and quality of performance. New employees usually start at the first step of a grade; however, if the position in question is difficult to fill, entrants may receive somewhat higher pay or special rates. Almost all physician and engineer positions, for example, fall into this category. In an effort to make federal pay more responsive to local labor market conditions, federal employees working in the continental U.S. receive locality pay. The specific amount of locality pay is determined by survey comparisons of private sector wage rates and federal wage rates in the relevant geographic area. At its highest level, locality pay can lead to an increase of as much as 26 percent above the base salary. Every January a pay adjustment tied to changes in private sector pay levels is divided between an across-the-board pay increase in the General Schedule and locality pay increases.

In December 2005, the average wage for full-time workers paid under the General Schedule was $63,812. All pay plans, average pay was $67,186. General attorneys, who earned $105,557 on average — represented one of the higher paid occupations, while average income for nursing assistants was only about half the average for all occupations.

For those in craft, repair, operator, and laborer jobs, the Federal Wage System (FWS) is used to pay these workers. This schedule sets federal wages so that they are comparable tp prevailing regional wage rates for similar types of jobs. As a result, wage rates paid under the FWS can vary significantly from one locality to another.

In addition to base pay and bonuses, federal employees may receive incentive awards. These one-time awards, ranging from $25 to $10,000, are bestowed for a significant suggestion, a special act or service, or sustained high job performance. Some workers also may receive "premium" pay, which is granted when the employee must work overtime, on holidays, on weekends, at night, or under hazardous conditions.

The *2007* "Base Rate" General Schedule (GS) pay chart is presented in this Chapter. Updated GS pay tables including all 32 Locality Pay Tables are posted on http://federaljobs.net — select "Pay Schedules" on the main menu. This site is the companion Web site for *The Book of U.S. Government Jobs* and many of this book's resources and Web links are listed on this site to assist you with your job search. Updated pay tables are published on http://federaljobs.net the first week of January each year.

General Schedule (GS) pay varies from the GS-1 level at $16,630 per annum to $120,981 per annum at step 10 of the GS-15 grade, not including locality pay adjustments. The Senior Executive Service salary tops out at $154,600 per annum. The president adjusts federal salaries to levels that are competitive with the private sector. The average annual salary for full-time non-postal employees increased to just over $63,000 in 2007. Starting pay depends on the level of experience, education and complexity of the position applied for.

Locality Pay Tables

The General Schedule Base Pay Table shows the "base rate" that is used to establish each of the 32 *Locality Pay Tables*. If you work in an area that isn't covered by a *Locality Area* your pay will be determined using the "Rest of the U.S." table. The adjustment to the basic rate ranges from a 12.64% for the "Rest of the U.S." to a high of 26.65% for the Houston, TX Locality Area.

Each GS grade has 10 pay steps. Currently, a GS-9 starts at $38,824 for step 1 and reaches $50,470 per year at step 10 (not including locality pay adjustments). At the GS-9 grade, each pay step adds $1,294 to the annual salary. Pay steps are earned based on time in service and the employee's work performance. General Schedule employees are referred to as white-collar workers under the federal classification system. There are 32 locality pay areas. Visit http://federaljobs.net for specific locality pay information for your area. All of the 32 locality pay areas adjust the base salary in a range from12.64% to 26.65%.

TABLE 1-3
Annual Salary Rates
2007 General Schedule (GS)

General Schedule (GS) Step Increases 1-10 in Dollars										
GS	1	2	3	4	5	6	7	8	9	10
1	16,630	17,185	17,739	18,289	18,842	19,167	19,713	20,264	20,286	20,798
2	18,698	19,142	19,761	20,286	20,512	21,115	21,718	22,321	22,924	23,527
3	20,401	21,081	21,761	22,441	23,121	23,801	24,481	25,161	25,841	26,521
4	22,902	23,665	24,428	25,191	21,954	26,717	27,480	28,243	29,006	29,769
5	25,623	26,477	27,331	28,185	29,039	29,839	30,747	31,601	32,455	33,309
6	28,562	29,514	30,466	31,418	32,370	33,322	34,274	35,226	36,178	37,130
7	31,740	32,798	33,856	34,914	35,972	37,030	38,088	39,146	40,204	41,262
8	35,151	36,323	37,495	38,667	39,839	41,011	42,183	43,355	44,527	45,699
9	38,824	40,118	41,412	42,706	44,000	45,294	46,588	47,882	49,176	50,470
10	42,755	44,180	45,605	47,030	48,455	49,880	51,305	52,730	54,155	55,580
11	46,974	48,540	50,106	51,672	53,238	54,804	56,370	57,936	59,502	61,068
12	56,301	58,178	60,055	61,932	63,809	65,686	67,563	69,440	71,317	73,194
13	66,951	69,183	71,415	73,647	75,879	78,111	80,343	82,575	84,807	87,039
14	79,115	81,752	84,389	87,026	89,663	92,300	94,937	97,574	100,211	102,848
15	93,063	96,165	99,267	102,369	105,471	108,573	111,675	114,777	117,879	120,981

Approximately 10 percent of total federal non-postal employment is classified under the Wage Grade (WG) blue-collar pay schedules. Wage Grade workers are placed in a five step pay system and the pay is based on competitive rates that are established by an annual wage survey. The Department of Defense employs the largest number of Wage Grade workers.

Sample of Wage Grade (WG) Occupations

WG-2502 Telephone Mechanic	WG-4204 Pipefitting
WG-2892 Aircraft Electrician	WG-4417 Offset Press Operating
WG-3314 Instrument Making	WG-4754 Cemetery Caretaking
WG-3502 Laboring	WG-5220 Shipwright
WG-3703 Welding	WG-5788 Deckhand
WG-3919 Television Equip.	WG-7304 Laundry Working
WG-4102 Painting	WG-7404 Cooking

See Appendix D for a complete list of WG occupations.

There are a number of special compensation systems that augment the general schedule. Physicians receive signing bonuses for a one-year continued-service agreement and additional bonuses for two years. The Federal Aviation Administration pays employees in safety-related careers under a "Core Com-pensation" multi-pay band system. Organizations such as the General Accounting Office (GAO), NASA, and the Commerce Department's National Institute of Standards and Technology either are exempt from or have exceptions to the GS pay system.

The SES is a corps of men and women, composed of those who administer public programs at the top levels of federal government. Some positions include additional recruitment incentives. The SES programs and application guidance are included in Chapter Six.

Structure of the SES Pay System	Minimum	Maximum
Agencies with a Certified SES Performance Appraisal System	$101,676	$168,000
Agencies without a Certified SES Performance Appraisal System	$111,676	$154,600

Pay reform has been implemented to offset competitive hiring pressures from private industry and local governments. Agencies can now offer allowances and bonuses when recruiting, match salary within certain limits, and are authorized to pay interview travel expenses under certain circumstances.

Table 1-4

Average annual salaries for GS full-time workers

Occupations *(Selected occupations)*	Salary
All Occupations	$63,812
General attorney	105,577
General engineer	95,456
Financial management	95,257
Economist	89,441
Computer science	86,443
Chemistry	83,777
Statistician	81,262
Microbiology	80,798
Architecture	80,777
Criminal investigating	79,100
Information technology management	77,003
Accounting	74,907
Chaplain	74,730
Librarian	74,630
Mine safety and health	72,601
Ecology	72,021
Human resource management	71,232
Air traffic control	70,555
Budget analysis	67,767
Nurse	60,935
Engineering technician	60,543
Border patrol agent	56,297
Customs and border protection	53,533
Correctional officer	47,400
Legal assistant	42,279
Fire protection and prevention	41,061
Secretary	39,938
Police officer	39,579
Human resource assistant	36,576
Medical technician	35,536

SOURCE: U.S. Office of Personnel Management, 2005 & CBO Report

VACATION AND SICK LEAVE

All employees receive 10 paid holidays, 13 days of vacation for the first three years service, 20 days of vacation with three to 15 years of service, and 26 days after 15 years. Additionally, 13 sick days are accrued each year regardless of length of service and employees can carry over any sick leave accumulation to the next year. Many federal employees accrue sick leave balances of a year or more during their career. The author had 2100 hours of sick leave, just over one year, accumulated when he retired in 2004. He was able to exchange his sick leave balance for an increase in his annuity payment. Military time counts toward benefits. If you have three years of military service you begin with four weeks of paid vacation. Military service time counts toward civil service retirement.

HEALTH BENEFITS AND LIFE INSURANCE

Medical health plans and the Federal Employees' Group Life Insurance (FEGLI) programs are available to all employees. The Federal Employees Health Benefits (FEHB) plan is an employee-employer contribution system and includes fee-for-service, consumer-driven, point-of-service, and HMO options. The costs are reasonable and the coverage excellent.

In 2007 the federal government started offering comprehensive dental and vision care under the new Federal Employees Dental & Vision Insurance Program (FEDVIP). Coverage is available from a number of healthcare providers and is competitively priced with standard and high options. The FEGLI program offers low-cost term life insurance for the employee and basic coverage for the family. FEGLI offers up to five times the employee's salary in death benefits.

One of the primary benefits of federal employment is the satisfaction you experience from working in a challenging and rewarding job. Positions are available with the level of responsibility and authority that you desire.

RETIREMENT

The federal retirement system is currently based on the following: Social Security contributions, an annuity based on 1 percent for each year of service times your three highest earning years, Social Security offset if you meet certain conditions, and an employee contribution system fashioned after a 401k defined contribution plan. You can elect to contribute up to 15 percent of your salary into a THRIFT savings 401k plan. The government matches your contributions. Employees receive 1 percent automatically and they match the next 3 percent contributed by the employee and 50 cents per dollar for the next 2 percent contributed. Therefore, if you contribute a minimum of 5 percent Uncle Sam matches 5 percent. New hires should consider contributing a minimum of 5 percent to receive a 5 percent match from the government.

New hires should consider contributing a minimum of 5 percent to receive a 5 percent match.

Contributions are tax-deferred and reduce taxable income by the amount contributed. The retirement benefit is determined by the amount accumulated during the employee's career. This includes the interest earned and capital gains realized from the retirement fund. Visit http://federaljobs.net/retire, our retirement planning Web site, for complete information and details about the federal retirement system.

There are many withdrawal options, including lump sum and various fixed term annuities. The THRIFT plan contribution payout is in addition to your federal retirement annuity and Social Security benefits that you will be eligible for at retirement.

CAREER DEVELOPMENT

Each department or agency determines the training that is required and offers workers opportunities to improve job skills and to gain qualifications to advance to other jobs. Career development training includes technical or skills training, tuition assistance or reimbursement, fellows programs outlined in Chapter Three, and executive leadership and management training programs, seminars, and workshops. Training may be offered on the job, by another agency, or at local colleges and universities. Visit http://fedcareer.info for detailed information on the government's *"Individual Development Plan"* program.

Visit http://fedcareer.info
for career development guidance

Today there are many diverse opportunities for self-development and one of the major initiatives is online and computer-based instruction. Most agencies offer extensive online courses for skills improvement to career development. I encourage all federal employees to take advantage of these programs to enhance their promotion potential and to improve their skills. Some courses are required by the position. However, most are designed to improve job performance.

Starting in my early thirties I took advantage of many agency-sponsored training programs that helped me prepare for — and eventually be selected for — supervisory and management positions. I completed evening college courses receiving reimbursement for up to 50 percent of my tuition, attended seminars, signed up for agency correspondence courses, and volunteered for temporary and lateral assignments throughout my 35-year career. I used the courses to improve my writing, automation, organizational, and interpersonal skills to gain promotions. When I was assigned to complete a course project, I developed the project around an actual work issue and eventually presented the project plans to management in the form of proactive work improvement plans and suggestions.

I encourage all federal employees to take advantage of these programs to enhance their promotion potential and to improve their skills.

The improvement plans and suggestions attracted the attention of upper management, and I believe this is why I was selected for my first supervisory position at the early age of 35. I was selected from a group of applicants who had considerably more experience and were considerably older. However, I was selected due in part to my personal career development activities.

At each juncture of my career I used career development training to improve my productivity, soft skills — such as interpersonal behavior, management skills— and technical expertise. I developed comprehensive Individual Development Plans (IDPs) shortly after reporting for my first job with the Federal Aviation Administration in 1975 and revised my plan annually throughout my career. I believe this is why I was successful in working my way up through the ranks from a GS-0856-07 step 1 grade to my final senior management position when I retired in late 2004 from the Federal Aviation Administration (FAA). My last position was air traffic control tower technical operations manager for the FAA at the Greater Pittsburgh International Airport. Learn more about the IDP process at www.fedcareer.info.

The federal government also offers college or graduate students employment training in the Presidential Management Fellows Program; college students may apply for one of the independent agency fellowships. More information on these programs are available in Chapter Three or contact your college's financial aid and placement office.

Federal Government Leadership Development Programs (FED LDP)

There are many government leadership programs available to help federal employees advance in their careers. Visit the Office of Personnel Management (OPM) Web site at http://opm.gov/fedldp/index.aspx for a comprehensive leadership program.

This site is the online home of the Catalogue of Federal Government Leadership Development Programs (Fed LDP). You will find a comprehensive searchable electronic library of programs offered by federal departments and agencies to foster the development of leadership skills in their employees. Information on programs can be found by searching the catalog by agency and/or pay level. Additional information can be accessed by selecting the URL or e-mail listed next to each program under *Get More Info*.

You will find extensive leadership programs in the form of conferences, seminars, residential courses, general coursework, developmental assignments, coaching initiatives, distance learning, lectures, mentoring , workshops, on-the-job training and much more. The programs are offered either to federal employees from specific agencies or to all federal employees, and there are opportunities for non-federal employees as well.

TYPES OF TRAINING

- Orientation Training (New Employees)
- Technical and Administrative Skills Training
- Professional Training
- Supervisory Training
- Executive and Management Training
- Career Development Training

Career development programs are offered by most agencies for target positions and personal long term career goals. Each agency offers its own unique programs. However, they are all authorized by the same federal regulations and many similarities exist between agencies. The following is a sampling of currently offered career development programs.

Career Development Program Examples

- **Aspiring Leaders Development Program** — A 12-month program designed to provide a series of developmental experiences for high potential employees. Participants remain in their current positions and attend program activities when scheduled. Participation in this program is based on a competitive selection process limited to individuals with at least one year in a position at the GS 7-12 levels or equivalent.

- **Individual Development Plans (IDP)** — This program offers employees the opportunity to sit down with their supervisor and design a personalized career development program. Training is provided to help the employee reach his/her goal. Training programs can include formal college courses at government expense. *(The amount of tuition reimbursement depends on availability of funds.)*

    Correspondence courses are also available and lateral work assignments are encouraged to provide exposure to diverse aspects of the target position. Correspondence, online, and computer-based instruction courses, and lateral assignments are available to provide exposure to skills necessary for the target position. Visit our site at http://fedcareer.info for detailed information on this program.

NOTE: Federal employees will benefit from the book titled *"Take Charge of Your Federal Career,"* published by Federal Employees News Digest. This book is a practical, action-oriented career management workbook for all federal employees that guides you step-by-step through the IDP process. It is available for $17.95 plus shipping by calling 1-800-782-7424. Information about this title is available online at http://fedcareer.info/.

- **The Presidential Management Fellows Program** (PMF) — The PMF program, previously known as the Presidential Management Intern Program, provides a career starting point in the federal government for graduate students who have demonstrated a commitment to the management or analysis of public programs and policies. Graduate students must be nominated by their college or university and undergo an extensive screening process to be chosen as a fellow. Those selected enter at the GS-9 level and receive two years of formal and on-the-job training and career planning. Those who successfully complete the program are eligible for career appointments at the GS-12 level. Chapter Three includes more information on this program. Visit their Web site at http://www.pmf.opm.gov for more information.

- **Leadership Challenge Course** — A one-week self-development course whose primary target audience is non-supervisory employees. The course is intended to provide participants with the tools for developing a plan of action to improve their leadership skills. The course is framed around the OPM Leadership Competencies and is focused on the belief that all employees have leadership capabilities and can make a difference.

WHERE THE JOBS ARE

Fifteen Cabinet departments and more than 100 independent agencies compose the federal government system. These departments and agencies have offices in all corners of the world. The size of each agency varies considerably. The larger the agency, the more diverse the opportunities. Appendix C provides a comprehensive federal agency and department directory.

Agencies are like corporations in the sense that each agency has a headquarters office, typically located in Washington D.C., regional offices located around the country to manage large geographic areas, and many satellite offices to provide public services and to perform agency functions. A good example is the Social Security Administration, which has offices in most areas to administer the Social

Appendix C provides a comprehensive federal agency & department directory.

Security program; manage disability claims, sign up those who retire at 62 and again at age 65 or older when they are required to elect Medicare B options, etc.

Jobs can be found in all parts of the country and overseas — even in places you might never imagine. Don't exclude any location regardless of size. In 1975 I was hired by the FAA to work at the Philipsburg Airport in central Pennsylvania. Philipsburg is a small town of 3,056 and I maintained navigational aids and communications facilities at the airport and the near by town of State College. One of the main reasons I was hired was that few bid on these remote-location jobs. If you want to be successful in your job search, expand your area of consideration. It took me three years to get trained and transfer back to my home town.

If you want to be successful in your job search, expand your area of consideration.

To locate potential employers and federal offices in your area, check the blue pages in your phone book, contact the regional Federal Executive Board — offices are listed in Appendix B — to obtain a comprehensive list of agency offices in your area, and start networking as described in Chapter four using the informational interview process outlined in that chapter. A comprehensive agency directory is available in Appendix C. Locate the agencies in your area to find out what potential jobs may be available or soon become available. Visit http://federaljobs.net and follow the links to 142 federal personnel offices and agency employment sites to explore available careers and locate job vacancies. Chapter three will take this one step further and show you how to find job vacancies throughout government and what jobs are available.

*If you desire to travel, the government
offers abundant opportunities to
relocate within the 50 states and
throughout the world.*

If you desire to travel, the government offers abundant opportunities to relocate within the 50 states and overseas. Chapter eight provides information on overseas employment opportunities including qualifications, hiring agency contact information, and much more. Twelve federal agencies and departments offer employment abroad for more than 93,000 workers. The Department of Defense Dependent Schools system employ hundreds of teachers for military dependent schools overseas.

The Washington, D.C. area, including D.C., Maryland and Virginia, has the largest number of federal workers, 327,270, and Vermont the least with 3,831. All of the 315 Metropolitan Statistical Areas (MSA) in the U.S. and Puerto Rico have federal civilian employment as listed in the Central Personnel Data File. Small towns and rural areas outside of MSAs have approximately 18 percent of total non-postal federal workers.[6] The actual number of federal civilian employees is greater

---

[6] Federal Civilian Employment by State & Metropolitan Areas (CPDF)

than the above figures. The Defense Intelligence Agency, Central Intelligence Agency, and the National Security Agency do not release their data. Chapter Three provides job resources including Internet Web sites, magazines and newspapers that list thousands of national job openings, and job placement services. Special hiring programs are explained for Outstanding Scholars, and Appendix C provides a comprehensive agency contact list that includes national and regional personnel office contacts. Go to the employment page on http://federaljobs.net to link direct to 143 federal agency personnel offices that advertise jobs. These Web sites typically have up to 20,000 jobs listed at any given time.

EDUCATION REQUIREMENTS

In the federal government, 58 percent of all workers do not have a college degree. The level of required education is dependent upon the job applied for. Each job announcement lists needed skills and abilities including education and work experience. However, the more education and work experience you have, the more competitive you will be when ranked against other applicants. A sample qualification statement is presented in Chapter Two for administration and management positions. The majority of positions within the government have a published qualifications standard similar to the provided example.

You can review and download a specific qualification standard online at http://federaljobs.net, http://opm.gov, or visit your local Federal Depository Library. Many large college and private libraries are designated depository status and they can help you locate specific government publications including the Qualification Standards Handbook for General Schedule positions.

Many look at the job announcement and see "Bachelor's Degree" and pass up the job not knowing that three years of general experience could qualify them for the position.

You can often substitute work experience for a college degree in many fields. For example, refer to the qualification standard in Chapter Two, and you will find that you can substitute three years, one year equivalent to at least a GS-4, of general work experience for a four-year course of study leading to a bachelor's degree. Many look at the job announcement and see *"Bachelor's Degree"* and pass up the job not knowing that three years general experience could qualify them for the position. If they would have only kept reading they would have discovered that fact in the job announcement. **READ** the entire job announcement, front to back, before eliminating the job from consideration.

CAREER SEARCH

If you are uncertain about which career to enter or if a government job is right for you, *The Book of U.S. Government Jobs* is a good place to start. Chapter Four outlines detailed informational interviewing techniques that will help you investigate primary and alternate career paths, and the all new and expanded 10th Edition provides more than 1000 resources to help you make a connection. The Federal Jobs Checklist in Appendix A guides job seekers through the federal employment system from beginning to end.

There are many excellent resources available to assist you with your job hunt. A few select books and software programs are offered for sale by the publisher in the back of this book for your convenience. Books and services that we mention but don't offer for sale will have ordering information printed with the notation.

CIVIL SERVICE EXAM INTRODUCTION

Over 80 percent of all jobs do not require a written entrance exam. Uncle Sam rates most applicants through an extensive review of their work experience and/or education that is stated on their application or federal style résumé. Tests are required for specific groups including secretarial/clerical, air traffic control, law enforcement and certain entry level jobs. However, there are exceptions to those occupations as well. For example, if you apply for clerical positions with many agencies, they often waive the entrance exam and require you to fill out a comprehensive *"Occupational Questionnaire"* and you may also be able to self-certify your typing speed.

Chapter Five provides sample test questions and offers detailed testing information and guidance. You will also be able to determine if the occupation that you are applying for requires a written entrance exam. Outstanding scholars, college graduates with top grades, can be hired on the spot. Entry-level professional and administrative job applicants who graduate from a four-year college with a grade point average of 3.5 or above — on a 4.0 scale — can be hired without competition if the applicant impresses agency recruiters with experience and technical abilities during an interview.

TABLE 1-5
FEDERAL EMPLOYMENT BY STATE — SEPTEMBER 2006

Non-Postal

STATE	TOTAL	STATE	TOTAL
Alabama	36,064	Nevada	10,065
Alaska	12,995	New Hampshire	3,997
Arizona	36,216	New Jersey	28,243
Arkansas	13,415	New Mexico	24,139
California	149,146	New York	62,204
Colorado	35,909	North Carolina	36,071
Connecticut	7,737	North Dakota	6,091
Delaware	3,087	Ohio	44,423
Florida	76,428	Oklahoma	20,380
Georgia	68,498	Oregon	20,380
Hawaii	22,186	Pennsylvania	64,166
Idaho	9,731	Rhode Island	6,503
Illinois	45,222	South Carolina	18,746
Indiana	20,463	South Dakota	7,936
Iowa	8,494	Tennessee	25,488
Kansas	16,506	Texas	118,225
Kentucky	21,767	Utah	29,226
Louisiana	20,125	Vermont	3,831
Maine	9,824	Virginia	124,791
Maryland	110,960	Washington	49,728
Massachusetts	26,034	Washington, D.C.	148,042
Michigan	11,211	West Virginia	14,067
Minnesota	16,241	Wisconsin	13,279
Mississippi	18,437	Wyoming	5,809
Missouri	32,472	Overseas	88,700
Montana	11,201	*Unspecified	37,082
Nebraska	9,549		

OPM Employment Statistics, September 2006

CHAPTER TWO
Understanding
Federal Recruitment

There are numerous misconceptions about federal civil service. Some believe that all federal applicants must take civil service entrance exams. Others think that federal workers have the same benefits as the military and that you have to be a veteran to land a job. Many qualified applicants don't read the entire job announcement and miss out on excellent job opportunities because they assume they don't qualify. Job seekers often submit private-sector résumés when applying for jobs, not realizing that federal style résumés require considerably more detail. All are gross misconceptions that can prevent highly qualified job seekers from landing a high paying and secure government job.

Adding further confusion to the recruitment process is the fact that government personnel specialists do not have the time to counsel the hundreds of thousands who apply for federal jobs each year. There are too many questions and too few counselors to answer them. This is why I wrote the first edition of this book in 1985. I was a federal manager and too many applicants didn't understand what was needed to successfully approach the federal sector, and more important, **LAND A JOB.**

Recruitment and retention incentives including Student Loan Repayment options for new and current employees are very attractive.

Recently, Uncle Sam started offering lucrative recruitment and retention incentives including student loan repayment programs for select new hires and current employees. The federal government paid over $60 million in student loan repayment benefits since the program started a few years ago.

CHAPTER OBJECTIVES

✎ Understand federal recruiting and how to apply for jobs

✎ Determine your eligibility and what jobs you qualify for

✎ Find out if civil service exams are required for your occupation

✎ Identify recruitment incentives such as student loan payoff, etc.

✎ Identify typical federal employee characteristics (*Table 2-3*)

The federal government's recruitment goals are to provide fair and equitable opportunities for all qualified applicants regardless of race, national origin, gender, age or religious beliefs. The system is designed to reduce and eliminate, wherever possible, outside influence such as nepotism and political affiliation to level the playing field for all QUALIFIED applicants. This is the primary reason for the *competitive examination* process. Don't confuse competitive examinations with written exams. A competitive examination can be either a written test or a thorough examination of your work experience, education and special skills, coupled with an interview.

The recruitment process needs to be thoroughly understood so that you will achieve the highest rated application possible. All examinations, written or review, are rated on a point system of up to 100 points. Essentially, the rating official will either look at your written exam score or rate your application on a point system to determine your final score. Only the top rated applicants are considered for employment and interviewed. The remainder of this chapter outlines what you need to know about this system so that you can obtain higher scores for the jobs you apply for.

COMPETITIVE SERVICE

Approximately 50 percent of civilian jobs are in the *competitive service,* which means that people applying for them must be evaluated by the Office of Personnel Management (OPM) either directly or through agency personnel offices that are delegated direct-hire or case-hire authority. Chapter Three explains the various services into which you can be hired.

All competitive and *excepted service* is based on your ability to perform the knowledge, skills, abilities, and other characteristics of the job. Job announcements outline the duties, responsibilities, and educational requirements for each job. Read the job announcement front to back to determine all requirements and options. Chapter Six shows you how to evaluate job announcements to improve your score.

Approximately 80 percent of government jobs are filled through a competitive examination of your background, work experience, and education, not through a written test.

COMPETITIVE EXAMINATIONS

Hiring for federal jobs is generally through a competitive examination. Don't be intimidated by the word "examination." The majority — approximately 80 percent — of government jobs are filled through a competitive examination of your background, work experience, and education, not through a written test. There are exceptions to this rule, and noncompetitive appointments are available for certain veterans, the physically challenged or disabled, and other groups. All hiring is based on the ability to perform the work advertised in the job announcement.

EMPLOYMENT TYPES

The government offers competitive and excepted service jobs. There are a multitude of employment options within these groups. Competitive service means individuals compete for positions and the most qualified applicant is selected. Hiring is based on the applicant's knowledge, skills, and ability as compared to all other applicants. Excepted service job benefits, pay, etc. are identical in most cases to competitive service positions. Certain jobs are excepted by statute or by the Office of Personnel Management (OPM). The federal courts, Library of Congress, the Federal Reserve System, the U.S. Foreign Service, the Tennessee Valley Authority, the FAA, the FBI, the CIA, and other federal intelligence agencies are excepted service by statute. OPM uses the excepted service to fill positions that are difficult to fill or have specific limitation or restrictive requirements.

The U.S. Postal Service, Veterans Readjustment Act Appointments, attorneys, teachers in dependents' schools overseas, the CIA and FBI, Secret Service, and most positions in the legislative and judicial branches are also in the excepted service. Foreign nationals who hold jobs overseas are excepted by executive order.

One disadvantage of the excepted service is the inability to transfer directly into a competitive service position. Excepted service employees who want to apply for a competitive service job must compete for jobs with all other applicants.

DETERMINING YOUR ELIGIBILITY

Eligibility is determined through the evaluation of an applicant's related education **AND/OR** work experience. For example, an entry level radio operator would start at a GS-2 pay grade, $18,698 per year, if he or she was a high school graduate **OR** had at least three months of general experience. That same radio operator could start at a GS-4, $22,902 per year, if he or she had six months of general experience and six months of specialized experience, **OR** two years of education above high school with courses related to the occupation. You would add 12 to 26 percent to the salary figures for a specific *"Locality Pay"* area.

College degree requirements can in many cases be substituted for work experience. Refer to the Job Qualification Standard for Administrative and Management Positions presented in this chapter. Applicants for jobs in this group can substitute three years of general experience for a four year bachelor's degree. Many job hunters without degrees see Bachelor's Degree listed as required in the job announcement, stop reading and look elsewhere. If they had read the entire job announcement they would have realized that work experience could be substituted for this degree requirement. Many highly qualified applicants miss out on lucrative jobs because of this one fact.

College degree requirements, in many cases, can be substituted for work experience.

General Experience

This is any type of work which demonstrates the applicant's ability to perform the work of the position, or any experience which provides a familiarity with the subject matter or process of the broad subject areas of the occupation. Specialized experience can be substituted for general experience.

Specialized Experience

This is experience which is in the occupation of the position to be filled, in a related occupation, or in one of the specialized areas within that occupation, which has equipped the applicant with the particular *knowledge, skills, abilities, and other characteristics* (KSAOs) to perform the duties of the position.

Written Tests

An examination announcement (job opening notice) may or may not require a written test. In many cases the examination consists of a detailed evaluation of your work experience, education, and schooling listed on your employment application. The Office of Personnel Management (OPM) eliminated the reliance on a written test as a single examining method and now provides agencies with additional examining options. Under this program, applicants apply for specific vacancies rather than broad occupational groups. While written tests will continue to be used for some jobs, taking a test is no longer the compulsory first step in the hiring process.

It should also be noted that if a written test is required, many agencies allow applicants to bypass the written test for select occupations by completing an "Occupational Questionnaire." This is a series of questions, often 30 to 75 or more, that you have to answer in detail, often online. See Chapter Six for more information on this subject. Occupational questionnaires are not KSAs. Many applicants confuse them for required KSA statements. If KSAs or KSAOs are required, the job announcement will clearly identify them as such. See Chapter Six for instructions on how to write effective KSAs for your jobs. KSAs and KSAOs are the same. Agencies refer to them as one or the other.

Don't confuse Occupational Questionnaires with KSA statements.

Applicants can complete one of several optional application formats including a federal style résumé or the Optional Application for Employment, OF-612 form. Many agencies now accept applications online. Review Chapter Six before applying online. It is best to compile your federal style résumé prior to starting an online application because of the considerable detail needed for the application. After you compile your federal style résumé you can then copy and paste it into the online application if needed. OPM or the hiring agency then scores the applicants' responses to determine the most highly qualified candidates. Hiring offices receive a list of the best qualified applicants from either OPM or the agency's human resource department for each vacancy. Agencies may require qualified applicants to take a written test for specific occupations.

Approximately 110 entry level professional and administrative jobs originally required written tests under the Administrative Careers With America (ACWA) program. A centralized list of qualified applicants was maintained by OPM until the program changed several years ago. Applicants now apply for individual openings that are announced on http://USAJOBS.gov or on individual agency Web sites. Agencies may still use the ACWA test to rate the best qualified applicants. Sample test questions are featured in Chapter Five for entry level professional and administrative applicants to study. Additionally, jobs in air traffic control, various security agencies, and other specialized fields require written tests.

The federal government evaluates each candidate strictly on his/her ability to perform the duties of the position. **Ability is obtained through education AND/OR experience.** Even engineering positions are rated this way. For example, there are several alternative non-degree paths that allow applicants to rate as eligible for engineering positions. OPM qualifications for engineering positions require either a four-year engineering degree OR four-year college level education, and/or technical experience. Chapter Three provides specific details on the Engineering Conversion Program.

JOB SERIES

There are over 900 job series — occupations — to choose from. Each job announcement describes the required experience, education, job location, pay and miscellaneous details needed to apply for a position within a *job series*. A complete occupational job series listing is provided in Appendix D. These series are from the General and Wage Grade Schedules in the competitive service. Excepted service job series are designated with different alpha characters; however, most follow the General Series Qualification Standards.

JOB SERIES EXAMPLES
General Schedule

TITLE	SERIES
Accountant	GS-0510
Secretary	GS-0318
Engineer-Electrical	GS-0801
Computer Specialist	GS-0334
System Specialist	GS-2101

Wage Grade

Equipment Mechanic	WG-5800
Laboring	WG-3502

FEDERAL REGISTERS

Most *federal registers* have been abolished. Applicants who passed an examination with a score of 70 out of a maximum of 100 points were added to a register and agencies would hire from the register as vacancies developed. Applicants for the most part no longer apply for general consideration. They apply for specific vacancies. Federal registers created problems for employer and potential employees alike. Agencies had to purge the registers of applicants no longer seeking employment, and applicants who scored high on the entrance tests could not understand why they didn't get called. Some agencies, especially those in excepted service agencies including the U.S. Postal Service, still maintain lists of eligible candidates. When job vacancies exist, those agencies select from active lists and retest to rebuild the list when it becomes outdated or depleted.

EXAMINATION ANNOUNCEMENTS

Examination announcements, most often referred to as job announcements, are issued by the Office of Personnel Management and by individual agencies that have direct hire or case examining authority. The Office of Personnel Management (OPM) operates a network of employment service centers, federal jobs touch-screen computers, USAJOBS telephone number, and an extensive Internet Web site at www.usajobs.gov that you can use to locate federal job announcements for anticipated job vacancies within their servicing area. OPM does not advertise jobs for all agencies. To locate all available jobs, contact individual agencies in your area. A list of federal agency employment Web sites is available on http://federaljobs.net. Refer to Chapter Three to locate Internet sites, job hotlines, and other services that offer federal job listings. A sample announcement is presented in Chapter Six.

Visit http://federaljobs.net for direct links
to over 150 agency recruiting sites.

Examination announcements are advertised for periods from several days to continuously open depending on the agency's critical needs. Exceptions to these rules apply to Veteran Recruitment Appointments (VRA) and recently discharged veterans, disabled veterans, and the disabled. You must obtain examination announcements through the resources mentioned above and in Chapter Three.

Case Examining

The Office of Personnel Management implemented case examining hiring procedures to assist agencies that have critical hiring needs. Agencies conduct targeted recruitment, issue a job announcement for the immediate filling of specific jobs, and close a case file when the selection process is completed. Applicants can apply direct to agencies with case examining authority for targeted positions. The announcements issued list the title, series and grade of the position, opening/closing dates and duty location; provide information concerning the duties, responsibilities and qualification requirements of the position; and provide the name and phone number of a contact person in the recruiting agency. To obtain announcements, applicants must visit the agency's Web site or contact the agency where the vacancy exists.

The agency reviews the applicant's basic eligibility. The final ratings are completed by OPM and the candidates are ranked according to total score. OPM maintains a centralized listing of open case examinations through USAJOBS. See Chapter Three for complete information on how to obtain current announcement information. Case examining procedures involve a one-time-only action with no expectation of filling other vacancies at a later date.

Direct Hire Authority

Direct hire authority is granted to agencies with specific hiring needs in one or several job series. The Office of Personnel Management allows agencies with this Delegated Examining Authority — often referred as Direct Hire Authority — to advertise job openings, rate applicants, establish their own eligibility lists and registers, conduct interviews and hire. Unlike case examining, which is a one-time action, Delegated Examining Authority grants agencies to conduct competitive examinations for all positions in the competitive service, except for administrative law judge positions.

Over 80 percent of all job vacancies are now advertised through either case examining or direct hire authority.

Job seekers can locate individual agency positions on their Web site or you can subscribe to one of several private companies' federal jobs listing services that are listed in Chapter Three. OPM is encouraging agencies to list their job openings on USAJOBS (see Chapter Three resources).

APPLYING FOR FEDERAL JOBS

It is important to remember that you must submit all required information and forms. You have the option of using a federal style résumé format, the OF-612 *Optional Application for Federal Employment,* or online applications that many agencies now use. If you don't include all required information as presented in Chapter Six, your application may be rejected, or at the very least you will lose valuable rating points if key data are missing.

There are vast differences between industry's standard brief résumé format and the detailed information you must supply on the new approved federal style résumé format. The résumé most people are accustomed to is a short one to two page introduction. Uncle Sam's federal style résumé must be highly structured with specific data or it may not be considered. The federal style résumé is probably your best bet because of your ability to send it as hard copy or copy and paste the federal style résumé into an online application. I suggest using the federal style résumé outline in Chapter Six to guide you when completing your application.

An excellent and comprehensive set of tools for obtaining a federal job, called Quick & Easy Federal Jobs Kit by DataTech Software, is available. It includes the optional forms, the original SF-171 application, generates résumés from data that you entered on your forms, provides for KSAs, and it includes spell check and various formatting options. The software includes nine additional employment forms and it is compatible with Windows 95, 98, NT, ME, 2000, XP and Vista.

The federal government rates applicants on their work experience and education. The personnel specialist rating your application generally knows little about the specific job you bid on. This administrative specialist will rate you as either eligible or ineligible by referring to the Federal Qualification Standards. (See a sample qualification standard in this chapter.) These standards break most job series down to general and specialized qualifying work experience and required education. You must have a certain number of years of both general and specialized experience for various starting pay grades. Past work experience and training must be noted in detail on your application. If your application is rated eligible, you will be ranked against all applicants and the best qualified candidates will be referred to the selecting official. The selecting official must select from the top-rated applicants. Interviews are optional; however, if one applicant is interviewed, generally all of the top-rated applicants will be interviewed. Refer to Chapter Six for guidance on how to complete your application.

*I*nadequately prepared application forms prevent many highly qualified candidates from making the eligible list.

LITTLE KNOWN FACTS

If you visit USAJOBS online or use one of the federal job touch screen computers located at federal buildings around the country and view their current list of job vacancies, the list may not be all-inclusive. Agencies in your area may have direct hire or case hiring authority for specific job skills, and many agencies can hire college graduates noncompetitively under the Outstanding Scholars Program. These agencies might not advertise openings through OPM. See Chapter Three for details.

To locate other potential job openings and networking resources, contact individual agency personnel or human resource departments where you wish to work. Also, contact the local Federal Executive Board (FEB) to obtain a list of agencies in your area. There are 28 FEBs located in cities that are major centers of federal activity. Many now have Web sites that you can access with a computer and modem. You will also find a list of FEBs in Appendix B. Most FEBs publish a comprehensive area federal agency directory that you can use to identify where the agency offices are located in your area. Many agencies have multiple staffed facilities in major metropolitan areas.

Review the blue pages in your white page telephone directory. Blue pages list government agencies in your area. The yellow pages also offer comprehensive government listings.

To obtain information about a particular agency, refer to Appendix C for contact information, addresses, Web sites, and a brief agency description. You can also explore over 140 federal agencies and departments online from links posted on http://federaljobs.net/federal.htm.

Don't overlook your local state employment office. The Office of Personnel Management supplies current employment lists to all state employment offices, and direct hire agencies may forward their lists to state agencies.

HOW JOBS ARE FILLED

Selecting officials can fill positions through internal promotions or reassignments, re-employing former employees through reinstatement, using special noncompetitive appointments such as the Veterans Recruitment Act, or by appointing a new employee through a vacancy announcement.

NONCOMPETITIVE APPOINTMENTS

Noncompetitive appointments are special hiring authority for special- emphasis hiring programs such as the Veterans Recruitment Program discussed in Chapter Seven, college graduates under with high QPAs under the Outstanding Scholar Program outlined in Chapter Three, and special hiring practices for people with physical or mental disabilities covered in Chapter Ten.

Federal managers fear that if they don't hire up to their authorized employment ceiling in the current fiscal year, Congress will, with the stroke of a pen, reduce their employment ceiling next year.

Agencies evaluate their attrition, projected retirements, and staffing allowances throughout the year. However, they often hold off hiring until close to the end of the fiscal year on September 30 because of budgetary concerns. Agencies are able to use the funds they save for positions that go unfilled for that fiscal year. However, they must be staffed at 100percent by September 30 or they risk losing that position next fiscal year. Therefore, one of the best times of the year to look for employment is July through September.

Adding to the confusion, many federal employees are eligible to retire at age 55 with 30 years service or at age 60 with 20 years service. Some job series offer early retirement with as little as 20 years service. Many eligible employees opt to remain long after their retirement anniversary date. After age 55 is reached, agencies don't know when employees will elect to retire. One day agencies are fully staffed and the next day they could have 50 people submit their retirement paperwork. More than 34 percent of the federal workforce is now eligible for retirement.

All this uncertainty causes agencies to go begging for new employees at or close to the end of the fiscal year, September 30. Unfortunately, if agencies advertise through the Office of Personnel Management or initiate hiring actions through delegated hiring authority it can take from several weeks to months before the job is advertised, the applicants rated, and the selection made.

Noncompetitive appointments including former employees with reinstatement rights can be selected and hired the same day. If you qualify for noncompetitive appointments, multiply your chances by contacting agencies in your area. Send them a signed copy of your application, a federal style résumé or the OF-612 form, and write a cover letter explaining who you are, what program you qualify for, and when you can start working. Be tactful and don't demand employment. Agencies don't have to hire anyone noncompetitively if they choose not to.

The term "noncompetitive" is misleading. Individuals within noncompetitive groups do compete for jobs. If there are three Veterans Recruitment Appointment (VRA) candidates vying for the same position, the best qualified candidate will be selected from this group, generally through the interview process.

REINSTATEMENT

Reinstatement is the noncompetitive re-entry of a former federal employee into the competitive service. Formal federal employees are not required to compete with applicants for federal employment. Reinstatement is a privilege accorded in recognition of former service and not a "right" to which the formal employee is entitled. Reinstatement is completely at the discretion of the appointing agency.

Career status is obtained when an employee works for three full years with the federal government in a career position. Former employees entitled to veterans preference who served, or who were serving, under appointment that would lead to career status and non-veteran employees with career tenure may be reinstated regardless of the number of years since their last appointment.

Former non-veteran career-conditional employees, those who worked less than three years with the federal government, may be reinstated only within three years following the date of their separation. Certain types of service outside the competitive service may be used to extend this limit. Employees seeking reinstatement should apply directly to the personnel office of the agency where they wish to work.

SAMPLE QUALIFICATION STANDARD

The following qualification standard example will give you an idea of what a rater looks for and how all job series standards are written:

GROUP COVERAGE QUALIFICATION STANDARD FOR ADMINISTRATIVE AND MANAGEMENT POSITIONS

This qualification standard covers positions in the General Schedule that involve the performance of two-grade interval administrative and management work. It contains common patterns of creditable education and experience to be used in making qualifications determinations. Section IV-B of the Qualification Standard Handbook contains individual occupational requirements for some occupations that are to be used in conjunction with this standard. Section V identifies the occupations that have test requirements.

A list of the occupational series covered by this standard is provided on pages IV-A-13 and IV-A-14 of the Qualification Standard Handbook. This standard may also be used for two-grade interval positions other than those listed if the education and experience pattern is determined to be appropriate.

EDUCATION AND EXPERIENCE REQUIREMENTS

Table 2-2 on the next page shows the amount of education and/or experience required to qualify for positions covered by this standard.

		EXPERIENCE	
GRADE	**EDUCATION**	**GENERAL**	**SPECIALIZED**
GS-5	4-year course of study to a bachelor's degree	3 years, 1 year equivalent to at least GS-4	None
GS-7	2 full years of graduate level education or superior academic achievement	None	1 year equivalent to at least GS-5
GS-9	2 full years of progressively higher level graduate education or master's or equivalent graduate degree (such as an LL.B. or J.D)	None	1 year equivalent to at least GS-7
GS-11	3 full years of progressively higher education or Ph.D. or equivalent doctoral degree	None	1 year equivalent to at least GS-9
GS-12 & above	None	None	1 year equivalent or at least next grade level

TABLE 2-2

EDUCATION OR EXPERIENCE

Some of the occupational series covered by this standard include both one - and two - grade interval work. The qualification requirements described in this standard apply only to those positions that typically follow a two-grade interval pattern. While the levels of experience shown for most positions covered by this standard follow the grade level progression pattern outlined in the table, users of the standard should refer to the "General Policies and Instructions" (Section 11 of the Qualifications Handbook) for guidance on crediting experience for positions with different lines of progression.

Undergraduate Education: Successful completion of a full four-year course of study *in any field* leading to a bachelor's degree, in an accredited college or university, meets the GS-5 level requirements for many positions covered by this standard. Others have individual occupational requirements in Section IV-B that specify that applicants must, in general, (1) have specific course work that meets the requirements for a major in a particular field(s), or (2) have at least 24 semester hours of course work in the field(s) identified. Course work in fields closely related to those specified *may* be accepted if it clearly provides applicants with the background of knowledge and skills necessary for successful job performance. One year of full-time undergraduate study is defined as 30 semester hours or 45 quarter hours, and is equivalent to nine months of general experience.

Superior Academic Achievement: The superior academic achievement provision is applicable to all occupations covered by this standard. See the "General Policies and Instructions" for specific guidance on applying the superior academic achievement provision.

Graduate Education: Education at the graduate level in an accredited college or university in the amounts shown in the table meets the requirements for positions at GS-7 through GS-11. Such education must demonstrate the knowledge, skills, and abilities necessary to do the work.

One year of full-time graduate education is considered to be the number of credit hours that the school attended has determined to represent one year of full-time study. If that information cannot be obtained from the school, 18 semester hours should be considered as satisfying the one year of full-time study requirement.

Part-time graduate education is creditable in accordance with its relationship to a year of full-time study at the school attended.

For certain positions covered by this standard, the work may be recognized as sufficiently technical or specialized that graduate study alone may not provide the knowledge and skills needed to perform the work. In such cases, agencies may use selective factors to screen out applicants without actual work experience.

General Experience: For positions for which individual occupational requirements do not specify otherwise, general experience is three years of progressively responsible experience (one year of which was equivalent to at least GS-4) that demonstrates the ability to:

1. Analyze problems to identify significant factors, gather pertinent data, and recognize solutions;

2. Plan and organize work; and

3. Communicate effectively orally and in writing.

Such experience may have been gained in administrative, professional, technical, investigative, or other responsible work. Experience in substantive and relevant secretarial, clerical, or other responsible work may be qualifying as long as it provided evidence of the knowledge, skills, and abilities (KSAs) necessary to perform the duties of the position to be filled. Experience of a general clerical nature (typing, filing, routine procedural processing, maintaining records, or other non-specialized tasks) is not creditable. Trades or crafts experience appropriate to the position to be filled may be creditable for some positions.

For some occupations or positions, applicants must have had work experience that demonstrated KSAs in addition to those identified above. Positions with more specific general experience requirements than those described here are shown in the appropriate individual occupational requirements.

Specialized Experience: Experience that equipped the applicant with the particular knowledge, skills, and abilities to perform successfully the duties of the position, and that is typically in or related to the work of the position to be filled. To be creditable, specialized experience must have an equivalent to at least the next lower grade level in the normal line of progression for the occupation in the organization. Applicants who have the one year of appropriate specialized experience, as indicated in the table, are not required by this standard to have general experience, education above the high school level, or any additional specialized experience to meet the minimum qualification requirements.

Combining Education and Experience: Combinations of successfully completed post-high school education and experience may be used to meet total qualification requirements for the grade levels specified in the table. They may be computed by first determining the applicant's total qualifying experience as a percentage of the experience required for the grade level, then determining the applicant's education as a percentage of the education required for the grade level, and then adding the two percentages. (See examples below.) The total percentages must equal at least 100 percent to qualify an applicant for that grade level. Only graduate education in excess of the amount required for the next lower grade level may be used to qualify applicants for positions at grades GS-9 and GS-11. (When crediting education that requires specific course work, prorate the number of hours of related courses required as a proportion of the total education to be used.)

The following are examples of how education and experience may be combined. They are examples only, and are not all-inclusive.

- The position to be filled is a Quality Assurance Specialist, GS-1910-5. An applicant has two years of general experience and 45 semester hours of college that included nine semester hours in related course work as described in the individual occupational requirements in Section IV-B. The applicant meets 67 percent of the required experience and 38 percent of the required education. Therefore, the applicant exceeds 100 percent of the total requirement and is qualified for the position.

- The position to be filled is a Management Analyst, GS-343-9. An applicant has six months of specialized experience equivalent to GS-7 and one year of graduate level education. The applicant meets 50 percent of the required experience but none of the required education, since he or she does not have any graduate study beyond that which is required for GS-7. Therefore, the applicant meets only 50 percent of the total requirement and is not qualified for the position. (The applicant's first year of graduate study is not qualifying for GS-9.)

- The position to be filled is a Music Specialist, GS-1051-11. An applicant has nine months of specialized experience equivalent to GS-9 and 2 ½ years of creditable graduate level education in music. The applicant meets 75 percent of the required experience and 50 percent of the required education, i.e., the applicant has ½ year of graduate study beyond that required for GS-9. Therefore, the applicant exceeds the total requirement and is qualified for the position. (The applicant's first two years of graduate study are not qualifying for GS-11.)

SELECTIVE FACTORS FOR COVERED POSITIONS

Selective factors must represent knowledge, skills, or abilities that are essential for successful job performance and cannot reasonably be acquired on the job during the period of orientation/training customary for the position being filled. For example, while the individual occupational requirements for Recreation Specialist provide for applicants to meet minimum qualifications on the basis of education or experience in any one of a number of recreational fields, a requirement for knowledge of therapeutic recreation may be needed to perform the duties of a position providing recreation services to persons with physical disabilities. If that is the case, such knowledge could be justified as a selective factor in filling the position.

FEDERAL STUDENT LOAN REPAYMENT PROGRAM

The federal government has paid over $60 million in student loan repayment incentives to new hires and current employees since the program's inception in 2002. Student loan repayment is intended to be a tool for agencies to use when necessary to help them achieve their recruitment and retention goals.[1] The federal student loan repayment program authorizes agencies to repay federally insured student loans as a recruitment or retention incentive for candidates or current employees of the agency.

The federal government has paid over $60 million in student loan repayment incentives to new hires and current employees since its inception.

The program authorizes agencies to set up their own student loan repayment programs to attract or retain highly qualified employees.[2] Any employee is eligible, except those occupying a position excepted from the competitive civil service because of their confidential, policy-determining, policy-making, or policy-advocating nature (e.g., Schedule C appointees).

Although the student loan is not forgiven, agencies may make payments to the loan holder of up to a maximum of $10,000 for an employee in a calendar year and a total of not more than $60,000 for any one employee.

Employees that accept loan payment are required to sign a service agreement to remain in the service of the paying agency for a period of at least three years. Employees must reimburse the paying agency for all benefits received if he or she

---

[1] Fiscal Year 2005 Federal Student Loan Repayment Program Report to Congress

[2] Authorized per 5 U.S.C. 5379, employee defined by U.S.C. 2105

is separated voluntarily or separated involuntarily for cause or poor performance. In addition, an employee must maintain an acceptable level of performance in order to continue to receive repayment benefits.

One word of caution. When you accept student loan reimbursement the payments sent to your loan holder are included in the employee's gross income and in wages for federal employment tax purposes. Therefore, your actual payment will be reduced by the taxes incurred.

Participating Agencies

The program began in 2002 and each year since inception the amount of reimbursement and employees receiving benefits have increased dramatically. Agencies may choose to provide student loan repayment benefits to recruit or retain employees across all job series, or target the incentive to a particular occupation or set of occupations.

Agencies may use student loan repayment benefits to recruit or retain employees across all job series, or target the incentive to a particular occupation or set of occupations.

Table 2-3

Student Loan Repayment Program Statistics

	2002	2003	2004	2005
Participating Agencies	16	24	28	30
Employees Benefiting	690	2,077	2,945	4,409
Amount of Benefits in Millions	$3.164	$9.183	$16.424	$27.982

Table 2-4

Top Five Agencies in FY 2005
Using Student Loan Reimbursement Incentives

Agency	Employee Count	Amount of Benefits Provided
Department of Justice	1,092	$10,063,954
Department of Defense	1,077	$4,818,492
Department of State	809	$3,859,737
Securities & Exchange Commission	414	$3,690,471
Government Accountability Office	218	$1,170,876
All Others	799	$4,379,150
Total	**4,409**	**$27,982,680**

Job Classifications

Agencies may choose to provide student loan repayment benefits to recruit or retain employees across all job series, or target the incentive to a particular occupation or set of occupations. Table 2-5 lists the occupations that agencies used student loan repayments most often.[3] Don't be discouraged if your occupation is not on this list. Employees from a diverse cross section of occupations (42.7 percent of all incentives awarded) have received tuition reimbursement and the list ranges from secretary, chemists, and program analysts to IT specialists, nurses, office managers and scientists and everything in between.

Table 2-5

2005 Student Loan Occupational Summary

Occupation	Employee Count	% of Total
Attorney	479	10.9
Criminal Investigator	445	10.1
Intelligence	201	4.6
GAO Analyst	164	3.7
Miscellaneous Administrative	161	3.7
Mechanical Engineer	149	3.4
Information Technology Management	148	3.4
Contract Specialist	135	3.1
Foreign Service Political Affairs Officer	121	2.7
Management and Program Analysis	118	2.7
Inspection, Investigation, and Compliance	106	2.4
Foreign Service Economics	104	2.4
Accounting	100	2.3
Foreign Service Public Diplomacy Officer	97	2.2
All Other Occupations	1,881	42.7
TOTAL	**4,409**	**100.00**

---

[3]OPM's *Fiscal Year 2005 "Federal Student Loan Repayment Program" Report to Congress*.

Agencies are often fighting tight budgets, and even when agencies have allocated funding for this program you may not receive an offer **UNLESS YOU ASK!** If you are selected for a position and there is no incentive initially offered don't hesitate to ask if the agency will pay your student loans under this program if you accept the position. Be tactful when asking the question. Remember that no agency has to pay incentives; they do it because they need to meet their recruitment goals and have to attract and keep competent and qualified employees in a highly competitive market. Don't be discouraged if they don't offer to pay your student loans when first employed; you can always request repayment after you are employed on the job and have some experience. The next section will discuss other incentives that you must often ask for, such as pay matching.

You may not receive an offer UNLESS YOU ASK!

Visit OPM's Web site at http://opm.gov/oca/PAY/StudentLoan/index.asp for additional information on this subject. You can also find current information and updated statistics at http://federaljobs.net.

RECRUITMENT, RELOCATION, AND RETENTION INCENTIVES

Thirty-four federal agencies paid 5,998 recruitment, relocation, and retention incentives worth more than $51 million in 2005. Agencies may pay recruitment incentives to newly appointed employees if the agency determines that the position is likely to be difficult to fill in the absence of an incentive.

In 2005 34 federal agencies paid 5,998 recruitment, relocation, and retention incentives worth more than $51 million.

Recruitment and Relocation Incentives

A recruitment incentive may be paid to an eligible individual who is appointed to a General Schedule (GS), senior-level (SL), scientific or professional (ST), Senior Executive Service (SES), Federal Bureau of Investigation and Drug Enforcement Administration (FBI/DEA) SES, Executive Schedule (EX), law enforcement officer, or prevailing rate position. OPM may approve other categories for coverage upon written request from the head of the employing agency.

Recruitment incentives may not be paid to presidential appointees; noncareer appointees in the Senior Executive Service; those in positions excepted from the competitive service by reason of their confidential, policy-determining, policy-making, or policy-advocating natures; agency heads; or those expected to receive an appointment as an agency head.

Agencies may pay a recruitment incentive to an employee newly appointed to a position that is likely to be difficult to fill in the absence of an incentive.[4] Recruitment incentive pay may not exceed 25 percent of the employee's annual rate of basic pay in effect at the beginning of the service period multiplied by the number of years in the service period, not to exceed four years, Agencies may also pay a relocation incentive to a current employee who must relocate to accept a position in

---

[4] 5 U.S.C. 5753 and 5 CFR part 575, subpart A & B

a different geographic area that is likely to be difficult to fill in the absence of an incentive. Employees who accept incentives must sign an agreement to fulfill a period of service with the agency.

Payment options

Recruitment and relocation incentives may be paid—

✓ As an initial lump-sum payment at the beginning of the service period;

✓ In equal or variable installments throughout the service period;

✓ As a final lump-sum payment on completion of the service period; or

✓ In a combination of these methods.

For example, an agency may decide to pay a portion of a recruitment incentive to an employee upon appointment to the new position, another portion when the employee completes half of the service period required by the service agreement, and a final payment when the employee completes the full service period required by the service agreement. An agency may decide to use different payment options for different incentive authorizations.

Retention Incentives

Agencies may pay a retention incentive to a current employee if they determine the unusually high or unique qualifications of the employee or a special need of the agency for the employee's service makes it essential to retain the employee and the employee would likely leave federal service without this incentive. Retention incentives may not exceed 25 percent of an employee's rate of basic pay. These incentives can also be awarded for a group or category of employees not to exceed 10 percent of the employee's rate of basic pay.

Participating Agencies

Many federal departments and agencies participate in this program. The largest number of incentives were offered by the Department of Defense. It paid $25,622,370 to 3,516 workers in 2005 of which 1331 were *recruitment incentives* averaging $8,527 per award. The national average recruitment incentive was $8,765 and it was paid to 2037 new hires from 34 agencies in 2005. The Justice Department was second with 143 recruitment incentives worth $1,224,188. The e program began in 2002 and each year since inception the amount of reimbursement and number of employees receiving benefits have increased dramatically. Agencies may choose to provide student loan repayment benefits to recruit or retain employees across all job series, or target the incentive to a particular occupation or set of occupations.

In 2005 the average recruitment incentive was $8,765.

Ask prior to accepting a position if they are offering recruitment incentives for the advertised position. If they aren't offering recruitment incentives or student loan payback, ask if they will at least match your previous employer's salary. Many new hires accept their first position at less salary than what they were earning in the private sector to get their foot in the door. Ask the hiring agency to match your previous salary (before you accept the position) and you could end up starting at other than a step 1 in your pay grade. You will have to provide copies of your most recent pay stubs and you have to request this **PRIOR** to accepting a position. Agencies can't match salary after you accept the initial offer by federal regulations. Salary matches are used to attract new hires when filling critical positions. It never hurts to ask.

Ask hiring agencies to match your previous salary BEFORE you accept the position.

TABLE 2-6
The "TYPICAL" Federal Civilian Employee

INDIVIDUAL CHARACTERISTICS	2000	2005
Average Age	46.3	46.8
Average Length of Service	17.1	16.6
Retirement Eligible		
CSRS	17.0%	30.0%
FERS	11.0%	13.0%
College Educated	41%	42%
Gender		
Men	55%	56%
Women	45%	45%
Race & National Origin		
Minority Total	30.4%	31.4%
Black	17.1%	17.0%
Hispanic	6.6%	7.3%
American Indian	4.5%	5.0%
Asian/Pacific Islander	4.5%	5.0%
Alaska Native	2.2%	2.1%
Disabled	7.0%	7.0%
Veterans Preference	24.0%	22.0%
Vietnam Era Veterans	14.0%	12.0%
Retired Military	3.9%	4.9%
Retired Officers	0.5%	0.9%

Sources: "The 'typical' Federal Civilian Employee"; OPM FACT Book, 2006

CHAPTER THREE
What Jobs Are Available

O ver 30,000 federal jobs are advertised on any given day. Yes, thousands of jobs just a few key strokes away if you know where to find them. With 50 percent of the federal work force eligible for either early or regular retirement, there are abundant opportunities for all who seek them out. Jobs are available nationwide and overseas. The Office of Personnel Management (OPM) maintains the largest government online jobs data base at http://www.usajobs.gov and you can take advantage of its FREE online résumé and automated job alert services. Visit http://federaljobs.net/federal.htm to link to hundreds of agency employment Web sites to locate ALL available jobs. Job seekers can also call OPM's **USAJOBS** hotline for updated job information at 1-703-724-1850, TTY 978-461-8404.

V isit, federaljobs.net to link to hundreds of agency employment sites to find ALL available jobs.

The USAJOBS jobs hotline is menu driven, and you can search jobs by answering specific questions using your telephone keypad. The phone prompts help you select jobs and salary ranges of interest. If you don't have access to a computer visit your local library to explore the easy to use referenced Web sites.

Not all government jobs are advertised on **USAJOBS**. Agencies with direct hire authority may advertise vacancies independently. A list of key Web sites is available in this chapter and you will find a master list of agency recruitment Web sites and links posted on this book's companion Web site at http://federaljobs.net.

CHAPTER OBJECTIVES

✎ Find federal job vacancies in your area

✎ How to improve your chances

✎ Discover useful & productive job resources *(periodicals, hotlines, web sites, directories, books, services & software, agency phone numbers)*

✎ Learn how former employees can be reinstated

✎ How to explore student employment opportunities

Many additional resources are available to locate job announcements including agency sponsored job hot lines, Internet Web sites, computer generated jobs databases, employment services, directories, and periodicals that publish job listings. These resources are listed in this chapter under Common Job Sources. Specific hiring programs such as student hiring, employee reinstatement, and engineering conversion paths are discussed following the job resource listings.

Individual agency personnel offices should be contacted to obtain job announcements and to find out about the agencies' recruitment plans. An agency directory is included in Appendix C. I also suggest that you contact your local Federal Executive Board; see listing in Appendix B. They publish federal office directories for their area. A consolidated listing of Washington, D.C. federal personnel departments is provided in this chapter. If an agency has direct hire or case examining authority, and most do today, they advertise jobs independently from the Office of Personnel Management. OPM does not list job vacancies for all agencies that have direct hire job authority. Occasionally OPM conducts job fairs throughout the country and they are announced on its USAJOBS Web site.

Chapter Seven explains the Veteran Recruitment Appointment (VRA) Program and Veterans Preference. Postal Service jobs are covered separately in Chapter Nine. The U.S. Postal Service (USPS) doesn't advertise job openings through OPM. The federal handicapped hiring program is presented in Chapter Ten, and we expanded the chapter on Homeland Security that includes many law enforcement occupations including federal airport screeners. If you are interested in overseas jobs, review Chapter Eight.

IMPROVING YOUR CHANCES

The more contacts you make, the greater your chances. **Don't get lost in the process.** Too many job seekers pin all their hopes on one effort. They find an open announcement, send in an application, then forget about the process until they receive a reply. Federal jobs are highly competitive and the more jobs you apply for the better your chances.

Good things come to those who wait,
as long as they work like hell while they wait.

Content, proper spelling, and grammar counts when sending in your application forms and/or federal style résumé. Complete your application using fill-in forms available online or computer programs like Quick & Easy Federal Jobs Kit that streamlines the process for you. Quick & Easy completes the entire application and comes with spell check and other functions to help you through the process. The standard private sector résumé is not sufficient to apply for a federal job, it's too brief and lacks the detail necessary to be properly rated. You can download free fill-in Microsoft Word OF-612 forms at http://federaljobs.net.

I participated in many selection panels during my 35 years of government service and was a certified rating official for the Federal Aviation Administration (FAA). I also coordinated and/or conducted hundreds of job interviews for our organization. The first impression that a rating official has of a new applicant is reflected by his or her application package. I can't tell you that many thousands of applications that I reviewed during my career were an absolute disgrace. The handwriting was illegible, spelling poor, and grammar left much to be desired. Half the time you couldn't read the application clearly, and unfortunately they often didn't get a high enough rating to be considered.

Don't make this same mistake — take the time to draft a coherent, clear, error free, and concise federal style résumé as outlined in Chapter Six. With today's word processors and spell check functions there isn't any reason to send in an application with misspelled words, and the word processor grammar check functions are also very helpful. If you don't have the inclination or time to do it right, hire a service to assist you with your federal style résumé. Notice that I say, assist you with your federal style résumé; it takes a lot of time and work for both the résumé service and client to complete a federal style résumé that will get you hired. So even if you hire a service to complete yours, understand that you will have to provide considerable input and devote time to reviewing drafts to get it right. Only the highest rated applicants are referred for interviews and eventually selected for a job.

Take the time to draft a coherent, clear, error free, and concise application.

One Size Doesn't Fit All

Too many applicants make the mistake of submitting the exact same résumé for all jobs they apply for. That may be fine if you are applying for the exact same job series for the same agency. However, there can be significantly different duties and responsibilities for the same job series with other organizations, and you must address those differences in the application package, otherwise you stand to loose valuable rating points. Tailor your federal style résumé, as described in Chapter Six, for each job that you bid on to increase your standing.

Use the list of OPM Service Centers, Federal Executive Boards and Regional Offices in Appendix B and C and the common job resources listed in this chapter to improve your chances. If you're willing to relocate, obtain job announcements from other areas and apply for as many jobs in similar or related occupations that you qualify for. One other word of advice; highlight the key duties and responsibilities listed in the job announcement and then use those exact terms in your work descriptions and Knowledge, Skills, and Abilities (KSA) statements that are described further in Chapter Six. Don't forget to use the *"Job Hunter's Checklist"* in Appendix A to steer you through the entire process.

Don't forget to use the "job Hunter's Checklist" in Appendix A to steer you through the entire process.

Several of the job resources listed in this chapter publish comprehensive national federal job listings. **USAJOBS** and individual agencies each maintain job listings, and most are accessible online databases. Also, contact local agency offices and find out what is currently available, what's coming up, and how to apply. This is especially true since the abolishment of centralized federal job registers. Now over 80 percent of all jobs are advertised by individual agencies. OPM may not list vacancies from excepted service agencies or for agencies with direct hire authority.

The informational interviewing methods presented in Chapter Four will help you develop agency contacts that may be able to help you land a job with Uncle Sam. You aren't locked into the first job or location that you are originally selected for. Once hired, you'll have ample opportunities to bid for jobs in-house.

I accepted my first federal civil service position after discharge from active military duty in Topeka, Kansas, and was able to transfer to my home town in less than a year. Several years later, I applied to the competitive service and accepted a position in a small town of 3,056 in central, Pennsylvania and was able to transfer back to Pittsburgh for a second time three years later. Many agencies have offices at hundreds of locations and you can bid to any one of those locations for future promotions or to enter a related field within your job series. Check with employing agencies to see if they have offices located in or close to the area where you want to relocate. If so, you will more than likely have an opportunity to bid on future openings as long as they employ your specialty at that location.

Our business in life is not to get ahead of others, but to get ahead of ourselves — to break our own records, to outstrip our yesterdays by our today.

Susan B. Johnson

Finally, use all tools available to assist you with your job search, including OPM's excellent *"Career Exploration Interactive Guide"* at http://career.usajobs.gov. This guide helps you select federal careers that match your education and work history. A **GREAT** tool.

COMMON JOB SOURCES

This section presents resources that can be used to locate federal job announcements. After reviewing the listed resources, refer to Appendix D for a complete list of federal occupations. Appendix B lists OPM Service Centers and FEB offices throughout the country. A number of the periodicals and directories listed in this chapter are available at public libraries. Many publishers will send complimentary review copies of their publications upon request.

Resource headings include job openings, Internet Web sites, directories, and general information. Job openings include publications with job ads and job hotlines. The general information section lists related books, pamphlets, informational services, brochures, and computer software. All job sources are listed alphabetically.

JOB OPENINGS

Periodicals and Newspapers with Federal Job Ads

Equal Opportunity Publications — 445 Broad Hollow Road, Suite 425, Melville, NY 11747; 631-421-9421, e-mail info@eop.com. This company publishes a number of excellent publications including **Minority Engineer, Woman Engineer, Equal Opportunity, CAREERS & The disABLED, Hispanic Career World** and **African–American Career World** magazines. Display ads feature national employers, including the federal government, seeking applicants for many varied fields. Each issue offers a dozen to 60 or more display job ads. Call for subscription rates or visit the Web site at http://www.eop.com/contact.html.

Federal Career Opportunities — Federal Research Service, PO Box 1708, Annandale, VA 22000; 1-800-822-5027 or 703-281-0200. You can e-mail question at info@fedjobs.com. Federal job listings, $19.95 per month, $39.97 for a three month subscription. Includes federal and private sector job listings. The vacancy listings are also available online at http://fedjobs.com. Other job hunting resources are available.

Federal Jobs Digest — Breakthrough Publications, P.O. Box 594, Millwood, NY 10546; 1-800-824-5000, http://jobsfed.com; publishes online database job listings for $7.95 per month, $11 for the "Super Search" package or $39.95 for a three month subscription.

Federal Times — 6883 Commercial Dr., Springfield, VA 22159; 1-800-368-5718, http://www.federaltimes.com, weekly subscription available. Call for rates. Publishes some vacancies with brief descriptions starting at the GS-7 level and provides abundant information about federal employment.

Federal Practitioner — Quadrant Health Com, Inc.,151 Fairchild Ave., Plainview, NY 11803-1709, published monthly. Call for subscription rates. Generally includes up to a dozen or so ads for Veterans Administration hospital nurses and physicians under the *"Career Center"* section. Visit their Web site at www.fedprac.com or email quadrantfp@emscirc.com.

SPOTLIGHT — National Association of Colleges and Employers, 62 Highland Ave., Bethlehem, PA 18042; 800-544-5272, 610-868-1421, annual subscriptions free to members. Call for online subscription rates. A newsletter to keep up with the latest trends in the job market; get up-to-the-minute information changes in hiring laws; and learn about what the technology professionals use to perform their jobs more efficiently. Twelve issues a year. Job listings are available on the Web site at http://www.naceweb.org..

The Black Collegian Magazine — Black Collegiate Services, 140 Carondelet St., New Orleans, LA 70130; phone 504-523-0154, published semiannually. Visit the Web site at http://www.black-collegian.com. Free copies are sent to over 800 schools. Subscription rate : $15 per year or $25/2 years. Your one year subscription entitles you to two Super Issues, which are published in October *(Career Planning and Job Search Issue)* and February *(Top 100 Employers and African American History Issue)*.

Federal Job Hotlines

USAJOBS Automated Telephone System — Federal government job national hotline, 703-724-1850, TTY 978-461-8404. You can also call one of the 10 OPM Service Centers located throughout the country for information on federal employment. These centers provide support to agencies in their geographic area. However, if you have a problem with an announcement, first call the contact number listed on the job announcement. If you can't get the information you need, call the OPM Service Center in your area. You can also e-mail or fax questions to them. Contact information is provided in Appendix B.

USA JOBS is operated by the Office of Personnel Management. The hotline phone answers 24 hours a day and provides federal employment information for most occupations. Callers can leave messages to receive forms and announcements by mail. Requested job announcements and applications are mailed within 24 hours. Easy-to-use online voice prompts and voice commands allow access with any touchtone or rotary dial telephone. **Note** — Not all job vacancies are listed on this service. Excepted agencies and agencies with direct hire authority announce vacancies through their individual human resources departments.

USA JOBS Web site http://www.usajobs.opm.gov.

Department of Veterans Affairs — Hotline for VA job information refers users to USAJOBS. The VA advertises job announcements on USAJOBS.

U. S. Postal Service — The Postal Service has a comprehensive employment Web site at http://www.usps.com/employment for vacancies including management, supervisory, administrative, professional and technical positions. Craft or bargaining unit positions such as clerk, carrier, custodian, mail handler, and maintenance technician, or any postal position that requires a test, will find exam testing dates on this site. Sample 473 tests for carriers and mail handlers are available in the 4th edition of Post Office Jobs; you can pick up a copy at your local bookstore or order with credit card by calling 1-800-782-7424. Also call 1-866-999-8777, TTY 1-800-800-8776 to apply by phone if you have the job announcement number. Most job announcements are listed on the Postal Service's Web site or you may find jobs advertised in your local newspaper.

WEB SITES

There are thousands of Internet Web sites now available to assist you with your job search. Many agencies have searchable online job databases available. Not all federal jobs are listed on OPM's USAJOBS Web site. You can review job vacancy announcements online, print them out, and apply for vacancies nationwide. You must contact individual agency personnel offices in your area or visit that department's Internet jobs database for complete listings.

Federal Jobs Network — (http://www.federaljobs.net) This career center will assist you with your federal government job search and guide you step-by-step through the process. You can search this site for key words and phrases. Includes a listing of over 143 federal agency employment Web sites that you can visit for up-to-date job listings and agency information. You will also find current pay scales and up-dates to the 10th Edition of *The Book of U.S. Government Jobs*. Visit this site often for updated information and e-mail contact and address changes to bookhaven@aol.com. We will research and post up-dates as needed.

Federal Online Job Search by FRS — (http://fedjobs.com) Federal Research Service, Inc.,PO Box 1708, Annandale, VA 22003; 1-800-822-5027 or 703-281-0200; e-mail *info@fedjobs.com*. A searchable database of thousands of federal job vacancies updated each weekday. Search thousands of federal job vacancies by GS series, grade, location, eligibility, agency or any combination of the above. Subscriptions are available. Call or visit the Web site for rates.

Federal Web Locator — (http://www.lib.auburn.edu/madd/docs/fedloc.html) The Federal Web Locator is a service provided by the Villanova Center for Information Law and Policy and is intended to be the one-stop shopping point for federal government information on the Internet. I found this site to be very use-ful, with links to hundreds of sites. If you are looking for anything in the federal sector, visit this site and just click on the agency, department, or any one of the selections that may interest you.

FedWorld — (http://www.fedworld.gov/) The FedWorld Federal Job Search uses files created by the Office of Personnel Management. FedWorld downloads source files from USAJOBS. This site allows job searches by various key words such as occupational title, series, and grade, and by state. Each job announcement on FedWorld has a link to the same announcement at USAJOBS. This site's job search capability is excellent, and should you find the USAJOBS site overloaded and slow, go to Fedworld for job listings.

FirstGov — (http://www.firstgov.gov) This site was developed by the administration to be the federal government's Internet directory. It provides abundant information on all aspects of federal government, including a jobs page that offers extensive links you can explore.

Health Care Jobs (Career Center) — (http://healthcarejobs.org) Explore health care services occupations or use this career center to locate jobs in all specialties including jobs with Uncle Sam. You will find a tremendous amount of up-to-date information and resources that you can use to explore lucrative and fast growing careers in the health care industry.

Federal Jobs Digest — (http://jobsfed.com) Breakthrough Publications, P.O. Box 594, Millwood, NY 10546; 1-800-824-5000. Online job search database available for registration fee. This firm also publishes a bi-weekly listing of federal job vacancies in newspaper format. Visit the Web site for registration fees and to review their site features.

Student Jobs — (http://www.studentjobs.gov) Use this site to explore student job vacancy announcements and draft your résumé. This excellent site also provides active links to agencies that recruit students.

USA.gov — (http://www.usa.gov) This site is the U.S. government's official Web portal and makes it easy for the public to get U.S. government information and services on the Web. There are five major channels to search; Citizens, Business and Nonprofits, Federal Employees, Government to Government, and Visitors to the U.S. Click on the Federal Employees link to learn about benefits and pay, policies and practices. A great place to look for government-specific information.

USAJOBS — (http://www.usajobs.opm.gov) Operated by the Office of Personnel Management (OPM). This site provides access to the national federal jobs database; full text job announcements; answers to frequently asked employment questions; and access to electronic and hard copy application forms. Listings are divided into professional career, entry level professional, senior executive, worker-trainee, clerical and technician, trades and labor, and summer positions. An e-mail job notification feature is available, and registered users can create and store up to three searches on this service. When jobs are announced you will be notified by e-mail.

This site offers a résumé builder that you can use to create a federal style résumé that can be printed, saved, and edited. It also offers résumé electronic transfers via e-mail. Agencies may choose to accept electronic résumés on a job-by-job basis.

Many federal job announcements don't make it into this database, and many agencies have their own employment Web sites. A good place to explore over 140 federal agency employment Web site listings that may not be featured on USAJOBS is to visit http://www.federaljobs.net/federal.htm.

USAJOBS Tools

- ✓ Post and store your résumé
- ✓ Search for jobs & receive automated job alerts via email
- ✓ *Career Interest Guide* — Explore career opportunities
- ✓ *Job Interest Match* — Investigate jobs that match your skills
- ✓ *e-SCHOLAR* — Locate student job, grants, and internships, scholarships, apprenticeships, and fellowships

Federal Department Internet Web Sites

Generally you can link to individual agencies of each department from the listed home page. For example, when you visit the Department of Transportation's Web site you will find links to the Federal Aviation Administration and other agency links. Visit http://www.federaljobs.net for a comprehensive and updated listing of agency employment sites.

Appendix C includes Web addresses for most agencies and major departments.

Executive Departments:

Agriculture	http://www.usda.gov
Commerce	http://www.doc.gov
Defense	http://www.persec.whs.mil/hrsc/index.html
Education	http://www.ed.gov
Energy	http://www.energy.gov
Health & Human Services	http://www.os.dhhs.gov
Homeland Security	http://www.dhs.gov/dhspublic/
Interior	http://www.doi.gov
Justice	http://www.usdoj.gov
Labor	http://www.dol.gov
State	http://www.state.gov
Transportation	http://www.dot.gov
Treasury	http://www.ustreas.gov
Veterans Affairs	http://www.va.gov
White House	http://www.whitehouse.gov

Independent Establishments and Government Corporations:

Central Intelligence Agency	http://www.cia.gov
Environmental Protection Agency	http://www.epa.gov
Federal Communications Commission	http://www.fcc.gov
Office of Personnel Management	http://www.opm.gov
U. S. Postal Service	http://www.usps.gov

DIRECTORIES

Congressional Staff Directory — CQ Press, 1255 22nd St. NW, Suite 400, Washington, DC 20037; 202-729-1800. Set lists over 20,000 staff members of the offices and agencies of Congress. Visit http://www.csd.cq.com/scripts/index.cfm to view samples of this helpful guide. Available at many libraries.

Directories In Print — Thomas Gale, 27500 Drake Road, Farmington Hills, MI 48331; 1-800-877-4253; request information on current edition. The 2007 edition costs $720 and it is available at most libraries. You will find over 15,500 active listings. Listed directories can provide locations for government facilities in your area that you can contact for job information and vacancy announcements. A good example is Gale's Government Research Directory. This resource lists more than 4,800 research facilities and programs of the U.S. and Canadian federal governments.

Federal Employees Almanac — (Published in January of each year), Federal Employees News Digest, PO Box 809, Herndon, VA 20172-0809, 1-800-989-3363. A comprehensive guide to federal pay, benefits, retirement and more. Includes pay scales, detailed information about special emphasis hiring programs, veterans benefits, with detailed contact information. Visit http://www.federaldaily.com for more information.

Federal Personnel Guide — (Published February 1 every year) - LRP Publications, 360 Hiatt Drive, Palm Beach Gardens, FL 33418; 1561-622-6520, annual guide, 300 pages, $14.95 plus shipping. This guide is a useful, accurate, time-saving source of valuable information on government organization, compensation, promotion, retirement, insurance, benefits, and other important and interesting subjects for Civil Service, Postal Service, and all other employees of the federal government. Available in print, CD and online at http://www.fedguide.com/.

Federal Yellow Book: Who's Who in Federal Departments and Agencies — Leadership Directories Inc., 104 Fifth Ave, New York, NY 10011; 212-627-4140, quarterly, $450 for one year subscription. The Federal Yellow Book is a comprehensive directory of individuals within the executive branch of the federal government located within the Washington, D.C. metropolitan area. Quarterly editions provide you with direct contact information for more than 44,000 federal officials. All of the information listed in the Federal Yellow Book is verified directly with each organization listed. Includes thousands of e-mail and fax numbers. Visit the Web site at http://www.leadershipdirectories.com/.

Military Installation Directory — A free military installation guide is available at http://www.military.com, click on *"Installation Guide"* in the left border. This comprehensive guide allows you to browse by service, location or alphabetically. It includes a phone directory, medical services, community listings, employment and school information. Military.com offers free membership and connects service members, military families and veterans to benefits and services including government benefits, scholarships, discounts, and much more.

Washington Information Directory — Congressional Quarterly Inc., 1255 22nd St. NW, Washington, DC 20037; 202-729-1800; published June of each year. Call for pricing or visit the Web site at http://www.cq.com. Discusses 18 federal government subject categories and provides abundant information on federal departments and agencies.

The United States Government Manual — 2006/2007 edition, 700 pages, $22. Order by phone at 1-866-512-1800, 202-512-1530 (D.C. Metro area) or online at http://bookstore.gpo.gov/. Available at many libraries. The official handbook of the federal government provides comprehensive information on all agencies of the legislative, judicial, and executive branches. The manual also includes information on quasi-official agencies; international organizations in which the United States participates; and boards, commissions, and committees.

A typical agency description includes a list of principal officials, a summary statement of the agency's purpose and role in the federal government, a brief history of the agency, including its legislative or executive authority, a description of its programs and activities, and a "Sources of Information" section. This last section provides information on consumer activities, contracts and grants, employment, publications, and many other areas of public interest.

GENERAL INFORMATION

Books, Services, and Software

Federal Résumé Guidebook: *Strategies for Writing a Winning Federal Electronic Resume, KSAs, and Essays (4th Edition)* — by Kathryn Kramer Troutman, 2007, 448 pages, $21.95. Kathryn is a professional résumé writer and founder of The Résumé Place, where she manages her consulting practice and publishing business. This book takes readers step-by-step through the federal résumé writing process. It instructs readers on how to write and package their application package to achieve higher ratings and improver their changes of being referred for interviews. Tons of samples are provided for entry level to SES positions. Order from our back-of-book catalog; call our toll free number 1-800-782-7424 (answers 24/7) or online through http://federaljobs.net. A **MUST HAVE** Book for the serious federal job hunter.

Government Job Finder: *Where the Jobs are in Local, State, and Federal Government (4th Edition)* — by Daniel Lauber and Jennifer Atkin, 2007, 348 pages, $19.95. If you are interested in exploring state and local government jobs — over 12 million positions — this is a must have resource. Written by two of the leading experts in the field. Lauber and Atkin provide abundant resources for you to land government jobs in every state and overseas. This highly informative book introduces readers to over 2,000 resources and tools for finding jobs and getting hired in local, state, and federal government: online and print listings, job-matching services, directories, salary surveys, and job hotlines. Designed for professional, labor, trade, technical, and office staff in local, state, and federal government in the United States and overseas. Updates are available at http://jobfindersonline.com/.

Health Care Job Explosion! High Growth Health Care Careers and Job Locator (4th Edition) — by Dennis V. Damp, 2006, 320 pages, $19.95. The perfect book for anyone seeking work in the health care industry. Bursting with details on over 1,000 sources for locating health care jobs including jobs with the federal government, this comprehensive career guide and job finder steers readers to where they can actually find job openings. Lists hundreds of Web sites and e-mail addresses. Appendices include guidance on scholarships and tuition assistance programs and jobs with health care corporations. Available at bookstores or order from our back-of-book catalog; call our toll free number 1-800-782-7424 (answers 24/7) or online through http://healthcarejobs.org.

Military to Federal Career Guide; Ten Steps to Transforming Your Military Experience Into A Competitive Federal Résumé — by Kathryn Kramer Troutman, 237 pages with CD, $38.95. This military transition book is a comprehensive guide for military personnel seeking federal employment. It takes readers through 10 critical steps including networking, federal benefits for veterans, writing your résumé, determining where you fit in, understanding vacancy announcements, searching for jobs, and interview preparation. The accompanying CD provides abundant resources and sample resumes for various military specialties. Order from our back-of-book catalog; call our toll free number 1-800-782-7424 (answers 24/7) or online through http://federaljobs.net.

Post Office Jobs — (4th Edition) by Dennis V. Damp, 256 pages, $19.95. The USPS employs over 800,000 workers in 300 job categories for positions at 39,000 post offices, branches, stations, and community post offices throughout the United States. Approximately 40,000 postal workers are hired each year to backfill for retirements, transfers, deaths and employees who choose to leave. This book presents eight steps to successfully landing a high paying job with the Postal Service. It includes sample tests to help you pass the 470 Battery Exam, prepares you for the interview, and shows you how to apply. Available at bookstores or order from our back-of-book catalog; call our toll free number 1-800-782-7424 (answers 24/7) or online through http://postofficejobs.info.

Take Charge of Your Federal Career — by Dennis V. Damp, 224 pages, $17.95. Call 1-800-782-7424 to order. A practical, action-oriented career management workbook for federal employees. Packed with proved tips and valuable assessment and evaluation tools, this unique workbook provides federal workers with the know-how and guidance they need to identify, obtain, and successfully demonstrate the skills and experience required to qualify for new and better federal jobs.

Services

Résumé Writing Service — Visit http://www.federaljobs.net/applyfor.htm and click on *"Federal Résumé and KSA Writing Service."* This service offers expert federal and electronic résumé, KSA, and federal application writing services. Customers: both federal employees seeking advancement and private industry people seeking their first federal job.

Résumé Writing Referral Service — Visit http://federaljobs.net/referrals.htm for guidance on how to select a federal résumé, KSA and SES Executive Core Qualification (ECQ) Writing Service. The author discusses considerations and three reputable services to fit your needs based on your grade level and objectives. This service is designed to help you decide on what support level you will need to complete your application package. It could be as little as the purchase of a guide to one-on-one assistance with a professional writer, and several options in between.

Computer Software

Quick & Easy Federal Jobs Kit — by DataTech, $49.95 or the personal version plus shipping. Call 1-800-782-7424 to order. This Windows 98/NT/ME/2000/XP and VISTA compatible system offers an excellent and comprehensive set of tools for obtaining a federal job. Includes a résumé processor.

This software includes the **optional forms OF-306 and SF-612**, the **original SF-171 application**, and it **generates federal résumés** and KSAs from data that you enter in the program. It also includes the VA 10-2850 application, AID 1420-17 forms, OPM 1170/17 supplemental Qualifications Statement, SF-181, DA-3433, AD-799 and the SF-172 Amendment to Application for Federal Employment, SF-15 Veterans Preference.

Quick & Easy is designed to be easy to use, even for the person with little or no computer experience. You simply enter your information into the computer using a series of screens that look just like the forms you want to fill out. The program is completely menu driven, with advanced help at the touch of a button. It is a complete system with word processing and spell check, specifically designed to fill in and manage the new optional forms (OF-612), résumé, and the original SF-171. The *Quick & Easy Federal Jobs Kit* prints all forms on any Windows compatible system. Includes the new RESUMIX technology to scan résumés that are submitted. This program is available from the ad in the back of this book or call 1-800-782-7424.

TABLE 3-1
WASHINGTON D.C. AGENCY
OFFICE NUMBERS (June 2007)

TDD (Telephone Device for the Deaf)
Main office number ● *Job Hotline* ■ *Personnel Office*

References: Government Manual 2006-2007 / The Federal Blue Pages
http://www.usbluepages.gov / Federal phone listings at
http://www.info.gov/phone.htm

Agriculture Department	202/720-3631	Bureau of Reclamation	■ 202/513-0501
Research Services	202/720-3656	Fish & Wildlife Service	202/573-4500
Food/Safety	202/720-0351	Mineral Mgmt. Service	202/787-1000
Farm & Foreign Service	202/720-7107	National Parks Service	■ 202/619-7256
Forest Service	202/205-1661	U.S. Geological Survey	■ 888/275-8747
Graduate School	888/744-4723	**Justice Dept.**	● 202/514-2000
		Attorney Applications	■ 202/514-3892
Commerce Department	■ 202/482-2000	Bureau of Prisons	■ 202/307-3198
Bureau of Census	301/763-4748		● 800/995-6423
International Trade	800/872-8723	Drug Enforcement Admin.	202/305-8600
Nat'l Oceanic & Admin.	202/482-6090	FBI	202/278-2000
Patent/Trademark Office	571/272-1000	US Marshal Service	202/307-9400
Defense Department	■ 703/545-6700	**Labor Department**	● 877/872-5627
Defense Logistics Agency	703/767-6427		
Dept. of the Air Force	703/545-6700	**State Department**	202/647-4000
Dept. of the Army	703/545-6700	Foreign Service	■ 202/261/8888
Navy Department	■ 202/545-6700	Civil Service Positions	● 866/656-6830
Marine Corps	703/545-6700		
National Security Agency	301/688-6311	**Transportation**	202-366-4000
			● 800/525-2878
Education	■ 800/872-5327	Federal Aviation Admin.	202/267-3883
		Federal Highway Admin.	202/366-0530
Energy	■ 202/586-1234	Federal Transit Admin.	202/366-4043
		Maritime Administration	202/366-5807
			● 800/996-2723
Health & Human Services	202/619-0257	Surface Transportation	202/565-1500
Substance Abuse &			
Mental Health	800/789-2647	**Treasury**	202/622-2000
Food & Drug Admin.	■ 888/463-6332	Bureau of Public Debt	■ 304/480-6144
Indian Health Service	■ 877/696-6775	Alcohol, Tobacco & Trade	■ 202/927-5000
National Inst. of Health	301/496-4000	Comptroller of Currency	■ 202/874-4700
Housing & Urban Dev.	■ 202/708-0408	Engraving & Printing	■ 202/874-3747
		Financial Mgmt. Service	■ 202/874-8090
Homeland Security	202-282-8000	IRS	■ 202/622-5000
Coast Guard	877/669-8724	Thrift Supervision	■ 202/906-6000
Immigration & Customs	202-435-1000	US Mint	■ 202/354-7200
Secret Service	202-406-5800		800/872-6468
		Veterans Affairs	202/273-4800
Interior	■ 202/208-3100		800/949-0002

INDEPENDENT AGENCIES

African Development Foundation		202/673-3916
Central Intelligence Agency		703/482-0623
Commodity Trading Comm.		201/418-5009
Consumer Product Safety		301/504-7925
Defense Nuclear Facilities		202/694-7000
EEO Commission	■	202/663-4900
Environmental Protection	■	202/260-3300
Export-Import Bank of US		800/565-3946
Farm Credit Administration	■	703/883-4135
Federal Communications Commission	■	202/418-0101
Federal Deposit Ins. Corp.		877/275-3342
Federal Housing Finance		202/408-2500
Federal Labor Relations	■	877/303-8945
Federal Maritime Comm.	■	202/523-5773
Federal Mediation and Conciliation Service		202/606-8100
Federal Mine Safety & Health		202/434-9900
Federal Trade Commission	■	202/326-2021
Federal Reserve System		202/872-4984
General Accounting Office	■	202/512-6092
General Services Admin.	■	202/501-0370
Government Printing Office	■	202/512-1124
Inter-American Foundation		703/306-4301
Merit Systems Protection Bd.		202/653-6772
NASA	■	202/358-1543
National Labor Relations Bd		202/273-1000
TDD		202/273-4300
National Mediation Board		202/692-5000

National Archives/Records	●	877/272-6272
TDD		301/837-0482
National Capital Planning		202/482-7209
National Credit Union Admin.		703/518-6300
National Foundation of the Arts and the Humanities		202/682-5400
National Science Foundation	■	703/292-8180
	●	800/628-1487
National Transportation Safety Board	■	202/314-6239
Nuclear Regulatory Comm.		301/415-7000
Occupation Safety & Health		202/606-5398
Office of Government Ethics		202/482-9300
Office of Mgmt. & Budget		202/395-7250
Office of Personnel Mgmt.	■	202/606-2400
Peace Corps	■	202/692-1200
	●	800/818-9579
Postal Rate Commission		202/789-6800
Securities & Exch. Comm.	■	202/942-4150
Selective Service System	■	703-605-4056
Small Business Admin.		202/205-6600
Social Security Admin.		410-965-1234
		800/772-1213
Tennessee Valley Authority	■	865/632-3222
		866/620-8010
Trade & Development		703/875-4357
US Comm. On Civil Rights	■	202/376-8364
US International Trade Commission	■	202/205-2651
US Postal Service		202/636-1400
	●	800/562-8777

These numbers are subject to change. If you try a number and it has changed, go to the following Web sites to locate numbers:

■ http://www.usbluepages.gov
■ http://www.info.gov/phone.htm

TABLE 3-2
THE TYPICAL FEDERAL CIVILIAN EMPLOYEE

(NON-POSTAL EMPLOYMENT)

JOB CHARACTERISTICS	1990	2005
Annual Base Salary	$32,026	$61,714
Pay System		
General Schedule (GS)	73%	71%
Wage Grade	17%	11%
Other	10%	18%
Occupations		
White-Collar	83%	89%
Professional	21%	24%
Administrative	24%	33%
Technical & Other	38%	32%
Blue-Collar	17%	11%
Work Schedule		
Full-Time	93%	94%
Part-Time	4%	3%
Intermittent	3%	3%
Service		
Competitive	80%	73%
Excepted & SES*	20%	27%

* The SES is the Senior Executive Service.
Source: The Fact Book, September 2006.

EQUAL EMPLOYMENT OPPORTUNITY

The federal government is an Equal Opportunity Employer. Hiring and advancement in the government are based on qualifications and performance regardless of race, color, creed, religion, gender, age, national origin, or disability.

EMPLOYMENT OPTIONS

There are numerous employment paths available: full time, part time and job sharing positions, cooperative education hiring programs, student employment, job opportunities for veterans and the handicapped, and the Outstanding Scholar program. Military dependents and veterans can be hired under special appointment through the Family Member Preference, Military Spouse Preference Programs, or the Veterans Readjustment Appointment (VRA) Program. Military dependent and veterans' programs are explained in Chapter Seven.

The majority of applicants will seek federal employment through announcements from those listed on USAJOBS or individual agency sites. Alternate routes are categorized into special emphasis groups, such as student employment, military dependent, veteran and handicapped hiring programs. Refer to the related chapter for guidance on special emphasis hiring options.

STUDENT EMPLOYMENT OPPORTUNITIES

Student hiring programs are available to attract students into the public sector. These programs offer on-the-job experience that could lead to a full-time career with the government after graduation. Industry and government utilize student programs to identify prospects for future hiring and you will find OPM's Student site at http://www.studentjobs.gov very informative. An average of 63,000 students are employed each year in federal government.

Post your résumé on OPM's student jobs Web site and explore hiring programs and options.

The Student Educational Employment Program consolidated the Cooperative Education, Stay-in-School, Federal Junior Fellowship, and Summer Aid programs to combine key features of the old programs along with added functions to improve and streamline operations. This program consolidated 13 student hiring authorities into one program consisting of two components.

Most federal agencies hire students and some develop additional student programs to meet their needs. The Student Educational Employment Program introduces students to working for the United States Government.

Students must be working at least half-time for a:

❶ High school diploma or general equivalency diploma (GED),

❷ Vocational or technical school certificate, or

❸ Degree (associate, baccalaureate, graduate or professional).

The first component, the Student Temporary Employment Program (STEP), introduces students to the work environment and teaches basic workplace skills. Approximately 46,307 students were employed in this program in 2005. The second component, the Student Career Experience Program (SCEP), provides experience directly related to the academic and career goals of the student. Approximately 16,786 students were employed in the STEP program in 2005.

SCEP program participants may qualify for conversion to a career or career-conditional appointment. Eligibility for conversion requires that students graduate from an accredited school, complete a core amount of program work, and be hired into a position related to their academic training and career work experience. No competition is required.

Appointments to jobs under STEP are temporary and can range from summer jobs to positions that can last for as long as you are a student. Employing agencies, at their discretion, may establish academic and job performance standards that students must meet to continue in the program. There is no conversion element un-der the Temporary Employment Program.

Students interested in the Temporary Employment Program or the Career Experience Program can find out about job opportunities through their school guidance office, teachers, or federal agency employment office where they are interested in working. Visit http://www.studentjobs.gov/ to review the entire program, post your résumé, and search for job vacancies.

Getting Started

OPM initiated online student accounts at http://www.studentjobs.gov/. Visit this site and select *"New To Studentjobs.gov."* This will take you to the screen, show below, where you create your personal account, search for jobs, and manager your career. Setting up your account is easy and after setting up your account you can create and post your résumé online and request automated e-mail job alerts.

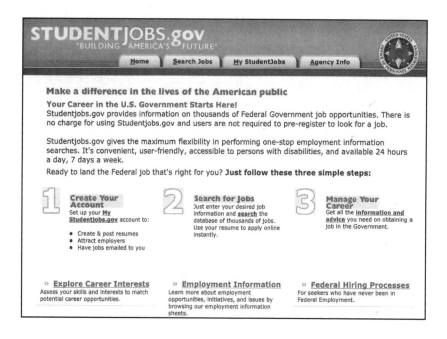

The e-SCHOLAR Resource

The e-SCHOLAR Web site at http://www.studentjobs.gov/e-scholar.asp is a one-stop portal for publicizing educational opportunities available to students (high school to doctorate) and career professionals (teaching faculty to lead scientist). OPM's goal is to simplify the process of finding educational opportunities and assist federal government agencies to attract talented professionals from diverse groups and academic areas.

Application requirements, including when to apply, will differ for each program. Programs are offered throughout the year (spring, summer, fall, and winter). Program durations vary from six weeks up to three years depending on the requirements. The different start times and length of programs provide the maximum flexibility for students and career professionals. You must read and comply with all application deadlines as specified by each program.

The following program list is featured on the e-SCHOLAR site. Visit the site and click on each heading to review the hundreds of available programs, agency sponsors, program descriptions, and application dates. Check this site frequently for new program additions and agency job announcements. Application dates for many of the programs are fixed to specific dates each year.

Student Domestic and International Programs

- Apprenticeships
- Cooperative
- Fellowships
- Grants
- Internships
- Scholarships
- Student Volunteers

Job Searches

Searches for student jobs on http://www.studentjobs.gov may be confusing initially. The search page has no mention of student jobs. I suggest just entering the location where you are looking for work from the drop-down menu, leave the *"Occupational Series"* entry blank and click *"Search For Jobs"* at the bottom of the page. This will bring up a list of ALL jobs available in your area. The results page allows you to narrow your search at the top of the page to *"Entry Level,"* *"Summer,"* *"Intern,"* *"Outstanding Scholars,"* and *"Other"* categories. Click on the type of job you are interested in to view those listings.

Presidential Management Fellows Program (PMF)

This program (formerly the Presidential Management Internship Program) is targeted for graduate students who would like to enter management in the federal government.

Entry into this program is considered an honor and recognized throughout government. In 2004 there were 412 selections made to over 28 major universities. Georgetown, American, and Columbia universities had the largest group of finalists in 2004. The Department of Justice was the biggest sponsor, selecting 57 Fellows for this program.

Professional, entry-level positions are available that provide exposure to a wide range of public management issues and offer career progression potential. Fellows candidates are appointed for a two-year period and most positions are located in the Washington, D.C. area. Visit http://www.pmf.opm.gov for complete information and guidance. At the end of the two-year appointment, Fellows upon program completion are converted to permanent positions as long as their performance was satisfactory.

Qualifications

Typical study areas that qualify include finance, economics, accounting, criminal justice, business administration, health administration, urban planning, social services, public administration, information systems management, law, political science, and information systems management. This list is not all-inclusive.

❶ You must be scheduled to receive or have received a graduate degree.

❷ During your studies you must have demonstrated an outstanding ability and personal interest in a government career in management of public policies and programs.

❸ You are currently a U.S. citizen or will soon become a citizen before being appointed to a PMF.

Your graduate school's dean, director, or chairperson must nominate you for the program. Nominations are made by December 1 of each year. Selections from each school are highly competitive and are based on skills, abilities, and knowledge.

The final selections from all nominees are made through a comprehensive individual and group interview, application assessment, writing samples, and a review of your school's recommendations.

Presidential Management Fellows announcements are mailed in September to graduate schools nationwide. If interested, contact your career placement and guidance office. Call the Career America Hotline for additional information and specific appointment details.

Student Volunteer Services

Students can volunteer to work with local agencies to gain valuable work experience. These jobs are not compensated. Schools coordinate participation, and high school and college students are eligible for this program. A number of colleges include volunteer service internships. Interested students can contact agencies directly.

The Student Volunteer program is an excellent path for students to develop agency contacts, work experience, and gain insight into various government careers. Often, participants receive career counseling and acquire first-hand information on upcoming paid student and full time openings.

All agencies are permitted to utilize this program. However, many don't participate for various reasons. Interested students should ask their career counselor for assistance when contacting agencies. Often, a counselor can persuade a manager to try out the program on a test basis. Student Volunteer Services is an excellent opportunity for aggressive students to get their foot in the door.

THE LARGEST OCCUPATIONS

White-collar workers are classified into 442 different occupations. Refer to Appendix D for a complete list of white-collar occupational groups and their descriptions. Average worldwide annual base salary for this group reached $61,714 in September 2004. The table on page 61 lists the 20 white-collar occupations with at least 16,000 employees.

Occupations ranged in size from several occupations with fewer than 10 employees each to 62,751 employees in the 2210 Information Technology Management job series.

Certain white-collar occupations are concentrated in particular federal agencies. The Department of Agriculture employed 62.2 percent of biological science employees and 91.6 percent of veterinary medical science workers. The Social Security Administration was the major employer of the social science, psychology and welfare group (37.4 percent). The Department of Veterans Affairs employed 71.2 percent of the medical hospital, dental and public health group. The Departments of Defense and Treasury combined employed 72.3 percent of the accounting and budget group. The Social Security Administration and Departments of Treasury and Justice altogether employed 64.9 percent of the legal and kindred group. The Department of Transportation had 68.6 percent of the transportation group employees. The Departments of Justice and Treasury together employed 73.3 percent of the investigative group.[1]

---

[1] Excerpted from Occupations of Federal White-Collar & Blue Collar-Workers

TABLE 3-5

WHITE-COLLAR OCCUPATIONS WITH
18,500 OR MORE EMPLOYEES

SERIES	JOB TITLE	TOTAL
2210	Information Technology Mgmt.	62,751
0301	Miscellaneous Administrative	57,248
0303	Miscellaneous Clerk & Assistant	54,484
0343	Management & Program Analyst	45,812
0019	Safety Technician	41,005
0610	Nurse	40,969
1811	Criminal Investigating	37,239
0318	Secretary	35,685
0105	Social Insurance Administration	26,750
1102	Contracting	26,535
0905	General Attorney	26,210
2152	Air Traffic Control	22,850
0962	Contract Representative	22,422
1101	General Business and Industry	22,399
0855	Electronics Engineer	20,452
0801	General Engineer	18,538
0855	Electronics Engineering	19,837
1801	General Inspection, Investigation, & Comp.	18,524
1895	Customs and Border Protection	17,453
0802	Engineering Technician	16,306

SOURCE: U.S. Office of Personnel Management Workforce Information & Planning Group Central Personnel Data File (CPDF) Sept. 2006

There are 213,500 full-time blue-collar workers classified into 300 occupations and organized into 37 job family groups. Refer to Appendix D for a complete description and list of blue-collar occupational groups.

TABLE 3-6
BLUE-COLLAR OCCUPATIONS WITH
2,700 OR MORE EMPLOYEES

SERIES	TITLE	TOTAL
8852	Aircraft Mechanic	9,728
3566	Custodial Worker	9,715
4749	Maintenance Mechanic	8,896
5803	Heavy Mobile Equipment Mechanic	8,579
6907	Materials Handler	8,089
2604	Electronics Mechanic	6,409
3806	Sheet Metal Mechanic	6,262
7408	Food Service Worker	5,228
5703	Motor Vehicle Operator	5,473
2805	Electrician	4,167
5823	Automotive Mechanic	3,970
3414	Machining	3,677
2610	Electronic Integrated System Mechanic	3,616
8602	Aircraft Engine Mechanic	3,370
4102	Painting	3,297
7404	Cook	3,245
4204	Pipefitting	2,762
3703	Welding	2,293
5716	Engineering Equipment Operating	2,278
5306	Air Conditioning Equip. Mechanic	1,904

SOURCE: U.S Office of Personnel Management Workforce Information & Planning Group Central Personnel Data File (CPDF) Sept. 2006

The federal wage system employment has decreased approximately 37 percent from 326,000 workers in 1994 to 205,233 in 2006. Wage system pay is based on locality, and wage surveys are conducted each year by the DOD to set wage rates for all areas. Over 85 percent of all wage grade jobs are with the Departments of Defense and Veterans Affairs and 47 percent are veterans. The national average base annual salary for full time wage grade employees was $45,156 in 2006. The state of California employs the largest number of wage grade workers, 15,821 with an average salary of $46,265. The largest pay area is Honolulu, with an average salary of $57,041, employing 5,400 workers. Most wage grade jobs are located at military or Veterans Administration installations throughout the country. Wage rate pay schedules are available online at http://federaljobs.net/. Click on the menu selection titled *"Pay Schedules."*

REINSTATEMENT ELIGIBILITY

If you had prior federal career or career-conditional service with the federal government you are eligible to reenter the federal competitive service workforce without competing with the public in a civil service examination.[2] You may apply for any open civil service examination, but reinstatement eligibility also enables you to apply for federal jobs open only to status candidates.

What Are the Eligibility Requirements?

If you held a career or career-conditional appointment at some time in the past there is no time limit on reinstatement eligibility for those who:

- Have veterans' preference, or
- Acquired career tenure by completing three years of substantially continuous creditable service.

If you do not have veterans' preference or did not acquire career tenure, you may be reinstated within three years after the date of your separation. Reinstatement eligibility may be extended by certain activities that occur during the three-year period after separation from your last career or career-conditional appointment. Examples of these activities are:

- Federal employment under temporary, term, or similar appointments.
- Federal employment in excepted, non-appropriated fund, or Senior Executive Service positions.
- Federal employment in the legislative and judicial branches.
- Active military duty terminated under honorable conditions.
- Service with the District of Columbia government prior to January 1, 1980 (and other service for certain employees converted to the District's independent merit system).

---

[2] 5 CFR Part 15.

- Certain government employment or full-time training that provided valuable training and experience for the job to be filled.
- Periods of overseas residence of a dependent who followed a federal military or civilian employee to an overseas post of duty.

Applying for Reinstatement?

You have to contact agencies and locate job vacancies. Reinstatement eligibility doesn't guarantee you a job. Agencies determine the sources of applicants they will consider. Individuals usually apply to agencies in response to advertised job vacancies. Some agencies accept applications only when they have an appropriate open merit promotion announcement, while others accept applications at any time. If you are seeking a higher grade or a position with more promotion potential than you previously held, generally you must apply under a merit promotion announcement and rank among the best-qualified applicants to be selected. Status applicants include individuals who are eligible for reinstatement.

To establish your reinstatement eligibility, you need a copy of your most recent SF 50, Notification of Personnel Action, showing tenure group 1 or 2, along with your application. You may obtain a copy of your personnel records from your former agency if you recently separated. Otherwise, send your request to Federal Records Center address:

FEDERAL RECORDS CENTER
National Archives and Records Administration
111 Winnebago Street
St. Louis, Missouri 63118
(314) 801-9250

Such inquiries should include your full name under which formerly employed, Social Security number, date of birth, and to the extent known, former federal employing agencies, addresses and dates of such employment. The Privacy Act of 1974 (5 USC 552a) and the Office of Personnel Management require a signed and dated written request for information from federal records. No requests for information from personnel or any other type of records will be accepted by telephone or e-mail.

Qualifications

You must meet the qualification requirements for the position. Written tests are not common, but if one is required, you must take it. You must also meet the suitability standards for federal employment. If you were removed for cause from your previous federal employment, it will not necessarily bar you from further federal service. The facts in each case as developed by inquiry or investigation will determine the person's fitness for re-entry into the competitive service.

A former employee who did not complete a required probationary period during previous service under the appointment upon which his/her eligibility for reinstatement is based is required, in most cases, to serve a complete one-year probationary period after reinstatement.

ENGINEERING CONVERSIONS

Many professional engineering jobs are open to non-degree applicants who meet the Office of Personnel Management's Engineering Conversion criteria. This is good news to those who have over 60 semester hours of college in specific areas of study. Federal regulations state that to qualify for professional engineering positions, GS-5 through GS-15, a candidate must meet basic requirements for all professional engineering positions. The GS-800 Engineering Position Qualification Standard provides an alternate and primary conversion path. A copy is available at http://federaljobs.net/quals2.htm.

Primary Path

The primary path consists of having an engineering degree from a four-year accredited college. The curriculum must be accredited by the Accreditation Board for Engineering and Technology (ABET) or include the specific courses and five of the specific study areas listed in Note 1 below.

Alternate Paths

Alternate paths are available to those without a four-year engineering degree but have the specific knowledge, skills, abilities, and work experience for an engineer position. Four years of college level education, training, and/or technical experience is required and can be obtained through the following paths:

1) Professional Engineering Registration Exam
2) Engineering-in-Training Examination
3) 60 semester hours in an accredited college including the courses and areas of study listed in Note 1 below
4) A degree in related curriculum

The first three alternate paths require appropriate training and work experience. If an applicant has the engineering experience and completed A, B, or C above, OPM will rate them as Professional Engineers.

The fourth alternate path is a related degree. For example, applicants who have a four-year degree in civil engineering and bid on a mechanical engineering job can be rated eligible if they have at least one year of experience under a professional mechanical engineer.

NOTE 1. Curriculum must include differential and integral calculus and courses (more advanced than first year physics and chemistry) in five of the seven areas including statics and dynamics, strength of materials, fluid mechanics, hydraulics, thermodynamics, electrical fields and circuits, nature and properties of materials, and other fundamental engineering subjects including optics, heat transfer, and electronics.

CHAPTER FOUR
The Interview Process

There are two primary interview types that you will encounter during your job search—the *informational interview* and the *employment interview*. The informational interview—initiated by the job seeker—is a valuable networking tool used to explore job opportunities. Employment interviews are initiated by prospective employers to assess your ability and weigh your strengths and weaknesses with other applicants. The person with acceptable qualifications and the ability to impress the interview panel gets the job.

CHAPTER OBJECTIVES

✎   Locate job prospects through informational interviews

✎   Prepare for the job interview

✎   Review commonly asked interview questions

✎   What to do after the interview

✎   Follow the "Interview Checklist" on page 106

Even under the best of conditions, interviews are often intimidating, and going to an interview without knowing the "rules" can be downright frightening. Understanding the interview process will help you throughout your career and just knowing what to expect will improve your mental stability as well. Before discussing interview specifics I'll introduce you to the interview process through an associate's true story. I changed the names to protect their privacy.

Understanding the interview process will help you throughout your career.

It was May 1969, and our main character — let's call him Tony — had recently been discharged from the Army. He decided to continue his college education and enrolled at a university in Pennsylvania. Shortly after Tony's discharge, he went on an ***informational interview*** — more on this type of interview later — at the Tobyhanna Army Depot, looking for any available position within his chosen electronics field.

He was informed that no opportunities were currently available; however, the Federal Aviation Administration (FAA) might be looking for someone with his electronic background that he could submit a "package" to the Office of Per-sonnel Management (OPM) in New York to determine his qualifications. That application package was nearly 100 pages thick. It questioned every aspect of Tony's background and knowledge. He completed the "package," made a copy for himself, and mailed it off to this thing called OPM, not knowing what to expect. Months later Tony received a letter from OPM advising him that he was qualified and an ***employment interview*** (more on this later, too) was scheduled with the FAA. He was given a phone number and told to contact the FAA for the exact date, time, and location for his interview. The interview would be in just three weeks. Tony was as excited as he was nervous. What was the FAA? What did they do? What were they looking for? Shouldn't they be calling him rather than vice versa? Lots of questions — few answers. How did Tony prepare for this interview? What was the outcome?

In 1969, information was not nearly as available as it is today. The Internet was a figment of our imagination and learning about the FAA was not easy. A trip back to Tobyhanna helped Tony find out some basic information about the FAA and what the different General Schedule (GS) levels were. Apparently they were just like ranks in the service and determined your salary and status. Tony then pulled out the copy of his "package" and began to study what he had submitted. Finally, he wrote down some key questions for which he needed answers. Here are his questions:

1.   What is the FAA and exactly what does it do?
2.   What is the mission of the FAA?
3.   How does someone with my credentials (microwave radio equipment repairman) fit in with this agency's mission and goals?
4.   Where is the job located?
5.   What additional training will I need, if any?
6.   What is my career development potential?

Tony then called the number and scheduled his interview for January 10, 1970 at the New York Air Route Traffic Control Center (ARTCC) — whatever that was — on eastern Long Island, N.Y. He made sure he got clear directions on how to get to the location and that he knew the full names of those he was to contact upon arrival. He then went back to reviewing his package and determined how he would answer questions testing his knowledge of all the skills he had listed. He also identified what he would take along with him. Since the ARTCC was nearly 200 miles from his home, Tony took along a friend, Frank — nice to have someone you know for moral support on those long drives — a change of clothes (since Tony didn't know the exact nature of the positions available, he chose a suit and tie for the interview — better to dress up than to dress down, he surmised) in case there might be a delay and the interview would be postponed, a copy of his "package" and a notepad with his questions written on it. Apparently Tony had also been a Boy Scout and knew that being prepared was the key to any successful venture.

The big day came, and Tony arrived at his destination about 30 minutes prior to his interview. Nancy, the receptionist, greeted Tony and his friend at the entrance, showed them into the facility and told them where they could freshen up. She showed Frank to the cafeteria and said he could wait there for Tony.

Tony straightened his tie, brushed out the wrinkles, splashed a bit of water on his face and then took a seat and waited for his interview. Nancy was very helpful and conveyed a sense of informality and ease. Tony noted that this wasn't a "stiff upper lip" kind of environment and that the atmosphere was relaxed. Clearly a very professional environment, but most of the staff seemed comfortable, relaxed and joked easily with one another. Tony noted these behaviors on his pad and thought, "I could like working here."

As he was reviewing his notes and questions Tony was taking slow, deep breaths, and silently repeating a positive affirmation to himself, *"I was successful in my interview because I was prepared and confident."*

Nancy's phone broke the silence. She listened for a minute, said okay, and hung up. She motioned to Tony and said, "You can go in now. Val is ready for you." "Val?" asked Tony. "Mr. Lawrence," said Nancy.

Val greeted Tony, extended his hand and announced, "Hi, I'm Val Lawrence. Welcome to the FAA." During that handshake, Tony introduced himself and said, "Mr. Lawrence, I'm glad to meet you and really appreciate your taking the time to interview me for this position." "Please call me Val," was the response. "Have a seat," Val said. As Tony sat down, he noticed that Val had a copy of his "package" on his desk.

After a few minutes of small talk about Tony's trip and the like, Val said, "okay, let's get started." Tony agreed and asked if it would be okay if he took some notes during the interview. Val agreed and began to describe the FAA and what the work entailed. It was clear that Val had read and become familiar with Tony's background and qualifications. He asked numerous specific questions concerning the data Tony had listed in his "package" and even asked about some specific pieces of equipment that Tony had worked on while in the Army. As Val described some of the functions required for the positions available, Tony took notes on terminology, industry-specific acronyms and other items with which he was not familiar.

During the interview Tony asked for clarification on all the notes he had taken. After about an hour of this give-and-take, Val took Tony and Frank on a tour of the facility. This tour answered numerous questions and Tony began to see what would be involved with the job and to realize this would be a great place to work. When they returned to Val's office, Fred, one of the supervisors, was waiting for them. Val introduced them and told Fred of Tony's qualifications and that he might be a candidate for employment. Fred pointed to a piece of sophisticated-looking electronic equipment in the corner of Val's office and asked Tony if he knew what it was. There sat a small piece of waveguide with a small dent in one side. Tony had worked with lots of waveguide in the Army and had noted that in his package.

Clearly, Fred was not just a casual observer in this process. It was obvious that he, too, had read Tony's "package" and this was a serious test. Tony realized that any dents in waveguide made it inoperative and said, "Hmm, looks like a piece of broken waveguide to me." Fred said, "Well I'll be damned!" nodded to Val and left. Tony realized that he had passed the test.

Val shook Tony's hand, and said, "I don't know what the outcome will be right now; however, I think you will fit in here just fine. Someone will get back to you within two weeks and let you know."

Tony thanked Val again for his time and for the tour and asked if he should call if he didn't hear anything within those two weeks. Val said, "Sure, but don't worry, you'll hear from us."

Tony and Frank left the facility and returned home. A week later, Tony received a telegram from the FAA offering him a job starting at the highest pay grade for which he qualified. On February 16, 1970, Tony began his career with the FAA. On June 3, 2006, he retired from that same FAA.

As you read through the remainder of this chapter and learn more about the interviewing process, refer to this story and see how Tony addressed the concerns and challenges of the different types of interviews. Then ask yourself, "How would I respond to these challenges? What would my questions be?" Once you find and document those answers, you, too, will be prepared for whatever comes your way, and using your newfound information and skills, you will be able to find a long and successful career as did Tony. Good luck!

INFORMATIONAL INTERVIEWS

The first step is to call agencies in your area and ask to talk with a supervisor who works in your specialty, e.g, administration, technical, computer operations, etc. If an immediate supervisor isn't willing to talk with you in person, ask to talk with someone in the human resources department. Briefly explain to this individual that you are investigating government careers and ask if he/she would be willing to spend 30 minutes talking with you in person about viable federal career paths with the agency.

If you're uncertain whether or not your job skills are needed by an agency, contact the personnel or human resources department.

If an informational interview is granted, take along a signed copy of your employment application or federal résumé and a cover letter describing your desires and qualifications. The informational interview will help you investigate available employment opportunities in many diverse agencies. You will need to identify persons to interview through the methods mentioned above. You don't have to limit your informational interviews strictly to supervisors. Any individual currently employed in a position you find attractive can provide the necessary information. The outcome of these interviews will help you make an objective career decision for specific positions. There is one key element you must stress when requesting an informational interview:

***When asking for the interview, make them aware that you
only desire information and
are not asking for a job.***

This should be brought to their attention immediately after requesting an interview. Many supervisors and employees are willing to talk about their job even when no vacancies exist. These interviews often provide insight into secondary careers and upcoming openings that can be more attractive than what you were originally pursuing.

Place a time limit on the interview. When contacting supervisors, request the interview by following the above guidelines but add that you will only take 30 minutes of their time. Time is a critical resource that must be respected and used wisely. When going for the interview you should be prepared to ask specific questions that will get the information you need. The following questions will help you prepare:

INFORMATIONAL INTERVIEW QUESTIONS

Experience and Background

1. What are the training and educational requirements of this position?

2. How would you suggest that I prepare for a career in this field?

3. What experience is absolutely essential?

4. How did you get started?

5. What do you find most and least enjoyable about this work?

Credentials

How would you rank these items with respect to their importance concerning a position with your agency?

1. Education

2. Special skills

3. Former work experience

4. Personality

5. Organizational knowledge

6. Other (name specific skills)

General Questions

1. What advice would you give to someone interested in this field?

2. How do I find out about available jobs and how they are advertised?

3. Does this agency hire from regional offices or does it hire through the Office of Personnel Management (OPM)?

4. Does this position have career development potential, and if so, what is the highest grade achievable?

5. What are the travel requirements of the job?

6. Is shift work a requirement? If yes, what are the shifts?

Referral

1. As a result of our conversation today, who else would you recommend I speak with?

2. May I use your name when I contact them?

If an interview is not granted: Ask permission to send a résumé or the new optional application forms for their prospective employee file. In many cases agencies do not have direct hire authority. However, if upcoming positions open they can notify you when the job will be advertised. Positions created through these methods bring aboard highly desirable employee prospects under future competitive announcements.

Certain agencies do have direct hire authority. To determine if an agency has this ability you must contact its regional HR or personnel department. Send direct hire agencies a cover letter and application for the prospective employment file. Office addresses and phone numbers can be obtained by calling local area agency offices and asking for the address and phone number of that agency's regional office. You can also use the Agency Directory in Appendix C.

It is hard to imagine the diversity of jobs needed by most agencies. Don't exclude any agency in this process. Most agencies hire a broad spectrum of skills and professions. When going for the interview, dress appropriately for the position applied for. You can expect numerous rejections while pursuing these methods. Don't become discouraged. Good managers, in industry, as well as the federal government, are always on the lookout for qualified employees. If you present yourself in a professional manner, demonstrate a good work ethic, and have the appropriate educational background, you will make a connection. Persistence pays off when dealing with the government. Many promising candidates give up prematurely before giving their efforts a chance to work. You must realize that it may take some time for a desirable position to become available.

Most government job openings are first advertised within the agency, and current employees have the first chance to bid for a higher-paying position. If the job can't be filled in-house it is advertised in the private sector by the Office of Personnel Management or in certain cases by the agency itself. These are the jobs you will be bidding on. The reason for going to the private sector is that no qualified in-house bidders applied for the available positions.

EMPLOYMENT INTERVIEWING

There are several different types of interviews you may encounter. You probably won't know in advance which type you will be facing. Below are descriptions of the different types of interviews and what you can expect in each of them.[1]

Types of Interviews

- **Screening Interview**. A preliminary interview either in person or by phone, in which an agency or company representative determines whether you have the basic qualifications to warrant a subsequent interview.

- **Structured Interview**. In a structured interview, the interviewer explores certain predetermined areas using questions which have been written in advance. The interviewer has a written description of the experience, skills and personality traits of an "ideal" candidate. Your experience and skills are compared to specific job tasks. This type of interview is very common and most traditional interviews are based on this format.

- **Unstructured Interview**. Although the interviewer is given a written description of the "ideal" candidate, in the unstructured interview the interviewer is not given instructions on what specific areas to cover.

- **Multiple Interviews**. Multiple interviews are commonly used with professional jobs. This approach involves a series of interviews in which you meet individually with various representatives of the organization. In the initial interview, the representative usually attempts to get basic information on your skills and abilities. In subsequent interviews, the focus is on how you would perform the job in relation to the company's goals and objectives.

    After the interviews are completed, the interviewers meet and pool their information about your qualifications for the job. A variation on this approach involves a series of interviews in which unsuitable candidates are screened out at each succeeding level.

- **Stress Interview**. The interviewer intentionally attempts to upset you to see how you react under pressure. You may be asked questions that make you

---

[1] Excerpted from the Job Search Guide, U.S. Department of Labor.
This excellent guide is available from the Government Printing Office.

uncomfortable, or you may be interrupted when you are speaking. Although it is uncommon for an entire interview to be conducted under stress conditions, it is common for the interviewer to incorporate stress questions as a part of a traditional interview. Examples of common stress questions are provided later in this chapter.

- **Targeted Interview**. Although similar to the structured interview, the areas covered are much more limited. Key qualifications for success on the job are identified and relevant questions are prepared in advance.

- **Situational Interview**. Situations are set up which simulate common problems you may encounter on the job. Your responses to these situations are measured against predetermined standards. This approach is often used as one part of a traditional interview rather than as an entire interview format.

- **Group Interview**. You may be interviewed by two or more agency or company representatives simultaneously. Sometimes one of the interviewers is designated to ask "stress" questions to see how you respond under pressure. A variation on this format is for two or more company representatives to interview a group of candidates at the same time.

NOTE: Many agencies have initiated quality-of-work life and employee involvement groups to build viable labor/management teams and partnerships. In this environment, agencies may require the top applicants to be interviewed by three groups. There are generally three interviews in this process, one by the selection panel and the other two by peer and subordinate groups. All three interview groups compare notes and provide input to the selection committee.

The interview strategies discussed in this chapter can be used effectively in any type of interview you may encounter.

BEFORE THE INTERVIEW

Prepare in advance. The better prepared you are, the less anxious you will be and the greater your chances for success. There is an old saying in the real estate business that value is determined by three things: location, location, location. In interviewing, it's preparation, preparation, preparation.

One very important consideration in your preparation is the role that stress plays in these situations. They say that public speaking is the most stressful situation for the majority of people. Well, interviewing for a career position is a close second, so let's talk a bit about stress and what you can do to ensure that stress works for you rather than against you.

Some level of stress will keep you focused and alert, while chronic stress can be a killer. Having those "butterflies" in your stomach is not a bad thing. If you feel they are getting the best of you, try some of Tony's techniques:

- Take long, slow, deep breaths. Breathe in through your nose for a count of 10, then slowly exhale through your mouth for the same count. Do this repeatedly and watch how much you calm down.

- Repeat to yourself some positive affirmation statements. Remember Tony's? *"I was successful in my interview because I was prepared and confident."* Positive affirmation statements always focus on the outcome, not the approach.

- Stay focused in the present. Don't frighten or alarm yourself with what "might" happen.

- Get comfortable. Avoid sitting on wallets or keys.

- Engage your sense of humor. Laughing releases tension and increases chemicals in your brain that enhance well-being.

- Stay fit! Exercise and eat a healthy diet. Your body cannot cope effectively with stress if it doesn't have the tools (nutrients) it needs. Follow the food guide pyramid.

- Role play. Find someone to role play the interview with you. This person should be someone with whom you feel comfortable and with whom you can discuss your weaknesses freely. The person should be objective and knowledgeable, perhaps a business associate.

- Use a mirror or video camera when you role play to see what kind of image you project.

Assess your interviewing skills

- What are your strengths and weaknesses? Work on correcting your weaknesses, such as speaking rapidly, talking too loudly or softly, and nervous habits such as hands shaking or inappropriate facial expressions.

- Learn the questions that are commonly asked and prepare answers to them. Examples of commonly asked interview questions are provided later in this chapter. Career centers and libraries often have books which include interview questions. Practice giving answers which are brief but thorough.

- Decide what questions you would like to ask and practice politely interjecting them at different points in the interview.

Evaluate your strengths

- Evaluate your skills, abilities and education as they relate to the type of job you are seeking.

- Practice tailoring your answers to show how you meet the federal agency's needs, if you have details about the specific job before the interview.

Assess your overall appearance

- Find out what clothing is appropriate for your occupation. Although some agencies now allow casual attire, acceptable attire for most federal professional positions is conservative.

- Have several sets of appropriate clothing available, since you may have several interviews over a few days.

- Your clothes should be clean and pressed and your shoes polished.

- Make sure your hair is neat, your nails clean and you are generally well groomed.

Research the federal department and agency. The more you know about the agency and the job for which you are applying, the better you will do on the interview. Get as much information as you can before the interview. (See Chapter Three and review Appendices C and D.)

Take along extra copies of your résumé, optional forms, or other appropriate application forms in case the interviewer ask for them. Make sure you bring along the same versions that you originally sent the agency. You may refer to your federal style résumé to complete other application forms such as the OF-306.

Arrive early at the interview. Plan to arrive 10 to 15 minutes early. Give yourself time to find a restroom so you can check your appearance.

It's important to make a good impression from the moment you enter the reception area. Greet the receptionist cordially. Be confident, positive and make eye contact. Introduce yourself and identify why you are there. If you shake hands with the receptionist, provide a firm handshake (don't crush his/her hand). Use appropriate salutations, e.g., Miss Johnson, Mr. Donald, etc. You never know what influence the receptionist has with your interviewer. With a little small talk, you may get some helpful information about the interviewer and the job opening. Remember, you only get one chance to make a positive first impression. Most people — not just interviewers — form their impressions about new acquaintances within the first 30 to 60 seconds of their initial meeting. Use this minute wisely. If you are asked to fill out an application while you're waiting, be sure to fill it out completely and print the information neatly.

DURING THE INTERVIEW

The job interview is usually a two-way discussion between you and a prospective employer. The interviewer is attempting to determine whether you have what the agency needs, and you are attempting to determine if you would accept the job if offered. Both of you will be trying to get as much information as possible in order to make those decisions. Ask your interviewer if you may take notes. (I've never heard of anyone who got a no to this question.) This lets your interviewer know that you are interested in learning and connecting with the process. You will certainly hear some terms or conditions with which you are not familiar. Rather than interrupting your interviewer, jot them down so you can ask the appropriate questions at the first available opportunity.

Don't make negative comments about anyone or anything, including former employers.

The interview that you are most likely to face is a structured interview with a traditional format. It usually consists of three phases. The introductory phase covers the greeting, small talk and an overview of which areas will be discussed during the interview. The middle phase is a question-and-answer period. The interviewer asks most of the questions, but you are given an opportunity to ask questions as well. The closing phase gives you an opportunity to ask any final questions you might have, cover any important points that haven't been discussed and get information about the next step in the process.

Introductory Phase

This phase is very important. You want to make a good first impression and, if possible, get additional information you need about the job and the agency.

- Make a good impression. You only have a few seconds to create a positive first impression which can influence the rest of the interview and even determine whether you get the job.

The interviewer's first impression of you is based mainly on non-verbal clues. The interviewer is assessing your overall appearance and demeanor. When greeting the interviewer, be certain your handshake is firm and that you make eye contact. Address your interviewer by name and thank him/her for the opportunity. Your initial conversation might go something like this: *"Thank you, Miss Henderson, for taking time from your schedule to interview me. I am very interested in learning...(more about your company, this position, etc)...and how I might be able to help you achieve your goals."* Wait for the interviewer to signal you before you sit down.

Once seated, your body language is very important in conveying a positive impression. Find a comfortable position and relax. Lean forward slightly and maintain eye contact with the interviewer. This posture shows that you are interested in what is being said. Smile, nod, and use active listening skills appropriately. There are numerous books available in local libraries on active listening and it would be advisable to do some research in this area. Some of the most common, and most effective, of these skills are quite simple. Saying *"uh-huh," "yes," "I see," "interesting,"* and other acknowledgments let your interviewer know that you are hearing what he/she is saying and are staying "connected" with the flow of the interview.

The use of paraphrasing, at appropriate times, also lets your interviewer know that you are truly hearing what is being discussed. Paraphrasing is another active listening technique where you repeat what you just heard, but put it in your own words. For example, your interviewer may mention that their organization has its technical training facility in Oklahoma City. You might respond with, *"So, I heard you say that based on my skill level, I may have to attend some technical school training courses at your Oklahoma City location?"* This may also generate some additional questions concerning things like the length of training courses, travel reimbursements, etc. Show that you are open and receptive by keeping your arms and legs uncrossed. Avoid keeping your briefcase or your handbag on your lap. Pace your movements so that they are not too fast or too slow. Remain relaxed and confident.

- Get the information you need. If you weren't able to get complete information about the job and the agency or department in advance, you should try to get it as early as possible in the interview. Be sure to prepare your questions in advance. Knowing the following things will allow you to present those strengths and abilities that the employer wants.

- ✎   Why does the company need someone in this position?
- ✎   Exactly what would they expect of you?
- ✎   Are they looking for traditional or innovative solutions to problems?

■ **When to ask questions.** The problem with a traditional interview structure is that your chance to ask questions occurs late in the interview. How can you get the information you need early in the process without making the interviewer feel that you are taking control?

Deciding exactly when to ask your questions is the tricky part. Timing is everything. You may have to make a decision based on intuition and your first impressions of the interviewer. Does the interviewer seem comfortable or nervous, soft-spoken or forceful, formal or casual? These signals will help you to judge the best time to ask your questions.

The sooner you ask the questions, the less likely you are to disrupt the interviewer's agenda. However, if you ask questions too early, the interviewer may feel you are trying to control the interview.

Try asking questions right after the greeting and small talk. Since most interviewers like to set the tone of the interview and maintain initial control, always phrase your questions in a way that leaves control with the interviewer. Perhaps say, *"Please tell me a little more about the job so that I can focus on the information that would be most important to the agency."* If there is no job opening but you are trying to develop one or you need more information about the agency, try saying, *"Please share your insight as to where the company is going so I can focus on those areas of my background that are most relevant."*

You may want to wait until the interviewer has given an overview of what will be discussed. This overview may answer some of your questions or may provide some details that you can use to ask additional questions. Once the middle phase of the interview has begun, you may find it more difficult to ask questions.

Middle Phase

During this phase of the interview, you will be asked many questions about your work experience, skills, education, activities and interests. You are being assessed on how you will perform the job in relation to the agency objectives.

All your responses should be concise. Use specific examples to illustrate your point whenever possible. Although your responses should be prepared in advance so that they are phrased-well and effective, be sure they do not sound rehearsed. Remember that your responses must always be adapted to the present interview. Incorporate any information you obtained earlier in the interview with the responses you had prepared in advance and then answer in a way that is appropriate to the question.

The following are some typical questions, with possible responses:

Question: *"Tell me about yourself."*

Reply:

"Briefly describe your experience and background." If you are unsure what information the interviewer is seeking, say, "Are there any areas in particular you'd like to know about?"

Question: *"What is your weakest point?"* (A stress question)

Reply: Mention something that is actually a strength. Some examples are:

"I'm something of a perfectionist."

"I'm a stickler for punctuality."

"I'm tenacious."

Give a specific situation from your previous job to illustrate your point.

Question: *"What is your strongest point?"*

Reply:

"I work well under pressure."

"I am organized and manage my time well."

If you have just graduated from college you might say,

"I am eager to learn, and I don't have to unlearn old techniques."

Give a specific example to illustrate your point.

Question: *"What do you hope to be doing five years from now?"*

Reply:

"I hope I will still be working here and have increased my level of responsibility based on my performance and abilities."

Question: *"Why have you been out of work for so long?"* (A stress question)

Reply:

"I spent some time re-evaluating my past experience and the current job market to see what direction I wanted to take."

"I had some offers but I'm not just looking for another job; I'm looking for a career."

Question: *"What do you know about our agency? Why do you want to work here?"*

Reply:

This is where your research on the agency will come in handy.

"You are a small/large agency and a leading force in government."

"Your agency is a leader in your field and growing."

"Your agency has a superior reputation."

"Your agency has a vision to provide superior service to its customers through teamwork and collaboration, and that matches my value system perfectly. I know that I can help you ensure that vision is a reality."

You might try to get the interviewer to give you additional information about the agency by saying that you are very interested in learning more about its mission, vision, philosophy, goals and objectives (MVP-GO). In doing your research on each prospective employer, find out this information, write it down and take it with you to the interview. Then keep it in your files for future reference. This will help you to focus your response on relevant areas.

Question: *"What is your greatest accomplishment?"*

Reply:

Give a specific illustration from your previous or current job where you saved the company money or helped increase profits. If you have just graduated from college, try to find some accomplishment from your school work, part-time jobs or extra-curricular activities.

Question: *"Why should we hire you?"* (A stress question)

Highlight your background based on the company's current needs. Recap your qualifications, keeping the interviewer's job description in mind. If you don't have much experience, talk about how your education and training prepared you for this opportunity.

Question: *"Why do you want to make a change now?"*

Reply:

"I want to develop my potential."

"The opportunities in my present company are limited."

Question: "Tell me about a problem you had in your last job and how you resolved it."

Reply:

The employer wants to assess your analytical, teamwork, communication and other necessary skills to determine your suitability. Think of a situation you encountered at a previous job. If your work experience is very limited, think of a personal situation. This should be a situation where you experienced a successful outcome. Describe clearly but briefly what you encountered, then describe the steps you took to resolve the problem, implement the solution, create the process, or whatever other action was required. You may need to think about this for a minute or two.

This is an important question and you should prepare for it well in advance of your interview so you are not caught off guard.

Some Questions You Should Ask

- ✎ "What are the agency's current challenges?"
- ✎ "Could you give me a more detailed job description?"
- ✎ "Why is this position open?"
- ✎ "Are there opportunities for advancement?"
- ✎ "To whom would I report?"

Closing Phase

During the closing phase of an interview, you will be asked whether you have any other questions. Check your notes and ask any relevant questions that have not yet been answered. Highlight any of your strengths that have not been discussed. If another interview is to be scheduled, get the necessary information. If this is the final interview, ask when the decision will be made and if/when you may call. As you are leaving, shake hands with your interviewer, make solid eye contact, thank the interviewer by name and say goodbye.

ILLEGAL QUESTIONS

During an interview, you may be asked some questions that are considered illegal. It is illegal for an interviewer to ask you questions related to gender, age, race, religion, national origin or marital status, or to delve into your personal life for information that is not job-related. What can you do if you are asked an illegal question? Take a moment to evaluate the situation. Ask yourself questions like:

- ✎ How uncomfortable has this question made you feel?
- ✎ Does the interviewer seem unaware that the question is illegal?
- ✎ Is this interviewer going to be your boss?

Then respond in a way that is comfortable for you.

If you decide to answer the question, be succinct and try to move the conversation back to an examination of your skills and abilities as quickly as possible. For example, if asked about your age, you might reply, "I'm in my forties, and I have a wealth of experience that would be an asset to your company." If you are not sure whether you want to answer the question, first ask for a clarification of how this question relates to your qualifications for the job. You may decide to answer if there is a reasonable explanation. If you feel there is no justification for the question, you might say that you do not see the relationship between the question and your qualifications for the job and you prefer not to answer it.

AFTER THE INTERVIEW

You are not finished yet. It is important to assess the interview shortly after it is concluded. Following your interview you should:

- Write down the name, phone number, e-mail address, and title (be sure the spelling is correct) of the interviewer.

- Review what the job entails and record what the next step will be.

- Note your reactions to the interview; include what went well and what went poorly.

- Assess what you learned from the experience and how you can improve your performance in future interviews.

Send a thank-you note within 24 hours. Your thank-you note should:

- Be hand-written only if you have very good handwriting. Most people use a word processor to prepare the thank-you note.

- Be on good quality white or cream colored paper.

- Be simple and brief.

- Express your appreciation for the interviewer's time.

- Show enthusiasm for the job.

- Get across that you want the job and can do it.

Here is a sample thank-you letter:

(Current date)

Dear Mr. Adams:

Thanks for taking the time to meet with me this afternoon. I enjoyed the interview and I am excited about the possibility of working for the Treasury Department. I believe that my military background, education, and work experience in law enforcement will be beneficial to your criminal investigation unit. I look forward to hearing from you, and if additional follow-up interviews are necessary just let me know the place and time and I will clear my schedule to attend.

As we agreed, I will call you next Thursday if I don't hear from you beforehand.

Sincerely,

PHONE FOLLOW-UP

If you were not told during the interview when a hiring decision will be made, call after one week.

At that time, if you learn that the decision hasn't been made, find out whether you are still under consideration for the job. Ask if there are other questions the interviewer might have about your qualifications and offer to come in for another interview if necessary. Reiterate that you are very interested in the job.

- If you learn that you did not get the job, try to find out why. You might also inquire whether the interviewer can think of anyone else who might be able to use someone with your abilities, either in another department or at another agency.

- If you are offered the job, you have to decide whether you want it. If you are not sure, thank the employer and ask for several days to think about it. Ask any other questions you might need answered to help you with the decision.

- If you know you want the job and have all the information you need, accept the job with thanks and get the details on when you start. Ask whether the employer will be sending a letter of confirmation, as it is best to have the offer in writing.

Who Gets Hired?

In the final analysis, the agency will hire someone who has the abilities and talents which fulfill its needs. It is up to you to demonstrate that you are the person they want by submitting a comprehensive and thorough application package and by doing well in the interview. Don't leave the interview to chance. Proper preparation can mean the difference between success and failure.

INTERVIEW CHECKLIST

Remember the three rules for a successful interview: 1) Preparation; 2) Preparation; and 3) More Preparation.

☐ Know the type of interview for which you are preparing. Is it informational or for employment?

☐ Make a list of all the questions you need to ask.

☐ Watch your time and don't abuse that privilege.

☐ Dress appropriately and err on the side of caution. It is better to be slightly overdressed than vice versa.

☐ Remember, the only information your interviewer will have about you is what you submitted in your "package." Keep a copy of this data and review it thoroughly prior to your interview.

☐ Create scenarios that you would ask yourself if you were the interviewer and prepare responses. This will prevent you from being caught off guard.

☐ Don't make stuff up! If you don't know the answer to a specific question, say so. Then, if it is an essential question, write it down and ask the interviewer if he or she needs you to call back with the answer.

☐ Incorporate positive body language such as solid eye contact, a firm handshake, proper posture and the like. This conveys a sense of confidence and maturity.

☐ Incorporate the stress management techniques identified in this chapter.

☐ Be positive, persistent and patient. It was nearly nine months from Tony's initial "informational interview" to his "employment interview" with an entirely different agency.

☐ Keep files on all your interviews. You never know when someone may call you back — even if you have already found employment with another agency. Be prepared to follow the opportunities.

☐ Re-read this chapter as often as necessary to comprehend the principles identified here.

☐ Finally, do some research. Topics like stress management, body language, dressing for success, active listening and other "soft skills" are too extensive to cover in this chapter. Numerous volumes are available on these topics in your local libraries and on the Internet. Take the time to read some of these so your tool box will be full.

Good luck, and have a long and fruitful government career.

CHAPTER FIVE
Civil Service Exams

The first question most government job applicants ask is whether or not they have to take a Civil Service exam. Many assume that **ALL** federal jobs require an entrance test, and in general no one likes taking written exams, including myself! For many years, the federal government relied on standardized tests for filling jobs in many career fields. That has changed as agencies moved to improve hiring practices. The government, like business, must quickly fill positions as vacancies develop and employees retire. The Civil Service testing system delayed recruiting initiatives considerably.

Approximately 80% of government jobs are filled through a comprehensive analysis of your background, work experience, and education, not through a written test.

Today, written tests are required for specific occupations including mail handlers, certain law enforcement occupations, air traffic controllers, foreign service specialists, and a few entry level jobs. The majority — more than 80 percent — of government jobs are filled through a competitive analysis of your background, work experience, and education — not through a written exam. Read the job announcement thoroughly to determine if a test or self-certification of a skill is necessary. Table 5-1 lists tested occupations.

CHAPTER OBJECTIVES

✎ Determine if a written exam is required for your occupation

✎ Understand the application rating process

✎ Learn the differences between a federal style & private sector résumé

✎ How to apply under the *Outstanding Scholar & Bilingual hiring* programs

✎ How to practice for clerical and administrative exams *(if required)*

Mandatory testing for administrative careers, originally administered through the **Administrative Careers With America (ACWA)** program, was eliminated with a few rare exceptions. OPM and individual agencies advertise professional and administrative job vacancies and interested parties request and receive application material through the mail or Internet. When ACWA or "written"

93

is listed as the required test in Table 5-1, substitute the process described in the following paragraph for a written exam. Agencies may still use the original ACWA tests to screen and rate applicants in the occupational groups listed in Table 5-2. You will find sample test questions for this exam later in this chapter just in case the job you apply for is one of the rare exceptions I mentioned above.

When entrance tests aren't used, applicants are typically required to complete and return an **occupational questionnaire** and a **federal style résumé** or an **optional application form**. Many agencies now allow applicants to apply online. Personnel offices score applications and generate hiring lists within several weeks of the job announcement's closing date. The top-rated applicants are referred to a selection official for interviews. The occupational questionnaire is discussed in Chapter Six.

Regardless of which method, written test or evaluation of your work experience, education and other qualifications, you will be rated on a point system up to a maximum of 100 points in most cases. Written test scores are based on the test results — how well you did on the exam. When you are not required to take an entrance exam, human resource specialists are trained to rate your application based on the quality and quantity of your work experience, education, and specialized qualifications such as college degrees, licenses, certifications, language skills if required, and so on. This is why it is extremely important to tailor your **federal style résumé** to the job announcement that you are applying for. Chapter Six will show you how to evaluate the job announcement and tailor your federal style résumé to a specific announcement. If you don't tailor your résumé you may lose valuable rating points. Only the higher rated applicants generally make it to a job interview.

Notice that I mentioned federal style résumé several times. I emphasize *"federal style"* because a resume in the federal sector is nothing like most private sector one-page résumés. A federal style résumé is highly structured and requires 43 specific blocks of information as listed in Chapter Six, and the format is standardized. A typical federal style résumé is between three and six pages long and if Knowledge, Skills, Abilities and Other Characteristic statements are required your résumé could easily reach seven to 10 pages or more. If you submit an improperly formatted résumé it may be rejected or at the very least you may lose valuable points because you more than likely excluded pertinent information.

Most people who first approach the federal sector are taken aback by the amount of time, energy, and paperwork required to apply for jobs. Applicants who put the extra effort and time into compiling their own unique federal style résumé and tailor it to the job announcement are more likely to succeed.

Agencies have the option to use a written test if they wish and Table 5-2 lists professional and administrative occupations that were originally tested under the ACWA program. This table now identifies occupations that can be hired using the Outstanding Scholar and Bilingual/Bicultural recruitment programs.

CAREERS WITH MANDATORY TESTING

Some occupations require specialized testing and assessments. The tests are used to validate physical and mental ability and skills required for the position. The exams vary in length from several hours to half a day or more. You will find required exams in law enforcement, the Foreign Service, postal workers, air traffic control specialists, and other related occupations. See the chapters on law enforcement and the Postal Service for more information. The information listed below provides a brief summary of the major occupations that require written exams and a list of their web sites where you can go for additional information.

Air Traffic Control Specialist — http://www.faa.gov/

Applicants for the Federal Aviation Administration's (FAA) Air Traffic Control positions must graduate from an accredited Air Traffic Certified Training Institution (AT-CTI). AT-CTI schools send names of students enrolled in their program to the FAA. There is an AT-CTI database of names for tracking purposes until graduation and recommendation. After enrollment in an AT-CTI program, students take **FAA's authorized pre-employment test**. This test determines an individual's aptitude to become an air traffic control specialist.

Border Patrol — http://www.cbp.gov/

The Department of Homeland Security (DHS) employs thousands of Border Patrol agents. Applicants must pass **The U.S. Border Patrol Logical Reasoning Test** to be considered for positions. The test evaluates how well applicants can read, understand, and apply critical thinking skills to factual situations. Agents must read and study laws, legal commentary, and regulations. Applicants who successfully pass the entrance screening exam and are hired will receive extensive training at their Border Patrol Academy. A free 60-page study guide is available on the Web site. Border Patrol vacancies are advertised at http://usajobs.gov.

Central Intelligence Agency — https://www.cia.gov/careers/

All applicants must successfully complete a thorough medical and psychological exam, a polygraph interview and an extensive background investigation. U.S. citizenship is required. Other proficiency tests may be required to verify language skills, etc.

Federal Bureau of Investigation — http://www.fbijobs.gov/

In order to apply for a job, you must first register online. After registering, you can apply to any vacancy currently posted. When applying to a vacancy, carefully read and respond to the application questions.

The application process can take up to one year to complete depending upon an applicant's qualifications and the current hiring needs of the FBI. It includes passing a written test, interview, polygraph examination, physical fitness test, physical, and a thorough background investigation.

Foreign Service Written Exam — http://www.careers.state.gov/

Application procedures for employment with the Department of State vary according to your career choice. Foreign Service Officers, for example, must pass the **Foreign Service Officer Selection Process**. Students must also meet certain criteria and deadlines for the program they choose to enter.

Internal Revenue Service — http://www.jobs.irs.gov/

Various positions with the IRS require assessment tests. IRS agents must complete an accounting assessment process that takes approximately four to five hours. It is composed of an accounting assessment and an interview with a panel of experienced Revenue Agent managers.

Mail Handlers USPS — http://www.usps.com/employment

The Postal Service has developed a new entrance exam titled **Test 473 for Major Entry-Level Jobs.** The new exam is also referred to as the 473 Battery Exam. All mail carriers must pass this exam with a score of 70 or higher. Check for exam dates in your area on the USPS employment Web site.

Secret Service — http://www.secretservice.gov/

The Secret Service is a federal law enforcement agency with headquarters in Washington, D.C. and more than 150 offices throughout the United States. The agency is mandated by Congress to carry out dual missions: protection of the nation's leaders and extensive criminal investigations. Special Agent applicants must pass the **Treasury Enforcement Agents (TEA) written examination**.

Transportation Security Agency — http://tsa.gov/join/index.shtm/

TSA jobs require U.S. citizenship and successful completion of a full background investigation. In addition, persons interested in security officer positions must pass a medical examination, be able to read, speak, and write English, and pass a physical ability test, a drug and alcohol screening, and an **aptitude test**.

U.S. Customs — http://www.ice.gov/careers/

Some Immigration and Custom Enforcement (ICE) entry-level law enforcement occupations require applicants to pass a written test as part of the application process. Two of these tests include the **ICE Immigration Enforcement Agent Test** and the **ICE Special Agent Test**. Test preparation manuals are provided on the Web site to assist prospective applicants with sample questions, test-taking tips and other guidance.

TABLE 5-1
TESTING BY OCCUPATIONAL GROUPS

P = Performance Test, W = Written Test, L = Language Abilities,
A = Assessment, ACWA = American Careers With America Test

SERIES	TITLE/POSITION	GRADE/s	REMARKS
Miscellaneous Occupations Group			
011	Bond Sales Promotion	5/7	ACWA
018	Safety & Occupational Health		
	Management	5/7	ACWA
020	Community Planning	5/7	ACWA
023	Outdoor Recreation Planning	5/7	ACWA
025	Park Ranger	5/7	ACWA
028	Environmental Protection		
	Specialist	5/7	ACWA
029	Environmental Protection		
	Assistant	2/3/4	W
072	Fingerprint Identification	2/3/4	W
080	Security Administration	5/7	ACWA
082	United States Marshal	5/7	W
083	Police	2	W
083	Park Police	5	W
083a	Police (Secret Service)	4/5	W
085	Security Guard	2	W
086	Security Clerical & Assist.	2/3/4	W
Social Science, Psychology, and Welfare Group			
101	Social Science	5/7	ACWA
105	Social Insurance Admin.	5/7	ACWA
106	Unemployment Insurance	5/7	ACWA
107	Health Insurance Admin.	5/7	ACWA
110	Economist	5/7	ACWA
130	Foreign Affairs	5/7	ACWA
131	International Relations	5/7	ACWA
132	Intelligence	5/7	ACWA
134	Intelligence Aid & Clerk	2/3/4	W
140	Manpower Research		
	and Analysis	5/7	ACWA
142	Manpower Development	5/7	ACWA
150	Geography	5/7	ACWA
170	History	5/7	ACWA
180	Psychology	5/7	ACWA
184	Sociology	5/7	ACWA
186	Social Services Aid & Assist.	2/3	W
187	Social Services	5/7	ACWA
190	General Anthropology	5/7	ACWA
193	Archeology	5/7	ACWA
Human Resources Management Group			
201	Human Resources Mgmt	5/7	ACWA
244	Labor Mgmt Relations Exam.	5/7	ACWA
249	Wage & Hour Compliance	5/7	ACWA
General Administration, Clerical, and Office Services Group			
301	Misc Admin. & Program	5/7	ACWA
302	Messenger	2/3/4	W
303	Misc Clerk & Assistant	2/3/4	W
304	Information Receptionist	2/3/4	W
305	Mail & File	2/3/4	W
309	Correspondence Clerk	2/3/4	W
312	Clerk-Stenographer	3/4/5	W, P

SERIES	TITLE/POSITION(S)	GRADE/s	REMARKS
318	Secretary	3/4	W
319	Closed Microphone Reporting	6/7/8/9	P
322	Clerk-Typist	2/3/4	W, P
326	Office Automation Clerical	2/3/4	W, P
332	Computer Operation	2/3/4	W
334	Computer Specialist	5/7	ACWA
335	Computer Clerk & Assistant	2/3/4	W
341	Administrative Officer	5/7	ACWA
343	Management and Program		
	Analysis	5/7	ACWA
344	Management, Clerical &		
	Assistance	2/3/4	W
346	Logistics Management	5/7	ACWA
350	Equipment Operator	2/3/4	W
351	Printing Clerical	2/3/4	W
356	Data Transcriber	2/3/4	W, P
357	Coding	2/3/4	W
359	Elect. Accounting Machine Op	2/3/4	W
382	Telephone Operating	2/3/4	W
390	Telecommunications Processing	2/3/4	W
391	Telecommunications	5/7	ACWA
392	General Telecommunications	2/3/4	W
394	Communications Clerical	2/3/4	W
Biological Sciences Group			
421	Plant Protection Technician	2/3	W
455	Range Technician	2/3	W
458	Soil Conservation Technician	2/3	W
459	Irrigation System Operation	2/3	W
462	Forestry Technician	2/3	W
809	Construction Control	2/3	W
817	Surveying Technician	2/3	W
818	Engineering Drafting	2/3	W
856	Electronics Technician	2/3	W
895	Industrial Engineering Tech.	2/3	W
Accounting and Budget Group			
501	Financial Admin. & Program	5/7	ACWA
503	Financial Clerical & Assistance	2/3/4	W
525	Accounting Technician	2/3/4	W
526	Tax Specialist	5/7	ACWA
530	Cash Processing	2/3/4	W
540	Voucher Examining	2/3/4	W
544	Civilian Pay	2/3/4	W
545	Military Pay	2/3/4	W
560	Budget Analysis	5/7	ACWA
561	Budget Clerical & Assistance	2/3/4	W
570	Financial Institution Examining		
	for FDIC positions (exception)	5/7	ACWA
592	Tax Examining	2/3/4	W
593	Insurance Accounts	2/3/4	W
Medical, Hospital, Dental, and Public Health Group			
636	Rehabilitation Therapy Assistant	2/3	W
640	Health Aid & Technician	2/3	W

SERIES	TITLE/POSITION(S)	GRADE/s	REMARKS
642	Nuclear Medicine Technician	2/3	W
645	Medical Technician	2/3	W
646	Pathology Technician	2/3	W
647	Diagnostic Radiologic Technologist	2/3	W
648	Therapeutic Radiologic Technologist	2/3	W
649	Medical Instrument Technician	2/3	W
651	Respiratory Therapist	2/3	W
661	Pharmacy Technician	2/3	W
667	Orthotist & Prosthetist	3	W
673	Hospital Housekeeping Mgmt	5/7	ACWA
675	Medical Records Technician	2/3/4	W
679	Medical Clerk	2/3/4	W
683	Dental Lab Aide & Technician	2/3	W
685	Public Health Program Specialist	5/7	ACWA

Veterinary Medical Science Group

SERIES	TITLE/POSITION(S)	GRADE/s	REMARKS
704	Animal Health Technician	2/3	W

Engineering and Architecture Group

SERIES	TITLE/POSITION(S)	GRADE/s	REMARKS
802	Engineering Technician	2/3	W

Legal and Kindred Group

SERIES	TITLE/POSITION(S)	GRADE/s	REMARKS
965	Land Law Examining	5/7	ACWA
967	Passport & Visa Examining	5/7	ACWA
986	Legal Clerk & Technician	2/3/4	W
987	Tax Law Specialist	5/7	ACWA
990	General Claims Examining	4	W
901	General Legal and Kindred Administration	5/7	ACWA
950	Paralegal Specialist	5/7	ACWA
958	Pension Law Specialist	5/7	ACWA
962	Contact Representative	5/7	W
963	Legal Instruments Examining	2/3/4	W
991	Workers' Comp Claims Exam.	5/7	ACWA
993	Railroad Retirement Claims Examining	5/7	ACWA
994	Unemployment Comp Claims Examining	5/7	ACWA
996	Veterans Claims Examining	5/7	ACWA
998	Claims Clerical	2/3/4	W

Information and Arts Group

SERIES	TITLE/POSITION(S)	GRADE/s	REMARKS
1001	General Arts and Information	5/7	ACWA
1015	Museum Curator	5/7	ACWA
1016	Museum Specialist & Tech.	2/3	W
1035	Public Affairs	5/7	ACWA
1046	Language Clerical	2/3/4	W
1082	Writing & Editing	5/7	ACWA
1083	Technical Writing & Editing	5/7	ACWA
1087	Editorial Assistance	2/3/4	W

Business and Industry Group

SERIES	TITLE/POSITION(S)	GRADE/s	REMARKS
1101	General Business and Industry	5/7	ACWA
1102	Contracting	5/7	ACWA
1103	Industrial Property Mgmt.	5/7	ACWA
1104	Property Disposal	5/7	ACWA
1105	Purchasing	2/3/4	W
1106	Procurement Clerical & Tech.	2/3/4	W

SERIES	TITLE/POSITION(S)	GRADE/s	REMARKS
1107	Property Disposal Clerical & Technician	2/3/4	W
1130	Public Utilities Specialist	5/7	ACWA
1140	Trade Specialist	5/7	ACWA
1140	International Trade Specialist	5/7	W
1145	Agricultural Program Specialist	5/7	ACWA
1146	Grain Marketing Specialist	5/7	ACWA
1146	Agricultural Marketing	5/7	ACWA
1147	Agricultural Market Reporting	5/7	ACWA
1150	Industrial Specialist	5/7	ACWA
1152	Production Control	2/3/4	W
1160	Financial Analysis	5/7	ACWA
1163	Insurance Examining	5/7	ACWA
1165	Loan Specialist	5/7	ACWA
1169	Internal Revenue Officer	5/7	ACWA
1170	Realty	5/7	ACWA
1171	Appraising & Assessing	5/7	ACWA
1173	Housing Management	5/7	ACWA
1176	Building Management	5/7	ACWA

Physical Sciences Group

SERIES	TITLE/POSITION(S)	GRADE/s	REMARKS
1316	Hydrologic Technician	2/3	W
1341	Meteorological Technician	2/3	W
1371	Cartographic Technician	2/3	W
1374	Geodetic Technician	2/3	W

Library and Archives Group

SERIES	TITLE/POSITION(S)	GRADE/s	REMARKS
1411	Library Technician	2/3/4	W
1412	Technical Information Services	5/7	ACWA
1420	Archivist	5/7	ACWA
1421	Archives Specialist	5/7	ACWA

Mathematics and Statistics Group

SERIES	TITLE/POSITION(S)	GRADE/s	REMARKS
1521	Mathematics Technician	2/3	W
1531	Statistical Assistant	2/3/4	W

Equipment Facilities and Services Group

SERIES	TITLE/POSITION(S)	GRADE/s	REMARKS
1654	Printing Management Specialist	5/7	ACWA

Education Group

SERIES	TITLE/POSITION(S)	GRADE/s	REMARKS
1701	General Education and Training	5/7	ACWA
1702	Education & Training Tech.	2/3	W
1715	Vocational Rehabilitation	5/7	ACWA
1720	Education Program	5/7	ACWA

Investigation Group

SERIES	TITLE/POSITION(S)	GRADE/s	REMARKS
1801	Civil Aviation Security Specialist	5/7	ACWA
1801	Center Adjudications Officer	5/7	ACWA
1801	District Adjudications Officer	5/7	ACWA
1802	Compliance Inspection & Support	2/3/4	W
1810	General Investigating	5/7	ACWA
1811	Criminal Investigating	5/7	ACWA
1811	Treasury Enforcement Agent	5/7	W
1812	Game Law Enforcement	5/7	ACWA
1812	Special Agent (Wildlife)	7	W
1816	Immigration Inspection	5/7	ACWA
1831	Securities Compliance Examining	5/7	ACWA
1854	Alcohol, Tobacco, & Firearms Inspection	5/7	ACWA
1863	Food Inspection	5/7	A

SERIES	TITLE/POSITION(S)	GRADE/s	REMARKS	SERIES	TITLE/POSITION(S)	GRADE/s	REMARKS
1864	Public Health Quarantine Inspection	5/7	ACWA	2050	Supply Cataloging	5/7	ACWA
1884	Customs Patrol Officer	5/7	W	2091	Sales Store Clerical	2/3/4	W
1889	Import Specialist	5/7	ACWA				
1890	Customs Inspection	5/7	ACWA	**Transportation Group**			
1895	Customs and Border Protect Officer	5/7	W	2101	Transportation Specialist	5/7	ACWA
1896	Border Patrol Agent	5/7	W, L	2101	ATSS DOT, FAA	5/7	W
1897	Customs Aide	2/3/4	W	2102	Transportation Clerk & Assistant	2/3/4	W
				2110	Transportation Industry Analysis	5/7	ACWA
Quality Assurance, Inspection and Grading Group				2125	Highway Safety	5/7	ACWA
				2130	Traffic Management	5/7	ACWA
1910	Quality Assurance	5/7	ACWA	2131	Freight Rate	2/3/4	W
				2135	Transportation Loss & Damage	2/3/4	W
Supply Group							
				Claims Examining			
2001	General Supply	5/7	ACWA	2150	Transportation Operations	5/7	ACWA
2003	Supply Program Management	5/7	ACWA	2151	Dispatching	2/3/4	W
2005	Supply Clerical & Technician	2/3/4	W	2152	Air Traffic Control	5/7	W
2010	Inventory Management	5/7	ACWA				
2030	Dist Facilities & Storage Mgmt	5/7	ACWA	**Information Technology Group**			
2032	Packaging	5/7	ACWA	2210	Information Technology	5/7	ACWA

OUTSTANDING SCHOLAR PROGRAM

Outstanding Scholars can apply for 112 professional and administrative job series (refer to **Table 5-2**) by using one of two options:

- A written examination (no longer mandatory) or
- An application based on scholastic achievement, reflected by your grade point average (GPA), and work experience.

Although the Outstanding Scholar and Bilingual / Bicultural programs are aimed at addressing under representation of African Americans and Hispanics, the programs have never been restricted to those designated minorities.

The merit principle, that "Recruitment should be from qualified individual from appropriate sources in an endeavor to achieve a work force from all segments of society, and selection and advancement should be determined solely on the basis of relative ability, knowledge, and skills..." applies.[1]

Entry level grades, generally starting at the GS-5 and GS-7 or equivalent pay grades, are filled through a review of standardized optional applications or federal style résumés, occupational questionnaires, self certification of required skills such as typing speed, and interviews. College graduates with top grades can be hired on the spot at OPM college fairs or by agencies under the Outstanding Scholar Program. Applicants who meet the requirements of the Outstanding Scholar Program are generally not required to take a written test.

---

[1] Reference http://www.opm.gov/employ/luevano-archive.asp and 5 U.S.C. 2301(b)(1)

Outstanding Scholar entry-level professional and administrative job applicants now earn eligibility by either:

- Earning a college **grade point average of 3.5 or above** on a 4.0 scale or having graduated in the upper 10 percent of a baccalaureate graduating class or major university subdivision such as a college of arts and sciences, and impressing agency recruiters with experience and abilities during an interview.[2] This method is referred to as the **Outstanding Scholar Program**.

- Passing an examination of your education and/or experience for a specific job vacancy. Agencies may use the original ACWA written tests to assess an applicant's abilities prior to appointment. Practice exams are included in this chapter.

These appointments may be made without going through an examination procedure for jobs at grades GS-5 and GS-7 in covered occupations. Covered occupations are listed in Table 5-2. A major university subdivision is a college or school and is not merely a department or program of study. For class standing to be used, it must be determined formally by the college, school, or university.

Announcing Vacancies

Prior to making appointments under the program, an agency must advertise positions, including posting them through OPM's job information system. There are three basic reasons why the positions must be announced:

- By law, the principle of merit requires fair and open competition, which in turn requires public notice of vacancies so all who are eligible may apply [5 U.S.C. 2301];

- Another law requires agencies to report to OPM and to the United States Employment Service of the Department of Labor each vacant position in the agency which is in the competitive service or the Senior Executive Service and for which the agency seeks applications from persons outside the Federal service [5 U.S.C. 3327]; and

- The regulation establishing the Interagency **Career Transition Assistance Plan (ICTAP)** for displaced employees requires agencies to report all vacancies to OPM when accepting applications from outside the agency (including applications for temporary positions lasting 120 or more days)[5 CFR 330.705]. Applicants who meet the ICTAP requirements must be selected before Outstanding Scholars.

---

[2] Your GPA can be rounded in the following manner: a 3.44 is rounded down to 3.4; a 3.45 is rounded up to 3.5.

Other Considerations

Outstanding Scholars cannot be appointed until they have actually become **college graduates.** They may, however, be given conditional offers pending graduation. Although Outstanding Scholar candidates do not have to appear on a certificate, their consideration must be concurrent with the priority consideration of displaced employees eligible for ICTAP selection.

Applicants under this program are prevented from using graduate grades in calculating grade point averages (GPAs). It also requires using grades received in **all undergraduate courses** leading to the degree. This would include courses from all undergraduate schools attended, not just courses taken at the school providing the degree. That requirement also means that the candidate **MUST HAVE** the 3.5 GPA at the time of graduation; any conditional offers made prior to graduation must be rescinded if the GPA is not maintained. Since the grade point average must be calculated on a 4.0 scale, agencies also need to adjust GPAs that were based on a scale that allows a 4.5 (A+) grade.

To be selected through this program, a candidate must meet both the eligibility requirements for the Outstanding Scholar program and the **qualification standards** for the position. Basic qualifications are described in OPM's Operating Manual, Qualifications Standards for General Schedule Positions.[3] You can also locate qualification standards online at http://federaljobs.net. Go to the *Apply For Jobs* page and select *Qualification Standards*.

Education must be from accredited colleges and universities, and the agencies use the established procedure of rounding GPAs to the nearest tenth of a percent (e.g., 3.45 rounded to 3.5). There is also a **Superior Academic Achievement (S.A.A.)** provision. The S.A.A. designation is solely grade-determining. It establishes eligibility to appoint at the GS-7 level instead of at GS-5, but does not in itself provide an appointment opportunity.

Although the term *"direct hire"* is used, the program essentially provides for a noncompetitive appointment to the competitive service. **Direct hire** means the ability to hire without having to rank candidates, but only when there are fewer than four candidates and there are no candidates eligible for veterans' preference. The Outstanding Scholar program does not have that restriction. Rating and ranking are not required, so neither the "rule of three" nor veterans' preference are applied. There are requirements, however, that the positions be announced, that displaced employees be given preference, and that the program only be used as a supplement to competitive examining.

---

[3] Operating manual located at https://www.opm.gov/qualifications/SEC-IV/B/GS1800/1881.asp

TABLE 5-2
Occupational Groups Approved For the
Outstanding Scholar and Bilingual/Bicultural Programs

Group 1 — Health, Safety and Environmental Occupations

Series	Title
0018	Safety & Occupational Health Management
0023	Outdoor Recreational Planning
0028	Environmental Protection Specialist
0673	Hospital Housekeeping Management
0685	Public Health Program Specialist

Group 2 — Writing and Public Information Occupations

Series	Title
1001	General Arts & Information
1035	Public Affairs
1082	Writing & Editing
1083	Technical Writing & Editing
1147	Agricultural Market Reporting
1412	Technical Information Services
1421	Archives Specialist

Group 3 —Business, Finance and Management Occupations

Series	Title
0011	Bond Sales Promotions
0106	Unemployment Insurance
0120	Food Assistance Program Specialist
0346	Logistics Management
0393	Communications Specialist
0501	Financial Administration
0560	Budget Analysis
0570	Financial Institution Examining
1101	General Business & Industry
1102	Contract Specialist
1104	Property Disposal
1130	Public Utilities
1140	Trade Specialist
1145	Agricultural Program Specialist
1146	Agricultural Marketing
1149	Wage and Hour Law Administration
1150	Industrial Specialist
1160	Financial Analysis
1163	Insurance Examining
1165	Loan Specialist
1170	Realty
1171	Appraising & Assessing
1173	Housing Management
1176	Building Management
1910	Quality Assurance Specialist
2001	General Supply
2003	Supply Program Management
2010	Inventory Management
2030	Distribution Facilities & Storage Management
2032	Packaging
2050	Supply Cataloging
2101	Transportation Specialist
2110	Transportation Industry Analysis
2125	Highway Safety Management
2130	Traffic Management
2150	Transportation

Group 4 — Personnel, Administration and Computer Occupations

Series	Title
0142	Manpower Development
0201	Personnel Management
0205	Military Personnel Management
0212	Personnel Staffing
0221	Position Classification
0222	Occupational Analysis
0223	Salary & Wage Administration
0230	Employee Relations
0233	Labor Relations
0235	Employee Development
0244	Labor Management Relations Examining
0246	Contractor Industrial Relations
0301	Misc. Admin & Program
0334	Computer Specialist (Trainee)
0341	Admin Officer
0343	Management Analysis
0345	Program Analysis
1715	Vocational Rehabilitation

Group 5-Benefits Review, Tax & Legal Occupations

Series	Title
0105	Social Insurance
0187	Social Services
0526	Tax Technician
0950	Paralegal Specialist
0962	Contact Representative
0965	Land Law Examining
0967	Passport & Visa Examining
0987	Tax Law Specialist
0990	General Claims Examining
0991	Worker's Compensation Claims Examining
0993	Social Insurance Claims Examining
0994	Unemployment Compensation
0995	Claims Examining
0996	Veteran Claims Examining
0997	Civil Service Retirement Claims Examining

Group 6 — Law Enforcement & Investigation

Series	Title
0025	Park Ranger
0080	Security Administration
0132	Intelligence
0249	Wage & Hour Compliance
1169	Internal Revenue Officer
1801	Civil Aviation Security Specialist
1810	General Investigator
1811	Criminal Investigator
1812	Game Law Enforcement
1816	Immigration Inspector
1831	Securities Compliance Examining
1854	Alcohol, Tobacco, and Firearms Inspection
1864	Public Health Quarantine Inspection
1889	Import Specialist
1890	Customs Inspector

Group 7 — Positions with Positive Education Requirements

Series	Title
0020	Community Planning
0101	Social Science
0110	Economist
0130	Foreign Affairs
0131	International Relations
0140	Manpower Research & Analysis
0150	Geography
0170	History
0180	Psychology
0184	Sociology
0190	General Anthropology
0193	Archeology
1015	Museum Curator
1420	Archivist
1701	General Education & Training
1720	Education Program

BILINGUAL/BICULTURAL PROGRAM

Eligibility

An agency may appoint applicants who obtain a passing score in an examination, without further regard to rank, provided that:

1. The job is one in which interaction with the public or job performance would be enhanced by having bilingual and/or bicultural skills and is at grade GS-5 or GS-7 in a covered occupation; and

2. The agency has determined through use of a reasonable questionnaire or interview that the applicant to whom appointment is to be offered has the required level of oral Spanish language proficiency and/or the requisite knowledge of Hispanic culture. Agencies must maintain documentation that these requirements have been met.

Rating Candidates

Unlike the Outstanding Scholar program, the Bilingual / Bicultural program requires that applicants receive a passing score through the alternative examining procedure. The examining procedure in current use is OPM's rating schedule used in case examining. A candidate who meets the minimum qualifications for the position will be rated as having "passed" the examination.

GENERAL CONSIDERATIONS FOR ALL POSITIONS

Basic Qualifications

It's important to note that a college degree isn't necessarily required to qualify for most of these jobs. Equivalent experience is acceptable as an alternative to a college degree. For example, to qualify for a administrative GS-5 position you would need four years of education leading to a bachelor's degree, three years of responsible experience, **OR** an equivalent combination of education and experience.

Applicants have three avenues to explore. If you don't have three years of experience or a bachelor's degree you can use a combination of education and experience to qualify.

Responsible Experience

You can combine education and experience to meet the qualification requirements. One academic year of full-time study (30 semester hours or 45 quarter hours) is equivalent to nine months of responsible experience. A bachelor's degree is equivalent to three years of responsible experience. To be considered, your experience must be related to the position applied for.

Courses Taken at Non-Accredited Institutions Are Acceptable if They Meet the Qualifying Conditions:

- The courses are accepted for advanced credit at an accredited institution.
- The institution is one whose transcript is given full credit by a State university.
- The courses have been evaluated and approved by a state department of education.
- The course work has been evaluated by an organization recognized for accreditation by the Council of Post-secondary Accreditation.

ADMINISTRATIVE CAREERS SAMPLE EXAM

The following sample test questions are excerpted from the original Administrative and Professional Testing Background Information Guides. They are provided to familiarize applicants with tests that may be used to qualify applicants in the administrative and professional job series. Agencies have the option to use a written test to assess applicant skills. Most agencies now use the **occupational questionnaire** instead of written tests.

Tests consist of:

    ✎   Vocabulary

    ✎   Reading

    ✎   Tabular Completion

    ✎   Arithmetic Reasoning *

    ✎   The Individual Achievement Record (IAR)

    * NOTE: The Careers in Writing and Public Information Occupations do not have an arithmetic reasoning section.

Vocabulary Questions

The following questions present a key word and five suggested answers. Your task is to find the suggested answer that is closest in meaning to the key word. Wrong answers may have some connection with the word, but the meanings will be essentially different from that of the key word. Sample questions 1, 2 and 3 are examples of the vocabulary questions in the test.

1. *Stipulation* means most nearly

A) essential specification
B) unnecessary addition
C) unnecessary effort

D) required training
E) required correction

The word *stipulation* refers to a required condition or item specified in a contract, treaty, or other official document. Therefore, response A, *essential specification*, is the best synonym. A *stipulation* could be an addition to a contract or other document, but even without the word *unnecessary*, response B is incorrect. Responses C and D are clearly unrelated to the meaning of *stipulation*. Response E, *required correction*, shares with *stipulation* the idea of being necessary, as well as an association with something written. However, a correction is an alteration made to remedy or remove an error or fault, so its basic meaning is completely different from that of *stipulation*.

2. *Allocation* means most nearly

A) prevention
B) site
C) exchange

D) assignment
E) ointment

An *allocation* is the act of setting something apart for a particular purpose. Response D, *assignment*, refers to the act of specifying or designating something exactly or precisely, and is, therefore, the best synonym for *allocation*. Responses A, C, and E are clearly unrelated to the meaning of *allocation*. Response B, *site*, means to put something in a location or position; however, the emphasis with *site* is on the physical location given to an object, rather than on the purpose of the object.

3. To *collaborate* means most nearly to work

A) rapidly
B) together
C) independently

D) overtime
E) carefully

The word *collaborate* means to work with another, especially on a project of mutual interest. Therefore, response B, *together*, is the best answer. Responses A, D, and E are clearly unrelated to the meaning of *collaborate*, and response C, *independently*, is the opposite meaning.

> Questions 1 and 2 relate to the careers in benefit review, tax, and legal occupations. Question 3 deals with careers in personnel, administrative, and computer occupations.

Reading Questions

In each of the questions you will be given a paragraph which contains all the information necessary to infer the correct answer. Use only the information provided in the paragraph. Do not speculate or make assumptions that go beyond this information. Also, assume that all information in the paragraph is true, even if it conflicts with some fact known to you. Only one correct answer can be validly inferred from the information contained in the paragraph.

Pay special attention to negative verbs (for example, "are <u>not</u>") and negative prefixes (for example "<u>in</u>complete" or "<u>dis</u>organized"). Also pay special attention to qualifiers, such as "all," "none," and "some." For example, from a paragraph in which it is stated that "it is not true that all contracts are legal," or that "some illegal things are contracts," but one **cannot** validly infer that "no contracts are legal" and "all contracts are two-sided agreements," one can infer that "some two-sided agreements are legal," but one **cannot** validly infer that "all two-sided agreements are legal."

Bear in mind that in some tests, universal qualifiers such as "all" and "none" often give away incorrect response choices. That is not the case in these tests. Some correct answers will refer to "all" or "none" of the members of a group.

Be sure to distinguish between essential information and unessential, peripheral information. That is to say, in a real test question, the example above ("all contracts are legal" and "all contracts are two-sided agreements") would appear in a longer, full-fledged paragraph. It would be up to you to separate the essential information from its context and then to realize that a response choice that states "some two-sided agreements are legal" represents a valid inference and hence the correct answer.

4. Personnel administration begins with the process of defining the number of people needed to do the job. Thereafter, people must be recruited, selected, trained, directed, rewarded, transferred, promoted and perhaps released or retired. However, it is not true that all organizations are structured so that workers can be dealt with as individuals. In some organizations, employees are represented by unions, and managers bargain only with these associations.

- A)   no organizations are structured so that workers cannot be dealt with as individuals.
- B)   some working environments other than organizations are structured so that workers can be dealt with as individuals.
- C)   all organizations are structured so that employees are represented by unions.
- D)   no organizations are structured so that managers bargain with unions.
- E)   some organizations are not structured so that workers can be dealt with as individuals.

The correct answer is response E. This conclusion can be derived from information contained in the third sentence of the paragraph, which states that *it is not true that all organizations are structured so that workers can be dealt with as individuals*. From this statement, it can be inferred that some organizations are not structured so that workers can be dealt with as individuals

.

> In this question, the correct answer follows basically from one sentence in the paragraph — the third sentence. The rest of the paragraph presents additional information about personnel administration which is relevant to the discussion, but not necessary to make the inference. Part of your task in the reading section is to understand what you read, and then discern what conclusions follow logically from statements in the paragraph. Consequently, in the test you will find some questions in which it is necessary to use all or most of the statements presented in the paragraph, while in others, such as this one, only one statement is needed to infer the correct answer.

5) One use of wild land is the protection of certain species of wild animals or plants in wildlife refuges or in botanical reservations. Some general types of land use are activities that conflict with this stated purpose. All activities that exhibit such conflict are, of course, excluded from refuges and reservations.

A)   all activities that conflict with the purpose of wildlife refuges or botanical reservations are general types of land use.

B)   all activities excluded from wildlife refuges and botanical reservations are those that conflict with the purpose of the refuge or reservation.

C)   Some activities excluded from wildlife refuges and botanical reservations are general types of land use.

D)   no activities that conflict with the purpose of wildlife refuges and botanical reservations are general types of land use.

E)   some general types of land use are not excluded from wildlife refuges and botanical reservations.

The correct answer is response C. The answer can be inferred from the second and third sentences in the paragraph. The second sentence tells us that *some general types of land use are activities that conflict with* the purpose of wildlife refuges and botanical reservations. The third sentence explains that *all activities that exhibit such conflict are...excluded from refuges and reservations*. Therefore, we can conclude that *some activities excluded from refuges and reservations* (the ones that conflict with the purpose of refuges and reservations) *are general types of land use.*

> Question 4 directly relates to the careers in personnel, administrative, and computer occupations. Question 5 deals with the careers in health, safety, and environmental occupations.

Tabular Completion Questions

These questions are based on information presented in tables. Only two sample questions of this type appear below, although, in the actual test, you will have to find five unknown values in each table. You must calculate these unknown values by using the known values given in the table. In some questions, the exact answer will not be given as one of the response choices. In such cases, you should select response E, "none of these." Sample questions 6 and 7, which are based on the accompanying table, are examples of the tabular completion questions in this test.

LOCAL GOVERNMENT EXPENDITURES OF FINANCES:
2000 TO 2003 *(in millions of dollars)*

ITEM	2000	2001	2002	2003	
				TOTAL	PER-CENT*
Expenditures	(I)	432,328	485,174	520,966	100.0
Direct General Expenditures	326,024	367,340	405,174	(IV)	83.2
Utility and Liquor Stores	30,846	(II)	43,016	47,970	9.2
Water and electric	20,734	24,244	28,453	31,499	6.0
Transit and other	10,112	11,947	14,563	16,471	3.2
Insurance Trust Expenditure	23,504	28,797	36,582	39,466	(V)
Employee retirement	12,273	14,008	(III)	17,835	3.4
Unemployment compensation	11,231	14,789	20,887	21,631	4.2

Hypothetical data.   * Rounded to one decimal place

6. What is the value of I in millions of dollars?

    A) 380,374
    B) 377,604
    C) 356,870
    D) 349,528
    E) none of these

The answer is A. It can be calculated by adding the values for Direct General Expenditures, Utility and Liquor Stores, and Insurance Trust Expenditure. Numerically, 326,024 + 30,846 + 23,504 = 380,374.

7. What is the value of II in millions of dollars?

    A) 338,543   D) 40,744
    B) 64,988   E) none of these
    C) 53,041

The answer is E. The correct value (not given as an answer) is calculated by adding the value for water and electric and the value for transit and other. Numerically, 24,244 + 11,947 = 36,191.

Questions 6 and 7 relate to the careers in benefits review, tax, and legal occupations.

Arithmetic Reasoning Questions

In this part of the test you have to solve problems formulated in both verbal and numeric form. You will have to analyze a paragraph in order to set up the problem, and then solve it. If the exact answer is not given as one of the response choices, you should select response E, "none of these."

8. An investigator rented a car for four days and was charged $200. The car rental company charged $10 per day plus $.20 per mile driven. How many miles did the investigator drive the car?

A) 800
B) 950
C) 1,000
D) 1,200
E) none of these

The correct answer is A. It can be obtained by computing the following: 4 (10) + .20X = 200.

9. In a large agency where mail is delivered in motorized carts, two tires were replaced on a cart at a cost of $34 per tire. If the agency had expected to pay $80 for a pair of tires, what percent of its expected cost did it save?

A) 7.5%
B) 17.6%
C) 57.5%
D) 75.0%
E) none of these

The answer is E. The correct answer is not given as one of the response choices. The answer can be obtained by computing the following:

$$(80/2 - 34)/40 = X$$
$$X = 6/40 = .15$$
$$.15 \times 100 = 15\%$$

The expected $80 cost for a pair of tires would make the cost of a single tire $40. The difference between the actual cost of $34 per tire and the expected cost of $40 per tire is $6, which is 15% of the $40 expected cost.

10. It takes two typists three 8-hour work days to type a report on a word processor. How many typists would be needed to type two reports of the same length in one 8-hour work day?

A) 4   D) 12
B) 6   E) None of these
C) 8

The correct answer is D. It can be obtained by computing the following:

$$3 \times 2 \times 2 = X.$$

The left side of the equation represents the total number of 8-hour work days of typing required for two reports: three days times two typists times two reports equals 12 8-hour work days of typing. If all of this had to be accomplished in on 8-hour work day, 12 typists would be needed.

NOTE: Question 8 deals with careers in law enforcement and investigation occupations. Question 9 relates to the careers in business, finance, and management occupations and question 10 relates to the careers in benefit review, tax, and legal occupations.

CLERICAL TESTS

Many agencies now use the occupational questionnaire and skills self certification instead of the clerical written exam. Applicants submit an optional application or federal style résumé and self certify typing speed. Agency human resource offices rate bidders on their education and/or experience. Some agencies continue to use the multiple choice clerical test, and a practice exam is included in this chapter just in case the job you apply for requires a written test.

The written test measures the clerical and verbal abilities needed to:

✎ Design, organize, and use a filing system
✎ Organize effectively the clerical process in an office
✎ Make travel, meeting and conference arrangements
✎ Locate and assemble information for reports and briefings
✎ Compose non-technical correspondence
✎ Be effective in oral communication
✎ Use office equipment

TABLE 5-2
QUALIFICATION REQUIREMENTS

For Clerk Typist positions:

GRADE	GENERAL EXPERIENCE		EDUCATION	PROFICIENCY
GS-2	3 months	OR	High school or equivalent	40 wpm typing
GS-3	6 months	OR	1 year above high school	40 wpm typing
GS-4	1 year	OR	2 years above high school	40 wpm typing

For Clerk Stenographer positions:

GRADE	GENERAL EXPERIENCE		EDUCATION	PROFICIENCY
GS-3	6 months	OR	High school or equivalent	40 wpm typing
GS-4	1 year	OR	2 years above high school	40 wpm typing
GS-5	2 years	OR	4 years above high school	40 wpm typing

For all other clerical and administrative support positions covered:

GRADE	GENERAL EXPERIENCE		EDUCATION
GS-2	3 months	OR	High school or equivalent
GS-3	6 months	OR	1 year above high school
GS-4	1 year	OR	2 years above high school

Some clerical and administrative support positions also require typing and/or stenography proficiency.

General Experience

High school graduation or the equivalent may be substituted for experience at the GS-2 level for all listed occupations except Clerk-Stenographer, where it may be substituted for experience at the GS-3 level. Equivalent combinations of successfully completed education and experience requirements may be used to meet total experience requirements at grades GS-5 and below. Table 5-3 lists the positions and grades covered under the Clerical and Administrative Support Positions test.

Positions at higher grade levels in listed occupations are covered under separate examinations.

TABLE 5-3
Clerical and Administrative Support Positions
Clerk GS 2/3, Clerk Typist GS-2/4
Clerk Stenographer GS-3/5
Secretary GS-3/4

Business
Business Clerk GS-2/4
Procurement Clerk GS-2/4
Production Control Clerk GS-2/4
Property Disposal Clerk GS-2/4
Purchasing Agent GS-2/4

Communications
Communications Clerk GS-2/4
Communications Technician GS-2/4
Communications Relay Operator GS-2/4
Cryptographic Equip. Operator GS-2/4
Teletypist GS-2/4

Finance
Accounting Clerk GS-2/4
Budget Clerk GS-2/4
Cash Processing Clerk GS-2/4
Financial Clerk GS-2/4
Insurance Accounts Clerk GS-2/4
Military Pay Clerk GS-2/4
Payroll Clerk GS-2/4
Tax Accounting Clerk GS-2/4
Time & Leave Clerk GS-2/4
Voucher Examining Clerk GS-2/4

Legal
Claims Clerk GS-2/4
Legal Clerk GS-2/4
Legal Records Clerk GS-2/4

Office Clerk
Correspondence Clerk GS-2/4
Information Reception Clerk GS-2/4
Mail and File Clerk GS-2/4

Office Clerk (continued.)
Office Equipment Operator GS-2/4
Personnel Clerk GS-2/4
Personnel (Military) Clerk GS-2/4
Printing Clerk GS-2/4
Statistical Clerk GS-2/4
Supply Clerk GS-2/4
Telephone Operator GS-2/4

Transportation
Dispatching Clerk GS-2/4
Freight Rate Clerk GS-2/4
Passenger Rate Clerk GS-2/4
Shipping Clerk GS-2/4
Transportation Clerk GS-2/4
Travel Clerk GS-2/4

Miscellaneous
Archives Clerk GS-2/4
Arts & Information Clerk GS-2/4
Coding Clerk GS-2/4
Compliance Inspection Clerk GS-2/4
Computer Clerk GS-2/4
Editorial Clerk GS-2/4
Electronic Accounting Machine Operator GS-2/4
Environmental Protection Assistant GS-2/4
Fingerprint Identification Clerk GS-2/4
Intelligence Clerk GS-2/4
Language Clerk GS-2/4
Library Clerk GS-2/4
Management Clerk GS-2/4
Messenger GS-2/4 *
Security Clerical & Assistant GS-2/4

* Under 5 U.S.C 3310, appointment to a messenger position is restricted to persons entitled to veterans preference as long as such persons are available.

Typing Proficiency

Typing proficiency is determined in several ways. You can present a speed certification statement from a typing course, take a typing test with OPM, or personally certify that you type 40 or more words per minute. If you self certify your typing speed you may have to take a typing test upon reporting for duty.

Testing Process

The written clerical test consists of two parts: clerical aptitude and verbal abilities. To pass the written test, applicants must make a minimum score of 33 on the verbal abilities and a minimum combined total score of 80 on both the clerical and verbal parts. A score of 80 converts to a numerical rating of 70. In addition to written tests, applicant's must complete the Occupational Supplement for Clerical Positions (OPM Form 1203-A1). With this form OPM will be able to determine an applicant's minimum qualifications based on a review of his or her education and work experience.

A final rating results from the written examination and Form 1203-Al, with five or 10 additional points added for veterans preference. After taking the exam and filling out the additional forms OPM will send you a *Notice of Rating* (NOR) with-in five to 10 work days of testing.

Sample Clerical Tests

There are several books on the market that provide sample tests for government clerical positions. You can find test preparation manuals published by *ARCO* at most book stores. When you apply to take an OPM test, they generally send out sample questions and explain the test in detail. The tests are multiple choice in the areas described above.

The following sample questions were provided by OPM.

SAMPLE QUESTIONS (Clerical Test)

The following sample questions show types of questions found in the written test you will take. Your answers to the questions are to be recorded on a separate answer sheet. The questions on the test may be harder or easier than those shown here, but a sample of each kind of question on the test is given.

Read these directions, then look at the sample questions and try to answer them. Each question has several suggested answers lettered A, B, C, etc. Decide which one is the best answer to the question. During the test you will be provided with an answer sheet. When taking the actual test, find the answer space that is numbered the same as the number of the question, and darken completely the oval that is lettered the same as the letter of your answer. All questions are multiple choice. The answers to the sample questions are provided on the following pages. For some questions an explanation of the correct answer is given.

Vocabulary. For each question like 1 through 3, choose the one of the four suggested answers that means most nearly the same as the word in *italics.*

1.   *Option* means most nearly
    A) use   C) value
    B) choice   D) blame

2.   *Innate* means most nearly
    A) eternal   B) well-developed
    C) native   D) prospective

3. To *confine* means most nearly to
    A) restrict   C) eliminate
    B) hide   D) punish

Grammar. In questions 4, 5, and 6, decide which sentence is preferable with respect to grammar and usage suitable for a formal letter or report.

4.   A)   If properly addressed, the letter will reach my mother and I.
    B)   The letter had been addressed to myself and my mother.
    C)   I believe the letter was addressed to either my mother or I.
    D)   My mother's name, as well as mine, was on the letter.

The answer to question 4 is D). The answer is not A because the word me (reach . . . me) should have been used, not the word I. The answer is not B. The expression, to myself, is sometimes used in spoken English, but it is not acceptable in a formal letter or report. The answer is not C, because the word I has been used incorrectly, just as it was in A.

5.   A)   Most all these statements have been supported by persons who are reliable and can be depended upon.
    B)   The persons which have guaranteed these statements are reliable.
    C)   Reliable persons guarantee the facts with regards to the truth of these statements.
    D)   These statements can be depended on, for their truth has been guaranteed by reliable persons.

6.   A)   Brown & Company employees have recently received increases in salary.
    B)   Brown & Company recently increased the salaries of all its employees.
    C)   Recently Brown & Company has increased their employees' salaries.
    D)   Brown & Company have recently increased the salaries of all its employees.

Spelling. In questions 7 through 9, find the correct spelling of the word among the choices lettered A, B, or C and darken the proper answer space. If no suggested spelling is correct, darken space D.

7.   A) athalete   C) athlete
    B) athelete   D) none of these

In question 7 an extra letter has been added to both A and B. The fourth letter in A makes that spelling of *athlete* wrong. The fourth letter in B makes that spelling of *athlete* wrong. Spelling C is correct.

8.   A) predesessor   C) predecesser
    B) predecesar   D) none of these

All three spellings of the word are wrong. The correct answer, therefore, is D because none of the printed spellings of *predecessor* is right.

9.   A) occassion   C) ocassion
    B) occasion   D) none of these

Correct Answers to Questions		
1. B	4. D	7. C
2. C	5. D	8. D
3. A	6. B	9. B

Word Relations. In questions like 10, 11, and 12 the first two words in capital letters go together in some way. The third word in capital letters is related in the same way to one of the words lettered A, B, C, or D).

10. PLUMBER is related to WRENCH as PAINTER is related to
    A) brush   C) shop
    B) pipe   D) hammer

The relationship between the first two words in capital letters is that a PLUMBER uses the tool called a WRENCH in doing his work. A PAINTER uses the tool called the BRUSH in doing his work. Therefore, the answer to question 10 is A. The answer is not B because a pipe is not a tool. The answer is not C for two reasons. A *shop* could be used by either a plumber or a painter and a shop is not a tool. The answer is not D. A hammer is a tool but it is not a tool used by a painter in his work.

11. BODY is related to FOOD as ENGINE is related to
    A) wheels   C) motion
    B) smoke   D) fuel.

You soon saw that the relationship between the words in question 10 does not fit the words in question 11. The relationship here is that the first runs on the second – the BODY runs on FOOD; and ENGINE runs on D) fuel.

12. ABUNDANT is related to CHEAP as SCARCE is related to
    A) ample   C) costly
    B) inexpensive   D) unobtainable

Reading. In questions like 13,14, and 15, you will be given a paragraph, generally from 4 to 10 lines long.

Read the paragraph with great care for you will have to decide which one of four statements is based on the information in the paragraph. The statement may not be based on the main thought of the paragraph.

13. What constitutes skill in any line of work is not always easy to determine; economy of time must be carefully distinguished from economy of energy, as the quickest method may require the greatest expenditure of muscular effort and may not be essential or at all desirable.

The paragraph best supports the statement that

A)   the most efficiently executed task is not always the one done in the shortest time
B)   energy and time cannot both be conserved in performing a single task
C)   a task is well done when it is performed in the shortest time
D)   skill in performing a task should not be acquired at the expense of time

The answer is A. You can see that the paragraph points out that the task done most quickly is not necessarily the task done best. The paragraph does not compare energy and time although it mentions both, so B is not an answer. The paragraph does not support C, which is almost the opposite of the answer, A. The statement in D may be true, but it is not contained in the paragraph.

14. The secretarial profession is a very old one and has increased in importance with the passage of time. In modern times, the vast expansion of business and industry has greatly increased the need and opportunities for secretaries, and for the first time in history their number has become large.

The paragraph best supports the statement that the secretarial profession

A)   is older than business and industry
B)   did not exist in ancient times
C)   has greatly increased in size
D)   demands higher training than it did formerly

15. It is difficult to distinguish between bookkeeping and accounting. In attempts to do so, bookkeeping is called the art, and accounting the science, of recording business transactions. Bookkeeping gives the history of the business in a systematic manner; and accounting classifies, analyzes, and interprets the facts thus recorded.

The paragraph best supports the statement that

A)   accounting is less systematic than bookkeeping
B)   accounting and bookkeeping are closely related
C)   bookkeeping and accounting cannot be distinguised from one another
D)   bookkeeping has been superseded by accounting.

Correct Answers to Sample Questions
10. A   11. D   12. C   13. A   14. C   15. B

Sample questions 16 through 20 require name and number comparisons. In each line across the page there are three names or numbers that are very similar. Compare the three names or numbers and decide which ones are exactly alike. On the sample answer sheet, mark the answer:

A   if ALL THREE names or numbers are exactly ALIKE
B   if only the FIRST and SECOND names or numbers are exactly ALIKE
C   if only the FIRST and THIRD names or numbers are exactly ALIKE
D   if only the SECOND and THIRD names or numbers are exactly ALIKE
E   if ALL THREE names or numbers are DIFFERENT

16. Davis Haven	David Hexane	David Haven
17. Lois Appal	Lois Appal	Lois Apfel
18. June Allan	Jane Allan	Jane Allan
19. 10235	10235	10235
20. 32614	32164	32614

In the next group of sample questions, there is an underlined name at the left, and four other names in alphabetical order at the right. Find the correct space for the underlined name so that it will be in alphabetical order with the others, and mark the letter of that space as your answer.

A) →
    Goodyear, G. L.
B) →
    Haddon, Harry
21. Jones, Jane   C) →
    Jackson, Mary
D) →
    Jenkins, Williams
E) →

A) →
    Olsen, C. A.
B) →
    Olsen, C. D.
23. Olsen, C. C.   C) →
    Olsen, Charles
D) →
    Olsen, Christopher
E) →

A) →
    Kessel, Carl
B) →
    Kessinger, D. J.
22. Kessler, Neilson   C) →
    Keesler, Karl
D) →
    Kessner, Lewis
E) →

A) →
    DeLong, Jesse
B) →
    DeMatteo, Jesse
24. DeMattia, Jessica   C) →
    Derbie, Jessie S.
D) →
    DeShazo, L. M.
E) →

Correct Answers to Sample Questions
16. E 17. B 18. D 19. A 20. C 21. E 22. D 23. B 24. C

In questions like 25 through 28, solve each problem and see which of the suggested answers A, B, C, or D is correct. If your answer does not exactly agree with any of the first four suggested answers, darken space E.

25. Add: Answers
        A) 44 B) 45
    22   C) 54 D) 55
   +33   E) none of these

27. Multiply: Answers
        A) 100 B) 115
    25   C) 125 D) 135
    x5   E) none of these

26. Subtract: Answers
        A) 20 B) 21
    24   C) 27 D) 29
    -3   E) none of these

28. Divide: Answers
        A) 20 B) 22
        C) 24 D) 26
   6√126   E) none of these

There is a set of five suggested answers for each of the groups of sample questions appearing below. Do not try to memorize these answers, because there will be a different set on each page in the test.

To find the answer to each question, find which one of the suggested answers contains numbers and letters all of which appear in that question. These numbers and letters may be in any order in the question, but all four must appear. If no suggested answers fits, mark E for that question.

29. 8 N K 9 G T 4 6
30. T 9 7 Z 6 L 3 K
31. Z 7 G K 3 9 8 N
32. 3 K 9 4 6 G Z L
33. Z N 7 3 8 K T 9

34. 2 3 P 6 V Z 4 L
35. T 7 4 3 P Z 9 G
36. 6 N G Z 3 9 P 7
37. 9 6 P 4 N G Z 2
38. 4 9 7 T L P 3 V

Suggested
Answers
A = 7, 9, G, K
B = 8, 9, T, Z
C = 6, 7, K, Z
D = 6, 8, G, T
E = none of these

Suggested
Answers
A = 3, 6, G, P
B = 3, 7, P, V
C = 4, 6, V, Z
D = 4, 7, G, Z
E = none of these

Correct Answers to Sample Questions
25. D, 26. B, 27. C, 28. E, 29. D, 30. C, 31. A, 32. E, 33. B, 34. C, 35. D, 36. A, 37. E, 38. B

CHAPTER SIX
Completing Your
Employment Application

The key to landing a job with Uncle Sam is to tailor your federal style résumé and application to the core duties and responsibilities listed in the job announcement. Those who take the time to develop a comprehensive and properly formatted application package will improve their rating and get the attention of the selecting official.

I reviewed and rated hundreds of federal applications during my 35-plus years of federal service and participated in many interview and selection panels. I was also a rating official for select occupations for our organization and can tell you from first-hand experience that many highly qualified applicants never made the cut because they didn't devote the time or effort to properly complete their application packages. The old saying still stands, especially in government:

> The job isn't completed until the paperwork is done — and DONE RIGHT!

CHAPTER OBJECTIVES

- ✎ What information is required for a federal style résumé
- ✎ Understand and evaluate federal job announcements
- ✎ How to write a federal style résumé, target it to the job announcement, and get the attention of selecting officials
- ✎ Write Knowledge, Skills, & Abilities (KSA) statements *(review sample KSA formats)*
- ✎ How to apply for Senior Executive Service (SES) positions

This chapter guides you through the application process. Unlike in the private sector, applicants have to submit detailed *federal style résumés or* the *OF-612 Optional Application for Federal Employment,* and submit replies to *Occupational Questionnaires and Knowledge, Skills & Abilities (KSA) statements* if required. A hard copy *Standard Form C* may still be required in some cases. Applicants must prepare their résumés and applications in accordance with the guidelines published in the job announcement. Most agencies encourage online application submission.

The examples used in this chapter and book are cross referenced to give you a better understanding of the application process. The six page sample federal style résumé for John Q. Adams beginning on page 143 is targeted to job announcement number 0916 LV starting on page 133. This chapter helps individuals assess and evaluate job announcements that interest them and write a targeted federal style résumé for that position using the guidance and sample résumé formats provided. I actually applied for this position so that I could describe first-hand what you can expect during the process. The Qualification Standard for the GS-0343 Analyst position is featured in Chapter Two as well. Qualification Standards list the required work experience and/or education that's needed for each pay grade in the job series. Refer to this document during your review of the federal style résumé in this chapter for insight into the evaluation process.

The examples used in this chapter and book are tied together to give you a better understanding of the application process.

Tailor your application to the job vacancy that you are applying for to improve your chances. Applicants who tailor their applications to the job vacancy are typically rated higher and are far more likely to be referred to the selecting official for interviews.

You may be familiar with the original SF-171 application. This six-page application is no longer available; however, many federal employees continue to use it to bid on internal job vacancies. OPM and other federal agencies offer the following enhanced application services:

- Diverse application submissions, online to hard copy.

- Online résumés are encouraged. The OF-612 Optional form is still available; however, it is used less frequently as automation takes over.

- Online career services at www.usajobs.gov/.

- Online résumé writer, electronic submissions, and job notification available with onsite registration.

It is misleading to assume that a standard résumé will land you a job.

Federal style résumés have become the application of choice and are fast replacing the OF-612 Optional Application form in most cases. The OF-612 form does include the essential information that is required when bidding on federal jobs. If you decide — and most do — to use a federal style résumé format, use the OF-

612 form as a guide to ensure that you include ALL essential information in your résumé or follow the guidance listed in this chapter under *"Required Information."*

Standard application software programs such as *Quick & Easy Federal Jobs Kit* or OPM's online résumé builder guide you through the process. Many agencies now use online automated application systems that allow applicants to submit résumés or questionnaires electronically. When you complete your résumé online, read the instructions carefully. OPM's Web site at http://www.usajobs.gov allows visitors to register and set up a personalized account to compile an online resume and to receive e-mail alerts for job vacancies. Not all agencies use OPM's services and those agencies have slightly different online application processes such as the eRecruit or COAST systems. For example, some sites don't save your data and they have time limits for completing the forms. Others not only save the data but allow you to revise your résumé when needed to apply for other jobs. Agency requirements vary; follow the instructions listed in the job announcement.

When you complete your résumé online read the instructions carefully.

A federal style résumé is completely different from the simple one-page private sector résumé. There are over 40 specific blocks of data required and much of it repeats for each work experience. Before attempting to complete you résumé online, review the samples in this chapter and use the next section for your résumé template. All the information listed on the OF-612 form with the exception of the Applicant Certification is required on your federal style résumé. You must also include all requested information and forms, and answer occupational questionnaires that may be listed in the job announcement.

All of the information listed on the OF-612 form is required on your federal style résumé.

I suggest writing your federal résumé on your computer word processor prior to attempting to post it online. Some agencies still require hard copy submissions, and this way you can produce both a paper hard copy and electronic format as discussed later in this chapter. You will be able to spell check your résumé in your word processor and you will have time to compose coherent work histories without time limits. If the job announcement accepts online submissions, simply cut and paste each section from your draft into the online résumé builder.

This process can dramatically improve your résumé, resulting in higher ratings, and you will be able to keep your résumé updated on your desktop. When you bid on other jobs in the same or similar occupational group you may be able to simply change the job announcement number and title and send it in. However, review each job announcement carefully. Even occupations in the same job series within the same agency can have significantly different requirements, and you must tailor your résumé to those criteria to improve your chances.

REQUIRED INFORMATION

It is misleading to assume that a standard private sector résumé will land you a job with Uncle Sam. Most résumés are loosely structured and simply introduce the applicant to the company. Follow the guidance in this chapter to write successful applications and résumés for the job you want in government. The application is your first introduction to your potential new employer and one of the keys to successfully landing a federal job. You must write a professional federal style résumé and develop job search strategies that work. This book will help you achieve those goals.

> If your application or résumé doesn't include all the information that is requested in the job vacancy announcement, your application may be rejected.

In addition to information requested in the job vacancy announcement, your application or résumé **MUST** contain the following information:[1]

JOB INFORMATION

☐   Announcement number, title and grade(s) of the job for which you are applying.

PERSONAL INFORMATION

☐   Full name, mailing address *(with Zip code)* and day and evening phone numbers.

☐   Social Security number.

☐   Country of citizenship *(most federal jobs require United States citizenship)*.

☐   Veterans' Preference

  ✔   If you served on active duty in the United States military and were separated under honorable conditions, you may be eligible for veterans' preference. To receive preference if your service began after October 15, 1976, you must have a Campaign Badge, Expeditionary Medal, or a service-connected disability. Review Chapter Seven.

  ✔   Veterans' preference is not a factor for Senior Executive Service Jobs or when competition is limited to status

---

[1] Reprinted from OPM brochure OF 510

candidates *(current former federal career or career-conditional employees).*

✔ To claim five-point veterans' preference, attach a copy of your DD-214, *Certificate of Release* or *Discharge from Active Duty* or other proof of eligibility.

✔ To claim 10-point veterans' preference, attach an SF-15, *Application for 10-Point Veterans' Preference,* plus the proof required by that form.

❑ Reinstatement eligibility *(former federal employees must attach a SF-50 proof of their career or career-conditional status).*

✔ Highest federal civilian grade held *(also give job series and dates held).*

EDUCATION

❑ High School

✔ Name, city, and state *(Zip code if known)*

✔ Date of diploma or GED

❑ Colleges and universities

✔ Name, city, and state *(Zip code if known)*

✔ Majors

✔ Type and year of any degrees received *(if no degree, show total credits earned and indicate whether semester or quarter hours).*

❑ Send a copy of your college transcript only if the job vacancy announcement requests it.

WORK EXPERIENCE

❑ Give the following information for your paid and non-paid work experience related to the job for which you are applying. *(Do not send job descriptions.)*

✔ Job title *(include series and grade if federal job)*

✔ Duties and accomplishments

✔   Employer's name and address

✔   Supervisor's name and phone number

✔   Starting and ending dates (month and year)

✔   Hours per week

✔   Salary

❑   Indicate whether the agency may contact your current supervisor.

OTHER QUALIFICATIONS

❑   **Job-related** training courses *(title and year)*.

❑   **Job-related** skills; for example, other languages, computer software/hardware, tools, machinery, typing speed.

❑   **Job-related** certificates and licenses *(current only)*.

❑   **Job-related** honors, awards, and special accomplishments; for example, publications; memberships in professional or honor societies; leadership activities; public speaking; and performance awards. *(Give dates, but do not send documents unless requested.)*

AGENCY FORMS

In the past you had the option of using the *federal style résumé* or the *"Optional Application for Federal Employment"* OF-612 form. Most jobs now require at least partial online résumé submission using agency résumé builder software.

If you use the OF-612 form to apply for a job you will discover that it only includes space to enter work history from your current and previous employer. **Don't stop there**. To earn a rating as high as possible, include all related work experience as far back as necessary, including your military time. Many applicants do not add supplemental sheets to include related work experience that can earn them a higher rating for the job. Programs like *Quick & Easy Federal Jobs Kit* and online résumé builder programs automatically expand to capture additional work experiences. *Quick & Easy Federal Jobs Kit* software will also convert your application to any approved format including the OF-612, SF-171, federal résumé, or RESUMIX. If you are submitting a hard copy OF-612 application and not using a software program, add supplemental sheets to capture **ALL** previous employment.

The government also uses the *"Declaration for Federal Employment,"* OF-306 form to collect information on conduct and suitability and also on other matters. Agencies have the option of asking applicants to complete this form at any time during the hiring process, and once selected for a position it is required. Generally, only the final few applicants, who have a good chance of receiving a job offer, would complete this form. The OF-306 warns applicants of the consequences of submitting fraudulent information, and by signing it you are certifying the accuracy of your application. Fraudulent applications are a basis for immediate dismissal.

OPM Form 1203, Form C, was used often in the past to assist agencies with rating job applicants. This form is an optical scan form designed to collect applicant information and qualifications in a format suitable for automated processing. The OPM Form 1203 form is a standard computer-graded form; however, the questions are tailored to the job announcement and vary by occupation and agency. You could bid on the same job series with two different agencies and have different qualification questions. Many agencies collect these same data through online questionnaires and do not use Form C.

Many agencies collect this same data through online questionnaires and do not use Form C.

You can download copies of the OF-612 form at http://federaljobs.net. All the information listed on the OF-612 is REQUIRED on *federal style résumés*.

Agency-specific Forms

When using an electronic application system, or for unique occupations with highly specialized requirements, agency-specific forms may be required. They are needed to address special qualifications necessary for the position. In addition, agency-specific questions are permitted to cover areas unique to certain agencies or positions and therefore are not included on the optional forms or résumé. Read the job announcement section titled *"How to Apply"* to determine exactly what forms are required — typically a *résumé* or standard forms — and answer mandatory screening questions, KSAs or Occupational Questionnaires.

Optional Job Application Methods

Applicants have several avenues available, including applying online at OPM or agency Web sites, mailing paper copies, or submitting forms via fax that are scanned by agencies. Many positions also require that applicants answer screening questions or complete a questionnaire that is read and scored by computer.

The online and electronically submitted applications dramatically reduce the time it takes to rank candidates and fill positions. Where automation is not used, applicants are given a choice in how to submit job applications on the job announcement.

Computer Generated Applications

USAJOBs sponsored by OPM at http://www.usajobs.gov offers a comprehensive online résumé builder with online registration. Many agencies direct applicants to OPM's site to register and submit required application material. Other agencies use their own online résumé builder programs such as the National

Science Foundation's *eRecruit* site or the Department of Homeland Security's *COAST* system used by the U.S. Coast Guard. In most cases you don't have an option except for reasonable accommodation that must be coordinated through the hiring agency for certain disabilities.

Take advantage of these services. However, it is best to know their limitations. They don't help you compose your work histories or answer occupational questionnaires. They will take the input you provide but the content is up to you. The more time and effort that you put into composing your résumé and tailoring it to the job announcement's required duties and specialized experience, the better chance you have of landing the job. Draft your résumé offline as suggested earlier in this chapter to produce a professional, complete, and well written application tailored to the job announcement.

DataTech Software offers a comprehensive set of tools for completing your applications and résumés, called **Quick & Easy Federal Jobs Kit**. This software package includes a built-in browser with a list of Internet Web sites that have federal job listings. With a click, you can go instantly to any of these sites, find a job, and save the vacancy announcement on your computer.

The software includes the optional forms, the original SF-171 application and agency-specific employment forms. It also generates federal style résumés from data that you enter on your forms. You can upload your résumé to various online federal résumé databases or copy and paste data from your Quick & Easy files into online résumé builders. Many federal employees use this software to keep their applications updated so they can bid on promotions without all the stress of staring the application all over from scratch. I personally used Quick & Easy throughout my federal career when bidding on promotions or to different positions. Whenever I would go on a special detail or completed new training, I updated the file and had it ready on a minute's notice when job announcements opened.

Quick & Easy Federal Jobs Kit prints all forms on any Windows compatible system including Windows 95, 98, 2000, NT, ME, XP and VISTA systems. If your federal application was completed on an earlier version, the new version imports your application file and generates all new forms. The personal version is available for $49.95 plus shipping by calling 1-800-782-7424. The version with security forms costs $69.95. You can order multiple user versions by calling 1-412-494-6926.

COMPLETING THE
OF-612 OPTIONAL APPLICATION

The following instructions will help you complete the OF-612 form or the federal style résumé. A blank OF-612 form follows the instructions. The information required on either the OF-612 or résumé is exactly the same; only the format is different. Use this guidance to tailor your application to the job announcement and don't leave anything out. All data listed are **REQUIRED** on either format, and if you leave out critical information your application may be rejected. Review this information and sample federal style résumés included in this chapter to better understand what is needed. Needless to say, it will take time and patience to complete your résumé and paperwork. Don't cut this process short; take one step at a time, and if you need help putting pen to paper, seek assistance from a competent federal résumé writing service. You will find several résumé writing services featured on http://www.federaljobs.net under *"Applying for Jobs"* on the main menu and in Chapter Three resources.

INSTRUCTIONS FOR COMPLETING
OPTIONAL APPLICATION FORM OF-612

Job Title Sought and Personal Information (Questions 1 - 7)

1. – 2. Job Title and Grade(s) Applying For

In block 1, fill in the job title listed in the announcement. Grade is the level of difficulty. If you aren't sure what grade you're qualified for, put in the entire range indicated on the announcement. EXAMPLE: Electronic Technician, GS-856-9/11.

3. Announcement Number

Fill in the number on the job announcement.

4-7. Full Name, Social Security Number, Mailing Address, and Phone Numbers

Fill in all blanks with the requested information.

Work Experience

8. Describe your paid and non-paid work experience related to the job for which you are applying.

The optional form includes two job blocks. You may need additional space to describe your duties and accomplishments or additional jobs that relate to the position you are applying for. A typical work description will range from a third of a page to a page or more, using a 12 pitch font depending on the job applied for. If you use the OF-612 form, add as many work experiences that you determine to be relevant by simply adding additional pages to your application. Make sure you include all the required information on the supplemental pages for each work experience. See the sample résumés to see how additional work experiences are compiled in that format.

Many applicants provide only work experience for their current and previous jobs, because the OF-612 form includes just two work experience blocks. This is a mistake and can cost you valuable rating points.

I suggest that you include **ALL** work experience that is relevant as far back as necessary, and don't forget your military experience as well. If you were on active duty or in the military reserves and you are applying for a job that requires the skills learned in the military, include it. You may also be eligible for Veterans Preference; see Chapter Seven for details.

Read the job announcement thoroughly for the position you are applying for and pay attention to the required *Duties and Responsibilities*. Look for special skills or other evaluation factors that are needed. Highlight the key duties and responsibilities and then incorporate them frequently in your work experience, occupational questionnaire and KSA write-ups. You must provide specific examples of the work experience you have that is relevant to the job you are bidding on.

Don't use the exact same application for all jobs that you apply for. The key is to read the job announcement and then tailor your application to that specific job. Detailed guidance on how to tailor your résumé is included in this chapter. Jobs within the same series from different agencies often have different skill sets or required experience. Read the announcement and ensure that your application includes the required knowledge, skills and abilities.

9. May we contact your current supervisor?

Answer *yes* only if you have discussed your interest in other employment with your supervisor.

10-12. Education

List all requested information completely, including Zip codes. You may need to add supplemental pages for schools you attended. The standard form only provides space for three schools.

If you anticipate graduating within the next year, list the year and note "EXPECTED" next to the year. EXAMPLE: B.S., 2006 (EXPECTED). If you are rated eligible for the position based on your education, you will be required to furnish an official transcript. Some positions may require a transcript or a list of courses. Job announcements indicate whether or not a transcript is required.

13. Other Qualifications

The categories under other qualifications call for training, skills, licenses, honors, awards and special accomplishments as they relate to the job you've targeted. Limit this to related qualifications, and it isn't recommended that you send unnecessary attachments with your application. Don't send samples of your work unless requested. Your application should be thorough but not full of unrelated material or material that will cause the reviewer to search through a mountain of papers to find the information he or she needs.

14. Are you a U.S. citizen?

Answer yes or no; if no, give country of citizenship. Generally speaking, you must be a citizen to get a federal job.

15. Do you claim Veterans' Preference?

Answer yes or no. Veterans' Preference is the special consideration given to qualified veterans. Refer to Chapter Seven for complete details.

16. Were you ever a federal civilian employee?

Answer yes or no. Give the job series number for the highest grade held during your federal civilian service, the grade level and the dates you held that grade. Example: *GS 856* (series), *12* (grade), *11/89 - 9/94* (from, to). Remember that the question asks for "highest," not last or present grade.

17. Are you eligible for reinstatement (based on career or career-conditional federal status)?

Answer yes or no. Previous federal employees who are eligible for reinstatement must attach a copy of their last Standard Form SF-50 as proof of employment.

18. Applicant Certification

First read the certification thoroughly, then sign and date in ink. Applicants must submit this page with an original signature. Some agencies allow copies to be faxed. Signature certification isn't required on résumés.

OPTIONAL APPLICATION FOR FEDERAL EMPLOYMENT – OF 612

Form Approved
OMB No. 3206-0219

Section A – Applicant Information

★ Use Standard State Postal Codes (abbreviations). If outside the United States of America, and you do not have a military address, type or print "OV" in the State field (Block 6c) and fill in the Country field (Block 6e) below, leaving the Zip Code field (Block 6d) blank.

1. Job title in announcement	2. Grade(s) applying for	3. Announcement number
4a. Last name	4b. First and middle names	5. Social Security Number

6a. Mailing address ★	7. Phone numbers (include area code if within the United States of America) 7a. Daytime

6b. City	6c. State	6d. Zip Code	7b. Evening

6e. Country (if not within the United States of America)

8. Email address (if available)

Section B – Work Experience

Describe your paid and nonpaid work experience related to this job for which you are applying. Do not attach job description.

1. Job title (if Federal, include series and grade)

2. From (mm/yyyy)	3. To (mm/yyyy)	4. Salary per $	5. Hours per week

6. Employer's name and address	7. Supervisor's name and phone number 7a. Name
	7b. Phone

8. May we contact your current supervisor?   Yes ☐   No ☐
If we need to contact your current supervisor before making an offer, we will contact you first.

9. Describe your duties and accomplishments

Section C – Additional Work Experience

1. Job title (if Federal, include series and grade)

2. From (mm/yyyy)	3. To (mm/yyyy)	4. Salary per $	5. Hours per week

6. Employer's name and address	7. Supervisor's name and phone number 7a. Name
	7b. Phone

8. Describe your duties and accomplishments

U.S. Office of Personnel Management
Previous edition usable

NSN 7540-01-351-9178
50612-101

Page 1 of 2

Optional Form 612
Revised December 2002

Section D – Education

1. Last High School (HS)/GED school. Give the school's name, city, state, ZIP Code (if known), and year diploma or GED received:

2. Mark highest level completed: Some HS ☐   HS/GED ☐   Associate ☐   Bachelor ☐   Master ☐   Doctoral ☐

3. Colleges and universities attended. Do not attach a copy of your transcript unless requested.			Total Credits Earned		Major(s)	Degree (if any), Year Received
			Semester	Quarter		
3a. Name						
City	State	Zip Code				
3b. Name						
City	State	Zip Code				
3c. Name						
City	State	Zip Code				

Section E – Other Qualifications

Job-related training courses (give title and year). Job-related skills (other languages, computer software/hardware, tools, machinery, typing speed, etc.). Job-related certificates and licenses (current only). Job-related honors, awards, and special accomplishments (publications, memberships in professional/honor societies, leadership activities, public speaking, and performance awards). Give dates, but do **not** send documents unless requested.

Section F – General

1a. Are you a U.S. citizen?   Yes ☐   No ☐   →   1b. If no, give the Country of your citizenship

2a. Do you claim veterans' preference?   No ☐   Yes ☐   →   If yes, mark your claim of 5 or 10 points below.

2b.   5 points ☐   →   Attach your *Report of Separation from Active Duty* (DD 214) or other proof.

2c.   10 points ☐   →   Attach an *Application for 10-Point Veterans' Preference* (SF 15) and proof required.

3. Were you ever a Federal civilian employee?   No ☐   Yes ☐   →   If yes, list highest civilian grade for the following:

3a. Series	3b. Grade	3c. From *(mm/yyyy)*	3d. To *(mm/yyyy)*

4. Are you eligible for reinstatement based on career or career-conditional Federal status?   No ☐   Yes ☐
    If requested in the vacancy announcement, attach *Notification of Personnel Action* (SF 50), as proof.

Section G – Applicant Certification

I certify that, to the best of my knowledge and belief, all of the information on and attached to this application is true, correct, complete, and made in good faith. I understand that false or fraudulent information on or attached to this application may be grounds for not hiring me or for firing me after I begin work, and may be punishable by fine or imprisonment. I understand that any information I give may be investigated.

1a. Signature	1b. Date *(mm/dd/yyyy)*

JOB ANNOUNCEMENTS

The sample job announcement included in this chapter and the résumés that follow it will help you understand the federal job application process. This process is considerably more complex than what you would typically find in the private sector. Applicants who fully understand this process have the greatest chance of successfully landing a job. This job announcement is for a GS-0343-7 Management Analyst. You can review the *Qualification Standard* for the GS-0343 in Chapter Two starting on page 39.

Each announcement is typically a little different from the others; however, the process is the same. You must submit **ALL** required applications and supporting information, including transcripts if required. You will find shadow boxes located throughout the following documents that clarify specific issues and guide you through the procedures needed to successfully apply for positions. Underlined text also points out key information you should review.

I applied for this job using a fictitious name and information, and I followed the checklist supplied in the announcement on the upcoming pages. This announcement permits partial online application submission, which does simplify the process. Many jobs now allow applicants to submit the Qualifications and Availability Form C, OPM Form 1203-AW, and their résumé online. Form C is often misunderstood and many don't realize its importance. If you don't complete Form C *(or its online equivalent)* you won't be considered for the job.

Form C

Form C in its hard copy format is simply an answer sheet. The applicant fills in the blanks with a No. 2 lead pencil. The form is then scanned by a computer to retrieve and compile the results. There are 25 sections; each section has multiple questions. This form supplies availability information such as geographic preferences, contact information, and Social Security number. However, agencies may also require that you answer up to 160 *Supplemental Qualification Questions* that focus on core competencies for the job.

You will find several of the 23 total pages reproduced here. The remaining 15 pages include the Form C instructions and 160 questions related to the requirements of the job for which you are applying. The first 16 questions are about your educational and work experience background and are multiple choice. The remaining questions focus on your accomplishments and require an answer YES or NO to each question, A for YES and B for NO. Several examples of the types of questions follow. These questions were excerpted from the bid package.

Most agencies now collect this data online, therefore you won't have to complete a hard copy in most cases.

1. Outstanding Scholar Eligibility — Do you possess a bachelor's degree and possess a cumulative grade point average of at least a 3.5 on a 4.0 point scale?
          A. Yes   B. No

10. I have been employed in work similar to that of the job covered by this examination:

          A. = never employed in a similar job

          B. = less than 1 year

          C. = 1 - 2 years

          D. = 3 - 4 years

          E. = over 5 years

17. Have you successfully done work where your primary responsibility was to help others work out their problems (for example, worked as a therapist)?

          A. = Yes   B. = No

51. Have you been given additional responsibilities because of your ability to organize and complete your regular work more quickly than expected?

          A. = Yes   B. = No

106. Have you successfully done work that regularly involved verifying the accuracy of information or the relevance of information to a problem or a situation (for example, investigative work)?

          A. = Yes   B. = No

CAUTION

When I submitted form C online it came back with an error statement that read, *"Response to an Occupational Question is invalid. Valid responses are A through I or blank."* When answering Yes or No questions it's easy to forget that A = Yes and B = No. I entered Y and N in several responses. After correcting my errors the application was accepted. Print out the job announcement. You need the instructions because the first few questions must be answered exactly as noted from the announcement instructions.

     Typically, the government may add a checklist at the end of a job announcement. I like to pull it out and put it in the front. Use the checklist as your guide to completing your application. It will help to ensure that you comply with all requirements of the bid.

APPLICANT CHECKLIST

To ensure that you file a correct and complete application package, see the list below. Each of these is explained in detail in the announcement, so be sure to refer to the corresponding section of the announcement for complete instructions.

❑   Answers to the Supplemental Qualifications Statement. These can be submitted in either of the following ways:

> Form C — Explained in detail under the "Hard Copy" section of the announcement. DO NOT FAX THIS FORM - IT MUST BE MAILED.
>
> -OR-
>
> Electronic Filing — Explained in detail under the "Electronic Application Options" section of the announcement. REMEMBER: Print out your "Thank You Message" or "Notice of Applicant Responses" as confirmation of your filing status; and write "Electronic Filer" at the top of your written application.

❑   Written application of your choice. You may submit an OF-612, SF-171, or personal résumé. Whichever you choose, be sure it contains all of information outlined in the "Written Application" section of the announcement. NOTE: Electronic résumés are not being accepted for this vacancy.

❑   **Transcripts.** If you qualify and/or claim to qualify for this position based on education, you must submit transcripts or a list of college courses detailing each course, the course number and department, course title, number of credit hours, and grade earned.

❑   **Proof of Veterans Preference.** If you are claiming five-point veterans' preference, please submit a DD-214. If claiming 10-point veterans' preference, submit a Standard Form 15 and any other documentation required on the reverse of the Standard Form 15.

❑   **Proof of Eligibility for Priority Consideration.** See the "Special Selection Priority Consideration Provisions for Surplus and Displaced Federal Employees" section at the end of the announcement.

USAJOBS   **CONTROL NO CK0916**

MANAGEMENT ANALYST
OPEN PERIOD 09/15/2006 - 10/05/2006
SERIES/GRADE: GS-0343-07/09
SALARY: $ 36,839 TO $ 47,888, ANNUAL
PROMOTION POTENTIAL: GS-09
ANNOUNCEMENT NUMBER: 0916 LV

SALARY — The starting salary may be negotiable. GS-07 salary ranges from $36,839, step 1, to $47,888, step 10. Your initial offer will be at the lowest step, $36,839. If you are currently earning more than step 1, ask them to match your current salary and give them a copy of your most recent pay stub for verification. Your starting salary can't exceed the maximum step 10 pay. **You MUST ask for this prior to accepting an offer**. An agency can't adjust your salary after you accept the position.

PROMOTION POTENTIAL — Generally this means that you are hired into a position that has promotion potential to a specified grade — GS-9 in this bid without competition, if your performance is acceptable.

HIRING AGENCY: NAT ARCHIVES AND RECORDS ADMINISTRATION
DUTY LOCATIONS: 0001 SUITLAND, MD
REMARKS: APPLICATION RECEIPT **DEADLINE: 10/9/06.**

DEADLINE: The closing date is 10/5/06. They will accept your application if it is postmarked no later than 10/5/06 and if it is received on or before 10/9/06.

CONTACT: USAJOBS BY PHONE
                 PHONE: (703) 724-1850
                 INTERNET ADDRESS: http://www.usajobs.gov
                 NTNL ARCHIVES & RECORDS ADMIN
                 C/O US OFC OF PERSONNEL MGMT
                 601 EAST 12TH STREET, ROOM 131
                 KANSAS CITY, MO 64106

FEDERAL EMPLOYMENT OPPORTUNITY ANNOUNCEMENT
U.S. Office of Personnel Management

Kansas City Service Center
601 East 12th Street
Kansas City, MO 64106

Candidates' requests to obtain the appropriate application forms must be postmarked no later than the closing date. In order to be accepted, completed application packages must be RECEIVED in this office by 10-9-2006.

> **IMPORTANT** — Postmark by closing date.

PLACE OF EMPLOYMENT: National Archives & Records Administration;
                                  Office of Records Services — Washington, DC
                                  Modern Records Program
                                  Washington National Records Center
                                  Suitland, Maryland

SPECIAL PROVISIONS: This position may be filled through competitive procedures or through the Outstanding Scholar appointment authority. Please see the Outstanding Scholar section of this vacancy announcement for further details.

IMPORTANT NOTE: Relocation costs **WILL NOT be paid**. In accordance with 5 USC 3303, recommendations by a senator or representative may not be considered except as to the character or residence of the applicant. Enrollment in Direct Deposit/Electronic Funds transfer is required as a condition of employment for all new employees. Position requires a background investigation.

> **DUTIES** — I underlined words that identify the key duties of the position and that are an integral part of the Qualification Standard. Do this with all job announcements and then include these key words and duties in your résumé work descriptions. If you have that skill or a related skill, include it in your application. Tailor your application on key duties and responsibilities to obtain higher ratings. The sample résumé that follows incorporates many of the underlined terms.

DUTIES: The incumbent analyzes elements of the Center's program and office automation systems and recommends improvements. Conducts analytical and management studies related to program and office automation applications and their effect on operational efficiency. Acts as technical expert on, analyzes and advises management on all aspects of the manpower tracking system, TASK; the records location system, NARS-5; and the space information system, SIS. Provides training to users and managers. Gives training on accessing and using the systems, and interpreting management reports. Makes recommendations concerning the desirability and feasibility of automating manual processes. Develops written reports which describe findings, describe scope of study, and include statistical and cost/benefit. Develops systems products to facilitate programs and administration. Designs office automation applications. Coordinates with Center branches on office automation applications. <u>Analyzes hardware and software requirements</u>; identifies <u>data elements</u>, <u>input and output requirements</u>; and <u>designs data entry screens</u> and <u>report formats</u>. <u>Tests applications</u> prior to implementation. <u>Creates and maintains</u> appropriate <u>user and technical documentation</u>. Provides <u>office automation training</u>. <u>Prepares annual ADP training plan</u>. Maintains a <u>technical reference library</u>. Acts as a <u>System Administrator</u> for the Center's Information Processing System (CIPS). Provides <u>system maintenance.</u>

QUALIFICATION REQUIREMENTS: Applicants will not be required to take a written examination, but will be rated on the extent and quality of their education and/or experience according to information provided in their application forms. To be rated eligible, applicants must meet one of the requirements described below, AND the Selective Factor, which follows.

> **QUALIFICATION REQUIREMENTS** — In most cases you **DON'T** need a degree to qualify. Even engineers can qualify using alternative non-degree avenues. At first glance it appears that a four-year bachelor's degree is required. Uncle Sam permits substitution of three-years of general work experience at an equivalent GS-4 to be eligible for this position. This is another reason why you must be thorough when describing your work experience and include all key duties and responsibilities in your write-up. See the sample OF-612.

Specialized Experience: One year of specialized experience equivalent to the GS-5 level of the federal service that provided the applicant with the knowledge, skills, and abilities to successfully perform the work of this position as described above. Specialized experience is experience <u>analyzing</u> and <u>evaluating the effectiveness of line program operations</u>; or <u>developing life cycle cost analyses</u>; or <u>performing cost benefit evaluations</u> of <u>projects</u> or <u>automated equipment</u>; or <u>advising on the distribution of work</u>; or <u>analyzing new or proposed legislation or regulations</u> for their impact on a program; or <u>developing new or modified administrative policies or regulations.</u>

> Underline key **Specialized Experience** requirements and focus your written application on these requirements as well as the functional duties of the position.

– OR –

Education: One full year of graduate level study, or a master's or higher degree in a field that provided the knowledge, skills, and abilities necessary to do the work of this position. Such fields include business administration, industrial management, industrial engineering, industrial psychology, public administration, political science, or government.

– OR –

Combination of Experience and Education: Combinations of successfully completed college level education and specialized experience may be used to meet the total experience requirements of this position. NOTE: Only graduate level education may be combined with experience.

– OR –

Alternative Requirement: Completion of all requirements for a bachelor's degree that, by itself, is fully qualifying for the position which meets one of the following Superior Academic achievement standards:

1. A standing in the upper third of your class or major subdivision (e.g., school of business) at the time you apply;
2. A grade average of "B" (3.0 of a possible 4.0) or its equivalent for all courses completed: (a) at the time of application; or (b) during the last two years of your undergraduate curriculum;
3. A "B+" (3.5 of a 4.0) average or its equivalent for all courses completed in a qualifying major field of study, either: (a) at the time of application; or (b) during the last two years of your undergraduate curriculum;
4. Election to membership in one of the national honorary societies (other than freshman societies) that meet the   requirements of the Association of College Honor Societies.

**If more than 10 percent of your courses were taken on a pass/fail basis, your claim must be based on class standing or membership in an honorary society.

SELECTIVE FACTOR: (ALL APPLICANTS MUST MEET)You MUST provide a narrative in your written application describing your experience/education in relation to the following Selective Factor: <u>Demonstrated ability to identify, analyze, and solve problems, especially those related to office automation by conducting management studies and issuing findings</u>.

SPECIAL PROVISIONS FOR OUTSTANDING SCHOLAR ELIGIBILITY: This position may be filled through the Outstanding Scholar appointment authority. All persons with a bachelor's degree and a cumulative grade point average of at least 3.5 on a 4-point scale will be referred as Outstanding Scholar eligibles. To be considered under this authority, applicants MUST INCLUDE A COPY OF THEIR COLLEGE TRANSCRIPT(S), and must follow the instructions for Outstanding Scholars in the <u>Supplemental Qualifications Statement on Form C</u>.

BASIS OF RATING: Applicants will be rated on their responses to items in the Supplemental Qualifications Statement as recorded on the Qualifications and Availability Form (Form C) or through the electronic application process.

HOW TO APPLY: Please read and follow the two-step process described below to ensure that you submit a complete application package. Applicants will be evaluated on the basis of information provided in their initial application forms only. This office will not solicit information which is missing or seek clarification of unclear information, nor will additional information be accepted after the final receipt date. Failure to provide complete information and/or supporting documentation may result in receipt of a lower or ineligible rating.

STEP 1) WRITTEN APPLICATION

Submit a résumé, Optional Application for Federal Employment(OF-612), or other written application format of your choice. E-mailed résumés are not being accepted for this vacancy. Please mail or fax your written application to the address below. Be sure your résumé contains all the information requested below: ***(Most agencies now accept online submissions)***

> The résumé outline must be followed. If you leave out requested data your application might not be considered. The OF-612 Form includes all the information, and if you fill in the blanks you will be providing all required data. Using one of the computer programs mentioned above will also ensure that your résumé is complete.

- Job Information: Public Announcement Number, title, and grade(s) for which you are applying.
- Personal Information: Full name, mailing address (with Zip code) and day/evening telephone numbers (with area code); Social Security number; and country of citizenship. If ever employed by the federal government, show the highest civilian grade held, job series, and dates of employment in the grade.
- Education: High school name, city, state, and Zip code, date of diploma or GED; colleges and/or universities attended, city, state, and Zip code; major field(s) of study; and type and year of degree(s) received. If no degree received, show total credit hours received in semester or quarter hours. If you qualify and/or claim to qualify for this position based on education, or if you are applying as an Outstanding Scholar, YOU MUST SUBMIT A COPY OF YOUR COLLEGE TRANSCRIPTS OR A LIST OF COLLEGE COURSES DETAILING FOR EACH COURSE, THE COURSE NUMBER AND DEPARTMENT (I.E., BIO 101, MATH 210, ETC.), COURSE TITLE, NUMBER OF CREDIT HOURS, AND GRADE EARNED. Failure to do so will result in an ineligible rating.
- Work Experience: Provide the following for each paid and non-paid position held related to the job for which you are applying (do not provide job descriptions): job title; duties and accomplishments; employer's name and address; supervisor's name and phone number; starting and ending dates of employment (month and year); hours per week; and salary. Indicate whether your current supervisor may be contacted.
- Other Qualifications: job-related training courses (title and year); job-related skills (e.g., other languages, computer software/hardware, tools, machinery, typing speed, etc.); job-related certificates and licenses; job-related honors, awards, and special accomplishments (e.g., publications, memberships in professional or honor societies, leadership activities, public speaking, performance awards, etc.). Do not send documents unless specifically requested.

- Veterans Preference: If you are applying for five-point Veterans Preference, submit a copy of your DD-214. If you are applying for 10-point Veterans Preference, submit a Standard Form 15, Application for 10-Point Veteran Preference, and the proof requested by the form. More information on veterans' preference is available in the Vets' Guide that can be found on the Internet at www.opm.gov.
- Federal employees: If you are or have been a federal employee, submit a copy of your latest Notification of Personnel Action, Form SF-50, and your most recent or last performance appraisal. If you are applying for priority consideration under the Agency Career Transition Assistance Program (CTAP) or the Interagency Career Transition Assistance Program (ICTAP), you must submit additional documentation. See the Special Selection Priority Consideration Section on this announcement for further information, instructions, and requirements.

STEP 2) SUPPLEMENTAL QUALIFICATIONS STATEMENT

Respond to the questions on the attached Supplemental Qualifications Statement (SQS). This may be done either electronically or by completing OPM Form 1203-AW, Qualification and Availability Form "C", in hard copy format.

- Electronic Application Options: This is the most convenient option if you have access to a computer with communications and/or Internet capability. If you choose to file electronically, you must do so by the CLOSING DATE of this announcement (10-05-04). If this equipment is not available to you, or you fail to file electronically by the CLOSING DATE, you must submit a hard copy (Form C) with your written application (refer to the "Hard Copy" section below).

- **Online Questionnaire**

    1. Connect to the USAJOBS Web site at http://www.usajobs.gov
    2. Click on online application from the USAJOBS logo or the text line below the logo
    3. Click on "Complete Online Supplemental Qualifications Statement"
    4. Scroll down the online application screen until the "Enter Control Number" box appears
    5. Enter Control Number CK0916 and click on "Submit" to begin the online application
    6. Follow the instructions on the Supplemental Qualifications Statement Questionnaire for the rest of the items

NOTE FOR ELECTRONIC FILERS: After completing the online application, you will know if your electronic submission through the Internet has been successful when you receive a "thank you" message stating that your online application for the control number has been received. If you applied through the USAJOBS Bulletin Board, you will receive a message indicating that you can receive a Notice of Applicant Responses through that system's E-mail, which you can then view or download. IF YOU DO NOT RECEIVE SUCH MESSAGES, PLEASE TRY AGAIN, AS THIS INDICATES YOUR RESPONSES HAVE NOT BEEN ENTERED INTO THE OPM DATABASE. When you do receive these messages, please print or save them, as they are your only confirmation of a timely submission.

THIS IS THE REPLY I RECEIVED AFTER APPLYING

Thank you. Your online application for CK0916 has been received. Please be sure to review the *"How to Apply"* information on the vacancy announcement for this position to see if additional application steps are required. Once you have submitted your complete application, you can usually expect to receive a Notice of Results in about 4 - 8 weeks. We are sorry, but we are unable to respond to requests to verify receipt of individual applications at the USAJOBS Web site. If you have questions concerning this vacancy, please write to the Office of Personnel Management Service Center shown on the job announcement.

After filing your SQS responses online, your résumé and any other requested documentation must be faxed to XXX-456-7890 or mailed to the address below. Your résumé must be received in our office by the filing deadline and must include the written notation "ATTN: ELECTRONIC FILER."

- Hard Copy: Complete the hard copy Form "C" and mail it (the Form C cannot be faxed) and all other requested forms (résumé, etc.) to the mailing address listed below. You may request a Form "C" by phone in the following manner:

    1. Call USAJobs by phone at 703-724-1850
    2 Press 1 for the main menu
    3. At the main menu, select 3 to request application forms
    4. Press 1 to continue (indicating you are sure of the application material you need to request)
    5. Follow the prompts to ASK THAT A FORM "C" BE MAILED TO YOU, and to record your name and address

Mailing Address:	U.S. Office of Personnel Management
	ATTN: 99-0916 LV
	601 East 12th Street, Room 131
	Kansas City, MO 64106

Where to get forms: If you **DO NOT** have all the required application forms listed on page 113 under the "Basis of Rating" and "How to Apply" sections, you may write to our office at the address listed above or request them by phone in the following manner:

1. Call USAJOBS by phone at 703-724-1850.
2. Press 1 for the main menu

3.   At the main menu, select 3 to request application forms
4.   Press 1 to continue (indicating you are sure of the application material you need to request)
5.   Follow the prompts to ASK FOR ANNOUNCEMENT NUMBER 0916 LV, and to record your name and address.

Eligibility: <u>Applicants will not be considered for other positions on the basis of this application.</u>

SPECIAL SELECTION PRIORITY CONSIDERATION PROVISIONS FOR SURPLUS AND DISPLACED FEDERAL EMPLOYEES:

Individuals who have special selection priority rights under the Agency Career Transition Assistance Program (CTAP) or the Interagency Career Transition Assistance Program (ICTAP) must be well qualified for the position to receive consideration for special priority selection. CTAP and ICTAP eligibles will be considered well qualified if they receive a score of 90 or above(excluding veterans preference points).

Current or former federal employees seeking priority selection consideration under CTAP/ICTAP provisions must submit proof that they meet the requirements of 5 CFR 330.605(a) for CTAP and 5 CFR330.704(a) for ICTAP. This includes a copy of the agency notice, a copy of their most recent performance rating and a copy of their most recent SF-50 noting current or last position, grade level, and duty location. Annotate your application to reflect you are applying as a CTAP or ICTAP eligible.

IMPORTANT!!
THE FEDERAL GOVERNMENT IS AN EQUAL OPPORTUNITY EMPLOYER

FEDERAL STYLE RÉSUMÉ

The following federal style résumé is targeted to the Management Analyst position, job announcement number 0916LV, featured in this chapter. Read the job announcement and review the résumé to observe how the duties, responsibilities, and specialized experience are integrated into the application. You need to capture required specialized experience, skills, duties and accomplishments to obtain a higher rating and to be referred to a selecting official for an interview. The Qualification Standard for this position is also available for your review in Chapter Two. The more time you spend refining your application to include required duties and specialized experience, the higher your rating.

Prepare two résumé formats, hard copy (paper) and online submission. Two formats are needed because the majority of federal job announcements permit either full or partial electronic submissions. The hard copy format can use different size, bold and italic type, bullets, symbols and offset margins to enhance its appearance. The hard copy format is used when you are permitted or requested to submit hard paper copies either through the mail, in person, or by fax to agencies. You can also hand them out when going for job interviews.

Prepare two résumé formats, hard copy (paper) and electronic.

Those same formatting attributes can scramble electronic submissions, and it is best to use plain 12 pitch type, flush left text, without any enhancements such as bullets and offset margins when cutting and copying information into online résumé builder programs. You may also be instructed by personnel offices to structure your résumé to a specific agency's unique automated format. You will copy and paste sections of your electronic formatted résumé into online résumé builders or fax this format to Resumix systems that search for the key words and phrases listed in the job announcement's duties and specialized experience.

Both résumé types are presented in this chapter. The hard copy (paper) format is shown first, followed by the online submission version so that you can compare the two. Hard copy versions are more attractive and if properly formatted can attract the attention of selecting officials. However, content outweighs this benefit in the federal sector and you have to consider that, in most cases today, your application package is being read by a computer, rating specialist, and the selecting official. After your application package is rated by the personnel or human resource office they send paper copies or printouts to the selecting official and/or interview panels.

The person rating your application is generally a human resource specialist and may not be familiar with all occupations. They rely on qualification and classification standards and other rating criteria to assign points to your application. Raters look for duties, responsibilities, and specialized experience — key words and phrases — to assign points to your application. Resumix and online submissions are electronically scanned for these data.

I was a trained and certified rater for several job series while working for the FAA, and reviewed and rated many hundreds of applications during my career. Your résumé will be rated on a point system of up to 100 points; veterans preference applicants can earn an additional five points if they served during a major military campaign or 10 points if they are disabled.

There is a balancing act to follow when completing your résumé and other application questionnaires. Use bullets in hard copy submissions to attract the reviewer's attention or add white space and line breaks between key points and topics in your online submission résumé. If you simply write a long narrative, it's hard for the rating official to pick out the required key duties and specialized experience. A typical federal résumé is between two and five pages; additional pages are added for KSAs. A typical KSA is between half and a full page in length.

Online résumé builders don't have a field for the OBJECTIVE or target position. This information is entered into the *Self Nomination* form. You will find several sample résumés in this chapter without target positions. The résumés were developed using on line résumé builder software and they are tailored to a specific job series. The target position will be listed prior to the sample résumé example.

Focusing on the job announcement's duties and specialized experience could earn you a higher rating.

Focusing on the job announcement's duties and responsibilities could earn you a higher rating, possibly a higher entry level pay grade, and it should help you get your foot in the door. If the job is advertised as a GS-7/9, and you have the required work experience and/or education, your chances of being hired at the GS-9 grade are much better if you follow the guidance in this chapter. I suggest making a list of the duties, responsibilities and specialized experience listed in job announcements that you are bidding on and keep this list handy when writing your work experiences.

You will find several résumé samples, following the two I developed for this edition, written by Kathryn Kraemer Troutman, owner of The Resume Place in Baltimore and author of the *Federal Résumé Guidebook.* The samples feature a student management analyst résumé, in both paper and electronic format, excerpted from Kathryn's *Student Federal Career Guide & CD-ROM* book, and a military transition electronic formatted résumé excerpted from her *Military to Federal Career Guide & CD-ROM* book..

Kathryn's book, the *Federal Résumé Guidebook*, covers strategies for moving up in government, federal résumé writing, electronic résumé submissions, and an excellent section on tailoring your résumé to specific occupations, with many samples and hints. If you need professional assistance, her book is available for $21.95 plus shipping by calling 1-800-782-7424. Kathryn's book is the next best thing to hiring a professional résumé writer. You can also order this title online at http://federaljobs.net/resbook.htm.

Management Analyst with IT Background Sample Résumé

The following sample paper hard copy résumé is formatted to attract the attention of the selecting official. It is a typical hard copy federal style résumé that you would either send in or hand deliver. You can also take extra copies to your interview. If you are applying online through a résumé builder you will need to plainly format your résumé, and an example of this same résumé in electronic format follows this example.

John Q. Adams

3401 Main Street
Hyattsville, MD 20782

Day Phone # 202-123-4567• Evening Phone # 301-234-5678 • jqadams79@gonext.com

Social Security Number:	xxx-xx-xxxx
Citizenship:	United States
Federal Status:	N/A
Veterans' Preference	Yes, 5 points *(DD-214 form available)*

OBJECTIVE

Management Analyst, GS-0343-07/09
National Archives & Records Administration
Announcement # 0916 LV, Closing Date 10/09/2006

PROFILE

Lead automation analyst for a large organization consisting of 797 workers located at seven offices in Maryland, Virginia, Pennsylvania, and Delaware. Novell, A+, Net+, and Microsoft Applications certified. Results-oriented analyst and computer specialist with sound analytical, automation applications, and technical expertise. Provides a full range of continuing automation technical and advisory services to operating offices, system users, company officials, and warehouse managers. Collateral duties included researching potential Local Area Network (LAN) deployment at branch and field offices, automation security administrator for the organization, and provided new system integration training. Attended numerous strategy sessions with vendors, managers, and staff to explore feasibility of expanding automation system capabilities.

PROFESSIONAL AND PERSONAL STRENGTHS

- Highly motivated, proven, and proactive leader recognized for sound judgment and entrusted with highly confidential and sensitive information.
- Conscientious and flexible when delegating and executing professional responsibilities and known for the ability to work effectively with work groups and teams to get the job done, and done right.
- Committed to the organization's mission and yet tactful and willing to work complex issues collaboratively to reach the desired outcome.
- Multi-task oriented and makes sound decisions due to technical expertise under pressure.

EXPERIENCE

Computer Analyst   April 1999 to Present
Hendricks Inc   40+ hours/week
435 Smithfield Drive, Smithfield, MD 20782   Salary: $47,956/yr
Supervisor: Gene Porter, 202-123-2456, Extension 410. You may contact my present and all previous supervisors.

Proficient in most Microsoft applications including Word, Excel, Powerpoint, Scheduler, Project, Frontpage 2003 and Access. Trained over 127 users in software applications over the past two years. Designed Hendricks' corporate Web site that received several internet design awards. Three of my articles were published in major national magazines concerning NOVELL upgrades and system integration issues. Copies available upon request.

DUTIES & RESPONSIBILITIES

- Technical automation expert for Leesburg, Virginia, headquarters of Novell LAN operations.
- Analyze and advise management of all aspects of system integration and LAN applications.
- Perform feasibility studies and analysis of staff and field office automation needs.
- Maintain DELL NT computer work stations at headquarters for 127 employees.
- Maintain company Lotus Notes email for the organization. Updated address databases and worked with vendors concerning major problems and software failures.
- Performed cost/benefit evaluation for work station upgrades and LAN automation expansion at field facilities.
- Train 127 users on new system functions and software applications.
- Company Web site Webmaster, proficient in html and htmls.
- Recommended filed system upgrade and LAN integration through Wynnframe deployment.
- Develop company's annual Information Resource Management (IRM) budget.
- Site automation administrator maintaining all user data, access levels, and system security passwords and documentation.
- Initiate daily LAN backups.
- Maintain a comprehensive technical and software applications user library.
- Debug, repair and service operating systems and software/hardware throughout the organization.

ACCOMPLISHMENTS

- Developed written automation configuration reports for upper management to consolidate three field offices into a central hub facility at Baltimore, Maryland.
- Management accepted my Wynnframe LAN field integration recommendation after I completed a comprehensive cost/benefit analysis and feasibility study for the upgrade. I developed gant and milestone charts using Microsoft Project to schedule,

coordinate, and complete the upgrade using internal resources. Trained users after field installation was complete.

- Designed the company's Internet Web site. Management accepted my proposal after viewing an interactive Powerpoint presentation that I developed and viewing a live online demonstration that featured the Web site's functionality. I received a substantial cash bonus for developing the site.
- Member of the company's strategic planning committee. The committee presented the CEO with plans for major Internet security improvements and a cost/benefit analysis for our automation needs through 2008. The study included a major expansion to two additional states scheduled for 2007.

Computer Specialist   June 1994 to April 1999
National Rental Corporation   40+ hours/week
101 Fifth St., Silver Spring, MD 20901   Salary: $32,545/yr
Supervisor: Charles Massie, 202-234-2345.

Computer specialist responsible for system administration, maintenance, and new software training for 47 specialists and five managers. Designed, updated, and modified office automation applications for the organization and serviced over 67 desktop and laptop computers and office Local Area Network (LAN). Worked closely with department managers and vendors to create and maintain appropriate technical documentation for all system users. Collateral responsibilities included researching potential LAN deployment at branch offices and new system integration training. Attended numerous strategy sessions with vendors and mangers to explore the feasibility of expanding office automation system capabilities.

DUTIES & RESPONSIBILITIES

- System administrator for the organization's information processing systems. Coordinated all upgrades, scheduled maintenance, and assigned user names and passwords.
- Performed daily LAN backups of critical office databases and assisted specialists with local computer backup as needed.
- Initiated and monitored special projects including automation software deployment for the entire organization. Team lead for LAN/WAN configuration and maintenance.
- Set up Internet accounts for all company vendors and trained staff on data collection applications.

ACCOMPLISHMENTS

- Team lead for recommending improvements, evaluating, coordination, and implementation of NOVELL server upgrades. The upgrade was accomplished with minimal system downtime and negligible impact to clients and staff.
- Developed numerous written reports and gave oral presentations to managers on various IRM and ADP issues including NOVELL deployment, user system upgrades, and automation security threats and system enhancements.

- Developed organization's IRM security directives/regulations. Trained managers and staff on security concerns and provided methods to improve online security at all levels of the organization.
- Performed a feasibility study to implement a paperless office. Researched options, developed plans, performed a cost/benefit analysis, and presented a proposal to the Chief Executive Officer. The plan was successfully implemented throughout the organization.

Communications System Repairman U.S. ARMY   May 1992 to June 1994
U.S. Army, National Training Center   40+ hours/week
11th Armored Regiment, Operations Group   Salary: $17,789/yr
Fort Irwin, CA 92310-5067
Supervisor: Msgt Don Riley, 760-999-9999

Attained the active duty rank of Sergeant. Responsible for maintaining and servicing the training center's field communications systems including Frequency Modulated (FM) handsets, telephone equipment, and Very High Frequency (VHF) and Ultra High Frequency (UHF) transmitters and receivers used to communicate with air support and armored cavalry command units. Assigned collateral duties to maintain field computers used to direct and coordinate troop movements with headquarters command. Responsible for analyzing and advising training command staff of communication problems and concerns.

DUTIES & RESPONSIBILITIES

- Provided field and shop level maintenance for FM handheld transceivers and VHF/UHF transceivers.
- Programed field computers used for troop movement and developed user technical documentation for critical field deployments.
- Assisted computer specialists with field computer repair.
- Logistical support including ordering of spare parts and supplies and storage of line replaceable units.
- Troubleshot telephone and switching equipment problems.

ACCOMPLISHMENTS

- Coordinated the utilization of limited communication resources for field deployment at the training center for over 2,000 active duty and reserve troops. Prioritized order of delivery communication needs for all deployments.
- Crypto trained for Top Secret scrambled communications between command centers and senior field command officers. Responsible for safeguarding equipment and destroying it at all costs if enemy infiltration discovered.
- Hold a Top Secret clearance.
- Developed, evaluated, and performed a cost/benefit analysis for a communications deployment scheme at the training centers that was implemented at all Department of Defense training facilities.

EDUCATION

Community College of Baltimore, Baltimore, MD 21201,
Associates Degree in Computer Technology, graduated with high honors, 1990

Additional Training

Communications Electronics School, US Army, 1992 (6 months)
Microsoft Office, April (40 hours), 1993
Work Station Integration & LAN Connectivity (160 hours), 1994
NOVEL Certification Course (80 hours), 1995
Microsoft Office Professional (40 hours), 1996
Quality of Worklife & Team Work (40 hours), employer sponsored
LAN/WAN Office Configuration Management Course (240 hours), 1999
A+ / Net + Software/Hardware Certification Course (200 hours), 2003

OTHER QUALIFICATIONS

Awards

- (1991) US ARMY Dickens Award for Outstanding Achievement. Awarded for developing a communications deployment strategy that was accepted by the DOD for all Army training centers.
- (2002) Designed, developed and published Hendricks' Web site. Received a substantial cash bonus for developing the site.

Licenses/Certifications

- FCC Radio Telephone License with Ship Radar endorsement (current)
- NOVEL Certified in 1999
- A+ / NET + Certified June 2003

In addition to the courses I have taken to acquire further knowledge for the positions I have held, I also have experience and expertise in the following areas:

Interpersonal Relations

- Deal effectively and professionally with people. A team player as evidenced by my military background and success at Hendricks Corp. to integrate and consolidate branch offices. I enjoy working in groups and have been trained in Quality Worklife (QWL) and Partnership initiatives.

Communications and Writing Skills

- Joined Toastmasters International in 1995 and achieved Competent Toastmaster status in 1997. Several of my networking integration studies were published in national journals in 2002. In 2004 I completed oral communications and report writing courses at a local community college. Maintain an excellent grasp of the English language and have experience in a variety of different writing styles including reports, grant requests, informational material, speeches, brochures, and promotional material.

Training Skills

- Conducted classes for office automation and software applications to over 200 employees. I also provide on-the-job training to individual users on an as-needed basis and frequently train managers on new applications and Internet security options and procedures.

Computer Skills

- Since 1985 my interest in computers has led to experience with all types of personal computers and software applications, and I have expertise in word processing, database management, spreadsheets, desktop publishing, form design, and BASIC and HTML programing and design. I have an associate degree in IRM Automation and completed numerous evening courses in all facets of automation. During my tenure with Hendricks I designed their corporate web site and was the site's webmaster. Design Web sites for small companies. I have A+ / NET +/ NOVELL and Microsoft Certifications and have worked in the field since 1990.

Office Skills

- Knowledgeable in all aspects of office operations and proficient in operating a wide variety of office machinery including word processors, copiers, postage meters, telephone systems (including PBX), fax machines, electronic mail, and computer modems, as well as all types of audiovisual equipment. Able to set up, calibrate, and configure all types of electronic equipment from printers and telephone systems, to recorders, cameras and other ancillary equipment. Knowledgeable with Powerpoint.

ELECTRONIC SUBMISSION RÉSUMÉ FORMAT

There are a number of options to consider when completing your electronic submission résumé. Different online résumé builders require different information and formatting. Unfortunately, not one size fits all. Don't let this confuse or dissuade you from applying. There are ways to work around this and not go crazy in the process.

Many automated data collection systems exist, including USAJOBS Résumé Builder, Resumix, QuickHire, eRecruit and COAST, to name a few. It would be so much easier if there was just one standard format. The reason there are so many different systems is because agencies have unique hiring and recruiting needs and they tailor their systems to those needs.

Fortunately, most online résumé builders have sufficient flexibility to accommodate your information. Notice in the following résumé example that I use the term PROFILE. This same data could be included under SUMMARY, SKILLS SUMMARY or QUALIFICATIONS AND SKILLS SUMMARY. It's just a title. Cut and paste information from your electronic formatted résumé into the online format as appropriate. The headings may be different but the content will be the same. If you can't find a match, add the data to the *Other Information* heading or something similar. Resumix doesn't have a Profile or Summary section; however, it does have space for other information.

You will also find different character and page limits per field between online résumé builder programs. It is important to be concise when writing your work descriptions, Knowledge, Skills, and Abilities (KSAOs), Occupational Questionnaires (OQs), and Executive Core Qualifications (ECQs) statements. You don't want to hide your core skills in too much text. Write, and rewrite your work experiences until your descriptions are to the point and concise. If you paste a work experience into an online résumé builder and the key data cut off, condense the write-up to make sure all key data are included.

Electronic Résumé Format Checklist

☐ Use white space and line breaks to separate topics and sections
☐ Use 10 or 12 point type size
☐ Use a margin of at least one inch on all sides
☐ Use CAPITAL LETTERS to highlight sections
☐ No graphics of any kind, including bullets
☐ Don't use symbols including &, #, *, or /
☐ Use date format mm-yyyy (example: May, 1988 would be 05-1988)
☐ No bold, italic, or underlined text
☐ Don't use parentheses

JOHN Q. ADAMS
SSN: xxx-xx-xxxx

3401 Main Street
Hyattsville, MD 20782
Work telephone: 202-123-456
Home telephone: 301-234-5678

E-mail address: jqadams79@gonext.com

Citizenship: United States
Federal Status: N/A
Veterans' Preference: Yes, 5 points / DD-214 form available

OBJECTIVE

Management Analyst, GS-0343-07/09
National Archives and Records Administration
Announcement Number: 0916 LV, Closing Date 10/09/2006

PROFILE

Lead automation analyst for a large organization consisting of 797 workers located at
seven offices in Maryland, Virginia, Pennsylvania, and Delaware. Novell, A+, Net+, and
Microsoft Applications certified.

Results-oriented analyst and computer specialist with sound analytical, automation
applications, and technical expertise. Provides a full range of continuing automation
technical and advisory services to operating offices, system users, company officials, and
warehouse managers.

Collateral duties included researching potential Local Area Network (LAN) deployment
at branch and field offices, automation security administrator for the organization, and
provided new system integration training. Attended numerous strategy sessions with
vendors, managers, and staff to explore feasibility of expanding automation system
capabilities.

PROFESSIONAL AND PERSONAL STRENGTHS

LEADERSHIP CHARACTERISTICS: Highly motivated, proven, and proactive leader
recognized for sound judgement and entrusted with highly confidential and sensitive
information.

PROFESSIONAL RESPONSIBILITIES: Conscientious and flexible when delegating and
executing professional responsibilities and known for the ability to work effective with
work groups and teams to get the job done, and done right.

MISSION ORIENTED: Committed to the organization's mission and yet tactful and willing to work complex issues collaboratively to reach the desired outcome. Multi-task oriented and makes sound decisions due to technical expertise under pressure

EXPERIENCE

COMPUTER ANALYST, 04-1999 to Present; 40 hours/week, Annual Salary $47,956
Hendricks Inc, 435 Smithfield Drive, Smithfield, MD 20782

Supervisor: Gene Porter, 202-123-2456, Extension 410. You may contact my present and all previous supervisors.

Proficient in most Microsoft applications including Word, Excel, Powerpoint, Scheduler, Project, Frontpage 2003 and Access. Trained over 127 users in software applications over the past two years. Designed Hendricks' corporate Web site that was awarded several Internet design awards. Three of my articles were published in major national magazines concerning NOVELL upgrades and system integration issues. Copies available upon request.

DUTIES & RESPONSIBILITIES

AUTOMATION EXPERT: Technical automation expert for Leesburg, Virginia, headquarters, Novell LAN operations.

LAN SYSTEM MANAGEMENT: Analyze and advise management on all aspects of system integration and LAN applications. Recommended file system upgrade and LAN integration through Wynnframe deployment. Initiate daily LAN backups.

FEASIBILITY STUDIES: Perform feasibility studies and analysis of staff and field office automation needs. Recommend automation system improvements and upgrade.

COMPUTER MAINTENANCE: Maintain DELL NT computer work stations at headquarters for 127 employees. Debug, repair and service operating systems and software/hardware throughout the organization.

E-MAIL SYSTEM ADMINISTRATOR: Maintain company Lotus Notes e-mail for the organization. Updated address databases and worked with vendors concerning major problems and software failures.

COST-BENEFIT ANALYSIS: Perform cost/benefit evaluation for work station upgrades and LAN automation expansion at field facilities.

COMPUTER TRAINING: Train 127 users on new system functions and software applications.

WEBMASTER: Company Web site Webmaster, proficient in html and htmls.

BUDGET ANALYSIS: Develops company's annual Information Resource Management (IRM) budget.

AUTOMATION SECURITY ADMINISTRATOR: Site automation administrator, maintaining all user data, access levels, and system security passwords and documentation.

TECHNICAL DOCUMENTATION: Maintain a comprehensive technical and software applications user library.

ACCOMPLISHMENTS

AUTOMATION CONFIGURATION: Developed written automation configuration reports for upper management to consolidate three field offices into a central hub facility at Baltimore, Maryland.

AUTOMATION NETWORK MANAGEMENT: Management accepted my Wynnframe LAN field integration recommendation after I completed a comprehensive cost/benefit analysis and feasibility study for the upgrade. I developed gant and milestone charts using Microsoft Project to schedule, coordinate, and complete the upgrade using internal resources. Trained users after field installation was complete.

WEBMASTER: Designed the company's Internet Web site. Management accepted my proposal after viewing an interactive Powerpoint presentation that I developed and viewing a live online demonstration that featured the Web site functionality. I received a substantial cash bonus for developing the site.

STRATEGIC PLANNING TEAM MEMBER: Member of the company's strategic planning committee. The committee presented the CEO with plans for major Internet security improvements and a cost/benefit analysis for our automation needs through 2008. The study included a major expansion to two additional states scheduled for 2007.

COMPUTER SPECIALIST, 06-1994 to 04-1999, 40 hours/week, annual salary $32,545
National Rental Corporation, 101 Fifth St., Silver Spring, MD 20901
Supervisor: Charles Massie, 202-234-2345.

Responsible for system administration, maintenance, and new software training for 47 specialists and five managers. Designed, updated, and modified office automation applications for the organization and serviced over 67 desktop and laptop computers and office Local Area network — LAN. Worked closely with department managers and vendors to create and maintain appropriate technical documentation for all system users. Collateral responsibilities included researching potential LAN deployment at branch offices and new system integration training. Attended numerous strategy sessions with vendors and mangers to explore the feasibility of expanding office automation system capabilities.

DUTIES & RESPONSIBILITIES

SYSTEM ADMINISTRATOR: System administrator for the organization's information processing systems. Coordinated all upgrades, scheduled maintenance, and assigned user names and passwords.

LAN MAINTENANCE: Performed daily LAN backups of critical office databases and assisted specialists with local computer backup as needed.

SPECIAL PROJECTS: Initiated and monitored special projects including automation software deployment for the entire organization. Team lead for LAN/WAN configuration and maintenance.

WEB SITE MANAGEMENT: Set up Internet accounts for all company vendors and trained staff on data collection applications.

ACCOMPLISHMENTS

TEAM LEAD: Recommended improvements, evaluated, coordinated, and implementation of NOVELL server upgrades. Upgrades were accomplished with minimal system downtime and negligible impact to clients and staff.

WRITTEN REPORTS AND ORAL PRESENTATIONS: Developed numerous written reports and gave oral presentations to managers on various IRM and ADP issues including NOVELL deployment, user system upgrades, and automation security threats and system enhancements.

IRM SECURITY: Developed organizations IRM security directives/regulations. Trained managers and staff on security concerns and provided methods to improve online security at all levels of the organization.

FEASIBILITY STUDIES: Performed a feasibility study to implement a paperless office. Researched options, developed plans, performed a cost/benefit analysis, and presented a proposal to the Chief Executive Officer. The plan was successfully implemented throughout the organization.

Communications System Repairman, 05-1992 to 06-1994, 40 hours/week,
Annual Salary $17,789
U.S. Army, National Training Center, 11th Armored Regiment, Operations Group
Fort Irwin, CA 92310-5067
Supervisor: Msgt Don Riley, 760-999-9999

Attained the active duty rank of Sergeant. Responsible for maintaining and servicing the training center's field communications systems including Frequency Modulated-FM handsets, telephone equipment, and Very High Frequency-VHF and Ultra High Frequency-UHF transmitters and receivers used to communicate with air support and armored cavalry command units. Assigned collateral duties to maintain field computers used to direct and coordinate troop movements with headquarters command. Responsible for analyzing and advising training command staff of communication problems and concerns.

DUTIES AND RESPONSIBILITIES

ELECTRONICS MAINTENANCE: Provided field and shop level maintenance for FM hand held transceivers and VHF/UHF transceivers.

COMPUTER MAINTENANCE: Programed field computers used for troop movement and developed user technical documentation for critical field deployments. Assisted computer specialists with field computer repair.

LOGISTICS SUPPORT: Logistical support including ordering of spare parts and supplies and storage of line replaceable units.

TELEPHONE SYSTEM MAINTENANCE: Troubleshoot telephone and switching equipment problems.

ACCOMPLISHMENTS

COMMUNICATIONS SYSTEMS MANAGEMENT: Coordinated the utilization of limited communication resources for field deployment at the training center for over 2,000 active duty and reserve troops. Prioritized order of delivery communication needs for all deployments.

TOP SECRETE CRYPTO CLEARANCE: Crypto trained for Top Secret scrambled communications between command centers and senior field command officers. Responsible for safeguarding equipment and destroying it at all costs if enemy infiltration discovered.

COST-BENEFIT ANALYSIS: Developed, evaluated, and performed a cost/benefit analysis for a communications deployment scheme at the training centers that was implemented at all Department of Defense training facilities.

EDUCATION

Community College of Baltimore, Baltimore, MD 21201,
associates degree in computer technology, graduated with high honors, 05-1990

ADDITIONAL TRAINING

Communications Electronics School, US Army, 1992 (6 months)
Microsoft Office, April (40 hours), 1993
Work Station Integration & LAN Connectivity (160 hours), 1994
NOVEL Certification Course (80 hours), 1995
Microsoft Office Professional (40 hours), 1996
Quality of Worklife and Team Work (40 hours), - employer sponsored
LAN/WAN Office Configuration Management Course (240 hours), 1999
A+ / Net + Software/Hardware Certification Course (200 hours), 2003

OTHER QUALIFICATIONS

AWARDS

US ARMY Dickens Award for Outstanding Achievement. Awarded for developing a
communications deployment strategy that was accepted by the DOD for all ARMY
training centers, 1991.

Designed, developed and published Hendricks' web site. Received a substantial cash
bonus for developing the site, 2002.

LICENSES/CERTIFICATIONS

FCC Radio Telephone License with Ship Radar endorsement (Current)
NOVEL Certified 1999
A+ / NET + Certified 06-2003
Competent Toastmaster status 05-1997

In addition to the courses I have taken to acquire further knowledge for the positions I
have held, I also have experience and expertise in the following areas:

INTERPERSONAL RELATIONS

Deal effectively and professionally with people. A team player as evidenced by my
military background and success at Hendricks Corp. to integrate and consolidate branch
offices. I joy working in groups and have been trained in Quality Worklife (QWL) and
Partnership initiatives.

COMMUNICATIONS AND WRITING SKILLS

Joined Toastmasters International in 1995 and achieved Competent Toastmaster status in
May 1997. Several of my networking integration studies were published in national
journals in 2002. In 2004 I completed oral communications and report writing courses at
a local community college. Maintain an excellent grasp of the English language and have

experience in a variety of different writing styles including reports, grant requests, informational material, speeches, brochures, and promotional material.

TRAINING SKILLS

Conducted classes for office automation and software applications to over 200 employees. I also provide on-the-job training to individual users on an as needed basis and frequently train managers on new applications and Internet security options and procedures.

OFFICE SKILLS

Knowledgeable in all aspects of office operations and proficient in operating a wide variety of office machinery including word processors, copiers, postage meters, telephone systems, including PBX, fax machines, electronic mail, computer modems as well as all types of audiovisual equipment. Able to set up, calibrate, and configure all types of electronic equipment from printers, and telephone systems, to recorders, cameras and other ancillary equipment. Knowledgeable with Powerpoint.

> The electronic format is flush left without any bold, italic, or underlined text. Some sections were combined to improve formatting. Capitalization was used to lead off most sections, parentheses were used occasionally and the "&" sign was converted to "and." After you complete your electronic submission résumé copy and paste each section into the online résumé tool.

Entry Level Admin / Analyst GS 5/7 USAJOBS Résumé Sample

The résumé builder at www.usajobs.gov was used to compile Kathryn Richard's sample résumé. Kathryn worked as a part time information specialist for the past two years. She is now seeking a full time GS 5 or 7 management analyst, or management assistant position. This sample was provided by Kathryn Kraemer Troutman and excerpted from her book. Kathryn Troutman copied and pasted the data into the USAJOBS online résumé builder to show readers what you can expect when using the résumé builder.

www.usajobs.gov My Resume Builder
New Bachelor's Degree Graduate, Public Administration Major
Target positions: GS 5 or 7, Management Analyst, Management Assistant

<u>Click here to edit this resume</u> | <u>Print Resume</u> | <u>Edit My Confidentiality Settings</u>

KATHRYN K. RICHARD
655 West Lake Road
Harpers Ferry, WV 25425
Day Phone: 907-333-3333
Email: <u>kathrynkrich@yahoo.com</u>

Country of citizenship: United States of America

Veterans' Preference: No

AVAILABILITY

Job Type:	Permanent
	Temporary
Work Schedule:	Full Time

**DESIRED
LOCATIONS**   US-DC-Washington/Metro

WORK EXPERIENCE Vistronix   5/2006 - Present
McLean, VA US   Salary: $15.32 USD Per Hour
                                      Hours per week: 20

INFORMATION SPECIALIST II

PROGRAM ANALYSIS - COPS "MORE" - Making Officer Redeployment Effective - Program expands the amount of time current law enforcement officers can spend on community policing by funding technology, equipment, and the hiring of civilian personnel through grants to local communities. Use database, and contact grantees by phone to gather information needed to complete surveys.

DATA ANALYSIS AND CIVILIAN SURVEYS: Evaluate grantee calculations on actual Full Time Equivalents (FTEs) versus the required FTEs. Determine how much time the grantee is saving by hiring civilian personnel to staff positions that enable sworn officers to patrol the community and the public roads.

DATA ANALYSIS AND INVESTIGATIVE: Analyze data regarding time the grantee saves by purchasing equipment with grant money, which frees up sworn officers for re-deployment. For example, technology funded under COPS MORE, such as mobile in-car computers, enables officers to analyze and research local problems while on patrol, improving their ability to quickly and effectively address crime. (Contact Supervisor: Yes, Supervisor's Name: Sarah Whitmore, Supervisor's Phone: 1 888 999 0000)

George Mason University   9/2002 - Present
Fairfax, VA US

                                      Hours per week: 20

NEW GRADUATE, B.S., PUBLIC ADMINISTRATION

Will complete BS in Public Administration in May 2007. Seeking opportunity to utilize public policy, writing, research, analysis and computer skills in an Analyst or Administrative position.

Cubic Transportation Systems   10/2005 - 2/2006
Chantilly, VA US   Salary: $10.50 USD Per Hour

                                      Hours per week: 20

RESEARCH ASSISTANT

ADMINISTRATIVE SUPPORT: Provided engineering and business development support. Processed employee timecards, and maintained accurate records. Made travel arrangements for engineers. Finalized travel expense reports for Accounting. Maintained inventory of office supplies; prepared monthly order.

DATA ANALYSIS AND RESEARCH: Assisted transportation specialists with data collection, analysis and development of spreadsheets. Researched information via Internet and transportation firm statement of work.

EDUCATION

GEORGE MASON UNIVERSITY

Fairfax, VA US

Bachelor's Degree - 5/2007

Major: Public Administration

Relevant Coursework, Licensures and Certifications:
RESEARCH METHODS AND ANALYSIS. Research paper involved analyzing FBI criminal statistics on forensics activities at Headquarters having to do with Internet banking fraud. Wrote a survey and interviewed one FBI agent for clarification on questions and thesis of project. Produced quantitative and qualitative analysis of data. Designed and produced a 10-minute Power Point and gave presentation before the class.

LEGISLATIVE BEHAVIOR. Organization, processes, functions, and roles of the legislature and its members in the U.S. Congress. Topics include state legislatures and cross-national comparisons as time and resources permit.

PUBLIC POLICY MAKING. Studied processes, agencies, and politics involved in the proposal making, implementation, evaluation, and revision of public policy in the United States.

PUBLIC POLICY ANALYSIS. Methods of public policy analysis, evaluation, and research. Studies design and development of alternative courses of government action and evaluation of results, and problems in applying systematic analysis to political issues.

RESEARCH PRACTICUM in Public and International Affairs. Applied research methods, including library research, data collection, data analysis, and report construction.

LANGUAGES

French

Spoken:	Advanced
Written:	Intermediate
Read:	Intermediate

ADDITIONAL INFORMATION

TOP LEVEL SKILLS from course projects and major papers include:
+Management Analysis skills:
+Research, writing and analysis
+Project management and teamwork
+Writing and editing
+Completing project studies, including data analysis
+Data management with Excel and Statistical Analysis

COMPUTER SKILLS:
+60 words per minute typing.
+Computer proficiencies: MS Office Professional (Word, Excel, +Access, PowerPoint, and Outlook), WordPerfect, PhotoShop, ScheduALL, Citrix, Internet, and E-mail.

ADMINISTRATIVE SKILLS:
+Computers, office operations, business telephones, customer services, basic accounting, spreadsheet development and maintenance

COMPETENCIES:
+Self-reliant, focused, and committed to excellence in academic and professional pursuits.
+Outstanding skills in written and oral communications.
+Team player; identify needs and fill them.
+Intellectually curious about computer software applications and quick to learn how to apply them to business needs.
+Able to balance priorities and complete multiple tasks in a demanding work environment.

Military Transition Electronic Formatted Résumé Sample

The following electronic formatted résumé for Fernando Herboso targets a GS-1750 training instructor job at the 9 or 11 pay grade. This résumé was provided by Kathryn Kraemer Troutman and excerpted from her book. I included Kathryn's examples in this edition to expose readers to other acceptable résumé formats. You will notice that I use more white space in my electronic résumé example. Both formats are acceptable. Fernando was recently discharged from the military and is applying for training instructor positions. The names for all samples are fictional.

FERNANDO HERBOSO
SSN xxx-yy-zzzz
288th BSB
Unit 27777, Box 22225
APO AE 09234-7535
Home: (44) 999-98-89-888
Comm Work: (44) 999-33-38-888
DSN: 444-8888

E-mail Home: herboso6@aol.com
E-mail Work: herbosof@cmtymail.98asg.army.mil

Typing words per minute: 60;   Steno: 0

WORK EXPERIENCE
May we contact your current supervisor? Yes

77th Personnel Services Battalion (10/10/2000 - Present) - Operations Officer
APO, Armed Forces Overseas Germany
Supervisor: Lester Smith, (66) 999-97-72-222; contact: yes
Salary: $48,000 per year

CHIEF ADVISOR, PROGRAM MANAGER AND ADMINISTRATIVE OFFICER FOR COMMAND PLANS: Chief Advisor to Battalion Operation Manager and Executive Officer for personnel, budget, training, policies, procedures, resources, schools, inspections, travel, manpower needs, security, and correspondence. Evaluate findings and recommendations on efficiency reviews of operations. Develop plans of action and milestones to incorporate needed improvements to correct deficiencies. Arrange and provide numerous briefings on operation requirements. Prepare briefing slides for command visits. Plan and coordinate command inspections.

SUPERVISE THE LARGEST ARMY PERSONNEL SERVICE IN EUROPE: Directly supervise four military personnel supporting largest Army Personnel Services organization consisting of 289 soldiers and 93 civilian employees. Provide leadership and manage diverse military personnel programs including leave, awards, personnel requirements, advancement, performance evaluations, educational programs, transfer programs, and personnel assignments.

SUPPORT COMMAND MISSION AND OPERATIONAL TASKINGS: Manage administrative needs relevant to contingency program planning and force modernization, including command mission and function statements, military manning, distribution, classified information, range operations, battalion suspense and operational taskings, and military personnel programs. Plan and coordinate personnel deployments, redeployments. Plan and manage Command's military and civilian TDY travel program, including budget formulation, reports, orders, and arrangements. Oversee battalion's security program, Nuclear Biological Chemical program, communications section, and a $90,000 TDY budget.

Directly support the Executive Officer, Command Sergeant Major, and Commander in obtaining information, tabulating data, composing numerous command level correspondence and summaries. Research, develop, coordinate, and publish multiple command and community policies and review policy guidance. Maintain and track Command Group assignments to ensure timely receipt of actions by units and staff.

TRAINING TO MEET CONTINGENCY AND MISSION OBJECTIVES. Supervise quarterly training briefings and manage field training exercises. Liaison for German Partnership unit to plan, execute, conduct, train German and American units on weapons and physical fitness. Plan and coordinate transition-to-war, contingency peacetime missions, force modernization, and wartime emergency planning policies for the battalion. Review policy guidance for the battalion operation branch and recommend changes to exercise, force modernization, and mass casualty plans.

RECOMMEND LONG-RANGE TRAINING OBJECTIVES. Based on program evaluations, recommend training objectives in terms of organizational structure, programs, and milestones to meet training and operational resource requirements and objectives. Perform program evaluations to sustain deployment posture and ensure continued support of personnel and units moving through the 98th ASG and 100th ASG. Prepare and review policy letters, SOPs, and propose changes to USAREUR guidelines. Interview unit commanders and first sergeants to gain information about organizational missions, functions, and work procedures.

MANAGE AND ANALYZE MANPOWER TO MEET TRAINING AND BATTALION EXERCISES. Coordinate Command's military manpower management system. Assure FYDP data accurately reflects budgeted end-strength, billet requirements and authorizations, and accuracy of Command's Enlisted Distribution and Verification Report. Prepare and process unit status reports.

SUPERVISE INTERNAL SECURITY FOR EMERGENCY PLANS, EDUCATION, AND INVESTIGATIONS. Supervise Personnel Security Program directing subordinate unit level security managers, classified information and material control, personnel security, security education, emergency plans, security violations and compromises, classification management, security review of information proposed for public release, security records and foreign travel.

ACCOMPLISHMENTS:
Developed a management system that increased efficiency of processing $90,000 in business travel vouchers and achieved 100 percent accuracy during the annual 2002 audit.

Single-handedly coordinated all Force Protection missions for all subordinate companies in 5 different communities.

Flawlessly planned and executed 5 movements involving a total of 150 personnel to Albania, Macedonia, Kosovo, Turkey, and Iraq. Training and assessing these personnel prior to their movement resulted in all personnel accomplishing their jobs and returning safely home.

Began and developed company security program from scratch, resulting in a thriving section that was rated "best in the company" during inspection of the security and safety program.

Planned, coordinated, trained 260 military personnel in preparation for deployment to Iraq (2003-2004). During 12 month deployment, was tasked twice to deploy a personnel service, casualty and postal team to Najah, Iraq in support of Operation Iraqi Freedom, set up a post office and a Human Resource Center to provide casualty reporting, postal services, and human resources to 2,000 personnel.

77th Personnel Services Battalion (04/03/1994 - 10/09/2000) - Operations Manager
APO, Armed Forces Overseas Germany
Supervisor: Martin Cleary, (66) 999-66-61-111; contact: yes
Salary: $47,000 per year

PERSONNEL / MANPOWER EVALUATION: Supervised Military Personnel Company staffed by 15 civilians, 80 military personnel servicing 20,000+ military, civilians and family members. Provided technical expertise and guidance to managers, supervisors, and employees on training, safety, welfare, discipline, morale, leave, advancement, evaluations, applications for special schools, entitlements, and commissioning programs. Supported Equal Employment Opportunity and other management programs. Reviewed and ensured proper and timely administration of company programs.

Managed supply program, maintenance and serviceability of all assigned equipment; maintained accounts involving $900,000 worth of property and equipment without loss. Monitored procedures and programs for ensuring adequate and timely manpower requirements, and submitted needs projections to senior management. Provided division level supervision of employees.

Senior advisor to the commander. Managed Army Individual training requirements and resources, including weapons qualification and physical fitness program. Maintained quality of life program, social functions, protocol, receptions, and ceremonies. Maintained rosters on awards and assignments. Ensured soldiers were slotted properly based on military occupational specialty structure. Managed in and out-processing, issuance of meal cards, and accident reporting.

SUPERVISION / EMPLOYEE DEVELOPMENT: Planned work to be accomplished through employees, assigning work based on priorities. Prepared military evaluations for divisional military personnel. Evaluated training needs, developed lesson plan, delivered training, evaluated training effectiveness.

ACCOMPLISHMENTS:
Superb leadership enabled companies to exceed numerous U.S. Army Europe training standards while completing 100 percent of all directed training. Mentored 50 soldiers to complete Army Non-Commission Officers Educational courses. Expertly planned, executed battalion field training exercise that greatly increased the battalion's overall readiness. Key in planning and preparation of battalion command post exercise, focusing on communications, personnel services support, and maintenance operations training.

Greatly improved the company's maintenance readiness levels; raised company's rate from 73 to 100 percent. Coordinated five training exercises; executed all world wide contingency field exercise to include preparation of Operation Joint Endeavor in Bosnia.

Coordinated, implemented, led a company into Bosnia to provide personnel services support to 9,500+ soldiers in Operation Joint Endeavor. 100 percent re-enlistment of all eligible soldiers in 1995 due to high unit morale.

Reorganized company's personnel administrative center in two weeks upon returning from a 9 month deployment to Bosnia, achieving 100 percent passing on battalion command inspection. Accomplished more work with less resources during FY 98 when average strength levels were at 78 percent.

Personally established a proactive maintenance program, raising equipment readiness by more than 25 percent.

Selected as "best manager" in 1997 during battalion's command post exercise. Cited by brigade commander for winning brigade maintenance award for three consecutive quarters.

EDUCATION
College/University
City College of Chicago (10/01/1985 - 07/31/2002)
APO, Armed Forces Overseas, Germany
Degree: Associates in Arts - Major: Liberal Arts
GPA: 3.32   Semester Hours: 85

College/University
University of Maryland (09/01/1984 - 04/30/1994)
APO, Armed Forces Overseas, Germany
Semester Hours: 19

ADDITIONAL INFORMATION:
Secret Security Clearance (07/09/2002)

AWARDS
Meritorious Service Medal (04/27/1998): Selfless service and dedicated leadership greatly improved the company's readiness and performance

Army Commendation Medal (04/15/1997): Displayed superior talent and industry in completing all required task in preparation for deployment in support of Operation Joint Endeavor/Joint Guard. Directly responsible for leading a company into Bosnia without any safety accidents or injuries. Restructured the available work force, originated an ingenious and comprehensive training program for soldiers to qualify on casualty reporting, Enlisted Department of the Army Systems, and Human Resource Information Systems. Provided direct leadership and guidance to 52 soldiers in different technical and tactical fields.

Army Superior Unit Award (04/04/1997): Company received the Army Superior Unit Award while deployed to Bosnia.

Army Achievement Medal (05/31/1996): Outstanding leadership while preparing the company for a organization command inspection, which resulted in the company being rated as the best company. Commended for having the best safety, training, equal opportunity, personnel retention, physical security, leaves, and evaluations program.

Army Achievement Medal (08/23/1990): Transformed the monthly pre-separation briefings into an outstanding program. Personal efforts resulted in the smooth transition of soldiers to civilian life. Quality of work was complimented during the 7th Corps community inspector general's inspection.

CERTIFICATIONS
Master Facilitator Course 40 h (10/15/1999); Certified to conduct equal opportunity training to military personnel and civilians.

Unit Movement Officer Course 80 h (08/07/1996); Certification to plan, coordinate, and conduct rail load operations.

Master Fitness Course 80 h (11/03/1995); Master Fitness Trainer for the company.

Personnel Management 40 h (09/30/1984)

PROFESSIONAL DEVELOPMENT
First Sergeants Course 240 h (10/07/1998); Provide technical expertise, advice and guidance to managers, supervisors, and individual employees on training, safety, welfare, discipline, morale, leave, advancement, evaluations, entitlements and commissioning programs.

Equal Opportunity Leaders Workshop 40 h (05/15/1990); Equal Opportunity Training for leaders.

PROFESSIONAL SUMMARY
Fluency in reading, writing, and speaking Spanish.

Written / Oral Communications: Proficient in written communications, managing all incoming and outgoing correspondence. Professional oral communicator, providing full range of oral presentations, including training, executive briefings, and one-on-one communications.

Leadership and Managerial Skills: Exceptional record of retention and re-enlistments of soldiers exhibiting high productivity and morale. Respected supervisor, effective at gaining meaningful support of employees.

Information Technology: Demonstrated results in streamlining and using information technology to improve efficiency and effectiveness. Computer proficiencies in Microsoft Word, Excel, Outlook, PowerPoint, Works, Access.

Organized /Analytical: Evaluate work processes and apply creativity in developing options to arrive at smarter ways to carry out unit assignments. Professional knowledge of administrative regulations and operating procedures.

KNOWLEDGE, SKILLS AND ABILITIES (KSAs)

KSAs are also referred to as Knowledge, Skills, Abilities, and Other Characteristics (KSAOs). They are required for the selecting official to identify the best qualified candidate. Most people look at writing KSAOs as drudgery; however, it is a necessary part of your employment application, if requested on the job announcement. To qualify for a position you must meet two types of factors: *Selective Factors* and *Quality Ranking Factors*.

KSAOs are attributes needed to perform a specific job function that is demonstrated through qualifying training, education and experience. The following definitions will help you understand what the selecting official is looking for when reviewing your application and résumé:

Knowledge — An organized body of information, usually of a factual or procedural nature, which if applied, makes adequate performance on the job possible.

- Examples include knowledge of:

> Federal regulations and directives
> Operational systems and procedures
> Budget and accounting principals
> Engineering practices
> Environmental compliance law
> Administrative practices

Skill — The manipulation of data, things, or people through manual, mental or verbal means. Skills are measurable through testing, can be observed, and are quantifiable. Often refers to expertise that comes from training, practice, etc.

- Examples include skill in:

> Keyboard data entry
> Motor vehicle operation
> Computer software proficiency
> Electronic or computer repair
> Carpentry, plumbing and/or HVAC repair
> Second language proficiency

Ability — The capacity to perform a physical or mental activity at the present time. Typically, abilities are apparent through functions completed on the job. Abilities and skills are often interchangeable in KSAOs. The main difference is that ability is the capacity to perform, where a skill is the actual manipulation of data, things or people. You may have the ability, but unless observed through actions, that ability may not transfer to a skill set.

- Examples include the ability to:

> Organize and plan work (observed at work)
> Analyze situations, programs and problems
> Communicate orally and in writing
> Coach and mentor others

Other Characteristics — Mental or physical attributes or characteristics that don't fall under the other areas.

- Examples are:

> Proactive — takes initiative to get things done without prompting
> Copes well in stressful environments — handles complex tasks
> Reliability — assigned work is completed ahead of schedule and the quality of work is exceptional
> Multiple work assignments — capable of successfully handling various and sundry tasks

This factor is required for jobs that to a greater degree encounter these characteristics, such as jobs with the Federal Aviation Administration in air traffic control, work at nuclear power plants, and careers in law enforcement.

SELECTIVE FACTORS

All applicants must meet the *Selective Factors* for a position which are over and above the minimum experience and education requirements in the Qualification Standards Handbook. After meeting the basic *Selective Factors* you can achieve a higher ranking score if you meet or exceed the *Quality Ranking Factors* (QRFs) as annotated on the job announcement. QRFs aren't required to meet basic eligibility. Their purpose is to provide the selecting official with additional information that demonstrates how well you will perform the duties of the position.

QUALITY RANKING FACTORS

Quality Ranking Factors must be taken seriously for you to rate as high as possible. Most feel, "Why should I have to reinvent the wheel? I've already completed a comprehensive application — Just read it — it's all in there!" Don't get discouraged. This is a natural feeling and most applicants don't want to bother. After all, when you applied in the private sector all you gave them was a short one or two page résumé!

Remember, this is the federal government. You have to complete the paperwork to beat out your competition. Federal government jobs are rated this way to eliminate favoritism and to provide a level playing field for all those who apply. Keep this in mind when completing your application in order to improve your chances.

Each agency develops its own unique QRFs, and there can be as few as one to as many as a dozen or more. The most I've had to complete during my 33 years of government service was eight. The higher the grade position you are applying for, the more likely that QRFs will be required. Some agencies require special forms while others only specify the factor and ask you to address each one in detail on a separate piece of paper.

There are a number of rating systems used by various agencies and the methods even differ within agencies. Some use point systems from 1 to 10, others simply evaluate the KSA as meeting or exceeding the standard. Still others use designations such as "Below Expectations," "Average," or "Above Average." Follow the guidance in the announcement and provide all the information they require. KSAs require contact information including names, phone numbers, and addresses so the personnel specialist or selecting official can verify your information.

There are often limits on the amount of data you can submit. For example, many KSAOs are limited to one typewritten page per KSAO, etc. I suggest highlighting or underlining each requirement on the announcement so that you will provide all requested information.

INSTRUCTIONS FOR ADDRESSING KSAOs

If a special form isn't required, list each KSAO title on a separate sheet of plain bond paper, and follow it with a description of what you did to meet this KSAO and include in each KSAO any of these relevant elements:

- Education
- Training
- Experience
- Volunteer work
- Outside activities
- Awards, licenses, etc.

You must include a narrative that indicates the degree to which you possess the KSAO and include each of the bulleted items listed above that apply in that narrative. For each work example or accomplishment listed, describe the situation, problem, or objective of the assignment, what was done, and the results obtained. Statements should be limited to one typewritten page per KSAO. Following the narrative, the applicant must indicate: the duration (date) of the activity, and the name and telephone number of a person who can verify the information provided, if available. **Applicants may attach copies of any relevant documents that will help substantiate their statements, such as performance evaluations, awards, or work products.** The applicant's narrative must indicate exactly how these documents relate to the KSAO. DO NOT INCLUDE SUCH DOCUMENTS UNLESS THEY ARE DIRECTLY RELEVANT.

Applicants may attach copies of any relevant documents that will help substantiate their statements, such as performance evaluations, awards, or work products.

Formatting Your KSAOs

You can format your KSAOs in a narrative form starting with "I" or use bulleted items that start with a forceful verb such as organized, directed, managed, coordinated, analyzed, or conducted to provide action to your statements. If you don't refer directly to an experience block, be sure to summarize the experience and pro-vide the time period that you performed that function. If you are applying for a supervisory position, mention the number of people you supervised, their status such as part time or full time, and pay grade if applicable.

After writing your KSAOs review them a number of times, asking yourself, "What did I do," "When did I do it," "Where did I perform these functions," and don't forget the proverbial question, "How often and how much did I do it." If you didn't answer these questions, edit your work until it is included. Add examples either in the narrative or by attaching an example, which is permitted in most cases.

Another factor that many overlook is the depth of training completed. Include correspondence study, seminars, classes, lectures, computer-based instruction, on-the-job training, every facet of training that you received including software programs that you taught yourself.

Include special licenses, registration exams, or certifications that you obtained in your specialty. If you are a medical assistant and passed the RMA (Registered Medical Assistant Exam), annotate that on your application and in your KSAOs. If you are in the trades and have various equipment operators' licenses, list items such as "Fork Lift Operator" certification. List whatever is relevant to the job announcement.

The following KSAOs were excerpted from Announcement Number 02-ADP-156 that was located on OPM's USAJOBS Web site. Note that all of the KSAOs could apply to almost any position and that if you are bidding on the GS-05/07 you have only four to complete. If you bid on the higher grade positions, GS-09/11, you must complete an additional two KSAOs.

Sample Supplemental Qualification Statements are provided for each of the first four elements. If special forms are not provided or if specific formats are not specified, follow the sample outline to submit your narratives. Notice the use of bullets and short concise statements. You want to attract the selecting official to your key qualifications, and good formatting techniques and the use of bullets, bold and underlined type will focus the reader's attention to your qualifications. Include all required information and be sure to add your name, job announcement number and position title at the top of each page.

If the KSAs are submitted online, the formatting must be basic without bullets, bold type, or underlined text as described under the online résumé format discussed earlier in this chapter

You will find that some books suggest placing your Social Security number (SSN) at the top of each page of your KSAOs. I suggest that you use your SSN only if it is specifically requested. Your SSN is annotated on your OF-612 or in your federal style résumé; it really isn't needed here.

Ranking Factors

The following ranking factors are excerpted from the job announcement that listed the sample KSAs that are addressed in this section.

GS-05/07 Level Ranking Factors

QUALIFICATION REQUIREMENTS: One year experience at/or equivalent to the next lower grade for current/former federal employees. One year experience for non-federal employees. RANKING FACTORS: These are mandatory to be considered for a position and will be used to determine who the highest qualified candidates are.

1. Demonstrated ability to organize and coordinate work within schedule constraints and handle emergent requirements in a timely manner.
2. Demonstrated ability to monitor important and complex projects concurrently.
3. Knowledge of Microsoft Word, Excel, Powerpoint, and Lotus Notes software.
4. Demonstrated ability to communicate orally and in writing, including writing and preparing memorandums, letters, and other official correspondence.

GS-09/11 Level Ranking Factors

QUALIFICATION REQUIREMENTS: One year experience at/or equivalent to the next lower grade for current/former federal employees. One year experience for non-federal employees.

RANKING FACTORS: In addition to the above ranking factors, applicants at the GS-9/11 level must address the following two ranking factors. These are mandatory and will be used to determine who the highest qualified candidates are.

1. Demonstrated knowledge of administrative/office management skills.
2. Demonstrated ability to gather, assemble, and analyze facts to include drawing conclusions and recommending solutions.

SAMPLE KNOWLEDGE, SKILLS, & ABILITIES STATEMENTS

Sample KSAs for Administrative Officer Position

Job Title: Administrative Officer, GS-341-05/11
Announcement Number: 02-ADP-156
Applicant's Name: John Smith

KSA #1 *Demonstrated ability to organize and coordinate work within schedule constraints and handle emergent requirements in a timely manner.*

I performed the following duties in my current position (Block A):

- Managed the office suspense lists for supervisors. Transcribed meeting minutes and compiled action item lists, annotated due dates and assigned action items to the responsible party. Sent reminders, updated suspense file, and reported accomplishments to the office manager weekly.

- Planned and coordinated two annual shareholders meetings for over 700 stock owners, key management and staff. Drafted the itinerary, set up the registration booth, arranged for morning breakout sessions, planned lunch and the shareholders meeting from 1 to 3 p.m. Also, staffed the shareholders' information booth after the meeting.

Award: Received an award for exemplary service for planning and organizing the 2006 meeting, <u>copy attached</u>.

- Required to frequently complete short notice work assignments including reports, transcribing meeting minutes, and payroll accounting tasks. I am the chief headquarters payroll clerk and I provide backup to 12 field offices. If any of the field office clerks or supervisors are not available, I complete their payroll reports prior to the cutoff time.

- Responsible for notifying management of pending funding shortfalls and providing justification for additional fund requests. I analyzed budget reports for trends, calculated spend rates and recommended reallocation of funds to satisfy pending or potential shortages.

Training:

1. Certificate: 24-hour Meeting Preparation and Planning seminar, March 1999
2. 40-hour Time Management Course, RMC Services, April 2001

Job Title: Administrative Officer, GS-341-05/11
Announcement Number: 02-ADP-156
Applicant's Name: John Smith

KSA#2 *Demonstrated ability to monitor important and complex projects concurrently.*

Performed these duties in my present position from 1/1/99 to the present (Block A):

- Budget analyst duties — Trend tracking, monitor and control of the office's annual budget of $350,000. Performed budget data entry, compiled reports, tracked trends, anticipated fund shortages in various program areas and drafted requests for additional funds for management's signature. Audited program areas to ensure fund expenditures were justified and properly classified.

- Payroll chief clerk — Ensured timely submission of all payroll data before the cutoff date each pay period, entered amendments, and researched pay problems for 37 employees. I advised management of problems and notified them when to review and approve the attendance for each pay period.

Training: 80-hour Peachtree accounting software class, by Peachtree, January 1999.

Performed the following duties in my previous position as Administrative Officer, GS-0341-7, with the USDA from 10/4/96 to 12/31/98 (Block B):

- Organizational Charts & Staffing — Processed revisions to and generated complex organizational charts based on input from the management team. Reviewed proposed changes to ensure they conformed to authorized levels and that positions were properly classified. Concurrently, prepared and tracked personnel actions for 124 employees and provided support in various program areas including payroll, benefits, staffing, and budget areas.

- Office of Workers Compensation Program (OWCP) Specialist — Conducted annual (OWCP) seminars for managers and supervisors. Seminars included guidance on procedures, claims processing and posted accident interventions. Provided guidance to immediate supervisors of injured employees and maintained the OSHA 200 log for all accidents.

Award: Cash award, June 2003, for managing the OWCP program, copy attached.

Training: 60 hours Position Management and Position Classification Course, 012-V-933, Graduate School, USDA, Washington, D.C., June 1997.

Job Title: Administrative Officer, GS-341-05/11
Announcement Number: 02-ADP-156
Applicant's Name: John Smith

KSA #3 *Knowledge of Microsoft Word, Excel, Powerpoint, and Lotus Notes/other e-mail software.*

Performed these duties in my present position from 1/1/99 to the present (Block A):

- Proficient in Microsoft Office, Word, Excel, Powerpoint and Lotus Notes for office e-mail. Developed a 34 page Powerpoint presentation for our CEO to use at the 2002 annual stockholders meeting in Memphis. The presentation received rave reviews and I was asked to develop presentations for other meetings. Worked closely with accounting to compile the data and then integrated it into a visual presentation. I use WORD for all office correspondence.

- Conducted Microsoft Word and Excel mini-training sessions for those less proficient in the office. Typically sessions ran one to two hours in length. Attended various software system seminars including Microsoft Office, Peachtree Accounting, and our new Lotus Notes e-mail program.

Volunteer Work: Performed these duties while working as a volunteer for United Way over past six years. Approximately 12 hours a week. (Block E):

- Developed our chapter's Web site (http://www.HELPUnited.org) using Microsoft Frontpage 2002. I consider myself very proficient in Web site development and I learned Frontpage through self study and experimentation. This Web site consists of 48 pages and two databases and we use a secure server for confidential assistance requests. I'm the Webmaster. Contact the United Way chairperson, Ms. Mary Jones, for verification at 890-123-4567.

Performed the following duties in my previous position as Administrative Officer, GS-0341-7, with the USDA from 10/4/96 to 12/31/98 (Block B):

- Proficient in VISO. I used VISO to generate ORG Charts while at the USDA.

- Proficient in several payroll & T&A software systems including IPPS, the USDA's Integrated Personnel and Pay System.

Training Certificates: 24-hour VISO software course and a 16-hour IPPS software course, both completed at our regional office, May 1998.

Job Title: Administrative Officer, GS-341-05/11
Announcement Number: 02-ADP-156
Applicant's Name: John Smith

KSA #4 *Demonstrated ability to effectively communicate orally and in writing, to include writing and preparing memorandums, letters, and other official correspondence.*

Performed these duties in my present position from 1/1/99 to the present (Block A):

- **Written Guidance** — Developed Standard Operation Procedures (SOPs) for program areas including payroll administration, office suspense tracking, monitor and control, and general office procedures. Adopted by the regional office for use throughout the organization, samples attached. I also wrote numerous internal memorandums within my program areas that provided direction for specific functions and clarified company policy issues.

  I also prepare transmittal forms for project files, letters to share holders, fax cover letters, e-mail messages to team leads and customers, flip charts for meetings, Powerpoint presentations, proof and edit management draft correspondence, and prepare replies to organizational reports.

- **Oral Communications** — In current capacity I teach office software to small groups, brief management team of progress at meetings, give presentations at interoffice meetings and to small groups of shareholders.

Volunteer Work

- I speak at various fund raisers for our local United Way and prepare written presentations to our work group and chairperson. I organized and hosted a dozen fund raisers since 1994. Contact the United Way chairperson, Ms. Mary Jones, for verification at 890-123-4567.

Education: Completed 12 semester hours, 3 courses in communications, at Duke University in 1997; Report Writing, Communications I and Writing Techniques.

Training:

1) **Competent Toastmaster.** Joined Toastmasters International in 1995. Obtained Competent Toastmaster status in 1997. Chapter president, Dan McCormick, 321-654-0987. Certificate attached.

2) **Certificate.** Constructive Communications with the Public, USDA Course 01501, June 1996. Interpersonal Communications, seminar 1996, sponsored by OPM.

KSAO CHECKLIST

Use this list to ensure that you have included key information. It's important to consider these areas when drafting your KSAO statements. When you first start to draft your KSAOs, don't worry about the specifics such as exact dates, contact information, etc. You can add that later. It is best to simply write down anything and everything, even the least significant events. After you get it all down then add specifics and put them in logical sequence. Review and rewrite your KSAOs at least three times, and more if needed. Let your draft sit overnight and review it again the next day. You will be surprised at what you left out on the first draft.

❏ **Experience** — Include experience for all offices, departments or agencies that you worked for to show depth and range of experience. For example, include that you tracked interoffice correspondence at multiple locations, or that you tracked budgets for headquarters. Also show expertise in what you do well such as having A++ certification, maintain LANS/WANS for several locations, thoroughly familiar with Peachtree accounting software, proficient at office organization, etc.

❏ **Supervision** — If you don't have a supervisory background, did you work independently with minimal supervision and make decisions for your program areas? If so, state that in your KSAOs. Were you assigned to be an acting supervisor on several occasions? Do you draft memorandums and letters for your supervisor's signature? Do you manage/supervise programs or projects?

❏ **Complexity Factors** — Did you write reports or work on large projects coordinating activities for various groups? Does your job impact the safety of others, and what standards do you follow and utilize in your present and past jobs? Do you have certifications, licenses, specific training, or accreditation that would help you land this job?

❏ **Achievements and Impact** — How did you show initiative and creativity in your office while working under adverse conditions? Were you responsible for major programs, product, or activities? If so list them. What did you do to save time, money, and resources or to improve the work environment?

❏ **Awards/Recognition** — Include all awards – monetary awards, letters of achievement, time-off awards, or write-ups in your office newsletter. Include scholastic nominations as well, and any service awards or recognition received from volunteer work.

❏ **Contacts** — If you dealt with headquarters staff, the general public, EPA or OSHA inspectors, local authorities, or government officials, list them in your KSAOs.

❏ **Fashionable Trends** — Mention current trends such as "BPE" Business Process Engineering, Model Work Environment initiatives, MBO — Management by Objectives, Partnership, Quality Work Groups, etc. If you have exposure to these and other initiatives, list them in your write-up.

THE SENIOR EXECUTIVE SERVICE (SES)

The Senior Executive Service (SES) was established by the Civil Service Reform Act (CSRA) of 1978 and became effective in July 1979. CSRA envisioned a senior executive corps with solid executive expertise, public service values, and a broad perspective of government.

The SES is a corps of approximately 6700 men and women who administer public programs at the top levels of federal government. Positions are primarily managerial and supervisory. SES pay is linked to individual performance. Basic annual salaries range from $111,676 to $154,600; however, an agency with a certified SES performance appraisal system can set basic pay at rates up to $168,000. Members of the SES are not eligible for locality pay and some positions include additional recruitment incentives. Visit OPM's SES Web page for additional information about this program at http://www.opm.gov/ses/sesguide.html. [2]

Structure of the SES Pay System	Minimum	Maximum
Agencies with a Certified SES Performance Appraisal System	$101,676	$168,000
Agencies without a Certified SES Performance Appraisal System	$111,676	$154,600

The CSRA established a distinct personnel system that applies the same executive qualifications requirements to all SES members. The new system was designed to provide greater agency flexibility for selecting and developing federal executives within a framework that preserves the larger corporate interests of government. The SES covers managerial, supervisory, and policy positions above GS-15 (including Executive Schedule IV or V or equivalent positions) that are not filled by presidential appointment with Senate confirmation.

---

[2] USAJOBS "Working For America" Federal Employment Fact Sheet EI-30

How SES Jobs Are Filled

Each federal agency independently determines the qualifications required for SES positions, and whether to consider only current federal civil service appointees or all qualified candidates. There are two methods of entry into the SES:

- Apply directly to a federal agency for a specific SES position.

- Apply for a federal agency's *SES Candidate Development Program* (SESCDP). *Qualifications Review Board* (QRB) certified graduates of an SESCDP advertised to *"all qualified Civil Service appointees"* or *"all qualified persons"* are eligible for (but not guaranteed) career appointment to an SES position without further competition.

Qualifications Requirements

OPM convenes Qualifications Review Boards (QRBs) to provide an independent peer review of candidates proposed for initial career appointment to the SES. The candidate cannot be appointed to the SES until the QRB certifies his/her executive qualifications. The QRB review is the critical last step in the SES selection process. By focusing attention on executive qualifications, the QRB helps ensure that technical skills do not outweigh leadership expertise in the selection of new senior executives.

Applicants must meet two types of qualifications for SES positions:

1. The Executive Core Qualifications, which apply to every SES position; and

2. Specific, professional/technical qualifications (if any) for the position being advertised.

OPM has identified five *Executive Core Qualifications* (ECQs) common to all SES positions:

- **Leading Change** — The ability to bring about strategic change, both within and outside the organization, to meet organizational goals. Inherent to this ECQ is the ability to establish an organizational vision and to implement it in a continuously changing environment.

- **Leading People** — The ability to lead people toward meeting the organization's vision, mission, and goals. Inherent to this ECQ is the ability to provide an inclusive workplace that fosters the development of others, facilitates cooperation and teamwork, and supports constructive resolution of conflicts.

- **Results Driven** — The ability to meet organizational goals and customer expectations. Inherent to this ECQ is the ability to make decisions that produce high-quality results by applying technical knowledge, analyzing problems, and calculating risks.

- **Business Acumen** - The ability to manage human, financial, and information resources strategically.

- **Building Coalitions** - The ability to build coalitions internally and with other Federal agencies, State and local governments, nonprofit and private sector organizations, foreign governments, or international organizations to achieve common goals.

The ECQs are mandatory qualification standards for every SES position. Agencies may also identify specific, professional/technical qualifications for the position being filled. The qualification standards for an advertised SES position are listed in the agency's vacancy announcement. Applicants need to obtain a copy of the agency's vacancy announcement to respond to these requirements. Visit http://www.opm.gov/ses/qualify.asp#qualify for detailed application guidance.

Examination Process

Federal agencies review, rate, and rank applicants based on the executive qualifications and the professional/technical qualifications (if any) listed in the vacancy announcement. They also makes final selections from among the best-qualified applicants, and submit a case to OPM for *Qualifications Review Board* (QRB) consideration of the selectees.

Executive Core Qualifications

OPM convenes Qualifications Review Boards to determine whether agency selectees have the executive qualifications required for the SES. An agency may not appoint the selectee unless a QRB approves.

Recruitment Area

Agencies decide how to fill a vacant SES position. If they choose to advertise the position (as opposed to noncompetitive alternatives), they also determine the recruitment area. There are two choices: all qualified civil service appointees or all qualified persons.

Recruitment Incentives

Exceptional difficulty in recruiting highly qualified applicants for SES positions may result in payment of recruitment or relocation bonuses up to 25% of base pay (up to 100%, if approved by OPM), waiver of the dual compensation restrictions that apply to civil service retirees, or designation of the position for critical pay authority whereby total annual salary may be established up to the Executive Schedule Level I rate (currently $183,500 per annum). Recruitment incentives are noted in the "Application Information" column.

How to Apply

In OPMs USAJOBS system, check the specific job entry for a full text vacancy announcement. If the announcement is not available through the system, call the agency contact for a copy of the vacancy announcement. Ask for additional information about application procedures and detailed qualifications requirements. Print a copy of the SES Qualifications Guide available at the site listed earlier in this section. Be prepared to address the ECQs as outlined above and in the guide.

Read the job announcement thoroughly and pay special attention to any supplemental documentation that may be required. If you neglect to send in required documentation your package will be rejected. Use the same techniques outlined earlier in this chapter to evaluate the job announcement and focus on the ECQs. Your work descriptions must also showcase the required duties, responsibilities, expertise, and education required for the advertised position.

Send your application directly to the address shown on the vacancy announcement or submit it online if allowed. Required documentation is generally faxed or sent direct to the human resource office listed in the job announcement. Apply promptly to meet closing dates.

Candidate Development Programs

Some, but not all, federal agencies have SES Candidate Development Programs to identify and develop potential executive talent. QRB certified graduates of OPM approved SESCDPs advertised to "all qualified civil service appointees" or "all qualified persons" are eligible for a career appointment to the SES without further competition. However, graduates are not guaranteed a SES position.

CHAPTER SEVEN
Veterans and Military
Dependent Hiring Programs

Veterans can take advantage of special-emphasis civil service hiring programs including the *Veterans Preference*[1] and the *Veterans Recruitment Act (VRA)*. Unknown to many, military dependents and spouses of active duty personnel receive hiring preference for government jobs under the *Military Spouse Preference Program* and the *Family Member Preference Program*.

In 1973 I took advantage of a special-emphasis hiring program and was discharged nine months early from the U.S. Air Force under the **Palace Chase** program. I was hired full time as an avionics technician for the Air National Guard. The Palace Chase program helped reduce the size of the military as the Vietnam war was ending.

The federal government has a long and outstanding record of employing veterans. Veterans hold a far higher percentage of jobs in the government than they do in private industry. In large part, this is due to laws providing Veterans' preference and special appointing authorities for veterans, as well as the fact that agencies recognize that hiring veterans is just good business.

Over 24% of all federal employees are veterans.

CHAPTER OBJECTIVES

✎   Understand Veterans' Preference

✎   Explore the Veterans' Recruitment Program (VRA)

✎   Opportunities for disabled veterans

✎   Military Transition Planning *(Working for Uncle Sam Again)*

✎   Special hiring programs for military spouses and dependents

---

[1] Authorized by Law Title 5 USC, Section 2108 and Section 3501.

When filling a competitive service job from *outside* the civil service, agencies may:

■ Appoint a well-qualified candidate from a competitive list of eligibles developed by OPM or by an agency with delegated examining authority; or

■ Appoint someone who is eligible under one of a number of special appointing authorities (e.g., the VRA or Schedule B authorities, and others authorized by either law or executive order).

Alternatively, filling jobs from among "status" candidates, agencies may:

■ Appoint someone from an agency-developed merit promotion list (when these jobs are open to candidates outside the agency, the agency must allow eligibles under the Veterans Employment Opportunities Act of 1998, as amended to apply); or

■ Reassign a current agency employee, transfer an employee from another agency, or reinstate a former federal employee.

VETERANS PREFERENCE

Beginning with the Civil War, veterans of the armed forces have been given some degree of preference in appointments for federal jobs. Veterans' preference is a way to help make up for the economic loss suffered by those who answered the nation's call to arms. When an agency advertises job vacancies through the Office of Personnel Management or locally through direct hire authority, the agency must select from the top rated eligible applicants. The official may not pass over a Veterans' Preference eligible, however, and appoint a non-preference eligible lower on the list unless the reasons for passing over the veteran are sufficient.

Veterans' preference gives special consideration to eligible veterans looking for federal employment.[2] Veterans who are disabled or who served on active duty in the United States armed forces during certain specified time periods or in military campaigns are entitled to preference over nonveterans both in hiring into the federal civil service and in retention during *reductions in force*. There are two classes of preference for honorably discharged veterans:

Five-Point Preference

Five-point preference is given to those honorably separated veterans (this means an honorable or general discharge) who served on active duty (not active duty for training) in the armed forces:

---

[2] Reference OPM's "Vet Info Guide" available online at http://www.opm.gov/veterans/html/vetsinfo.htm.

- During any war (this means a war declared by Congress, the last of which was World War II); **or**

- For more than 180 consecutive days, other than for training, any part of which occurred after January 31, 1955 and before October 15, 1976; **or**

- During the period April 28, 1952, through July 1, 1955; **or**

- During the Gulf War from August 2, 1990, through January 2, 1992; **or**

- For more than 180 consecutive days, any part of which occurred during the period beginning September 11, 2001, and ending on the date prescribed by presidential proclamation or by law as the last day of Operation Iraqi Freedom; or

- In a campaign or expedition for which a campaign medal has been authorized, such as El Salvador, Lebanon, Grenada, Panama, Southwest Asia, Somalia, and Haiti.

A campaign medal holder or Gulf War veteran who originally enlisted after September 7, 1980, or entered on active duty on or after October 14, 1982, without having previously completed 24 months of continuous active duty must have served continuously for 24 months or the full period called or ordered to active duty.

Effective October 1, 1980, military retirees at or above the rank of major or equivalent are not entitled to preference unless they qualify as disabled veterans.

Ten-Point Preference

Ten-point preference is given to:

- Those honorably separated veterans who 1) qualify as disabled veterans because they have served on active duty in the armed forces at any time and have a present service-connected disability or are receiving compensation, disability retirement benefits, or pension from the military or the Department of Veterans Affairs; or 2) are Purple Heart recipients;

- The spouse of a veteran unable to work because of a service-connected disability;

- The unmarried widow of certain deceased veterans;

- The mother of a veteran who died in service or who is permanently and totally disabled.

When applying for federal jobs, eligible veterans should claim preference on their application or résumé. Applicants claiming 10-point preference must complete **form SF-15**, Application for 10-Point Veteran Preference. This form is included in the *Quick & Easy Federal Jobs Kit* Software program. See the ad in the back of this book for complete information. Veterans who are still in the service may be granted five points tentative preference on the basis of information contained in their applications, but they must produce a DD Form 214 prior to appointment to document entitlement to preference.

Note: Reservists who are retired from the reserves but don't receive retired pay are not considered "retired military" for purposes of veterans' preference.

The Veterans' Preference Advisor system allows veterans to examine the preferences for which they might be entitled with regard to federal jobs. This system was developed by the Veterans' Employment and Training Service.

To explore the Veterans' Preference program, visit OPM's web site at http://www.opm.gov/veterans and download their Veterans Preference Guide.

PURPLE HEART RECIPIENTS ARE CONSIDERED TO HAVE A SERVICE-CONNECTED DISABILITY

How Preference Applies in Competitive Examination

Veterans who are eligible for preference and who meet the minimum qualification requirements of the position have five or 10 points added to their passing score on a civil service examination. For scientific and professional positions at the GS-9 grade or higher, names of all eligibles are listed in order of ratings, augmented by veterans' preference points, if any. For all other positions, the names of 10-point preference eligibles who have a service-connected disability of 10 percent or more are placed ahead of the names of all other eligibles. Other eligibles are then listed in order of their earned ratings, augmented by veterans' preference points. A preference eligible is listed ahead of a nonpreference eligible with the same score.

What Does This Mean?

If you apply for a federal job, your knowledge, skills and abilities will be rated on a point system. You will receive points for related education, experience, special skills, awards, and written test if required. To qualify for a position you must have a score of 70 to 100 points. If an eligible five-point preference candidate accumulates 90 points, five additional points are awarded on preference for a total score of 95. Therefore, the preference veteran, in most cases, must be hired before an agency can hire anyone with 95 points or less in this example. If that same veteran accumulated 100 points his final score — with preference — would be 105 points. A 10-point preference veteran would have a total score of 110. Vets who ace the exam will go to the top of the list, since only veterans' preference veterans can exceed 100 points on the exams.

The agency must select from the top three candidates (known as the Rule of three) and may not pass over a preference eligible in favor of a lower-ranking non-preference eligible without sound reasons that relate directly to the veteran's fitness for employment. The agency may, however, select a lower-ranking preference eligible over a compensably disabled veteran within the Rule of Three.

A preference eligible who is passed over on a list of eligibles is entitled, upon request, to a copy of the agency's reasons for the pass-over and the examining office's response.

If the preference eligible is a 30 percent or more disabled veteran, the agency must notify the veteran and OPM of the proposed pass-over. The veteran has 15 days from the date of notification to respond to OPM. OPM then decides whether to approve the pass-over based on all the facts available and notifies the agency and the veteran.

> Entitlement to veterans' preference does not guarantee a job. There are many ways an agency can fill a vacancy other than by appointment from a list of eligibles.

Filing Applications After Examinations Close

A 10-point preference eligible may file an application at any time for any position for which a nontemporary appointment has been made in the preceding three years; for which a list of eligibles currently exists that is closed to new applications; or for which a list is about to be established. Veterans wishing to file after the closing date should contact the agency that announced the position for further information.

SPECIAL APPOINTING AUTHORITIES

The following special authorities permit the noncompetitive appointment of eligible veterans. Use of these special authorities is entirely discretionary with the agency; no one is **entitled** to one of these special appointments:

VETERANS' RECRUITMENT APPOINTMENT (VRA)

The VRA is a special authority by which agencies can appoint an eligible veteran without competition at any grade level through General Schedule (GS) 11 or equivalent. The VRA is an excepted appointment to a position that is otherwise in the competitive service. After two years of satisfactory service, the veteran is converted to a career-conditional appointment in the competitive service. (Note, however, that a veteran may be given a noncompetitive temporary or term appointment based on VRA eligibility. These appointments do not lead to career jobs.)

When two or more VRA applicants are preference eligibles, the agency must apply veterans' preference as required by law. (While all VRA eligibles have served in the armed forces, they do <u>not</u> necessarily meet the eligibility requirements for veterans' preference under section 2108 of title 5, United States Code.)

Eligibility Requirements

Eligibility requirements changed considerably under the Jobs for Veterans Act, Public Law 107-288, which amended title 38 U.S.C. 4214. The new eligibility requirements limited access to this program to veterans who served during a war, or in a campaign and to recently separated veterans as noted below:

- Disabled veterans; or

- Veterans who served on active duty in the armed forces during a war, or in a campaign or expedition for which a campaign badge has been authorized; or

- Veterans who, while serving on active duty in the armed forces, participated in a United States military operation for which an Armed Forces Service Medal was awarded; or

- Recently separated veterans.

There has been some confusion on what is considered to be *"recently separated."* Agencies are limiting VRA to those within three years of discharge in some cases. Veterans claiming eligibility on the basis of service in a campaign or expedition for which a medal was awarded must be in receipt of the campaign badge or medal.

In addition to meeting the criteria above, eligible veterans must have been separated under honorable conditions (i.e., the individual must have received either an honorable or general discharge).

Clarifications

Under the eligibility criteria, not all five-point preference eligible veterans may be eligible for a VRA appointment. For example, a veteran who served during the Vietnam era (i.e., for more than 180 consecutive days, after January 31, 1955, and before October 15, 1976) but did not receive a service-connected disability or an Armed Forces Service Medal or campaign or expeditionary medal would be entitled to five-point veterans' preference. This veteran, however, would not be eligible for a VRA appointment under the above criteria.

As another example, a veteran who served during the Gulf War from August 2, 1990, through January 2, 1992, would be eligible for veterans' preference solely on the basis of that service. However, service during that time period, in and of itself, does not confer VRA eligibility on the veteran unless one of the above VRA eligibility criteria is met.

Lastly, if an agency has two or more VRA candidates and one or more is a preference eligible, the agency must apply veterans' preference. For example, one applicant is VRA eligible on the basis of receiving an Armed Forces Service Medal (this medal does not confer veterans' preference eligibility). The second applicant is VRA eligible on the basis of being a disabled veteran (which does confer veterans' preference eligibility). In this example, both individuals are VRA eligible but only one of them is eligible for veterans' preference. As a result, agencies must apply the procedures of 5 CFR 302 when considering VRA candidates for appointment.

How To Apply

Veterans should contact directly the federal agency personnel office where they are interested in working to find out about VRA opportunities. Complete a résumé or an Optional Application for Federal Employment OF-612 and forward it with a cover letter to selected agencies. Refer to the resources listed in Chapter Three and the Appendices for specific agency addresses and telephone numbers. Also, visit http://federaljobs.net for direct links to more than 140 federal agency recruiting sites. Chapter Six will help you draft your federal style résumé.

Send a cover letter with your application explaining that you are a VRA candidate and would like to be considered for an appointment with that agency. Send a copy of your DD-214 form with your cover letter and application.

Follow up each submission with a phone call. It helps to call an agency first and obtain a name and address to which you can send an application. Send applications to every office and department that interests you.

Agencies **do not have to hire through the VRA program**. Only if your education and work experience meets their requirements, they have openings, and like what they see will they make you an offer. Be tactful and don't be demanding.

30% OR MORE DISABLED VETERANS

These veterans may be given a temporary or term appointment (not limited to 60 days or less) to any position for which qualified (there is no grade limitation). After demonstrating satisfactory performance, the veteran may be converted at any time to a career-conditional appointment.

Terms and conditions of employment

Initially, the disabled veteran is given a temporary appointment with an expiration date in excess of 60 days. This appointment may be converted at any time to a career conditional appointment. Unlike the VRA, there is no grade limitation.

How to Apply

Veterans should contact the federal agency personnel office where they are interested in working to find out about opportunities. Veterans must submit a copy of a letter dated within the last 12 months from the Department of Veterans Affairs or the Department of Defense certifying receipt of compensation for a service-connected disability of 30 percent or more.

Disabled Veterans Enrolled in VA Training Programs

Disabled veterans eligible for training under the Department of Veterans Affairs' (VA) vocational rehabilitation program may enroll for training or work experience at an agency under the terms of an agreement between the agency and VA. The veteran is not a federal employee for most purposes while enrolled in the program, but is a beneficiary of the VA.

The training is tailored to individual needs and goals, so there is no set length. If the training is intended to prepare the individual for eventual appointment in the agency (rather than just work experience), OPM must approve the training plan. Upon successful completion, the veteran will be given a Certificate of Training showing the occupational series and grade level of the position for which trained. This allows any agency to appoint the veteran noncompetitively for a period of one year. Upon appointment, the veteran is given a Special Tenure Appointment which is then converted to career-conditional with OPM approval.

VETERANS EMPLOYMENT OPPORTUNITIES ACT

The Veterans Employment Opportunities Act (VEOA) was passed in 1998 and it gives veterans access to federal job opportunities that might otherwise be closed to them. The law requires that:

- Agencies allow eligible veterans to compete for vacancies advertised under the agency's merit promotion procedures when the agency is seeking applications from individuals outside its own workforce.

- All merit promotion announcements open to applicants outside an agency's workforce include a statement that these eligible veterans may apply.

The law also establishes a new redress system for preference eligibles and makes it a prohibited personnel practice for an agency to knowingly take or fail to take a personnel action if that action or failure to act would violate a statutory or regulatory veterans' preference requirement.

This authority permits an agency to appoint an eligible veteran who has applied under an agency merit promotion announcement that is open to candidates outside the agency.

To be eligible a candidate must be a preference eligible or a veteran separated after three years or more of continuous active service performed under honorable conditions.

Terms and conditions of employment

Veterans given a VEOA appointment will be given a career or career conditional appointment in the competitive service. Veterans interested in applying under this authority should seek out agency merit promotion announcements open to candidates outside the agency. **Applications should be submitted directly to the agency.** Veterans who have career status or are reinstatement eligible are not eligible or VEOA appointments.

Applications should be submitted directly to the agency.

Positions Restricted to Preference Eligibles

Examinations for custodian, guard, elevator operator and messenger are open only to preference eligibles as long as such applicants are available.

MILITARY TO FEDERAL TRANSITION
Working for Uncle Sam After the Military

Military personnel approaching discharge or retirement often explore federal sector employment options. Most military retirees are in their late thirties or early forties and have 20 or more high income producing years to work before they stop working. Approximately 24 percent of the federal workforce are veterans and military personnel, and they are accustomed to federal regulations and the bureaucratic environment that's inherent with any government or military job.

Most military skills and training easily converts to federal occupations, and your military time can count towards federal retirement. Military retirees' war zone or campaign duty counts toward federal civilian retirement as well. There are many other benefits, including starting with four weeks or more of vacation time depending on how many years you served on active duty.

I made the transition from military to federal after completing active duty in 1972. I was drafted during the Vietnam War in 1968, and when I reported for my physical I was given the opportunity to join the Air Force. Two weeks after discharge I was hired by the Department of Defense (DOD) to maintain avionics systems, the same job I had on active duty. The big difference was that my pay increased dramatically. I was earning $2,500 a year as a sergeant in the Air Force in 1972, and my starting DOD annual salary was just under $10,000. Don't expect those big increases today. Military pay is now far more competitive due to the all volunteer service. After working for the DOD for three years, I applied to the Federal Aviation Administration and was hired to maintain ground-based navigation and communication systems.

The federal government uses the same National Stock Number (NSN) ordering system that I used in the military, and the regulations and manuals were similar as well, except you don't have the Uniform Code of Military Justice (UCMJ) to contend with or wear military uniforms. The FAA sent me to just under two years of training during my career. Most agencies provide comprehensive training so you don't have to have the specific equipment, systems, or software applications, just the basic qualifications that will help you succeed in your job.

An excellent guide to help you make the switch to the civilian federal sector is Kathryn Troutman's *Military to Federal Career Guide; Ten Steps to Transforming Your Military Experience Into a Comprehensive Federal Resume.* Copies are available by calling 1-800-782-7424, through our back-of-the-book catalog, or visit http://federaljobs.net/milfed.htm. The key to landing a federal job is to present your military training and skills in a federal style résumé that civilian classification specialists and selecting officials will understand. You have to demilitarize your résumé, explain the military acronyms that you use, and describe how your military work experience and education qualifies you for the jobs you apply for. The end result is to showcase your military knowledge, skills, and abilities to obtain the highest rating possible to improve your chances of being called for an interview.

Ms. Troutman is an expert in this area, and a sample of a military transition federal style résumé is presented in Chapter Six for your review. Her book, *Military to Federal Career Guide,* provides hundreds of samples and includes a resource CD that will help you write your federal style résumé. Review Chapter Six to better understand what you **MUST** do to land a high paying federal job, and use Kathryn's book to tailor your military skills to the jobs you apply for.

MILITARY DEPENDENT HIRING PROGRAMS

Dependents of military and civilian sponsors and spouses of active duty military personnel receive hiring preference when applying for civilian employment with Department of Defense agencies. The Military Family Act expanded hiring preference to many jobs previously not available to this program and for jobs within the states, territories, and U. S. Possessions.[3]

The U.S. Army in Europe hires the majority of civilian employees. Most are either residents of the host country or family members of military and civilians

---

[3] DOD Instruction (DODI) 1400.23 (Appendix 3)

officially stationed in Europe. The largest number of European vacancies is in Germany, with additional vacancies in Belgium, Italy, Saudi Arabia, the Mideast, and Africa. The majority of jobs in the Pacific region are in South Korea, Japan, and the Philippines. A limited number of positions are also available in the United States.

Family Member Employment Assistance Programs are available at most large bases. These programs are sponsored by local Civilian Employment Offices and Family Support Centers to provide employment information, career assistance and counseling, job skills training, and personal development workshops.

MILITARY SPOUSE PREFERENCE PROGRAMS

Military Spouse Preference Programs concentrate on placement into competitive civil service vacancies in the 50 states, the territories, the possessions, and the District of Columbia.[4] They do not apply to:

- Positions in the excepted service

- Positions filled from OPM certificates or under agency Delegated Examining Unit or Direct Hire Authority procedures

- Non-appropriated fund (NAF) positions

- Positions in foreign areas, whether in the competitive or excepted service

- Positions filled under component career program procedures (each component must establish procedures for the consideration of spouse preference eligibles)

- Positions filled at the full performance level that are covered by a mandatory mobility agreement

- Spouses who already obtained federal employment in an appropriated fund (AF) or NAF position within the commuting area of the sponsor's duty station on a full-time, part-time, or intermittent appointment expected to last for at least one year

Noncompetitive positions for spouse preference are generally Excepted Service and *Nonappropriated Fund Instrumentality (NAFI)* positions. NAFI jobs are in service clubs, exchanges, retail stores, snack bars, base services, and related activities.

---

[4] Section 806 of Public Law 99-145, Department of Defense Authorization Act of 1986

Preference is given for employment in Department of Defense (DOD) civilian positions for which a military spouse is *best qualified* at pay grades GS-1 through GS/GM-15 or equivalent.

Best qualified doesn't necessarily mean the highest rated candidate. This term is used to identify anyone who meets the basic requirements for the position. Generally, the only candidates with a higher preference are veterans and career civil service employees displaced from their jobs through a reduction in force.

Information regarding spouse preference is also available at installation family centers, and you can take advantage of a comprehensive military spouse career center offered at http://military.com/spouse. A searchable base facility database is available from the DOD at http://www.dod.mil/mapsite/famlocat.html.

Competitive Positions

Nonstatus applicants are those who have never worked for the government and must establish eligibility. Individuals can also establish eligibility at overseas Department of Defense (DOD) locations.

Previous federal employees, called *status* applicants, may have reinstatement eligibility. They must submit a current application and a copy of their most recent (SF) 50, Notification of Personnel Action, and a copy of their last government performance appraisal to the appropriate *Civilian Personnel Office* (CPO).

Excepted Service and NAFI Positions

The majority of overseas positions are *Excepted Service*. Each employing CPO maintains a list of qualified and available candidates. Excepted Service applicants must complete an employment application and supplemental forms required by the CPO. Applicants for NAFI positions require a service application form such as the Army's DA-3433. All required forms are provided by local CPOs.

Eligibility

A spouse's eligibility begins 30 days before the military sponsor's overseas reporting date. A spouse with less than six months time remaining in the area may be non-selected for permanent continuous positions. Also, preference entitlement ends when the spouse accepts or declines (whichever occurs first) any position expected to last longer than 12 months at any acceptable grade level. Preference is limited to positions in the same commuting area as that of the new duty station. However, a spouse may compete for positions, without preference, outside the commuting area. Spouse preference can be exercised only once for each permanent relocation of the military member.

How to Apply

Spouses can apply for preference at any armed forces or Defense agency facility within the commuting area of the military member's duty station. You can apply at any service branch in your area. Contact your local Civilian Personnel Office (CPO) for employment information and application forms.

You are encouraged to call the Human Resource Office (HRO) for an appointment to preregister within 30 days of your departure. For pre-registration, you will need to bring a copy of your Permanent Change of Station orders and application. Contact the local HRO for application details. You must submit an employment application along with a detailed statement that includes: your name; the name of the installation or activity at which you are applying; a statement that you have not been offered and declined a position for which you applied under spousal preference during your current PCS; the position title or number for which you are applying; and a copy of the service member's official orders, attached to the statement and application.

FAMILY MEMBER PREFERENCE

Most family member positions are clerical. However, family members are eligible to apply for any position for which they qualify. Family members of both military and civilian sponsors are given equal preference for positions designated for U.S. citizen occupancy, after military spouse and veterans' preference, for employment in nonsupervisory positions at pay grades of GS-8 or below.

Normally, family members are appointed under excepted appointments which cannot extend longer than two months beyond the sponsor's departure or separation date. Family members hired under this program do not acquire competitive civil service status, but may gain eligibility for federal Civil Service re-employment (under Executive Order 12362) when returning to the States.

Executive Orders 12362 and 12721

Eligible family members who worked overseas may be non-competitively appointed on a career-conditional basis to a competitive position in the U.S., including Guam, Puerto Rico, and the Virgin Islands. An eligible family members can apply to any position in the United States for which he or she meets all qualification requirements and time-in-grade restrictions, provided that he or she:

1. Is a citizen of or owes permanent allegiance to the United States;

2. Accumulated 52 weeks of creditable overseas service in an appropriated fund position(s) under an overseas local hire appointment(s) within any one-year period beginning after January 1, 1980. The service of regularly-scheduled employees, whether or not employed on a permanent, part-time basis, is computed on the basis of the calendar time the employee spent in the position;

3. Received a fully successful or better performance rating for the period of creditable overseas service;

4.   Was a family member of a federal civilian employee, a non-appropriated fund employee, or of a member of a uniformed service (the civilian or uniformed sponsor) who was officially assigned to the overseas areas during the period of creditable overseas service.

5.   Accompanied the civilian or uniformed sponsor on official assignment in the overseas areas while serving in the overseas position during the period of creditable overseas service.

6.   Is appointed by March 31, 1998 or three years from the date of his or her return to the United States (whichever is later) from the overseas tour of duty during which he or she acquired eligibility; and

7.   Meets the qualification requirements for the position in the United States for which he or she is applying.

The appointment can be made to any occupation and grade for which you are qualified. Non-competitive means you can apply for a position advertised on a local vacancy announcement which is open to transfer and reinstatement eligibles. Agencies can waive written tests after determining that the overseas position was similar to make the written test unnecessary. Executive Order eligibility entitles you to register in the DOD Priority Placement Program when you return to the U.S.

Application Procedures

Most Excepted Service and NAFI stateside and overseas vacancies are filled by local Civilian Personnel Offices (CPOs). Stateside competitive positions are controlled by OPM in most cases, while overseas competitive positions are often handled by CPOs who have direct hire authority.

Army, Air Force, Navy and Marine installation Family Support Centers work with local CPOs to offer family members employment assistance, career counseling and in some cases skills training. Family Support Centers have slightly different names within each military branch. In the Army they are called Army Community Service (AWS) offices. Contact your local Support Center for additional information.

If a military sponsor is relocating to a new duty station, family members should contact the CPO or Family Support Center at the new location and request employment information. CPOs provide detailed job information and often provide the names of other federal agencies in the commuting area, as well as non-federal personnel offices.

Family member counseling is provided by local CPO recruitment and placement offices upon request and at least 30 days prior to departing an area.

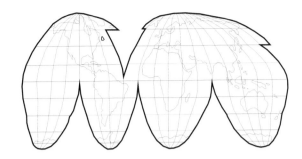

CHAPTER EIGHT
Overseas Employment Opportunities

There are over 88,700 federal employees working for the federal government in 140 foreign countries, in the United States territories, and in Alaska and Hawaii.[1] The positions that are most often available are administrative, technical and professional, accountants, auditors, foreign service officers, budget and program officers, management analysts, nurses, procurement officers, shorthand reporters, equipment specialists, engineers, social workers, housing officers, teachers, and alcohol and drug abuse specialists. Clerical (clerk-typist, stenographer) and secretary positions are normally filled locally overseas.

> The Defense Department is the largest overseas employer, with 48,151 workers, and the State Department is number two, with 20,712 employees stationed abroad.

CHAPTER OBJECTIVES

✎ Learn how positions are filled overseas

✎ Understand the conditions of overseas employment

✎ Locate hiring agencies and job opportunities *(includes a hiring agency directory and contact information)*

✎ Review overseas job resources *(periodicals with job ads, job hotlines, and Internet Web sites)*

---

[1] ARMY Civilian Personnel Office Online at http://acpol.army.mil

Job recruitment practices vary. In the U.S. territories, Hawaii, and Alaska most positions are filled through competitive civil service announcements. Various positions overseas are filled through Excepted Service and Nonappropriated Fund Instrumentality (NAFI) hiring programs. Excepted Service positions are described in Chapter Three. Nonappropriated Fund positions are paid using money generated within the Department of the Army and other military branches through sales revenues. These positions are primarily governed by military regulations.

When positions are filled locally overseas, U.S. citizens living abroad, dependents of citizens employed or stationed overseas, or foreign nationals can be hired. Most countries have agreements with U.S. installations that require the hiring of local nationals whenever possible to bolster the local economy. All positions held by foreign nationals are in the Excepted Service. Excepted Service positions are not subject to OPM's competitive hiring requirements.

Of the 88,700 overseas civilian federal employees, 67,804 U.S. citizens as of September 2006.[2] Since the last edition of this book, total overseas federal civilian employment decreased by 5,191 positions. The Department of Defense is the largest employer of civilians overseas. Consequently, the majority of jobs are located at military installations.

Most of the upper and mid-level positions are filled through internal placement. Internal placement allows government employees who desire to work overseas to apply for the positions in-house. If there are no in-house bidders, agencies then advertise through competitive announcements. Overseas applicants should contact individual Agency and OPM Web sites for job listings.

CONDITIONS OF EMPLOYMENT

Overseas workers must meet various requirements: physical, security, qualifications, tour of duty, etc. Announcements list specific restrictions, conditions, and special qualifications.

PHYSICAL EXAMINATIONS

Individuals wanting to work overseas must meet certain stringent requirements. Thorough physical exams for both the applicant and, in many cases, accompanying dependents require physicals. You must be able to physically adapt to the conditions at various locations that may not have adequate healthcare facilities. Individuals on medication or who require special care will not be considered for certain positions. Any physical impairment that would create a hazard to others or to the applicant, or would reduce performance level, will disqualify the applicant.

---

[2] Federal Civilian Workforce Statistics, Employment and Trends, September 2006.

SECURITY CLEARANCE CHECKS

All applicants considered for appointment must pass a comprehensive security clearance, character and suitability check. These investigations take from a few weeks to several months to complete. If you are selected for a position, you will be appointed conditionally, pending the results of the investigation.

TRANSPORTATION AGREEMENTS

Individuals selected for overseas assignment are generally required to sign a transportation agreement. Typically, overseas tours last from 12 to 36 months.

FOREIGN LANGUAGE REQUIREMENTS

A foreign language that would not be a position requirement in the States may be required for certain overseas positions. The job announcement will specify if a language is required. Several agencies appoint candidates without the required language skill and give them a period of time to develop acceptable language proficiency.

DEPENDENTS

Most agencies permit professional employees to take dependents with them. Professional positions are generally considered to be mid-level positions and above. Other employees can often arrange for dependents to follow them at a later date.

Government employees' dependents are often given priority employment consideration at U.S. overseas facilities. Your spouse may receive hiring preference.

PAY AND BENEFITS

Pay is generally the same overseas for the comparable stateside position. Additional allowances such as a post differential, cost-of-living and quarters allowance, are provided where conditions warrant. Military base privileges are authorized in many circumstances and Department of Defense schools are available for dependent children through grade 12.

Basic benefits are the same for all civil service employees. Overseas employees also receive free travel, transportation and storage of household goods, and extra vacation with free transportation to stateside homes between tours of duty. Review Chapter One for a list of available benefits.

COMPETITION

There are a limited number of overseas positions and competition is keen. However, if you are well qualified and available for most locations, there are opportunities available. The normal rotation of current employees back to the United States creates a large number of recurring vacancies.

CITIZENSHIP

Applications are accepted only from U.S. citizens and American Samoans. However, the hiring of locals at overseas military installations is authorized to bolster the local economy. All positions held by foreign nationals are in the Excepted Service.

APPLYING FOR OVERSEAS JOBS

Apply early. It pays to apply for federal jobs well in advance of the time you will be available for employment. Many overseas jobs, especially jobs with the Department of Defense, require submission of an online application or through the use of a RESUMIX (résumé) application. Applications submitted through the mail can take six to eight weeks for processing. Online application submission dramatically reduces the application processing time. It may take longer if written tests are required, especially in overseas areas. Applications are given out until the limit is reached or until the closing date of the announcement. Refer to Chapter Six for detailed federal employment application guidance.

TEMPORARY EMPLOYMENT

Federal agencies often hire temporary employees. You may be considered for both temporary and permanent positions. If you accept a temporary appointment, your name will remain on the register for consideration for permanent positions. Temporary employment is usually for one year or less, but may be extended for up to four years.

NAFI JOBS

Department of Defense agencies employ over 140,000 *Non-Appropriated Fund Instrumentalities (NAFI)* workers in post exchanges, military clubs and recreation services. These positions are not in the competitive service and they are funded by the revenue generated by the exchanges and clubs. Applications for these jobs must be submitted to the individual agencies or personnel offices. The NAFI personnel office can assist you with locating NAFI jobs worldwide:

- NAFI Personnel Policy Office
  1400 Key Boulevard, Suite B200
  Arlington, VA 22209-5144
  (703) 696-3318 or (703) 696-3310
  http://www.cpms.osd.mil/

OVERSEAS FEDERAL JOB SOURCES

This section presents resources that can be used to locate federal job announcements for overseas jobs. Refer to Chapter Three's Common Job Source lists for additional resources. Appendix D provides a complete list of federal occupations. Also, refer to Appendix C for detailed descriptions of government agencies and departments.

Resource headings include job openings, *Hiring Agency Directory*, and general information. The Hiring Agency Directory lists addresses of many agencies that offer overseas employment. Job openings include publications with job ads, job hotlines, and Internet Web sites. The general information section lists related books, pamphlets, brochures, and computer software. All job sources are listed alphabetically. A number of the periodicals and books listed in this chapter are available at libraries.

JOB OPENINGS

Periodicals with job ads

Federal Career Opportunities — Federal Research Service, PO Box 1708, Annandale, VA 22003; 1-800-822-5027 or 703-914-JOBS. Federal job listings for $19.95 per month, $39.97 for a 3 month subscription. Includes federal and private sector job listings. The online database at http://fedjobs.com is easy to use and lists thousands of vacancies, often more than OPM's web site. Other helpful services and job hunting resources are available.

Federal Jobs Digest — Breakthrough Publications, 326 Main Street, Emmaus, PA 18049; 610-965-5825 or 1-800-824-5000, http://jobsfed.com, publishes online database job listing plus job matching services. Two week free trial to access the job search database. After 14 day free trial, cost is only $7.95 per month or $39.95 for lifetime subscription. The lifetime subscription includes FREE job matching service. The jobs database is extensive.

Job Hotlines

Department of Defense Education Activity (DODEA)

The Department of Defense Education Activity (DODEA), ATTN: Teacher Recruitment, 4040 N. Fairfax Drive, Arlington, VA 22201-1634, phone: (703) 588-3983. Applications are processed online at http://www.dodea.edu. Select "Human Resource." On the Human Resources Page select "Employment" to locate job vacancy announcements with links to the online application. A description of the DODDS teacher program is featured later in this chapter.

USA JOBS by Phone - Federal government job hotline 1-703-724-1850 or TDD 978-461-8404. This service is operated by the Office of Personnel Management and the phone answers 24 hours a day. Provides federal employment information for most occupations. Callers can leave voice-mail messages with their name, address, and phone number. Requested job announcements and applications are mailed within 24 hours. Easy-to-use voice prompts and voice commands allow access with any touchtone or rotary dial telephone. (Note — Not all vacancies are listed on this service. Agencies with direct hire authority announce vacancies through their individual human resources departments.)

Peace Corps Recruiting Contacts (http://www.peacecorps.gov) The Peace Corps has numerous university programs, including: the Peace Corps Preparatory Program, the Master's Internationalist Program, the Community College Model, Campus Compact Internships, Student Internships, Cooperative Education, Volunteer Partners, and Research Collaboration programs. For specific information contact the Peace Corps, Office of Human Resource Management, Washington, DC 20526, phone 1-800-424-8580.

U.S. Department of State jobs (http://www.state.gov). Inquiries about employment in the Foreign Service should be directed to: HR/REE/REC, 2401 E Street NW, Suite 518H, Washington, DC 20322, phone: 202-261-8888. Employment 24 hour hotline: 703-875-7490. Call this number for current Foreign Service Specialist job openings. The State Department employs 32,997 persons, of whom 20,162 work overseas.

Internet Web Sites

Army Civilian Personnel Online (http://www.cpol.army.mil/) Very helpful with links to the Atlantic and Pacific employment Web sites. Includes RESUMIX application online forms, job listings, and much more.

Army CPO Links   (http://acpol.army.mil/employment) This page offers job listings worldwide with comprehensive searches for all occupations. Includes links to job vacancies in the Pacific, Atlantic, Korea, and all Army stateside regions as well.

Central Intelligence Agency (http://www.cia.gov/) Complete information on CIA employment opportunities, with job lists.

Federal Departments that deploy personnel overseas include:

Agriculture	http://www.usda.gov
Commerce	http://www.doc.gov
Defense	http://www.whs.mil/HRD/
Homeland Security	http://www.dhs.gov/dhspublic
Interior	http://www.doi.gov
Justice	http://www.usdoj.gov
State	http://www.state.gov/m/dghr/hr/
Transportation	http://www.dot.gov
Treasury	http://www.ustreas.gov/jobs
Veterans Affairs	http://www.va.gov

FBI (http://www.fbi.gov/employment/employ.htm) Visit its site for complete information on job opportunities and vacancy announcements.

Federal Jobs Network (http://federaljobs.net)

This career center helps anyone who is actively seeking government employment and current federal employees looking for career progression. The overseas section includes many of the links in this chapter. Visit this site for the latest updates to this book and to locate information on all government jobs. Use the direct links to more than 200 agency employment sites to locate job vacancies.

National Security Agency (http://www.nsa.gov/careers) Visit their employment page for vacancy announcements and for complete information on the agency and its mission.

USAJOBS — Sponsored by OPM (http://www.USAJOBS.gov)

This site provides a comprehensive listing with full search capability for many federal job vacancies, general employment information, with online applications for some jobs and a résumé builder.

HIRING AGENCY DIRECTORY

TABLE 8-1 OVERSEAS EMPLOYMENT BY DEPARTMENT		
Department	**Overseas Employment**	**Total Employment**
Agriculture	1,246	105,047
Commerce	787	40,079
Defense	48,151	677,744
Education	9	4,229
Energy	14	14,795
Health & Human Services	257	61,163
Homeland Security	3,978	154,100
Housing & Urban Development	74	9,935
Interior	329	72,274
Justice	1,903	106,781
Labor	37	16,195
State	20,712	34,160
Transportation	319	53,865
Treasury	672	106,925
Veterans Affairs	3,550	239,299

Data Obtained from Table 2 of OPM's September 2006 Employment Trends

The following list of agency personnel offices that hire overseas is not complete. Some agencies employ small numbers of workers for overseas assignments.

Foreign Agriculture Service (FAS) http://www.fsa.usda.gov/pas

Contact the Information Division, Mail Stop 0506, 1400 Independence Avenue SW, Washington, DC 20250. Phone, 202-720-5237.

Formed in 1953 by executive reorganization, FAS is one of the smaller USDA agencies, with about 900 employees. FAS operates worldwide with staff in more than 75 posts covering more than 130 countries. Washington-based marketing specialists, trade policy analysts, economists, and others back up the overseas staff.

In addition, FAS has four domestic outreach offices that provide a complete range of export services to new-to-export companies and trade organizations, to help expand their business knowledge of export opportunities and USDA export assistance programs.

Roughly 70 percent of the annual FAS budget is devoted to building markets overseas for U.S. farm products. This includes the funding for all FAS trade and attaché offices overseas, as well as the agency's work with U.S. commodity associations on cooperative promotion projects. The remaining funds cover other trade functions, including gathering and disseminating market information and trade policy efforts. Click on the careers tab at http://www.fas.usda.gov to locate FAS job vacancies.

Positions are generally filled from the Professional and Administrative Career Examination. Agricultural occupations that are assigned overseas include Agricultural Program Specialist GS-1145, Agricultural Marketing Series GS-1146, Agricultural Market Reporting GS-1147, and Agricultural Engineering GS-0890.

Economists start at the GS-9 pay grade and have promotion potential to the GS-12 grade. The Foreign Agriculture Service carries out its tasks through its network of agricultural counselors, attaches, and trade officers stationed overseas.

Department of Commerce — http://www.commerce.gov/

The United States & Foreign Commercial Service is one of four official Foreign Affairs Agencies under the Foreign Service Act of 1980. The Commercial Service is responsible for commercial affairs. Foreign service officers in the Commercial Service are assigned to foreign and domestic field offices, as well as Washington, D.C., to promote the export of United States goods and services and defend United States commercial interests abroad. The Commercial Service, through its customized business solutions, creates economic prosperity and more and better jobs for all Americans. Employment information and job vacancies are available online.

Department of Defense — http://www.whs.mil/HRD/

Human Resources Directorate, Washington Headquarters Services, 1155 Defense Pentagon, Washington, DC 20301, phone 703-604-6219. The DOD is the largest overseas employer and provides hiring support to other federal agencies, including the Departments of the Air Force and the Navy, through its Overseas Employment Program (OEP). The OEP gives first consideration to qualified employees currently working at federal installations overseas. Former employees with reinstatement rights, and current government employees, should contact DOD Civilian Personnel Offices (CPOs) at DOD installations. When positions can't be filled in-house, the human resources department opens a competitive register to fill the position.

Department of the Army — http://www.cpol.army.mil/

The Department of the Army consolidated all hiring, and you can search this site for jobs in any country. Generally locals are hired for trades, laborers, equipment operators, and crafts and clerical positions. Dependents of military and civilian U.S. citizens assigned abroad receive hiring preference for many of these positions. Contact Civilian Personnel Offices at local Army posts for vacancies.

This site links to the Atlantic and Pacific overseas employment Web sites. Includes RESUMIX application online forms, job listings, and much more.

PACIFIC Opportunities

Most federal jobs in the Pacific overseas areas are with the Department of Defense. Many positions in DOD agencies are currently filled under a special appointment authority for hiring family members of U.S. military or civilian personnel stationed in foreign areas. Jobs not filled by the special appointment authority are frequently filled by federal employees who transfer overseas or U.S. citizens living in the local areas on a temporary or time-limited basis. Generally, the greatest demand is for experienced engineering, administrative, educational, technical, and scientific occupations. Federal employees in Hawaii and Guam receive cost-of-living allowances (COLAs) in addition to their basic pay.

ATLANTIC Opportunities

The majority of positions are in Germany, Belgium, Italy, and Africa. Germany is where the largest number of employees are stationed. The majority of these jobs are filled by residents of the host country or by family members of military and civilians officially stationed in Europe. Approximately 5 percent are U.S. citizens who were recruited outside of Europe. Local Army Civilian Personnel Offices (CPOs) have primary responsibility within Europe for most noncareer, technical and administrative positions.

If you seek employment with the Departments of the Army, Navy or Air Force, or any other federal agency in the Atlantic region, the U.S. Army, Europe, and the Seventh Army (USAREUR), located in Leiman, Germany, is the delegated examining authority by the Office of Personnel Management for certain positions above the GS-7 grade level.

Status and Nonstatus applicants who are seeking employment in the Atlantic Overseas Area for GS-7 and above positions should apply through the online system listed on the above listed Web sites. You can fax applications, but they prefer online applications through the RESUMIX system.

A status applicant is one who previously worked for the federal government and obtained career status. Nonstatus applicants that have never worked for the federal government must establish eligibility with the Office of Personnel Management or with an agency that has been delegated examining authority, such as the USAREUR.

Department of Defense Dependent School System (DODDS)

The Department of Defense Education Activity (DODEA), ATTN: Teacher Recruitment, 4040 N. Fairfax Drive, Arlington, VA 22201-1634, phone: (703) 588-3983. Applications are processed online at http://www.dodea.edu.

Elementary and secondary schools have been operating on U.S. military bases overseas since 1946 for children of military and civilian personnel. The DODDS provides educational opportunities comparable to those offered in the better school systems in the United States. This segment of U.S. public education consists of 157 elementary, middle, and secondary schools. The schools are located in 14 foreign countries with an enrollment of approximately 77,000 students, and are staffed with approximately 6,500 employees.

School Locations:

European Region — Belgium, England, Iceland, Netherlands, Norway, Scotland, Germany, Azores, Bahrain, Greece, Italy, Spain, Turkey

Pacific Region — Japan, Korea, Okinawa (Japan)

Americas Region — Stateside, Puerto Rico, Cuba and Guam

Salary:

Overseas salaries are comparable to the average of the range of rates for similar positions in urban school jurisdictions in the U.S. having a population of 100,000 or more.

The school year consists of 190 duty days, with a minimum of 175 days of classroom instruction. Teachers are currently paid on several different pay bands (bachelor's degree, bachelor's degree plus 15 semester hours, master's degree plus 30 semester hours, and doctor's degree).

Housing and Living Conditions

In some areas, living quarters are provided by the U.S. government. These quarters may be in dormitories, apartments, old hotels, converted office buildings, or new modern facilities. These U.S. government quarters are usually provided without charge.

Visit the Web site for the overseas location where you desire to teach.

DODEA Worldwide Web Sites:

- Pacific   http://www.pac.dodea.edu/
- Europe   http://www.eu.dodea.edu/
- Guam   http://www.pac.dodea.edu/
- Cuba   http://www.am.dodea.edu/

Department of Homeland Security — http://www.dhs.gov

This department has 149,059 employees, of whom 3,978 are stationed overseas. The Department of Homeland Security (DHS) was founded to increase communication, coordination and resources and has three primary missions:

- Prevent terrorist attacks within the United States,
- Reduce America's vulnerability to terrorism, and
- Minimize the damage from potential attacks and natural disasters.

DHS was created to provide one single government agency with the primary mission of homeland security. It consolidates security functions from 100 government organizations to provide a single, unified homeland security structure that improves protection against today's threats and is flexible enough to help meet the unknown threats of the future.

The Department of Homeland Security has unique and challenging career opportunities. Homeland Security employees help secure our borders, airports, seaports and waterways; research and develop the latest security technologies; respond to natural disasters or terrorist assaults; and analyze intelligence reports.

The Department of Homeland Security was the most significant transformation of the U.S. government in over a half-century and is transforming and realigning government security activities into a single department.

Department of Justice — http://www.usdoj.gov

950 Pennsylvania Avenue NW, Washington, DC 20530. Phone, 202-514-2000. Agency-wide employment job line for attorneys and law students is available at 202-514-3397.

The DOJ's mission is to enforce the law and defend the interests of the United States according to the law; to ensure public safety against threats foreign and domestic; to provide federal leadership in preventing and controlling crime; to seek just punishment for those guilty of unlawful behavior; and to ensure fair and impartial administration of justice for all Americans.

Drug Enforcement Administration (DEA) — Office of Personnel, 2401 Jefferson Davis Highway, Alexandria, VA 22301. Phone 202-307-1000. Employs several hundred workers overseas. The DEA is an agency under the Department of Justice. Visit the Web site at http://www.dea.gov or Call 1-800-332-4288 for Special Agent employment opportunities.

Drug enforcement agents and administrative.

Department of Transportation (DOT) - http://www.dot.gov

Transportation Administrative Service Center (TASC) DOT Connection, Room PL-402, 400 Seventh Street SW, Washington, DC 20590. Phone, 202-366-9391 or 800-525-2878..

Employees work in hundreds of occupations including many professional and technical categories. Employs a large number of electronics technicians and engineers. The majority of overseas employment is with the Federal Aviation Administration (FAA).

I spent the majority of my 35 years with the federal government working for the FAA in Airways facilities, now called Technical Operations, working with Air Traffic Control.

Federal Aviation Administration (http://www.faa.gov). Visit the Web site for stateside and overseas employment listings.

Aviation safety inspectors, pilots, electronic system specialists.

Department of State — http://www.state.gov

The Foreign Service employs thousands of Foreign Service officers and specialists who serve in 180 countries and at more than 265 posts around the world. Application procedures for employment with the U.S. Department of State vary according to the direction in which you take your career. Foreign Service officers, for example, must pass the Foreign Service Officer Selection Process.

Of the 34,160 total employment, two-thirds or 20,712 employees work overseas. Visit the Web site and explore the many opportunities available in Foreign Service. Direct inquires to: Office of Recruitment, Examination and Employment, HR/REE, Room H-518m 2401 E Street NW, Washington, DC 20522. Phone, 202-262-8888. A 24 hour job information line is available at 202-647-7284.

Foreign Service officers, enforcement specialists, technical specialists, medical care specialists, administrative specialists, advisors, building operations, and internships.

The Foreign Service of the United States is America's diplomatic, commercial, and overseas cultural and information service. This agency assists the president and secretary of state in planning and carrying out American foreign policy at home and abroad. Personnel spend an average of 60 percent of their careers abroad, moving at two- to four-year intervals. Many overseas posts are in small or remote countries where harsh climates, health hazards, and other discomforts exist, and where American-style amenities frequently are unavailable.

English Language Skills

The Foreign Service requires all employees to have a strong command of the English language. All Foreign Service officers must be able to speak and write clearly, concisely, and correctly. The Departments of State and Commerce and the United States Intelligence Agency give high priority to English-language skills in selecting officers and evaluating their performance.

Foreign Language Skills

Knowledge of a foreign language is not required for appointment. Candidates without such knowledge are appointed as language probationers and must acquire acceptable competency in at least one foreign language before tenure can be granted. Officers can attend classes at the *National Foreign Affairs Training Institute*, which offers training in over 40 languages. These agencies seek persons with knowledge of Arabic, Chinese, Japanese, or Russian.

Department of the Treasury — http://www.treas.gov

1500 Pennsylvania Avenue NW, Washington, DC 20220. Phone, 202-622-6415. The Department of the Treasury is the primary federal agency responsible for the economic and financial prosperity and security of the United States, and as such is responsible for a wide range of activities including advising the president on economic and financial issues, promoting the president's growth agenda, and enhancing corporate governance in financial institutions.

In the international arena, the Department of the Treasury works with other federal agencies, the governments of other nations, and the International Financial Institutions (IFIs) to encourage economic growth, raise standards of living, and predict and prevent, to the extent possible, economic and financial crises.

Almost every major field of study has some application to the work of this service. A substantial number of positions are filled by persons whose major educational preparation was accounting, business administration, finance, economics, criminology, and law. There are, however, many positions that are filled by persons whose college major was political science, public administration, education, liberal arts, or other fields not directly related to business or law.

Department of Veterans Affairs — http://www.va.gov

The VA headquarters is located at 810 Vermont Avenue NW, Washington, DC 20420. Phone, 202-273-4950. The department operates programs to benefit veterans and members of their families. Benefits include compensation payments for disabilities or death related to military service; pensions; education and rehabilitation; home loan guaranty; burial; and a medical care program incorporating nursing homes, clinics, and medical centers. Most of the 3,550 overseas employees work in Hawaii, Alaska, and Puerto Rico.

Employs most medical specialties. This system does not require civil service eligibility.

CHAPTER NINE
The U.S. Postal Service

The U.S. Postal Service (USPS) has annual operating revenue exceeding $68 billion and it pays $2 billion in salaries and benefits every two weeks. There are more than 757,000 workers in 300 job categories for positions at 38,000 post offices, branches, stations, and community post offices throughout the United States. Approximately 40,000 postal workers are hired each year to backfill for retirements, transfers, deaths, and employees who choose to leave the Postal Service.

Adding benefits, overtime, and premiums, the average bargaining unit annual compensation rate was $62,348.

Vacancies are advertised internally by the USPS and not by the Office of Personnel Management. Visit the Web site at http://usps.com/employment for exam schedules and job vacancy lists. In 1971, the Postal Service became independent. Pay scales are determined by the Postal Pay Act.

Informative Sites:
www.usps.com/employment
www.postofficejobs.info

CHAPTER OBJECTIVES

✎ Learn about Postal Service opportunities

✎ Understand the employee pay and classification system

✎ Determine employee qualification requirements

✎ How to apply for exams

✎ Review postal clerk and mail carrier occupations *(nature of work, working conditions, training, job outlook, and earnings)*

SALARY EXPECTATIONS

Starting pay in 2007 was $19 per hour, $39,520 per year, for part time flexible mail carriers in 2007. Mail handlers start at $13.92 per hour, $28,953 per year, and clerks start at $18.26 per hour, $37,980 per year.[1] Mail handler workers are initially hired under the Postal Service's part time flexible pay scale and work 40 or more hours per week. The average pay and benefits for career bargaining unit employees was $62,348 per year, excluding corporate-wide expenses, in 2006.[2] The largest pay system in the Postal Service is predominantly for bargaining unit employees. There are also Executive and Administrative Schedules for non-bargaining unit members, with pay ranging from $20,875 up to an authorized maximum of $108,166.

EMPLOYEE CLASSIFICATIONS

Initial appointments are either casual (temporary) or part-time flexible (career). Hourly rates for part-time flexible employees vary depending upon the position's rate schedule. Some positions are filled full-time, such as the Maintenance (Custodial) classification.

Full-time, part-time regular, and part time flexible employees compose the *Regular Work Force*. This category includes security guards. Part-time flexible employees are scheduled to work fewer than 40 hours per week and they must be available for flexible work hours as assigned. Part-time employees are paid hourly and the rates vary from $14.25 at the P1 PS Schedule Step BB Grade 1 to $29.15 for Step P Grade 12.

A *Supplemental Work Force* is needed by the Postal Service for peak mail periods and offers casual (temporary) employees two 89-day employment terms in a calendar year. During the Christmas season an additional 21 days of employment can be offered to Supplemental Work Force employees.

College students may be considered for casual (temporary) employment with the Postal Service during the summer months. The rate of pay ranges from $8 to $12 per hour. Tests are not required and appointments cannot lead to a career position. Apply early for summer work. Contact post offices in your area by no later than February for summer employment applications.

---

[1] Beginning salary figures obtained from the Pittsburgh USPS human resource office.

[2] Comprehensive Statement on Postal Operations, 2006 — USPS

EMPLOYMENT RESOURCES

There are several resources that provide valuable information for those interested in working for the Postal Service. Visit these sites or call the listed number for additional information:

http://usps.com/employment (Official Postal Service recruitment site)

Job hotline: **1-866-999-8777**
(Sponsored by the USPS)

---

http://postofficejobs.info (Job information and links)

http://postalemployeenetwork.com/index.htm (Resources for postal workers. Offers a free electronic newsletter subscription.)

http://PostalReporter.com (Postal service employment information)

QUALIFICATION REQUIREMENTS

Various standards from age restrictions to physical requirements must be met before you can take one of the Postal Service exams.

Age Limit

You must be 18 to apply. Certain conditions allow applicants as young as 16 to apply. Carrier positions requiring driving are limited to age 18 or older. High school graduates or individuals who terminated high school education for sufficient reason are permitted to apply at age 16.

Entrance Exams

Applicants for clerk, carrier and other specific jobs must pass an entrance exam. Specialties such as mechanic, electronic technician, machinist, and trades must also pass a written test. The overall rating is based on the test results and your qualifying work experience and education. Professionals and certain administrative positions don't require an entrance exam or written test. They are rated and hired strictly on their prior work experience and education.

The Postal Service exam schedule dates are listed online by state at http://www.usps.com/employment. Exams are offered generally every two years in an area, depending on turnover rates and other factors.

The 473 Postal Examination covers the following entry level positions:

✔ **City Carrier**

✔ **Mail Processing Clerk**

✔ **Mail handler**

✔ **Sales, Services, and Distribution Associate**

The 473 Postal Examination covers the majority of entry level hiring, although some offices also maintain custodial registers which, by law, are reserved for veterans' preference eligibles. The USPS also maintains motor vehicle and tractor trailer registers and some highly skilled maintenance positions such as building equipment mechanic, engineman, electronics technician, and general mechanic. All the skilled maintenance positions require examination 931. A separate announcement, examination 932, is required for Electronics Technician positions.

Six sample exams are presented in Chapter Five, and a sample *473 Battery Test* is included in Chapter Six, along with a comprehensive study guide in the new Fourth Edition of *Post Office Jobs*, available at your local bookstore, library, or order with any major credit card by calling 1-800-782-7424 to help you prepare for this test. The 473 examination and completion of forms will require approximately three hours. Jobs with the U.S. Postal Service are highly competitive due to the excellent salary and benefits offered. It's essential that you pass the test with the highest score possible to improve your chances. Applicants scoring between 95 and 100 percent have a better chance of being hired.

Citizenship

Applicants do not have to be U.S. citizens. If you have permanent alien resident status in the United States of America or owe allegiance to the United States you can apply for Postal Service jobs.

Physical Requirements

Physical requirements are determined by the job. Carriers must be able to lift a 70-pound mail sack and all applicants must be able to efficiently perform assigned duties. Eyesight and hearing tests are required. Applicants must have at least 20/40 vision in the good eye and no worse than 20/100 in the other eye. Eyeglasses are permitted.

State Driver's License

Applicants must have a valid state driver's license for positions that require motor vehicle operation. A safe driving record is required and a Postal Service road test is administered for the type of vehicle that you will operate.

DRUG TESTING (SUBSTANCE ABUSE)

The Postal Service maintains a comprehensive program to ensure a drug-free workplace. A qualification for postal employment is to be drug free, and this qualification is determined through the use of a urinalysis drug screen. When you are determined to be in the area of consideration for employment, you will be scheduled for a drug screening test.

APPLICATION PROCEDURES

Positions Requiring Written Examinations

The USPS does not maintain a national directory or register of openings. It has a decentralized hiring process for personnel and examination related matters. The examinations are administered by examination center personnel from local Customer District Human Resources offices located in most large cities. A comprehensive listing of Customer Service District offices is provided in Chapter Four of *Post Office Jobs.*

To apply for postal positions you must contact a Management Sectional Center (MSC), Bulk Mail Center, General Mail Facility, Customer Service District Office or a Sectional Center Facility to register for the postal workers civil service exam. Contact your local post office to find out where the tests are administered in your area. A complete listing of postal facilities is available from the USPS in the National Five-Digit Zip Code and Post Office Directory (two volumes). A copy of this publication is usually available for use in the post office lobby.

A passing score of 70 percent or better on an exam will place the applicant's name on an eligible *register* for a period of two years. Registers are lists of job applicants that have passed an exam or evaluation process. Your score determines your placement on the register. Applicants can write to the postal examination office for a one-year extension. Requests for extension must be received between the 18th and 24th month of eligibility. Most people hired have a score of between 90 and 100 percent. There is a separate register for each job classification. To improve your chances, test for as many different positions as you can qualify for.

Positions That Don't Require a Written Exam

Vacancies in these positions—generally professional and administrative—are announced (advertised) first within the Postal Service. Postal employees who have the knowledge, education, credentials, and skills may apply for these openings. If there aren't any qualified applicants (called bidders in the federal sector), then the Postal Service will advertise the vacancies to the general public and accept résumés and applications for rating. All applicants must pass an entrance examination and/or an evaluation process to be placed on a register in numerical score order.

VETERANS PREFERENCE

Veterans receive five or 10-point preference. Those with a 10 percent or greater compensable service-connected disability are placed at the top of the register in the order of their scores. All other eligibles are listed below the disabled veterans group in rank order. The Veterans Preference Act applies to all Postal Service positions. Refer to Chapter Seven for detailed information on veterans' preference.

Custodial exams for the position of cleaner, custodian, and custodial laborer are exclusively for veterans and present employees. This exam is open only to veterans' preference candidates.

POSTAL CLERKS AND MAIL CARRIERS
(The Largest USPS Occupations)

Nature of the Work

Each week, the U.S. Postal Service delivers billions of pieces of mail, including letters, bills, advertisements, and packages.[3] To do this in an efficient and timely manner, the Postal Service employs about 757,000[4] individuals. Most Postal Service workers are clerks, mail carriers, or mail sorters, processors, and processing machine operators. Postal clerks wait on customers at post offices, whereas mail sorters, processors, and processing machine operators sort incoming and outgoing mail at post offices and mail processing centers. Mail carriers deliver mail to urban and rural residences and businesses throughout the United States.

Postal service clerks, also known as window clerks, sell stamps, money orders, postal stationery, and mailing envelopes and boxes. They also weigh packages to determine postage and check that packages are in satisfactory condition for mailing. These clerks register, certify, and insure mail and answer questions about postage rates, post office boxes, mailing restrictions, and other postal matters. Window clerks also help customers file claims for damaged packages.

Postal service mail sorters, processors, and processing machine operators prepare incoming and outgoing mail for distribution. These workers are commonly referred to as mail handlers, distribution clerks, mail processors, or mail processing clerks. They load and unload postal trucks and move mail around a mail processing center with forklifts, small electric tractors, or hand-pushed carts. They also load and operate mail processing, sorting, and canceling machinery.

Postal Service mail carriers deliver mail, once it has been processed and sorted. Although carriers are classified by their type of route, either city or rural, duties of city and rural carriers are similar. Most travel established routes, deliv-

---

[3] This section excerpted from the Occupational Outlook Handbook 2006-2007 edition, U.S. Department of Labor

[4] Federal Civilian Workforce Statistics — September 2006

ering and collecting mail. Mail carriers start work at the post office early in the morning, when they arrange the mail in delivery sequence. Automated equipment has reduced the time that carriers need to sort the mail, allowing them to spend more time delivering it.

Mail carriers cover their routes on foot, by vehicle, or a combination of both. On foot, they carry a heavy load of mail in a satchel or push it on a cart. In most urban and rural areas, they use a car or small truck. Although the Postal Service provides vehicles to city carriers, most rural carriers must use their own automobiles. Deliveries are made house-to-house, to roadside mailboxes, and to large buildings such as offices or apartments, which generally have all their tenants' mailboxes in one location.

Besides delivering and collecting mail, carriers collect money for postage-due and COD (cash-on-delivery) fees and obtain signed receipts for registered, certified, and insured mail. If a customer is not home, the carrier leaves a notice that tells where special mail is being held. After completing their routes, carriers return to the post office with mail gathered from street collection boxes, homes, and businesses and turn in the mail, receipts, and money collected during the day.

Some city carriers may have specialized duties such as delivering only parcels or picking up mail from mail collection boxes. In contrast to city carriers, rural carriers provide a wider range of postal services, in addition to delivering and picking up mail. For example, rural carriers may sell stamps and money orders and register, certify, and insure parcels and letters. All carriers, however, must be able to answer customers' questions about postal regulations and services and provide change-of-address cards and other postal forms when requested.

Working Conditions

Window clerks usually work in the public portion of clean, well-ventilated, and well-lit buildings. They have a variety of duties and frequent contact with the public, but they rarely work at night. However, they may have to deal with upset customers, stand for long periods, and be held accountable for an assigned stock of stamps and funds. Depending on the size of the post office in which they work, they also may be required to sort mail.

Despite the use of automated equipment, the work of mail sorters, processors, and processing machine operators can be physically demanding. Workers may have to move heavy sacks of mail around a mail processing center. These workers usually are on their feet, reaching for sacks and trays of mail or placing packages and bundles into sacks and trays. Processing mail can be tiring and boring. Many sorters, processors, and machine operators work at night or on weekends, because most large post offices process mail around the clock, and the largest volume of mail is sorted during the evening and night shifts. Workers can experience stress as they process ever-larger quantities of mail under tight production deadlines and quotas.

Most carriers begin work early in the morning—those with routes in a business district can start as early as 4 a.m. Overtime hours are frequently required for urban carriers. A carrier's schedule has its advantages, however. Carriers who begin work early in the morning are through by early afternoon and spend most of the day on their own, relatively free from direct supervision. Carriers spend most of their time outdoors, delivering mail in all kinds of weather. Even those who drive often must walk periodically when making deliveries and must lift heavy sacks of parcel post items when loading their vehicles. In addition, carriers must be cautious of potential hazards on their routes. Wet and icy roads and side-walks can be treacherous, and each year dogs attack numerous carriers.

Employment

The U.S. Postal Service employed 75,000 clerks, 335,000 mail carriers, and 209,000 mail sorters, processors, and processing machine operators in 2004. Most of them worked full time. Most postal clerks provided window service at post office branches. Many mail sorters, processors, and processing machine operators sorted mail at major metropolitan post offices; others worked at mail processing centers. The majority of mail carriers worked in cities and suburbs, while the rest worked in rural areas.

Postal Service workers are classified as either casual, part-time flexible, part-time regular, or full time. Casuals are hired for 90 days at a time to help process and deliver mail during peak mailing or vacation periods. Part-time flexible workers do not have a regular work schedule or weekly guarantee of hours but are called as the need arises. Part-time regulars have a set work schedule of fewer than 40 hours per week, often replacing regular full-time workers on their scheduled day off. Full-time postal employees work a 40-hour week over a five-day period.

Training, Other Qualifications, and Advancement

Postal Service workers must be at least 18 years old. They must be U.S. citizens or have been granted permanent resident-alien status in the United States, and males must have registered with the Selective Service upon reaching age 18. Applicants should have a basic competency of English. Qualification is based on a written examination that measures speed and accuracy at checking names and numbers and the ability to memorize mail distribution procedures. Applicants must pass a physical examination and drug test, and may be asked to show that they can lift and handle mail sacks weighing 70 pounds. Applicants for mail carrier positions must have a driver's license and a good driving record, and must receive a passing grade on a road test.

Job seekers should contact the post office or mail processing center where they wish to work to determine when an exam will be given. Applicants' names are listed in order of their examination scores. Five points are added to the score of an honorably discharged veteran and 10 points are added to the score of a veteran who was wounded in combat or is disabled. When a vacancy occurs, the appointing officer chooses one of the top three applicants; the rest of the names remain on the list to be considered for future openings until their eligibility expires — usually two years after the examination date.

Relatively few people become postal clerks or mail carriers on their first job, because of keen competition and the customary waiting period of one to two years or more after passing the examination. It is not surprising, therefore, that most entrants transfer from other occupations.

New Postal Service workers are trained on the job by experienced workers. Many post offices offer classroom instruction on safety and defensive driving. Workers receive additional instruction when new equipment or procedures are introduced. In these cases, workers usually are trained by another postal employee or a training specialist.

Postal clerks and mail carriers should be courteous and tactful when dealing with the public, especially when answering questions or receiving complaints. A good memory and the ability to read rapidly and accurately are important. Good interpersonal skills also are vital, because mail distribution clerks work closely with other postal workers, frequently under the tension and strain of meeting dispatch or transportation deadlines and quotas.

Postal Service workers often begin on a part-time, flexible basis and become regular or full time in order of seniority, as vacancies occur. Full-time workers may bid for preferred assignments, such as the day shift or a high-level non-supervisory position. Carriers can look forward to obtaining preferred routes as their seniority increases. Postal Service workers can advance to supervisory positions on a competitive basis.

Job Outlook

Employment of Postal Service workers is expected to decline through 2014. Still, many jobs will become available because of the need to replace those who retire or leave the occupation. Those seeking jobs as Postal Service workers can expect to encounter keen competition. The number of applicants should continue to exceed the number of job openings due to low entry requirements and attractive wages and benefits.

A small decline in employment is expected among window clerks over the 2004-14 projection period. Efforts by the Postal Service to provide better service may somewhat increase the demand for window clerks, but the demand for such clerks will be offset by the use of electronic communications technologies and private delivery companies. Employment of mail sorters, processors, and processing machine operators is expected to decline because of the increasing use of automated materials handling equipment and optical character readers, barcode sorters, and other automated sorting equipment.

A small decline in employment among mail carriers is expected through 2014. Competition from alternative delivery systems and the increasing use of electronic communication are expected to influence the demand for mail carriers. In addition, the Postal Service is moving toward more centralized mail delivery, such as the use of cluster boxes, to cut down on the number of door-to-door deliveries. The best employment opportunities for mail carriers are expected to be in less urbanized areas as the number of addresses to which mail must be delivered continues to grow, especially in fast-growing rural areas. However, increased use of the "delivery point sequencing" system, which allows machines to sort mail directly by the order of delivery, should reduce the amount of time that carriers spend sorting their mail, allowing them more time to handle longer routes.

The role of the Postal Service as a government-approved monopoly continues to be a topic of debate. Any legislative changes that would privatize or deregulate the Postal Service might affect employment of all its workers. Employment and schedules in the Postal Service fluctuate with the demand for its services. When mail volume is high, full-time employees work overtime, part-time workers get additional hours, and casual workers may be hired. When mail volume is low, overtime is curtailed, part-timers work fewer hours, and casual workers are discharged.

Earnings

Median annual earnings (not counting benefits) of Postal Service mail carriers was $44,450 in May 2004. The middle 50 percent earned between $37,590 and $50,580. The lowest 10 percent had earnings of less than $31,980, while the top 10 percent earned more than $54,240. Rural mail carriers are reimbursed for mileage put on their own vehicles while delivering mail.

Median annual earnings of Postal Service clerks were $40,950 in 2004. The middle 50 percent earned between $37,880 and $44,030. The lowest 10 percent had earnings of less than $36,040, while the top 10 percent earned more than $50,510.

Median annual earnings of Postal Service mail sorters, processors, and processing machine operators were $39,430 in 2004. The middle 50 percent earned between $36,240 and $42,620. The lowest 10 percent had earnings of less than $24,290, while the top 10 percent earned more than $44,540.

Postal Service workers enjoy a variety of employer-provided benefits similar to those enjoyed by federal government workers. The American Postal Workers union, the National Association of Letter Carriers, the National Postal Mail Handlers union, and the National Rural Letter Carriers Association together represent most of these workers.

ADDITIONAL REFERENCE MATERIAL

Post Office Jobs: How to Get a Job with the U.S. Postal Service

$19.95 (Fourth Edition)

by Dennis V. Damp

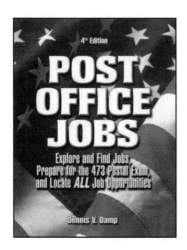

A one-stop resource for those interested in working for the Postal Service. Updated with all new contact information including Postal Service Internet sites and phone hot lines. It presents what jobs are available, where they are, and how to get one. *Post Office Jobs* dispels the myth that everyone in the Postal Service is a mail carrier or clerk. The 773,000 Postal Service workers are employed in hundreds of occupations—from janitors and truck drivers to accountants, personnel specialists, electronics technicians, and engineers. Many professional and administrative jobs do not require written examinations.

This book includes a comprehensive 473 & 473-C Postal Exam study guide and sample tests to help you prepare for the Clerk, Carrier and Mail handler exams.

Post Office Jobs presents eight steps to successfully landing a job and helps job seekers:

❶ Identify job openings

❷ Match your skills to postal jobs

❸ Locate postal exam test dates for your area

❹ Study for the 473 postal exam

❺ Complete job applications

❻ Prepare and practice for job interviews

❼ Apply for jobs that don't require written tests

❽ Explore viable civil service job options

This book is available at all bookstores and many libraries. You can also order it by phone toll free with all major credit cards including Visa, MasterCard, Discover, and American Express at **1-800-782-7424**.

OCCUPATIONS LIST

(Partial Listing)

Craft & Wage per hour positions:

Administrative Clerk	General Mechanic
Auto Mechanic	Letter Box Mechanic
Blacksmith-Welder	Letter Carrier
Building Equipment Mechanic	LSM Operator
Carpenter	Machinist
Carrier	Mail Handler
Cleaner, Custodian	Maintenance Mechanic
Clerk Stenographer	Mark Up Clerk
Data Conversion Operator	Mason
Distribution Clerk	Mechanic Helper
Electronic Technician	Motor Vehicle Operator
Elevator Mechanic	Painter
Engineman	Plumber
Fireman	Scale Mechanic
Garageman-Driver	Security Guard

Professional

Accounting Technician	Electronic Engineer
Architect/Engineer	Transportation Specialist
Budget Assistant	Industrial Engineer
Computer Programmer	Technical Writer
Computer System Analyst	Stationary Engineer

Management

Administrative Manager	Postmaster-Branch
Foreman of Mail	Safety Officer
General Foreman	Schemes Routing Officer
Labor Relations Representative	Supervisor-Accounting
Manager-Bulk Mail	Supervisor-Customer Service
Manager-Distribution	System Liaison Specialist
Manager-Station/Branch	Tour Superintendent

CHAPTER TEN
Employment Opportunities
For People with Disabilities

Seven percent of the total federal civilian workforce, over 189,000 employees, have disabilities.[1] Opportunities exist at all levels of government and in hundreds of occupations. The *Americans with Disabilities Act* (ADA) and Executive Order 13217 have increased awareness of hiring options by federal managers and those seeking employment. Both programs along with agency outreach efforts have expanded government employment opportunities for disabled persons.

*A*gencies have direct hire authority for trial appointments.

The Office of Personnel Management (OPM) established a comprehensive online portal to help the disabled explore and find employment in the federal sector. Its site at http://www.opm.gov/disability provides simple and straightforward guidance for both job seekers and federal managers, plus provides comprehensive resources and guidance for all concerned.

Informative and Helpful Site:

http://www.opm.gov/disability

CHAPTER OBJECTIVES

✎ Understand managers' hiring options

✎ Review types of appointments

✎ Learn about special accommodations *(includes testing arrangements and on-the-job assistance)*

✎ Review job resources *(periodicals with job ads, job hotlines, Internet Web sites, placement services, and association list)*

---

[1] OPM's Office of Workforce Information — 2006 FACT BOOK

The federal government offers special noncompetitive appointments — special emphasis hiring options — for people with physical or mental disabilities. There are distinct advantages for managers to hire individuals under special emphasis hiring appointments. Managers are able to hire individuals under special appointments within days, where it may take as long as several months to fill positions under the competitive process. Secondly, federal managers are tasked with specific performance targets, called *"critical job elements" (CJEs),* for maintaining workforce diversity. All agencies are required by law to develop outreach efforts to identify qualified candidates to meet agency workforce diversity goals.

This chapter explains the various hiring options for people with disabilities. Individuals seeking appointments with the federal government must be proactive and begin networking with local agencies, contacting listed resources, and aggressively seeking out all available federal employment opportunities.

FEDERAL MANAGERS' RESPONSIBILITIES

Federal agency managers and supervisors are responsible for the employment and advancement of people with disabilities.[2] This includes recruitment, hiring, training, career development, mentoring support and considering reasonable accommodations when requested.

Career development and promotion opportunities, training, awards, and other similar programs must be an integral part of an agency's responsibilities toward employees with disabilities. Federal employers are required to make reasonable accommodations to the known physical or mental limitations of a qualified applicant or employee with a disability, unless the agency can demonstrate that the accommodation(s) would impose an undue hardship on the agency. Absent undue hardship, agencies must remove physical barriers as a matter of reasonable accommodation to particular employees for whom necessary facilities are inaccessible.

Agencies are required to establish procedures to ensure that the employment and advancement of people with disabilities meets affirmative action program objectives, diversity planning, special emphasis, and accountability. They must also ensure that there are no personnel or management policies, practices or procedures which unnecessarily restrict hiring, placement, and advancement of people with disabilities.

It is illegal for a federal agency to discriminate in employment against qualified individuals with disabilities. Anyone who believes he or she has been subjected to discrimination on the basis of disability may file a complaint with the employing agency's equal employment opportunity (EEO) office.[3]

---

[2] Employment Guide for People With Disabilities in the Federal Government

[3] EEOC's MD-110 and 29 CFR, Part 1614. EEO complaint process.

Agencies have direct hire authority for Schedule A appointments. Therefore interested parties must contact individual agencies to determine what's available. Refer to the agency lists in Appendix C and the common resources listed in Chapter Three. Additional special hiring programs exist for disabled veterans. Refer to Chapter Seven for complete details.

Selective Placement Program Coordinators

Most federal agencies have a Selective Placement Program Coordinator, Special Emphasis Manager (SEP) for Employment of Adults with Disabilities, or equivalent, who helps agency management recruit, hire and accommodate people with disabilities at that agency. SEP managers develop, manage and evaluate the agency's Affirmative Employment Program for Individuals with Disabilities.

One of their primary responsibilities is to help persons with disabilities get information about current job opportunities, types of jobs in the agency and how these jobs are filled, and reasonable accommodation. SEP coordinators are subject to change due to transfers, retirements, and promotions. It is best to locate the most up-to-date contacts online at **http://apps.opm.gov/sppc_directory/**. The directory can be searched by agency or state. The SEP contacts are a primary resource for you to use to locate agencies in your area and potential employment prospects.

Many federal managers and HR specialists that you contact in the federal sector may not be aware of who their SEP contact is or that they even exist. You best bet is to contact the agency SEP first, and when you do talk to local HR specialists or managers, let them know who their agency SEP is and provide them with their contact information. The SEP serves a dual role, providing assistance to both disabled job seekers and managers.

Typical SEP Coordinator Directory Listing (by agency)

Alison Levy
Departmental Selective Placement Coordinator
Disability Resource Center
U.S. Department of Transportation
400 7th Street SW, Room 2110
Washington, DC 20590

Phone: (202) 366-5305
TTY: (202) 366-5273
Fax: (202) 366-3571
E-mail: alison.levy@dot.gov

The state search isn't very helpful, because most SEPs are located in headquarters offices in or around Washington, D.C. It is best to locate agencies in your area through your local Federal Executive Board, see listing in Appendix B, or your local phone book, and then contact that agency's SEP for assistance.

THE REHABILITATION ACT OF 1973

Section 501 of the Rehabilitation Act of 1973, as amended (29 U.S.C. Section 791) prohibits discrimination on the basis of disability in federal employment and requires the federal government to engage in affirmative action for people with disabilities. The law:

- Requires federal employers not to discriminate against qualified job applicants or employees with disabilities. Persons with disabilities should be employed in all grade levels and occupational series commensurate with their qualifications. Federal employers should ensure that their policies do not unnecessarily exclude or limit persons with disabilities because of a job's structure or because of architectural, transportation, communication, procedural, or attitudinal barriers.

- Requires employers to provide "reasonable accommodations" to applicants and employees with disabilities unless doing so would cause undue hardship to the employers. Such accommodations may involve, for example, restructuring the job, reassignment, modifying work schedules, adjusting or modifying examinations, providing readers or interpreters, and acquiring or modifying equipment and/or facilities (including the use of adaptive technology such as voice recognition software).

- Prohibits selection criteria and standards that tend to screen out people with disabilities, unless such procedures have been determined through a job analysis to be job-related and consistent with business necessity, and an appropriate individualized assessment indicates that the job applicant cannot perform the essential functions of the job, with or without reasonable accommodation.

- Requires Federal agencies to develop affirmative action programs for hiring, placement, and advancement of persons with disabilities. Affirmative action must be an integral part of ongoing agency personnel management programs.

HIRING OVERVIEW

In addition to competing for a position by applying through a vacancy announcement, the federal government's Selective Placement programs include special hiring authorities for hiring people with disabilities. You may apply for employment directly to agencies, which may use these authorities to streamline the appointment of people with disabilities. If you are interested in being considered under these special authorities, you should contact a state vocational rehabilitation agency or, if you are a veteran, a Department of Veterans Affairs vocational rehabilitation counselor, and request his/her assistance. Links to both groups can be found in the resources section of this chapter. You should ask the counselor to provide you with a "certification" statement that identifies you as a person with a disability and that describes your ability to perform the essential duties of the position in which you are interested. Then, once you have obtained this certification statement, you should contact the federal agency where you wish to work. Ask for the Selective Placement or Disability Employment coordinator or their equivalent.[4]

HIRING OPTIONS

The federal government provides opportunities for qualified persons with physical and mental disabilities. Applicants with handicaps must be considered fairly for all jobs in which they are able to perform the job duties efficiently and safely. To be eligible for these noncompetitive, Schedule A appointments, a person must meet the definition for being disabled. The person must have a severe physical, cognitive, or emotional disability; have a history of having such disability; or be perceived as having such disability. In addition, the person must obtain a certification letter from a state Vocational Rehabilitation Office or the Department of Veterans Affairs to be eligible for appointment under these special authorities.

Applicants with handicaps must be considered fairly for all jobs in which they are able to perform the job duties efficiently and safely.

Disabled veterans may also be considered under special hiring programs for disabled veterans with disability ratings from the Department of Veterans Affairs of 30 percent or more.

Agency human resource management departments encourage federal managers to give people with disabilities full and fair consideration, and to make accommodations when necessary. Although the majority of employees with handicaps obtain their jobs through competitive procedures, there are some for whom ordinary procedures do not function fairly or accurately. The competitive process is explained in Chapters Two and Three. To meet the needs of those with severe impairments, agencies may use the following special appointing techniques:

CERTIFICATION OF PERSONS WITH MENTAL RETARDATION, SEVERE PHYSICAL DISABILITIES, OR PSYCHIATRIC DISABILITIES

Agencies may appoint, on a permanent, time-limited, or temporary basis, a person with mental retardation, a severe physical disability, or a psychiatric disability if he or she meets the conditions described below.

---

[4] Federal Employment of People With Disabilities — OPM Web site

Proof of disability

The disabled applicant must present proof of his or her mental retardation, severe physical disability, or psychiatric disability prior to appointment. Agencies may accept, as proof of an individual's mental retardation, severe physical disability, or psychiatric disability, appropriate documentation (e.g., records, statements, or other appropriate information) issued from a licensed medical professional (e.g., a physician or other medical professional duly certified by a state, the District of Columbia, or a U.S. territory, to practice medicine); a licensed vocational rehabilitation specialist (i.e., state or private); or any federal agency, state agency, or an agency of the District of Columbia or a U.S. territory that issues or provides disability benefits.

Certification of job readiness

Certification that the individual is likely to succeed in the performance of the duties of the position for which he or she is applying is required. Certification of job readiness may be provided by any entity specified in the previous paragraph. In cases where certification has not been provided, the hiring agency may give the individual a temporary appointment under this authority to determine the individual's job readiness. The agency may also accept, at the agency's discretion, service under another type of temporary appointment in the competitive or excepted services as proof of job readiness.

APPOINTMENT TYPES

Permanent or time-limited employment options

Permanent or time-limited appointment is based upon proof of disability and certification of job readiness, or demonstration of job readiness through a temporary appointment.

Temporary employment options

Temporary appointments are based upon proof of disability as noted in the previous paragraphs. Temporary appointments are used when it is necessary to observe the applicant on the job to determine whether the applicant is able or ready to perform the duties of the position. When an agency uses this option to determine an individual's job readiness, the hiring agency may convert the individual to a permanent appointment whenever the agency determines the individual is able to perform the duties of the position or the individual has a certification of job readiness and the work is of a temporary nature.

Noncompetitive conversion to the competitive service

Agencies may noncompetitively convert an employee to the competitive service who completed two years of satisfactory service in a nontemporary appointment under this authority in accordance with the provisions of Executive Order 12125 as amended by Executive Order 13124 and Sec. 315.709. Disabled workers may receive credit for time spent on a temporary appointment towards the two-year requirement.

CONVERSION TO CAREER OR CAREER-CONDITIONAL EMPLOYMENT

A disabled employee who is appointed under 5 CFR Parts 213 and 315 may have his or her appointment converted to a career or career-conditional appointment when he or she:

1. Completes two or more years of satisfactory service, without a break of more than 30 days, under a nontemporary appointment;

2. Is recommended for such conversion by his or her supervisor;

3. Meets all requirements and conditions governing career and career-conditional appointment except those requirements concerning competitive selection from a register and medical qualifications; and

4. Is converted without a break in service of one workday.

Employees who are converted under these regulations becomes career-conditional employees, with a few exceptions, or career employee if he or she has completed three years of substantially continuous service in a temporary appointment.

TEMPORARY LIMITED APPOINTMENTS

Temporary appointments are made when the need for the position is short-term and not expected to last for more than one year. Temporary jobs are filled through competitive procedures with a requirement for public notice. Under limited circumstances, agencies may use "outside-the-register" procedures. Agencies may also give noncompetitive temporary appointments to individuals who qualify for positions and have a specific noncompetitive eligibility such as reinstatement or veterans readjustment appointment (VRA) (5 CFR 316.402).

Time Limits: Appointments are not to exceed one year; a one-year extension is allowed.

TERM APPOINTMENTS

Term appointments are made when the need for an employee's services will last for a period of more than one year, but no more than four years. Reasons for term appointments may include, but not be limited to, project work, extraordinary workload, and uncertainty of future funding. Term positions are filled through competitive procedures with the requirement for public notice.

These positions may also be filled by qualified individuals based on specific noncompetitive eligibility such as reinstatement and veterans readjustment appointment (VRA) (5 CFR Part 316.302).

Time Limits: Appointments are made for more than one year but not more than four years.

Conversion: This authority does not contain a provision for conversion to a permanent appointment when the term expires.

STUDENT VOLUNTEER PROGRAM

Agencies may provide educationally-related work assignments for student volunteers on a non-pay basis. (5 CFR 308.103)

Requirements: The student is enrolled at least half-time in a high school, trade school, vocational institute, university, or other accredited educational institution, and the school permits the participation of the student in a program established to provide educational experience.

Time Limits: No time limits have been established for these appointments, as long as the student continues to meet program requirements.

COMPETITIVE VERSUS EXCEPTED SERVICE

People with disabilities may start their federal career in the Excepted Service in temporary positions, while most federal jobs are in the Competitive Service.

Congress excepted certain jobs and groups from the Competitive Service. In the Competitive Service, individuals must compete for positions through examination. The end result is that individuals are placed on a competitive register in rank order of their rating. Agencies then can select from the top three candidates on the list when vacancies arise.

The Excepted Service includes a number of agencies such as the CIA, FBI, National Security Agency, Federal Aviation Administration, and about a dozen others. Specific jobs are also excepted and include the Stay-in-School program, student interns, veterans readjustment appointments, and the physically and mentally impaired programs discussed above. Excepted Service employees on permanent excepted appointments are eligible for all benefits including health insurance, life insurance, leave, retirement, and they are eligible for promotion and reassignment just like those in the Competitive Service. The first year of employment is a trial period similar to the one-year probationary period for the Competitive Service.

There are some differences between these two appointments. First, Excepted Service employees are not eligible for transfer to other agencies or for non-competitive reinstatement that is afforded to Competitive Service employees. Excepted Service employees are also placed in a separate category when agencies go through a reduction in force, typically referred to as layoffs in private industry.

These differences cease to exist after the two year period of acceptable performance is achieved. Workers with physical or mental impairments may be converted to the Competitive Service upon supervisory recommendation as noted above for many appointments.

UNPAID WORK EXPERIENCE

Most rehabilitation organizations include on-the-job training and job placement programs for participants. Vocational rehabilitation centers work with federal agencies to place people with disabilities in jobs that provide meaningful work experience. Agencies benefit from the services provided by these workers and they get an opportunity to evaluate a prospective employee.

Federal regulations limit unpaid services from a person with disabilities to those who are clients of a state *Office of Vocational Rehabilitation* (OVR). Applicants must be enrolled in an OVR program. Signed agreements must be initiated between the rehabilitation center and the federal agency. Agencies can negotiate these agreements individually with local Vocational Rehabilitation Facilities. Once an agreement is initiated, the agreement covers all participants. Individuals accepted into these programs don't receive any compensation from the government; however, many sponsors provide a small stipend to the worker.

Federal regulations limit unpaid services from a person with disabilities to those who are clients of a state OVR.

SPECIAL ACCOMMODATIONS

When appropriate, OPM uses special examination (testing) procedures for applicants who are physically handicapped to assure that their abilities are properly and fairly assessed.[5] Special testing arrangements are determined on an individual basis depending on the applicant's disability. For example: readers, examinations in Braille, tape, or large print for visually impaired competitors; interpreters for test instructions and modifications of parts of tests for hearing-impaired competitors.

Accommodations on the Job

When federal agencies hire a person with disabilities, efforts are made to accommodate the individual to remove or modify barriers to his or her ability to effectively perform the essential duties of the position. Agencies may, for example: (1) provide interpreter service for the hearing impaired, (2) use readers for the visually impaired, (3) modify job duties, (4) restructure work sites, (5) alter work schedules, and (6) obtain special equipment or furniture.

The Rehabilitation Act of 1973, as amended, requires federal agencies to provide reasonable accommodations to qualified employees or applicants with disabilities, unless doing so would cause an undue hardship to the agency. (An undue hardship means that a specific accommodation would require significant difficulty or expense.) A reasonable accommodation is any change to a job, the work environment, or the way things are usually done that allows an individual with

---

[5]U.S. OPM, Office of Affirmative Employment Programs, ES-5 (GPO 0-157-269).

a disability to apply for a job, perform the essential job functions, or enjoy equal access to benefits available to other individuals in the workplace.

Federal agencies are required to develop written procedures for providing reasonable accommodation. You may gain greater understanding of your specific situation and alternatives available to you by reading the agency's reasonable-accommodation procedures. Different agencies place responsibility for reasonable-accommodation in different offices. Contact the agency's personnel office, reason-able-accommodation coordinator, civil rights office, or EEO office to request a copy of the agency's written procedures.[6]

COMMON JOB SOURCES

This section presents resources that can be used to locate federal job announcements for people with disabilities. After reviewing the listed resources, refer to Appendix D for a complete list of federal occupations. A number of the periodicals and directories listed in this chapter are available at libraries. Many newsletter and periodical publishers will send complimentary review copies of their publications upon request.

Resource headings include job openings, placement services, directories, and general information. Job openings include publications with job ads, job hot lines, and Internet Web sites. The general information section lists related books, pamphlets, and Internet fact sheets. All job sources are listed alphabetically. For additional resources refer to Chapter Three's listings.

---

[6] Reasonable-accommodation policy per Executive Order 13164

JOB OPENINGS

Job Listings and Information Services

ABILITY Jobs & Resumes — 1001 W. 17th St., Costa Mesa, California 92627; 949-854-8700, e-mail generalinquiries@jobaccess.org. ABILITY provides information on new technologies, the "Americans with Disabilities Act," employment opportunities for people with disabilities and more. Call or visit their Web site for additional information and to post your résumé online. ABILITY also offers **JobAccess** to recruit qualified individuals with disabilities. Locate job opportunities on the Web site at http://www.jobaccess.org/.

Disabilities Resource Center — http://www.disabilityinfor.gov

A comprehensive federal government online resource designed to provide people with disabilities with quick and easy access to the information they need. The site provides access to disability-related information and programs available across the government on numerous subjects, including benefits, civil rights, community life, education, employment, housing, health, technology and transportation.

CAREERS & The DisAbled (Equal Opportunity Publications) — 445 Broad Hollow Rd, Suite 425, Melville, NY 11747, 631-421-9421, e-mail:info@eop.com, Web site: http://eop.com. This company publishes a number of excellent target audience publications. Call for subscription rates. A résumé matching service is also available to subscribers.

Diversity Services — http://www.diversity-services.com

Diversity Services was created to address the issues of diversity in today's ever-changing workplace. Diversity Services builds bridges to create workforce inclusion of all qualified individuals regardless of race, age, sexual orientation, or disability.

Federal Employment of People with Disabilities — http://opm.gov/disability/

This site provides a simple and straightforward mechanism to help Americans, with and without disabilities, better understand how to hire and retain persons with disabilities. The target audiences are applicants and employees with disabilities, federal managers and supervisors, and human resources professionals.

This excellent site provides access to information that is relevant to the recruitment, employment, and retention of individuals with disabilities in the federal government and includes federal and state laws as well as other governmental and non-governmental sites.

Federaljobs.net — http://federaljobs.net

This career center assists visitors with their federal government job search and guides them through the process. Search this site for key words and phrases. Includes a listing of over 200 federal agency employment Web sites that you can visit for up-to-date job listings and agency information.

Healthcarejobs.org — http://healthcarejobs.org

Explore high growth health care occupations, evaluate related occupations, and find job vacancies and networking contacts. Occupational descriptions include working conditions, qualifications, training and advancement, employment opportunities, required certifications and licenses, and job outlook and earnings.

JAN — Job Accommodation Network http://www.jan.wvu.edu/

A free consulting service designed to increase the employability of people with disabilities by providing individualized worksite accommodations, technical assistance regarding the ADA and other disability related legislation, and educating callers about self-employment options. The Job Accommodation Network (JAN) is a service of the U.S. Department of Labor Office of Disability Employment Policy, hosted by West Virginia University. This site is a wealth of information for job seekers. You can call **1-800-526-7234, voice and 877-781-9403 TTY.**

JobAccess — http://www.jobaccess.org

This site helps employers recruit qualified individuals with disabilities. The goal of JobAccess is to enable people with disabilities to enhance their professional lives by providing a dedicated system for finding employment. People with disabilities can locate viable employment opportunities at this Web site.

National Business and Disability Council — http://www.business-disability.com

The National Business and Disability Council links employers and college graduates with disabilities. It offers a free national résumé database, job search, career events and internship information. E-mail lbroder@abilitiesonline.org for additional information.

State Vocational & Rehabilitation Agencies *(2 resources listed)*

http://www.parac.org/svrp.html

http://www.jan.wvu.edu/cgi-win/TypeQuery.exe?902

The Rehabilitation Council and the JAN Network both offer a list of state vocational and rehabilitation agencies and contact information for disabled persons. These services can include counseling, evaluation, training and job placement. There are also services for the sight and hearing impaired. Visit this site for direct links to state Vocational and Rehabilitation Agencies. Call or write the office nearest you.

The ARC of the United States, 800-433-5255

1010 Wayne Ave., Suite 650, Silver Spring, MD 20910. National organization that you may find helpful in seeking job leads, placement, training, or assistance in the employment process such as résumé writing and interviewing techniques. You can join their online job registry at http://www.thearc.org.

Unemployment Offices Listings by State

http://www.servicelocator.org/OWSLinks.asp

This site offers Internet Web links to all 50 state unemployment offices. Visit this site to find the unemployment office nearest you.

Job Hotlines

Department of Veterans Affairs, 800-827-1000

The Department of Veterans Affairs supports a nationwide employment training program for veterans with service-connected disabilities who qualify for vocational rehabilitation. Regional or local offices are listed under federal government agencies in the telephone directory.

JAN — Job Accommodation Network, 800-526-7234 and 800-ADA-WORK (V/TTY)

The Job Accommodation Network (JAN) is *not* a job placement service, but an international toll-free consulting service that provides information about job accommodations and the employability of people with disabilities. JAN is a service of the President's Committee on Employment of People with Disabilities. It also provides information regarding the Americans with Disabilities Act (ADA). Visit the Web site at http://janweb.icdi.wvu.edu/.

USA JOBS by Phone — Federal government job hotline, **703-724-1850** or TDD 978-461-8404. Operated by the Office of Personnel Management. Phone answers 24 hours a day. Provides federal employment information for most occupations. Easy-to-use online voice prompts and voice commands allow access with any touch tone or rotary dial telephone.

PLACEMENT SERVICES

State Vocational and Rehabilitation Agencies

http://www.jan.wvu.edu/cgi-win/TypeQuery.exe?902

State vocational and rehabilitation agencies coordinate and provide a number of services for disabled persons. These services can include counseling, evaluation, training and job placement.

> NOTE: Many of the OVR and VA rehabilitation centers offer job placement services. Many associations also offer valuable services including job placement to their members. Refer to the association list that follow and contact local OVR and VA facilities in your area to identify available job placement services.

DIRECTORIES

ADA Technical Assistance and Resource Manual — U.S. Equal Employment Oppor-tunity Commission, 1801 L St. NW, Washington, DC 20507; 800-669-EEOC (Voice) or 800-800-3302 (TTY). Visit the Web site at http://eeoc.gov/ for ordering information and cost.

Encyclopedia of Associations 2007 — The Gale Group, 2700 Drake Road, Farmington Hills, MI 48331; 800-877-GALE, Internet http://www.gale.com/. Lists thousands of associations and it is available at most larger libraries. Use this resource to identify associations for your specific disability. This resource is also available in two additional formats including CD ROM and online. Most large libraries carry this title in their reference section.

Selective Placement Program Coordinators http://apps.opm.gov/sppc_directory/

Most federal agencies have a Selective Placement Program Coordinator, Special Emphasis Manager (SEP) for Employment of Adults with Disabilities who helps agency management recruit, hire and accommodate people with disabilities at that agency. They help persons with disabilities get information about current job opportunities, types of jobs in the agency and how these jobs are filled, and reasonable accommodation.

ASSOCIATIONS

Associations and Organizations

The following is a list of associations and organizations that offer numerous services to people with physical or mental impairments. Many offer job placement services, on-site accessibility surveys, job analysis, and advice and support to the group represented. Contact individual listings for details.

American Cancer Society — 1-800-ACS-2345; http://www.cancer.org. Refers employers to organizations offering help in recruiting qualified individuals with disabilities, and community programs offering consultation and technical assistance to cancer patients, survivors, and their families.

American Council of the Blind — 1155 15th St. NW, Suite 1004, Washington, DC 20005; 202-467-5081 or 800-424-8666, http://www.acb.org/. Provides information on topics affecting the employment of individuals who are blind, including job seeking strategies, job accommodations, electronic aids, and employment discrimination. Provides information on job openings for individuals who are blind and visually impaired. Offers free legal assistance.

American Speech-Language-Hearing Association — 10801 Rockville Pike, Rockville, MD 20852; 1-800-638-8255, http://www.asha.org/. Information and technical assistance on overcoming communication barriers.

The ARC—1010 Wayne Ave., Suite 650, Silver Spring, MD 20910, 301-565-3842, http://www.thearc.org/. (Formerly Association for Retarded Citizens of the United States). The country's largest voluntary organization committed to the welfare of all children and adults with mental retardation and their families.

Arthritis Foundation — P.O. Box 7669, Atlanta, Georgia 30357; 800-568-4045, http://Arthritis.org/. Helps people with arthritis and lupus obtain and retain employment.

Disabled American Veterans — 3725 Alexandria Pike, Cold Springs, KY 41076; 877-426-2838, http://www.dav.org/. Provides information on recruitment sources for veterans with disabilities. Offers a broad range of services.

Epilepsy Foundation of America — 8301 Professional Place, Landover, MD 20785; 800-332-1000 (Voice/TDD), http://www.efa.org/. Maintains a network of local employment assistance programs, which provide education and support to employers on epilepsy and employment issues, including employment referrals.

Helen Keller National Center for Deaf-Blind Youths and Adults — 141 Middle Neck Rd., Sands Point, NY 11050; 516-944-8900 (voice/TDD). Visit the Web site at http://www.helenkeller.org/. Provides job placement for deaf-blind individuals, and on-site support services for employers and employees.

Mental Health America — 1021 Prince St., Alexandria, VA 22314; 800-969-NHMA, TTY line 800-433-5959. Visit http://www.nmha.org. Mental Health America (formerly known as the National Mental Health Association) is a leading non-profit dedicated to helping all people live mentally healthier lives. With their more than 320 affiliates nationwide, they provide valuable services to promote mental wellness for the health and well-being of the nation.

National Center for Learning Disabilities — 381 Park Ave. South, Suite 1401, New York, NY 10016; 888-575-7373, http://www.ncld.org/. Provides information, referral, public education and outreach programs on the learning-disabled. Offers job placement and publishes a quarterly newsletter.

National Down Syndrome Congress —1370 Center Drive, Suite 102, Atlanta, GA 30328. Phone, 800-232-6372, http:/www.ndsccenter.org/. Provides general information on Down syndrome and the employment of individuals with Down syndrome.

National Multiple Sclerosis Society — 733 Third Avenue, New York, NY 10017. Phone: 1-800-344-4867. http://nationalmssociety.org. The society helps those with MS with the challenges of living with the disease through 50 state chapters. It funds MS research, provides services to MS patients, offers professional education and other helpful services.

National Spinal Cord Injury Association — 8701 Georgia Avenue., Suite 500, Silver Spring, MD 20910. Phone, 301-588-6959, visit the Internet Web site at http://www.spinalcord.org/. The mission of the National Spinal Cord Injury Association (NSCIA) is to enable people with spinal cord injury and disease (SCI/D) to achieve their highest level of independence, health, and personal fulfillment by providing resources, services, and peer support.

Spina Bifida Association of America — 4590 MacArthur Blvd. NW, Suite 250, Washington, DC 20007-4226. Phone, 1-800-621-3141, 202-944-3285. Visit the Web site at http://www.sbaa.org/. Since 1973, SBAA has served as the nation's only voluntary health agency dedicated to enhancing the lives of those with spina bifida and those whose lives they touch. Through its network of 57 chapters, SBA has a presence in more than 125 communities nationwide and serves thousands of people each year.

United Cerebral Palsy Association —1660 L Street NW, Suite 700, Washington, DC 20036. Phone, 800-872-5827, http://www.ucpa.org/. The United Cerebral Palsy Association's mission is to advance the independence, productivity and full citizenship of people with disabilities through an affiliate network.

Books, Pamphlets, and Brochures

Americans with Disabilities Act — A Guide for People with Disabilities Seeking Employment - U.S. Equal Employment Opportunity Commission Clearing House, 8280 Greenboro Drive, Suite 300, McLean, VA 22102; 800-669-3362 or 800-800-3302 (TTYS). Visit their Web site at http://www.eeoc.gov/ for ordering information and cost.

JAN (Job Accommodation Network) — It will send out an informational brochure upon request. Most of the pamphlets can be reviewed online at the Web site, http://janweb.icdi.wvu.edu. Call 1-800-526-7234 for free consulting and information about job accommodations and the employability of people with disabilities.

Most of the associations listed in this chapter provide information upon request or provide online pamphlets, databases, and directories to assist members. Visit the association relevant to your diagnosis and register online to join the organization. Upon registration you will have significant resources and contacts available to assist you with your job search.

CHAPTER ELEVEN
Law Enforcement and
Homeland Security Careers

The Department of Homeland Security (DHS) is constantly changing to better manage its diverse mission. DHS was formed after the September 11, 2001, attacks, to protect the nation against terrorism. The department was the first addition in over 40 years to the executive branch, and it is now the third largest department, employing over 154,000 federal workers. Homeland Security consolidated 22 agencies from various departments to unify the war on terror.[1]

Homeland Security has had a significant impact on federal law enforcement careers in general, and many functions were transferred to DHS. The federal government employs over 180,000 law enforcement personnel in more than 40 job series (see Table 11-1). Most federal agencies employ law enforcement specialists in one capacity or another. Work in law enforcement is not limited to investigative, police, compliance and security positions. There are tens of thousands of federal employees working in occupations that provide direct support to these groups.

Over 180,000 law enforcement personnel work for Uncle Sam.

CHAPTER OBJECTIVES

✎   Explore federal law enforcement occupations

✎   Learn about opportunities with Homeland Security

✎   Determine job qualifications *(review several qualification standards for the largest occupations)*

✎   Locate hiring agencies *(TSA security screeners, agents, investigators, FBI, CIA, Secret Service, and others)*

✎   Review typical working conditions, employment, training requirements, job outlook, and earnings

---

[1] Securing Our Homeland, U.S. Department of Homeland Security Strategic Plan 2004

The Department of Homeland Security transferred functions from the Departments of the Treasury, Justice, HHS, Defense, FBI, Secret Service, GSA, Energy, Agriculture, Transportation and the U.S. Coast Guard. The new organization was originally composed of five major Directorates, listed below. Agencies in parentheses were originally responsible for the listed service:

- **Border and Transportation Security**

  - U.S. Customs Service (Treasury)
  - Immigration& Naturalization Service (Justice)
  - Federal Protective Service
  - Transportation Security (Transportation)
  - Federal Law Enforcement Training Center (Justice)
  - Animal & Plant Health Inspection Service (Agriculture)
  - Office for Domestic Preparedness (Justice)

- **Emergency Preparedness and Response**

  - Federal Emergency Management Agency (FEMA)
  - Strategic National Stockpile & National Disaster Medical System (HHS)
  - Nuclear Incident Response Team (Energy)
  - Domestic Emergency Support Team (Justice)
  - National Domestic Preparedness Office (FBI)

- **Information Analysis and Infrastructure Protection**

  - Federal Computer Incident Response Center (GSA)
  - National Communications System (Defense)
  - National Infrastructure Protection Center (FBI)
  - Energy Security and Assurance Program (Energy)

- **Science and Technology**

  - CBRN Countermeasures Program (Energy)
  - Environmental Measurement Laboratory (Energy)
  - National BW Defense Analysis Center (Defense)
  - Plum Island Animal Disease Center (Agriculture)

- **Management**

The Secret Service and the Coast Guard are also with the DHS. They will remain intact and report directly to the secretary. In addition, the Immigration and Naturalization Service (INS) adjudications and benefits programs report directly to the deputy secretary as the U.S. Citizenship and Immigration Service.

In 2006 DHS established a new organizational structure that you can view online at http://www.dhs.gov/xabout/structure/editorial_0644.shtm. The elements of the original directorates remain with DHS.

LAW ENFORCEMENT

Many federal investigative jobs have age requirements, and applicants must be at least 21 years of age and under the age of 37 at the time of appointment. Other positions state that you must be 21 years of age and be a U.S. citizen. Each job announcement lists the required qualifications for that position. If you want to work in law enforcement, and you are over age 37, your options are limited; you may have to consider a support position that does not have an age limit.

The federal government maintains a high profile in many areas of law enforcement. Federal Bureau of Investigation (FBI) agents are the government's principal investigators, responsible for investigating violations of more than 200 categories of federal law and conducting sensitive national security investigations. Agents may conduct surveillance, monitor court-authorized wiretaps, examine business records, investigate white-collar crime, or participate in sensitive undercover assignments. The FBI investigates organized crime, public corruption, financial crime, fraud against the government, bribery, copyright infringement, civil rights violations, bank robbery, extortion, kidnaping, air piracy, terrorism, espionage, interstate criminal activity, drug trafficking, and other violations of federal statutes.[2]

U.S. Drug Enforcement Administration (DEA) agents enforce laws and regulations relating to illegal drugs. Not only is the DEA the lead agency for domestic enforcement of federal drug laws, but it also has sole responsibility for coordinating and pursuing U.S. drug investigations abroad. Agents may conduct complex criminal investigations, carry out surveillance of criminals, and infiltrate illicit drug organizations using undercover techniques.

U.S. marshals and deputy marshals protect the federal courts and ensure the effective operation of the judicial system. They provide protection for the federal judiciary, transport federal prisoners, protect federal witnesses, and manage assets seized from criminal enterprises. They enjoy the widest jurisdiction of any federal law enforcement agency and are involved to some degree in nearly all federal law enforcement efforts. In addition, U.S. marshals pursue and arrest federal fugitives.

Bureau of Alcohol, Tobacco, Firearms, and Explosives agents regulate and investigate violations of federal firearms and explosives laws, as well as federal alcohol and tobacco tax regulations.

The U.S. Department of State *Bureau of Diplomatic Security special agents* are engaged in the battle against terrorism. Overseas, they advise ambassadors on all security matters and manage a complex range of security programs designed to

---

[2] Occupational Outlook Handbook, 2006/2007 (OHH)

protect personnel, facilities, and information. In the United States, they investigate passport and visa fraud, conduct personnel security investigations, issue security clearances, and protect the secretary of state and a number of foreign dignitaries. They also train foreign civilian police and administer a counter-terrorism reward program.

The Department of Homeland Security employs numerous law enforcement officers under several different agencies, including *Customs and Border Protection, Immigration and Customs Enforcement,* and the *U.S. Secret Service. U.S. Border Patrol agents* protect more than 8,000 miles of international land and water boundaries. Their missions are to detect and prevent the smuggling and unlawful entry of undocumented foreign nationals into the United States; to apprehend those persons violating the immigration laws; and to interdict contraband, such as narcotics.

Immigration inspectors interview and examine people seeking entrance to the United States and its territories. They inspect passports to determine whether people are legally eligible to enter the United States. Immigration inspectors also prepare reports, maintain records, and process applications and petitions for immigration or temporary residence in the United States.

Customs inspectors enforce laws governing imports and exports by inspecting cargo, baggage, and articles worn or carried by people, vessels, vehicles, trains, and aircraft entering or leaving the United States. These inspectors examine, count, weigh, gauge, measure, and sample commercial and noncommercial cargoes entering and leaving the United States. Customs inspectors seize prohibited or smuggled articles; intercept contraband; and apprehend, search, detain, and arrest violators of U.S. laws. *Customs agents* investigate violations, such as narcotics smuggling, money laundering, child pornography, and customs fraud, and they enforce the Arms Export Control Act. During domestic and foreign investigations, they develop and use informants; conduct physical and electronic surveillance; and examine records from importers and exporters, banks, couriers, and manufacturers. They conduct interviews, serve on joint task forces with other agencies, and get and execute search warrants.

Federal Air Marshals provide air security by fighting attacks targeting U.S. airports, passengers, and crews. They pose as ordinary passengers and board flights of U.S. air carriers to locations worldwide.

U.S. Secret Service special agents protect the president, vice president, and their immediate families; presidential candidates; former presidents; and foreign dignitaries visiting the United States. Secret Service agents also investigate counterfeiting, forgery of government checks or bonds, and fraudulent use of credit cards.

Other federal agencies employ police and special agents with sworn arrest powers and the authority to carry firearms. These agencies include the Postal Service, the Bureau of Indian Affairs Office of Law Enforcement, the Forest Service, and the National Park Service.

WORKING CONDITIONS

Law enforcement work can be very dangerous and stressful. In addition to the obvious dangers of confrontations with criminals, officers need to be constantly alert and ready to deal appropriately with a number of other threatening situations. Many law enforcement officers witness death and suffering resulting from accidents and criminal behavior. A career in law enforcement may take a toll on officers' private lives.

Uniformed officers, detectives, agents, and inspectors are usually scheduled to work 40-hour weeks, but paid overtime is common. Shift work is necessary because protection must be provided around the clock. Junior officers frequently work weekends, holidays, and nights. Police officers and detectives are required to work at any time their services are needed and may work long hours during investigations. In most jurisdictions, whether on or off duty, officers are expected to be armed and to exercise their arrest authority whenever necessary.

The jobs of some federal agents such as U.S. Secret Service and DEA special agents require extensive travel, often on very short notice. They may relocate a number of times over the course of their careers. Some special agents in agencies such as the Border Patrol work outdoors in rugged terrain for long periods and in all kinds of weather.

EMPLOYMENT

There are approximately 180,000 law enforcement workers in the federal government. There are many more in support occupations such as administrative officers, clerks, logistics specialists, etc. The Justice Department is the largest employer of (GS-1811) criminal investigators, employing 22,448. The Department of Homeland Security is the second largest employer of this series with 9,509 criminal investigators. Total criminal investigator employment is 40,067. Correctional officers (GS-0007) are employed by two agencies — the Department of Justice has 16,167 officers, and Interior employs the remaining 106. All Internal Revenue officers (GS-1169) are employed by the Treasury Department.

Airport screeners and immigration inspection occupations are now in the GS-1802 job series.

Table 11-1 lists the major occupations, the total number employed in parentheses, the largest employing agency, and number of workers employed. There are two significant changes to this table since the last edition was published. Airport screeners, originally classified under the GS-0019 job series, and immigration inspection, originally classified under the GS-1816 series, are both included in the GS-1802 Compliance, Inspection, and Support series.

Use Table 11-1 to identify viable opportunities and then visit those agencies' recruiting sites or call their human resources departments. A list of agency phone numbers is included in Chapter Three, and Appendix C provides a description of each agency with contact information and Web site addresses.

You can use the job series or titles on the following table to search for job vacancy announcements on http://www.usajobs.gov. This site allows job series or occupational title searches and also offers e-mail notification for specific job series announcements. You can register on this site for free e-mail notification for job vacancies and compile your federal style résumé online. Also, visit the specific agency Web sites where law enforcement jobs are posted. Not all agencies advertise on OPM's Web site. You will find abundant information, and in some cases, online testing and applications on several law enforcement agency Web sites. Go to http://federaljobs.net/federal.htm to link direct to 140-plus federal agency recruitment sites.

Homeland Security advertises most jobs through OPM's Web site at http://usajobs.opm.gov. However, it does offer some online applications for specific jobs on http://www.dhs.gov and provides informative applicant study guides, career information, and videos. U.S. Immigration and Customs Enforcement (ICE) site at http://ice.gov offers career information for federal Air Marshal, Office of Intelligence, Detention and Removal, Air and Marine Operations, and Office of Investigations.

Table 11-1 does not list support occupations that are available, such as a number of occupations under general administration, clerical, office services, communications, IT professionals, chemistry and biological science. A number of positions in these occupations are recruited in support of most law enforcement organizations. Also, check out the Skills Index in Appendix E to locate other agencies that hire law enforcement specialists.

TABLE 11-1 Law Enforcement Employment Occupations			
Job Series (GS)	**Title**	**Total Employment**	**Largest Employing Department**
0006	Correctional Administration	1,678	Justice (1,642)
0007	Correctional Officer	16,273	Justice (16,167)
0025	Park Ranger	6,009	Interior (4,922)
0072	Fingerprint Identification	434	Justice (373)
0080	Security Administration	9,234	Defense (5,180)
0083	Police Officer	12,291	Defense (6,120)
0101	Social Science	7,597	Defense (1,962)
0132	Intelligence	8,793	Defense (3,957)
0180	Psychology	4,382	Vet. Admin. (2,471)
0249	Wage & Hour Compliance	938	Labor (938)
0390	Telecomm. Processing	513	Defense (228)
0436	Plant Protection/Quarantine	23	Agriculture (23)
1169	Internal Revenue Officer	6,032	Treasury (6,032)
1397	Document Analysis	111	Justice (50)
1801	General Insp., Investigation	23,689	Homeland Security (16,076)
1802*	Compliance Insp.& Support	53,212	Homeland Security (50,264)
1810	General Investigation	462	Agriculture (60)
1811	Criminal Investigation	40,944	Justice (22,448)
1812	Game Law Enforcement	67	Defense (51)
1822	Mine Safety & Health	1,218	Labor (1,218)
1854	Alcohol, Tobacco & Firearms	202	Treasury (152)
1889	Import Specialist	990	Homeland Security (990)
1896	Border Patrol Agent	12,278	Homeland Security (12,278)
2121	Railroad Safety	466	Transportation (466)
2151	Radio Dispatching	805	Defense (6203)
2181	Aircraft Operations	2,564	Defense (2,218)

Employment statistics obtained from OPM's September 2006 Employment & Trends
* Airport screeners and immigration inspection are now under the GS-1802 job series.

TRAINING AND QUALIFICATIONS OVERVIEW

Federal civil service regulations govern the appointment of law enforcement officers, police and detectives. Candidates must be U.S. citizens, usually at least 20 years of age, and must meet rigorous physical and personal qualifications. In the federal government, candidates must be at least 21 years of age but less than 37 years of age at the time of appointment. Physical examinations for entrance into law enforcement often include tests of vision, hearing, strength, and agility. Eligibility for appointment usually depends on performance in competitive written examinations and previous education and experience. Federal agencies typically require a college degree. Candidates should enjoy working with people and meeting the public.

Because personal characteristics such as honesty, sound judgment, integrity, and a sense of responsibility are especially important in law enforcement, candidates are interviewed and their character traits and backgrounds are investigated. In some agencies, candidates are interviewed by a psychiatrist or a psychologist, or given a personality test. Most applicants are subjected to lie detector examinations or drug testing. Some agencies subject sworn personnel to random drug testing as a condition of continuing employment.

Before their first assignments, officers usually go through a period of training. In federal departments, recruits get training in their agency's academy, often for 12 to 14 weeks. Training includes classroom instruction in constitutional law and civil rights, state laws and local ordinances, and accident investigation. Recruits also receive training and supervised experience in patrol, traffic control, use of firearms, self-defense, first aid, and emergency response.

Police officers usually become eligible for promotion after a probationary period ranging from six months to three years. Promotion may enable an officer to become a detective or specialize in one type of police work, such as working with juveniles. Promotions to corporal, sergeant, lieutenant, and captain usually are made according to a candidate's position on a promotion list, as determined by scores on a written examination and on-the-job performance.

The FBI has the largest number of special agents. To be considered for appointment as an FBI agent, an applicant must be either a graduate of an accredited law school or a college graduate with a major in accounting, fluency in a foreign language, or three years of related full-time work experience. All new agents undergo 16 weeks of training at the FBI academy on the U.S. Marine Corps base in Quantico, Virginia.

Applicants for special agent jobs with the Secret Service and the Bureau of Alcohol, Tobacco, and Firearms must have a bachelor's degree or a minimum of three years' related work experience. Prospective special agents undergo 11 weeks of initial criminal investigation training at the Department of Homeland Security's Federal Law Enforcement Training Center in Glynco, Georgia, and another 17 weeks of specialized training with their particular agencies.

Applicants for special agent jobs with the U.S. Drug Enforcement Administration (DEA) must have a college degree and either one year of experience conducting criminal investigations, one year of graduate school, or have achieved at least a 2.95 grade point average while in college. DEA special agents undergo 14 weeks of specialized training at the FBI Academy in Quantico, Virginia.

U.S. Border Patrol agents must be U.S. citizens, younger than 37 years of age at the time of appointment, possess a valid driver's license, and pass a three-part examination on reasoning and language skills. A bachelor's degree or previous work experience that demonstrates the ability to handle stressful situations, make decisions, and take charge is required for a position as a Border Patrol agent. Applicants may qualify through a combination of education and work experience.

Postal inspectors must have a bachelor's degree and one year of related work experience. It is desirable that they have one of several professional certifications, such as that of certified public accountant. They also must pass a background suitability investigation, meet certain health requirements, undergo a drug screening test, possess a valid state driver's license, and be a U.S. citizen between 21 and 36 years of age when hired.

Law enforcement agencies are encouraging applicants to take post-secondary school training in law enforcement-related subjects. Many entry-level applicants for police jobs have completed some formal post-secondary education and a significant number are college graduates. Many junior colleges, colleges, and universities offer programs in law enforcement or administration of justice. Other courses helpful in preparing for a career in law enforcement include accounting, finance, electrical engineering, computer science, and foreign languages. Physical education and sports are helpful in developing the competitiveness, stamina, and agility needed for many law enforcement positions. Knowledge of a foreign language is an asset in many federal agencies.

Continuing training helps police officers, detectives, and special agents improve their job performance. Through police department academies, regional centers for public safety employees established by the states, and federal agency training centers, instructors provide annual training in self-defense tactics, firearms, use-of-force policies, crowd-control techniques, sensitivity and communications skills, relevant legal developments, and advances in law enforcement equipment. Many agencies pay all or part of the tuition for officers to work toward degrees in criminal justice, police science, administration of justice, or public administration, and pay higher salaries to those who earn such a degree.

JOB OUTLOOK

The opportunity for public service through law enforcement work is attractive to many because the job is challenging and involves much personal responsibility. Furthermore, law enforcement officers in many agencies may retire with a pension after 25 or 30 years of service, allowing them to pursue a second career while still in their forties. Because of relatively attractive salaries and benefits, the number of qualified candidates exceeds the number of job openings in federal law enforcement agencies, resulting in increased hiring standards and selectivity by employers. Competition is expected to remain keen for the higher-paying jobs with state and federal agencies and police departments in more affluent areas. Applicants with college training in police science, military police experience, or both should have the best opportunities.

Employment of police and detectives is expected to increase about as fast as the average for all occupations through 2014. A more security-conscious society and concern about drug-related crimes should contribute to the increasing demand for police services. Employment growth at the federal level is currently being driven by the war on terror; however, employment will be tempered by continuing budgetary constraints faced by law enforcement agencies.

The level of government spending determines the level of employment for police officers, detectives, and special agents. The number of job opportunities, therefore, can vary from year to year and from place to place. Layoffs, on the other hand, are rare because retirements enable most staffing cuts to be handled through attrition. Trained law enforcement officers who lose their jobs because of budget cuts usually have little difficulty finding jobs with other agencies. The need to replace workers who retire, transfer to other occupations, or stop working for other reasons will be the source of many job openings.

EARNINGS

In May 2004, median annual earnings of detectives and criminal investigators were $53,990. The middle 50 percent earned between $40,690 and $72,280. The lowest 10 percent earned less than $32,180, and the highest 10 percent earned more than $86,010. Median annual earnings were $75,700 in federal government, $46,670 in state government, and $49,650 in local government.

Federal law provides special salary rates to federal employees who serve in law enforcement. Additionally, federal special agents and inspectors receive law enforcement availability pay (LEAP) — equal to 25 percent of the agent's grade and step — awarded because of the large amount of overtime that these agents are expected to work. For example, in 2005, FBI agents entered federal service as GS-10 employees on the pay scale at a base salary of $42,548, yet they earned about $53,185 a year with availability pay. They could advance to the GS-13 grade level in field nonsupervisory assignments at a base salary of $64,478, which was worth $80,597 with availability pay. FBI supervisory, management, and executive positions in grades GS-14 and GS-15 paid a base salary of about $76,193 and $89,625 a year, respectively, which amounted to $95,241 or $112,031 per year including availability pay. Salaries were slightly higher in selected areas where the prevailing local pay level was higher. Because federal agents may be eligible for a special law enforcement benefits package, applicants should ask their recruiter for more information.

Total earnings for local, state, and special police and detectives frequently exceed the stated salary because of payments for overtime, which can be significant. In addition to the common benefits — paid vacation, sick leave, and medical and life insurance — most police and sheriffs' departments provide officers with special allowances for uniforms. Because police officers usually are covered by liberal pension plans, many retire at half-pay after 25 or 30 years of service.

EMPLOYMENT RESOURCES

Further information about employment opportunities with specific agencies is included here. Use the information and resources provided in Chapter Three and Appendix C and E of this book to research opportunities with all agencies. Also, visit *http://federaljobs.net* for direct links to hundreds of resources and agency employment Web sites.

Department of Homeland Security

FBI Special Agent — Information is available from the nearest FBI office. The address and phone number are listed in the local telephone directory. Apply online at www.fbi.gov and explore careers.

Immigration and Customs Inspectors — Inspectors are stationed nationwide at air, land, and sea ports of entry. Visit the Web site at www.cbp.gov for complete information including a *"Career Finder"* tool that allows you to apply online through the Department of Homeland Security. Customs and Border Patrol Headquarters, 1300 Pennsylvania Avenue NW, Washington, DC 20229. Phone: 202-435-5708.

Intelligence Operations Specialist — Analyzes intelligence from DHS operating components, state and local partners, and other Intelligence Community (IC) agencies into Homeland Security assessments; ensuring analytic intelligence support to DHS elements that addresses the secretary's top priorities, serving as the primary interface between the IC and customers at state/local/tribal/territorial levels and in the private sector on Homeland Security issues; and coordinating intelligence analytic operations between I&A and DHS operating components as an integrated DHS intelligence enterprise. Locate vacancies at http://www.usajobs.gov. The DOD is the largest employer of this career field.

Security Screeners — Transportation Security Administration (TSA) This administration is in charge of the Airport Security Screener program. The TSA was transferred from the Department of Transportation to Homeland Security in 2002. Visit the Web site at www.tsajobs.com. See page 256 for additional information.

U.S. Secret Service Special Agents — Information is available from: U.S. Secret Service, 950 H St. NW, Washington, DC 20223. Web site: www.dhs.gov/.

Department of the Interior

Park Ranger — Park Rangers supervise, manage and perform work in the conservation and use of resources in national parks and other federally-managed areas. Park Rangers carry out various tasks associated with forest or structural fire control and they also operate campgrounds, including such tasks as assigning sites, replenishing firewood, performing safety inspections, providing information to visitors, and leading guided tours. Contact regional offices for employment information and visit http://usajobs.gov for job vacancy announcements. Career information is available at http://www.doi.gov/doijobs/employ1.html.

Regional Offices

Alaska
National Park Service
2525 Gambell St., Room 107
Anchorage, AK 99503
(907) 257-2574

Northeast
National Park Service
U.S. Custom House
200 Chestnut St., Room 322
Philadelphia, PA 19106
(215) 597-4971

Midwest
National Park Service
1709 Jackson St.
Omaha, NE 68102
(402) 221-3456

National Capital

National Park Service
1100 Ohio Dr. SW
Washington, DC 20242
(202) 619-7256

Intermountain
National Park Service
12795 Alameda Pkwy.
Denver, CO 80225
(303) 969-2020

Southeast
National Park Service
75 Spring St. SW, Suite 1130
Atlanta, GA 30303
(404) 331-5711

Pacific West
National Park Service
One Jackson Center
1111 Jackson St.
Suite 700
Oakland, CA 94607
(510) 817-1300

Department of Justice

DEA Special Agent — Information is available from the nearest DEA office, or call (800) DEA-4288. Internet, www.usdoj.gov/dea/. This Web site offers an assessment tool to help you determine what special agent jobs you may qualify for. The toll free phone line announces job openings and will forward your call to a recruiting officer if you select that option.

Deputy Marshal — Information is available from the United States Marshals Service, Human Resource Division, Washington, DC 20530. Phone 202-307-9625 or visit the Web site at www.usdoj.gov/marshals/.

Bureau of Prisons - Central Office, 320 First St. NW, Washington, DC 20534. Phone: 202-307-3082 or www.bop.gov/. The bureau is under the Department of Justice and consists of 114 institutions, 6 regional offices, a central office, two staff training centers, and 28 community corrections offices to care for 193,000 federal offenders. Approximately 85 percent of these inmates are confined in Bureau-operated correctional facilities or detention centers. Visit the online facility locator at http://www.bop.gov/locations/locationmap.jsp to explore employment opportunities in your area.

> *Correctional Officers with the Department of Justice (GS-0007)* — Job hotline at 202-514-3397. There are 16,167 correctional officers working for Justice. Correctional officers enforce the rules and regulations governing the operation of a correctional institution. This includes the confinement, safety, health, and protection of inmates, as well as supervising the various work assignments of inmates. On occasion, correctional officers are required to use firearms, and may at times require arduous physical exertion to subdue unruly inmates who may be armed or assaultive.

CIA Agents — Information is available from 703-482-1100 or www.cia.gov/. Visit the online career center at https://www.cia.gov/careers/index.html. Its mission is to provide our nation's first line of defense by collecting information, producing timely threat analysis, and conducting covert action at the direction of the president.

Department of the Treasury

IRS Special Agent — Agents combine their accounting skills with law enforcement skills to investigate financial crimes. Special Agents are duly sworn law enforcement officers who are trained to "follow the money." No matter what the source, all income earned, both legal and illegal, has the potential of becoming involved in crimes which fall within the investigative jurisdiction of the IRS Criminal Investigation. Because of the expertise required to conduct these complex financial investigations, IRS Special Agents are considered the premier financial investigators for the federal government.

Criminal Investigators - Investigate potential criminal violations of the Internal Revenue Code, and related financial crimes.

Visit http://www.irs.gov/compliance/enforcement/ to explore all IRS enforcement careers. You can also call the main number at 202-622-5000.

Treasury Department Office Human Resource Numbers:

> Bureau of Alcohol, Tobacco & Trade: (202) 927-5000
> Bureau of Public Debt: 304-480-6144
> United States Mint: (800) 872-6468

Not all occupations are included in the above listed resources. Research all occupations and agencies using Appendix C and Chapter Three of this book plus visit http://federaljobs.net/federal.htm for direct links to over 140 federal agency recruitment sites.

Table 11-1 lists the major law enforcement occupations and job classification series that you can use to search OPM's online federal job vacancy database at http://www.usajobs.gov and other job listing services that are listed in Chapter Three. Not all federal jobs are listed on OPM's Web site. Visit the 140 federal agen-cy recruitment sites noted above to locate even more jobs.

QUALIFICATION STANDARDS
FOR TWO MAJOR OCCUPATIONS

This section presents the federal qualification standards for two of the larger occupations: Correctional Officer GS-0007 and Criminal Investigator GS-1811.[3] The qualification standards are used by agency personnel department to develop the job announcements that you will see on USAJOBS and through other listing sites. They are also the primary guides that human resource departments use to rate your application. Review these standards closely for the occupation you are interested in to determine if you meet the basic qualification for the position. Visit http://federaljobs.net to locate qualification standards for all other occupations.

IMPORTANT

Read the entire standard before deciding whether or not you qualify. For example, look at education in the first standard. At first glance it appears that a four year B.S. degree is required for the position. There is a qualifier and this is NOT TRUE. You must have a four year degree **OR** three years of experience and they tell you exactly what experience qualifies. It may help to have a four year degree, but experience is also acceptable. Many applicants stop reading after they see a degree requirement and think they don't qualify.

READ THE ENTIRE STANDARD — FRONT TO BACK

---

[3] Excerpted from "Operations Manual, Qualifications Standards for General Schedule Positions, 2000."

Correctional Officer - GS-0007

EDUCATION AND EXPERIENCE REQUIREMENTS

EDUCATION

Undergraduate Education: Successful completion of a full four-year course of study in any field leading to a bachelor's degree, in an accredited college or university, is qualifying for GS-5 level positions.

Graduate Education: One full academic year of graduate education with major study in criminal justice, social science, or other field related to the position is qualifying for GS-7. Graduate education may be prorated according to the grade level of the position to be filled; however, it is not qualifying for positions above GS-7.

OR

EXPERIENCE

General Experience (for GS-5 positions): Three years of general experience, one year of which was equivalent to at least GS-4, are qualifying for positions at the GS-5 level. This experience must have demonstrated the aptitude for acquiring knowledge, skills, and abilities required for correctional work, and, in addition, demonstrate the possession of personal attributes important to the effectiveness of correctional officers, such as:

- Ability to meet and deal with people of differing backgrounds and behavioral patterns.
- Ability to be persuasive in selling and influencing ideas.
- Ability to lead, supervise, and instruct others.
- Sympathetic attitude toward the welfare of others.
- Ability to reason soundly and to think out practical solutions to problems.
- Ability to make decisions and act quickly, particularly under stress.
- Poise and self-confidence, and ability to remain calm during emergency situations.

Qualifying general experience may have been gained in work such as:

- Social case work in a welfare agency or counseling in other types of organizations.
- Classroom teaching or instructing.
- Responsible rehabilitation work, e.g., in an alcoholic rehabilitation program.
- Supervising planned recreational activities or active participation in community action programs.
- Management or supervisory work in a business or other organization that included directing the work flow and/or direct supervision of others.
- Sales work, other than taking and filling orders as in over-the-counter sales.

Specialized Experience (for positions above GS-5): One year of specialized experience equivalent to at least the next lower level in the normal line of progression is qualifying for positions at grade GS-6 and above. Specialized experience must have equipped the applicant with the particular knowledge, skills, and abilities to perform successfully the duties of the position to be filled. Experience may have been gained in work such as police officer, mental health counselor in a residential facility, or detention officer.

EMPLOYMENT INTERVIEW

The personal qualities and characteristics of the applicant are the most critical of all the requirements for correctional officer positions. The applicant must be willing to perform arduous and prolonged duties on any of three shifts. In addition, the applicant must possess certain personal qualities in order to relate to inmates effectively in a correctional setting. These include empathy, objectivity, perceptiveness, resourcefulness, adaptability and flexibility, stability, and maturity.

Before appointment, candidates may be required to appear before a panel of specialists in correctional administration for an employment interview to determine the extent to which the candidates possess these and other qualities necessary to perform correctional officer duties adequately. The interview will also serve to acquaint applicants with further details of, and the environment surrounding, the position. A determination by the panel that a person who is otherwise qualified does not possess such personal characteristics to the required degree may result in removal of his/her application from further consideration.

MEDICAL REQUIREMENTS

The Department of Justice, Bureau of Prisons, has established the following medical requirements for correctional officer positions:

General: The duties of these positions involve unusual mental and nervous pressure, and require arduous physical exertion involving prolonged walking and standing, restraining of prisoners in emergencies, and participating in escape hunts. Applicants must be physically capable of performing efficiently the duties of these positions, and be free from such defects or disease as may constitute employment hazards to themselves or others. The duties of a correctional officer are arduous, sound health as well as physical fitness is required.

Vision: Must have at least 20/30 vision with or without correction. If only one eye is present or functional, the examining health care practitioner shall determine if an applicant can safely perform the physical ability test, the firearms component, and the self-defense component at the training center.

Hearing: Must be capable of hearing conversational voice, with or without a hearing aid, in at least one ear, as measured by normal findings in the decibel ranges of 500, 1000, 2000. This determination is made via a hearing booth test.

Mental/Emotional Stability: Must display mental and emotional stability. The examining health care practitioner shall evaluate mental and emotional stability based upon a thorough medical/psychiatric history as well as a current medical/psychiatric examination. Additionally, any history of psychiatric hospitalizations and outpatient psychiatric treatments shall be considered when evaluating an applicant's mental health.

Active Disease: Active diseases that are infectious and may be spread by routine means, such as handshakes, skin contact, and breathing, preclude an applicant from employment. Once this disease is cured or is considered by the examining health care practitioner to be no longer infectious, the applicant may be considered for employment. Active disease processes or conditions cannot (solely on the basis of the existence of such process, disease, condition, impairment or disability) exclude an otherwise qualified applicant from consideration for employment (i.e., HIV positive, AIDS, cancer, epilepsy, diabetes, heart disease, and loss or injury of one or more limbs).

Disability: Similarly, history of a disease, medical condition, or impairment, particularly if deemed a permanent "disability," cannot, solely on the basis of the existence of such disease, condition, or impairment, exclude an otherwise qualified applicant from consideration for employment. If the applicant is otherwise qualified and can, with or without reasonable accommodation, safely perform the essential functions of the position, the physical ability tests, the firearms component, and the self-defense component, then the individual may be considered for employment.

Criminal Investigating Series GS-1811

Use these individual occupational requirements in conjunction with the "Group Coverage Qualification Standard for Administrative and Management Positions." Individual occupational requirements for Treasury Enforcement Agent positions are identified separately. Visit http://federaljobs.net to view the entire Group Coverage Qualification Standard for Administrative and Management Positions.

MEDICAL REQUIREMENTS

The duties of positions in this series require moderate to arduous physical exertion involving walking and standing, use of firearms, and exposure to inclement weather. Manual dexterity with comparatively free motion of finger, wrist, elbow, shoulder, hip, and knee joints is required. Arms, hands, legs, and feet must be sufficiently intact and functioning in order that applicants may perform the duties satisfactorily. Sufficiently good vision in each eye, with or without correction, is required to perform the duties satisfactorily. Near vision, corrective lenses permitted, must be sufficient to read printed material the size of typewritten characters. Hearing loss, as measured by an audiometer, must not exceed 35 decibels at 1000, 2000, and 3000 Hz levels. Since the duties of these positions are exacting and responsible, and involve activities under trying conditions, applicants must possess emotional and mental stability. Any physical condition that would cause the applicant to be a hazard to himself/herself or others is disqualifying.

Criminal Investigator / GS-1811

Treasury Enforcement Agent

Use these individual occupational requirements in conjunction with the "Group Coverage Qualification Standard for Administrative and Management Positions."

EDUCATION

Undergraduate and Graduate Education:

All Treasury Enforcement Agent (TEA) positions in Treasury bureaus and offices, except Internal Revenue Service (IRS) Special Agent positions: Major study—any field of study in an accredited college or university.

IRS Special Agent positions: Major study — any field of study that included or was supplemented by at least 15 semester hours in accounting, and nine semester hours from among the following or closely related fields: finance, economics, business law, tax law, or money and banking.

OR

EXPERIENCE

General Experience (for GS-5 positions):

TEA positions except IRS Special Agent: Successful, responsible experience in the criminal investigative or law enforcement fields that required knowledge and application of laws relating to criminal violations, and the ability to deal effectively with individuals or groups in stressful or controversial situations, collect and assemble pertinent facts for investigations, and prepare clear, concise written reports.

IRS Special Agent positions: Successful, responsible accounting and business experience that required knowledge and application of accounting and auditing principles and general business practices, and that demonstrated the ability to analyze and comprehend accounting and bookkeeping records, financial statements, related reports and automated systems.

Nonqualifying General Experience: Experience as a uniformed law enforcement officer where the principal duties consisted of investigations and arrests involving traffic violations, minor felonies, misdemeanors, and comparable offenses; or in which the major duties involved guarding and protecting property, preventing crimes, and/or legal research without the application of investigative techniques.

Specialized Experience (for positions above GS-5):

TEA positions except IRS Special Agent: Experience in or related to investigation of criminal violations that provided the specific knowledge, skills, and abilities to perform successfully the duties of the position. Examples of qualifying specialized experience include:

- Leadership or membership of a military intelligence or criminal investigative team or component in which the principal duties consisted of security investigation, intelligence gathering, or criminal prosecution.

- Analyzing or evaluating raw investigative data and preparing comprehensive written investigative reports.

- Investigating complex claims involving suspected crimes or alleged fraud.

- Investigating criminal cases requiring the use of recognized investigative methods and techniques and that may have included appearing in court to present evidence.

- Supervising or conducting interviews or interrogations that involved eliciting evidence, data, or surveillance information.

- Law enforcement work in which 50 percent or more of the time involved criminal investigations requiring the use of surveillance, undercover, or other criminal detection methods or techniques.

- Investigating computerized business and/or accounting systems and forming sound conclusions as to related criminal business practices and compliance with federal laws and regulations.

- Investigative work that required rapid, accurate judgments and sound decision-making in applying regulations, instructions, and procedures.

- Successful completion of formalized programs of in service training for any of the above.

IRS Special Agent positions: Specialized experience required for IRS Special Agent positions is essentially the same as that described above for other TEA positions, except that the experience must have been acquired in investigative work related to the accounting, auditing, business, or commercial practices of subjects investigated.

CERTIFICATE AS A CERTIFIED PUBLIC ACCOUNTANT (CPA)

Proof of possession of a CPA certificate (certificate number and date of issuance) obtained through written examination in a state, territory, or the District of Columbia meets the GS-5 level requirements for positions requiring accounting knowledge. Applicants with such certificates may also qualify for higher grade levels based on their education and/or experience.

PERSONAL QUALITIES

Appointment is conditional on a satisfactory report of character and background investigation, including a tax audit. This investigation is conducted in order to secure evidence of candidates' loyalty to the U.S. government, honesty, and integrity. For some positions, a top secret security clearance will be required.

INTERVIEW

Applicants who pass the written test, as required, and who meet the experience or educational requirements will be required to appear for an interview at the time of consideration for appointment. The interview is to evaluate observable personal qualifications essential for successful performance of the duties of the position, such as poise, tact, and ability in oral expression. An otherwise qualified applicant who is found to lack the personal qualifications necessary for successful performance of the duties of the position will be removed from further consideration.

MOTOR VEHICLE OPERATION

Applicants must possess a valid automobile driver's license at the time of appointment. Candidates must qualify after appointment for authorization to operate motor vehicles in accordance with applicable OPM regulations and related Department of the Treasury requirements.

USE OF FIREARMS

All positions require basic and periodic qualification in the use of firearms; proficiency with standard issue firearms must be demonstrated for successful completion of training. All agents are required to carry a handgun in the performance of duties.

MAXIMUM ENTRY AGE

The date immediately preceding an individual's 37th birthday is the maximum entry age for original appointment to a position within the Department of the Treasury as a law enforcement officer as defined in title 5 U.S.C. 8331(20) or in 5 U.S.C. 8401(17). Consideration will be restricted to candidates who have not yet reached age 37 at the time of referral for positions.

MEDICAL REQUIREMENTS

General: The duties of these positions require moderate to arduous physical exertion involving walking and standing, use of firearms, and exposure to inclement weather. Manual dexterity with comparatively free motion of fingers, wrists, elbows, shoulders, hips and knee joints is required. Arms, hands, legs, and feet must function sufficiently in order for applicants to perform the duties satisfactorily.

Vision: For all positions, near vision, corrected or uncorrected, must be sufficient to read larger type 2 at 14 inches. Normal depth perception and peripheral vision are required, as is the ability to distinguish shades of color by color plate tests. For all positions covered by this standard, applicants who have undergone refractive surgery (i.e., surgery to improve distant visual acuity) must meet Treasury-approved requirements which include documentation that they have passed specific exam and protocol testing. Visual acuity requirements for each bureau listed below are expressed in terms of the Snellen vision test:

U.S. Secret Service — Uncorrected distant vision must test 20/60 in each eye, and corrected distant vision must test 20/20 in each eye.

Bureau of Alcohol, Tobacco and Firearms — Uncorrected distant vision must test 20/100 in each eye, and corrected distant vision must test 20/20 in one eye, 20/30 in the other.

All other bureaus — Uncorrected distant vision must test 20/200, and corrected distant vision must test 20/20 in one eye, 20/30 in the other.

Hearing: Hearing loss, as measured by an audiometer, must not exceed 30 decibels (A.S.A. or equivalent I.S.O.) in either ear in the 500, 1000, and 2000 Hz ranges. Applicants must be able to hear the whispered voice at 15 feet with each ear without the use of a hearing aid.

Special Medical Requirements: Since the duties of these positions are exacting and involve the responsibility for the safety of others under trying conditions, applicants must possess emotional and mental stability. Any condition that would hinder full, efficient performance of the duties of these positions or that would cause the individual to be a hazard to himself/herself or to others is disqualifying.

Appointment will be contingent upon a candidate's passing a pre-employment medical examination and drug test to ascertain possession of the physical and emotional requirements for the position. For certain positions involving particularly arduous or hazardous duties, there are specific medical requirements where a direct relationship exists between the condition and the duties of the position being filled. Certain diseases or conditions resulting in indistinct speech may be disqualifying. Any chronic disease or condition affecting the respiratory system, the cardio-vascular system, the gastrointestinal, musculoskeletal, digestive, nervous, endo-crine or genitourinary systems that would impair full performance of the duties of the position is disqualifying. Prior to completion of the one-year probationary period following initial appointment, an incumbent may be required to undergo a physical examination and meet the same medical requirements as those for appointment. Supervisory positions excepted, these medical requirements must be met in service placement actions, including reinstatement of former employees and transfers from positions not covered by this standard. The presence of medical conditions that would be aggravated by the environmental conditions of these positions will ordinarily disqualify an applicant for appointment.

SECURITY SCREENING POSITIONS

The Transportation Security Administration (TSA) constantly reviews screening procedures to ensure that measures are targeted to counter potential threats. Originally, the TSA was under the Department of Transportation. When Homeland Security was established, all TSA functions and personnel transferred to HLS. There are approximately 28,000 federal screeners — originally job series 0019, now GS-1802 — and these positions were established by the Transportation Security Agency on November 19, 2001.

Job vacancies and applications are available online at www.tsajobs.com. Individuals unable to complete an online application may call toll-free 1-800-887-1895 or TTY 1-800-887-5506. All interested applicants are encouraged to fully review job vacancy announcements and Frequently Asked Questions on the TSA Web site prior to applying.

Job Description

Screeners perform a variety of duties related to providing security and protection of air travelers, airports and aircraft. They are responsible for identifying dangerous objects in baggage, cargo and/or on passengers, and preventing those objects from being transported onto aircraft. Screeners perform various tasks such as: wanding, pat-down searches, operation of x-ray machines, lift and carry baggage (weighing up to 70 pounds), and screening and ticket review using electronic and imaging equipment. As a Transportation Security Officer (TSO), they perform passenger screening, baggage screening or both and they are expected to perform these duties in a courteous and professional manner.

Qualification Standards

The Transportation Security Act made airport security a direct federal responsibility. As a result of this legislation a significant number of federal security screeners were hired over the past three years. The new security force is comprised of highly qualified and well-trained U.S. citizens.

One requirement of the Transportation Security Act was to establish qualification standards for screeners to be employed by the federal government. In response to this requirement, on December 19, 2001 the Department of Transportation published the basic eligibility requirements for federal security screeners.

All screeners must:

- Possess a high school diploma or general education diploma or have one year of any type of work experience that demonstrates the applicant's ability to perform the work of the position.

- Be a U.S. citizen.

- Pass a background and security investigation, including a criminal records check, in accordance with federal law and standards established by the Transportation Security Administration.

- Possess certain basic aptitudes and physical abilities as measured through a medical examination. These include color perception, visual and aural acuity, physical coordination, and motor skills, to the following standards:

1) Be able to distinguish objects on the screening equipment monitor at the appropriate imaging standard as specified by the Transportation Security Administration;

2) Be able to distinguish each color displayed on every type of screening equipment and explain what each color signifies;

3) Be able to hear and respond to the spoken voice and to audible alarms generated by screening equipment in an active checkpoint environment;

4) Be able to efficiently and thoroughly manipulate and handle baggage, containers, and other objects subject to security processing; and

5) Have sufficient dexterity and capability to thoroughly conduct hand metal detector and pat-down search procedures over an individual's entire body.

- Be able to read, speak, and write English well enough to:

    1) Carry out written and oral instructions regarding the proper performance of screening duties;

    2) Read English language identification media, credentials, airline tickets, and labels on items normally encountered in the screening process;

    3) Provide direction to, and understand and answer questions from, English-speaking individuals undergoing screening; and

    4) Write incident reports and statements and log entries into security records in the English language.

Any applicant tentatively selected for this position will be subject to a pre-employment or pre-appointment drug screening. Persons occupying these positions will be subject to random drug and/or alcohol testing and will be required to pass a Federal Civil Aviation Security Screener Aptitude test. The test will measure:

- Aptitude necessary to conduct screening;
- Ability to deal effectively with the public; and
- English proficiency.

SECRET

CHAPTER TWELVE
Employment Secrets

Why is it that some who land jobs with Uncle Sam have half the experience, education, and special qualifications than you have — and you're still looking? Many who approach the federal sector lose out because they didn't take the time to understand the federal hiring process. Others get frustrated by the required paperwork and give up prematurely. Decades later they will regret their impatience and wish they had done what it takes to land a high-paying and benefit-loaded government job.

The secret to success is that the harder you work the luckier you get.

If you take the time to understand the differences between the private and public sectors, thoroughly complete your application package, and seek out all available job vacancies, your chances for employment will increase substantially. Job applicants who successfully land government jobs have to deal with the application process throughout their careers. During my 35-plus years of government service I submitted over 14 application packages while working for the Departments of Defense and Transportation. My last federal application, for a senior management position, was over 60 pages long.

CHAPTER OBJECTIVES

✎   Achieve higher résumé/application ratings

✎   Learn how to improve your chances

✎   Identify job options *(apply for all job series that you can qualify for)*

✎   Understand the *"Keys to Success"*

APPLY EARLY

It pays to start your employment search early for federal jobs, well in advance of the time you will be available for employment. Applications can take six to eight weeks or even longer for processing. It can take even longer than that if written tests are required. From the time you first identify an opening to actual interviews and hiring can take up to six months in some cases.

All individuals interested in federal employment should start researching the system, identifying jobs, visiting agency Web sites, and preparing for tests — if required — months in advance.

> Most federal agencies have comprehensive Internet Web sites. Over 80 percent of all federal jobs are now advertised by individual agencies instead of OPM. It's imperative that you visit agency Web sites to locate **ALL** job vacancies in your area. A comprehensive list of federal agency employment Web sites is available in this book with direct online links located on this book's companion web site at http://federaljobs.net.

YOUR APPLICATION AND RÉSUMÉ

Review Chapter Six to learn how to evaluate job announcements and complete your federal style résumé and KSAs if required. There are a number of application methods available including the traditional paper copy résumés that are sent through the mail, online résumé submissions, standard forms, RESUMIX, e-mail, and telephone application processes. You should also be familiar with the optional application forms including the OF-612 and OF-306. All forms listed in the job announcement must be submitted with your package. If you need forms, most can be downloaded from various Internet sites.

The most popular application method today is the federal style résumé, for a number of reasons. First, most people are familiar with résumés and secondly, with the increase in online submissions, the résumé format makes the most sense because it is easy to copy and paste from your federal style résumé into online résumé builders.

DON'T SUBMIT A PRIVATE SECTOR RÉSUMÉ

Many applicants submit a private sector résumé, which is insufficient for federal jobs. The major differences between the federal style résumé and private sector is explained in Chapter Six and you will find sample résumés to assist you with yours. The differences are significant. Considerably more detail is required for the federal style résumé and if you don't provide the exact information requested your application may be rejected. At the very least you will lose valuable rating points for omitting required information and you will be less likely to be referred for interviews.

Details, Details, and More Details

First and foremost, when applying for any federal job READ the job announcement front to back. The job announcement will explain everything you need to know to apply for that specific job. Every job announcement is unique, so don't assume because you read one for the exact same job series and grade that the requirements are the same for this new job. This is especially true for the required key *Duties, Responsibilities* and *Specialized Experience*. Each advertised job has specific requirements such as proficiency and experience with computer software, equipment, programs, reporting systems, skills, and other factors.

When applying for any federal job read the job announcement front to back.

Rate Higher and Be Referred for Interviews by:

✓ Reading the job announcement completely — front to back

✓ Using a highlighter to mark key words and phrases listed on the job announcement under Duties, Responsibilities and Specialized Experience.

✓ Tailoring your résumé, KSAs, and Occupational Questionnaire by incorporating the key words and phrases identified in the previous step into your work descriptions and KSAs.

✓ Preparing two federal style résumé formats, an attractively formatted paper copy to use when sending copies through the mail or in person and a second minimally formatted version as described in Chapter Six for online submissions.

I can't stress enough the importance of tailoring your federal style résumé to the job announcement's key duties, responsibilities and specialized experience. If you do as suggested above you will potentially rate higher and you will improve your chances of being referred for interviews. Everything is about points, and your application will be rated on a point system up to 100. Your résumé will be awarded points based on meeting the criteria for the job, and the key words and phrases are what rating officials and electronic ratings systems scan for.

Another factor to consider is that most résumés — about 70 percent or more — are now submitted online through federal résumé builders. I suggest completing your federal style résumé offline on your desktop computer rather than going straight to a résumé builder. You need quality time to compose and tailor your résumé, and many of the online résumé builder and submission programs have time limits and other constraints. Some allow you to save your work, while others don't.

You may be asking why you need to prepare two résumé formats, as noted in the above list. This is suggested because highly formatted résumés when copied and pasted into online résumé builders can scramble the text and confuse the online scanning software. Be aware that the fancy formatting is great for hard copy submissions and to take along to interviews, but they could reduce your rating if you copy and paste from the formatted version into online documents. Most résumé services will provide both versions if requested.

APPLY FREQUENTLY

Many job hunters send in an application for only one job announcement. Seek out all available job vacancies and continue to send in applications with every opportunity. Don't limit yourself to http://www.usajobs.gov. This excellent site does advertise about 70 percent of all federal jobs; however you may be passing up job opportunities in your own back yard by not visiting individual agency recruitment sites in your area. Visit http://federaljobs.net/federal.htm, this book's companion Web site, for direct links to over 140 federal agency recruiting sites.

The more often you apply, the greater your chances. Many agencies now allow job seekers to apply online. Review the Appendices to identify all the job series you can possibly qualify for. If you are having difficulty identifying job series that fit your training, experience, and abilities, review the qualification standards for those positions and review the Skills Index in Appendix E. Qualification standards can be reviewed online at either http://federaljobs.net or http://opm.gov.

You will find that you can qualify for several to 20 or more job series. Don't overlook Wage Grade (WG) positions. When requesting job announcements, obtain copies of announcements that cover all the job series that interest you. You will be surprised by how many you qualify for.

Consider the electronics technician field. For example, all of the following job series require basic electronic technician skills:[1]

GS-856	Electronics Technician
GS-802	Electronics Engineering Technician
GS-2101	Transportation Specialist (FAA System Specialists)

WG-2500 — Wire Communications Equip/Installation/Maintenance Family

WG-2502 Telephone Mechanic
WG-2504 Wire Communications Cable Splicing
WG-2508 Communications Line Installing/Repairing
WG-2511 Wire Communications Equipment Install/Repair

WG-2600 — Electronic Equipment Installation and Maintenance Family

WG-2602 Electronic Measurement Equipment Mechanic
WG-2604 Electronic Mechanic
WG-2606 Electronic Industrial Controls
WG-2698 Electronic Digital Computer Mechanic

---

[1] Publication TS-56, March 1990, Part 3, Definitions of Trades and Labor Job Families and Occupations.

WG-2800   Electrical Installation Maintenance Family (4 occupations)
WG-3300   Instrument Work Family (5 occupations)
WG-4800   General Maintenance Family (7 occupations)

Over 40 Electronic Related Jobs Are Listed Under
Various Wage Grade Families

GETTING IN THE FRONT DOOR

Getting in is half the battle. If you want to enter a specific career field with an agency and there are currently no openings, apply for other related jobs with that agency. For instance, if you qualify for a logistics/supply position and they only have clerk openings, it may be to your benefit to apply and get on board. Agencies generally advertise in-house first to offer qualified workers opportunities for advancement. You will have a good chance to bid on other jobs if you have the qualifications and a good track record.

LOCATE ALL JOB VACANCIES

Locate announcements from all sources including OPM's USAJOBS, individual agency personnel offices and Web sites. Even if you wouldn't consider relocating, you will at least be aware of the job availability in other areas. Identify local agency offices and send them a copy of your application or federal style résumé along with a short cover letter. In the letter explain what jobs you are interested in and provide some background information. This is a good way to introduce yourself and your qualifications to a perspective employer. Each year additional agencies apply for and receive direct hire or case examining authority for specific job series. The more contacts you make the better.

Visit http://federaljobs.net/federal.htm, this book's companion Web site, for direct links to over 140 federal agency recruiting sites. Consider subscribing to *Federal Career Opportunities* (http://fedjobs.com) published by Federal Research Services or *Federal Jobs Digest* (http://jobsfed.com). Online job vacancy listing services compile job vacancies from over 200 federal personnel offices. **The larger the area of consideration the better your chances**. Choice jobs with certain agencies often require an applicant to accept a job in a not-so-desirable location. Often, agencies have to advertise jobs to the general public because the area isn't desirable and they can't get in-house applicants. Once hired, you may have an opportunity to apply to better locations after you are trained and have the required agency experience.

During my early government career I accepted a job with an agency in a small town of 3,056 inhabitants in central Pennsylvania. After completing the re-

"There are two things to aim at in life: first, to get what you want; and after that to enjoy it. Only the wisest of people achieve the second."

quired initial training and receiving required system certifications I was able to successfully relocate to the area of my choice. It took me three years to gain the training and experience needed to apply for jobs in other areas. When I did relocate, the agency paid for the complete move, including real estate expenses.

One important fact to remember: In most cases **your first move is at your expense**. If you are willing to relocate you will be responsible for the cost of the move in most cases. However, if you relocate to other areas after your first year of employment the government picks up the tab. The moving allowances are generous. Agencies often buy your house from you at close to market rates, pay to move your household goods, and pay real estate sales commissions and closing costs at your new location. On top of this, you will receive 60 to 90 days of temporary quarters expenses at your new location, 64 hours of leave for the move, and a free house hunting trip may be authorized.

CAUTION

Don't jump blindly at an employment offer. Many agencies have difficulty filling jobs in high-cost of living areas such as New York, Los Angeles, and Washington, D.C. Investigate the cost of living in the area you are selected for before saying yes. If you can't afford to live in the area you may have to turn down the initial offer.

"LOOK BEFORE YOU LEAP"

TRAINING AND EXPERIENCE

Often, applicants neglect to add valuable work experience and training to their application package. Go back as many years as your related education and experience go. For example, if you were a supply specialist in the military in 1980, and you are applying for a supply/logistics position, then by all means add your military experience and training to your application.

Many agencies require supplemental application qualification forms. If you are applying for an electronics position these forms often capture your math, electronics training and specific experience background. List all of your math training back through high school. Trigonometry and algebra are required for many electronics positions. If you had these subjects in high school and you don't list them you might not be rated eligible for the position.

KEYS TO SUCCESS

There are six basic ingredients to successfully finding federal employment for qualified applicants:

- Understand the differences between the private and federal sectors.

- Seek out all job vacancies and bid on multiple positions.

- Completely read and analyze each job announcement.

- Package a professional federal style résumé *(two formats)*.

- Don't give up when you receive your first rejection.

- Prepare for interviews.

You can learn from rejections by contacting the selecting official. Ask what training and/or experience would have enhanced your application package for future positions. If the selecting official suggests obtaining certain education, training or experience, work to achieve his recommendations.

You may discover that you did have the specific skills needed. However, you either neglected to include these facts in your application or considered them unimportant for the job applied for. This happens frequently. It doesn't pay to debate your qualifications over spilled milk. The job has already been filled. Thank the selecting official for his candor and time, then revise your bid for the next opening.

Write the selecting official a BRIEF letter of thanks and explain that you neglected to incorporate the recommended skills in the original application. Send him or her a copy of your revised application for future reference. **Managers appreciate dealing with rational and mature individuals, and you will be remembered.**

I used the Individual Development Plan (IDP) process throughout my federal career to target promotions and to work with management to obtain valuable career-enhancing lateral assignments and temporary details. You can do the same. Visit http://fedcareer.info to learn how to target your career goals and achieve them. During my tenure as a manager for the Federal Aviation Administration I encouraged employees seeking promotions to develop viable IDP plans in concert with management to achieve their career goals.

It took me two years to land my first competitive federal civil service job. I was not aware of the employment options available at that time and I simply sent written requests for bids every two weeks to the local OPM office. Today there are many options available through special emphasis hiring, direct hire authority, Outstanding Scholar programs, student employment, veterans' preference, and internships, to name a few. Add to this list the more than 1,000 job resources provided throughout this book. Take advantage of as many of the programs as you qualify for to enhance your career search. Don't give up or get overly frustrated with the paperwork that is required when applying for federal employment. Look at the long-term view and remind yourself that if you do the paperwork — and do it right — you can end up with a high-paying, benefit-loaded job for the rest of your career.

If you should get frustrated, and many do, just think of this: The average annual total compensation in 2005 for federal civilian workers was **$106,871,** compared to **$53,288** for the private sector.[2] The benefits are outstanding and according to the Congressional Budget Office's March 2007, *Characteristics and Pay of Federal Civilian Employees* report, federal employees' benefits ranged between 26 percent and 50 percent of pay based on time in service, the employee's age, and retirement system. Federal jobs are well worth the time and effort that you **INVEST** in the process.

Finally, I must add that is unwise to get angry with the process; instead of getting mad, **GET INVOLVED**.

NETWORKING

Networking is a term used to define the establishment of a group of individuals who assist one another for mutual benefit. You can establish your own network by talking to personnel specialists, contacting regional agency employment departments, conducting informational interviews, and bidding on all applicable job announcements. By following the guidelines outlined in the book and using your innate common sense your chances of success are magnified tenfold.

Use the more than 1,000 contacts presented in this book to begin your personal employment network. Add to this information individual contacts that you make with local agencies.

*"We grow great by dreams. All
big men are dreamers.
They see things in the soft haze of a
spring day or in the red fire of a
long winter's evening. Some of
us let these dreams die, but others
nourish and protect them, nurse
them to the sunshine and light
which come always to those who
sincerely hope that their dreams
will come true."*

— Woodrow Wilson

---

[2] Bureau of Economic Analysis, National Income & Product Account Tables 6.2D and 6.5D, 2005.

APPENDIX A
Job Hunter's Checklist

WHAT TO DO NOW

☐ Review the federal occupations lists in Appendix D and the skills index in Appendix E. These appendices provide lists of specific federal jobs that you may qualify for.

☐ Review Chapter One for an overview of the federal hiring system.

✔ Visit **USAJOBS** at http://usajobs.gov and link direct to over 140 federal agency recruitment sites at http://federaljobs.net/federal.htm. If you don't have access to the Internet, call **USAJOBS by phone** at 703-724-1850 or TTY 978-461-8404. However, you will need a vacancy number. The best way to obtain a vacancy number for a specific job is online or directly from a federal human resource department. Many libraries now have online access capabilities. Obtain job announcements for specific job series *(online or by phone)*.

✔ Review the application process in Chapter Six, including the sample job announcement and résumés.

☐ Contact regional and local agency personnel offices. See Appendix C for office addresses, Web sites, and phone numbers.

✔ Request agency career opportunity brochures online or from agencies.
✔ Visit http://federaljobs.net for direct links to over 140 agency employment Web sites.
✔ Talk with agency personnel offices and request job announcements and information on special hiring programs.
✔ Obtain local government office phone numbers from your phone

directory. Look under "U.S. Government" in the blue pages. Also contact Federal Executive Boards, Appendix B.

> Applications will only be accepted for open job announcements. If you are applying for an analyst position and no openings exist, they will not accept your application.

☐ Visit **Federal Jobs Network** at http://federaljobs.net/, this book's companion Web site for updates to *The Book of U.S. Government Jobs*. If hiring programs are modified, or Web site addresses or contact information change, those changes will be posted on this site. You can also link direct to hundreds of federal agency employment sites.

☐ Review Chapter Three's listings to identify job announcement resources including Internet Web site addresses. Also review:

   ✔ Chapter Three for Student Hiring Programs.

   ✔ Chapter Seven for Veterans Hiring Programs.

   ✔ Chapter Eight for overseas job resources.

   ✔ Chapter Nine for postal jobs. (Includes the 470 Battery Test.)

   ✔ Chapter Ten for job resources for people with disabilities.

   ✔ Chapter Eleven for Homeland Security and law enforcement jobs.

☐ Locate your high school and college transcripts, military records, awards, and professional licenses. Collect past employment history; salary, addresses, phone numbers, dates employed, etc.

☐ Visit your local library for these resources:

   ✔ *The United States Government Manual* — This book provides agency descriptions, addresses, contacts and basic employment information.

   ✔ *The Occupational Outlook Handbook* — If your library doesn't have this publication, check with a local college placement office. It is also available online at http://bls.gov/. This handbook is a nationally recognized source of career information and includes detailed descriptions of working conditions for over 250 jobs.

✔ *Computer access* - Visit your local library if you need to research careers, find job announcements, and apply using online resume builders.

✔ You will find this book in most large libraries. If you don't have the cash to purchase a copy, visit your local library's reference department and ask for a copy of the book. *The Book of U.S. Government Jobs* is recommended by **Library Journal**.

WHAT'S AVAILABLE

☐ Call local agencies listed in the phone directory. Also visit local federal buildings. Request informational interviews per instructions in Chapter Four. Visit the following sites to locate job announcements:

✔ http://www.usajobs.gov *(OPM Sponsored — approximately 70 percent of all federal jobs are advertised on this site. Average 30,000 daily listings.)*

✔ http://federaljobs.net/federal.htm *(Companion Web site for this book; direct links to over 140 federal agency recruiting sites.)*

☐ Research agencies in Appendix C of this book including agency Web sites. Department Web sites are listed in Chapter Three.

☐ Consider subscribing to Federal Research Services' *Federal Career Opportunities at* http://fedjobs.com or *visit Federal Jobs Digest's* Internet Web site at http://jobsfed.com. Both publish online databases and bi-weekly listings of job vacancies from over 200 federal personnel offices.

☐ Review Chapters Three, Seven, Eight, Nine, and Ten.

APPLYING FOR A JOB

☐ You will receive requested job announcements instantly via the Internet or within a week by mail. Each announcement will either be accompanied by all required application forms or downloadable from the Internet. Many job sites now permit online résumé submissions and allow you to draft and archive your federal style résumé online. Forms can also be downloaded from OPM's Web site or visit http://federaljobs.net.

☐ Review Chapter Six and follow the guidance for completing your federal style résumé. Chapter Six provides guidance on the federal style résumé and takes you step-by-step through the application process. You'll learn how to tailor and write a professional federal résumé and application using key words and phrases noted in the job announcement.

❏   If no vacancies exist for your specialty, visit http://www.usajobs.gov/ and agency Web sites frequently. Jobs can be advertised for very short periods. You can register on USAJOBS to compile and save your online résumé and for e-mail notification for specific job openings. Job vacancies can be located through USAJOBS, direct from local agencies, agency Web sites, various non-federal job listing services, local state employment offices, or through various publications.

❏   Contact individual agencies. The more contacts, the greater your chance of finding open announcements and special emphasis programs.

❏   Complete and sign ALL application forms received with the bid. Follow the step-by-step instructions presented in Chapter six and that are listed in the job announcement.

❏   Retain a copy of each job announcement that you applied for, along with all application forms that you submitted with your package. You may need to review them prior to the interview.

❏   Send in your completed résumé and application to the address specified on the announcement or submit it electronically if available. You must send your résumé by the closing date of the bid.

RESULTS

Your application will be processed and results returned to you within several weeks. You will receive a *Notice of Rating or Notice of Results* informing you of your eligibility by mail. If rated eligible, your name will be placed on the list of eligible applicants for that position. Your name and application will be forwarded to a selecting official for consideration.

THE INTERVIEW

❏   Prepare for the interview. Review Chapter Four's Employment Interviewing section.

APPENDIX B
Federal Service Centers & Executive Board Listings

OPM FEDERAL SERVICE CENTERS

The Office of Personnel Management (OPM) staffs these locations to provide services to all federal agencies. These offices provide a nationwide link to the automation and assessment services provided by the Employment Service's Technology Support Center and Personnel Resources and Development Center. Federal Service Centers typically service federal agencies; however, you can also call for assistance with application problems.

ATLANTA

75 Spring Street SW, Suite 1000
Atlanta, GA 30303
(404) 331-3455
(404) 730-9738 (FAX)
E-mail: Atlanta@opm.gov

CHICAGO

230 S. Dearborn St., DPN 30-3
Chicago, IL 60604
(312) 353-6234
(313) 353-6211 (FAX)
E-mail: Chicago@opm.gov

DENVER

12345 Alameda Pkwy, P.O. Box 25167
Denver, CO 80225
(303) 236-8580 (FAX)
E-mail: Denver@opm.gov

KANSAS CITY

601 E.12th St., Room 131
Kansas City, MO 64106
(816) 426-5706
(816) 426-5104 (FAX)
E-mail: KansasCity@opm.gov

NORFOLK

200 Granby St., Room 500
Norfolk, VA 23510-1886
(757) 441-3373
(757) 441-6280 (FAX)
E-mail: Norfolk@opm.gov

PHILADELPHIA

600 Arch St., Room 3400
Philadelphia, PA 19106
(215) 861-3074
E-mail: Philadelphia@opm.gov

RALEIGH

4407 Bland Rd., Suite 200
Raleigh, NC 27609-6296
(919) 790-2817
(919) 790-2824 (FAX)
E-mail: Raleigh@opm.gov

SAN ANTONIO

8610 Broadway, Room 305
San Antonio, TX 78217
(210) 805-2423
(210) 805-2429 (FAX)
E-mail: SanAntonio@opm.gov

SAN FRANCISCO

120 Howard St., Room 735
San Francisco, CA 94105
(415) 281-7094
(415) 281-7095 (FAX)
E-mail: SanFrancisco@opm.gov

WASHINGTON, DC

1900 E St. NW, Room 2469
Washington, DC 20415
(202) 606-2575
(202) 606-1768 (FAX)
E-mail: Washington@opm.gov

FEDERAL EXECUTIVE BOARDS (FEBs)

Federal Executive Boards (FEBs) were established to improve coordination among federal activities and programs outside of Washington. Approximately 84 percent of all federal employees work outside the national capital area. For job seekers the FEBs offer a wealth of information. Primarily, most of them compile directories of all agency offices in their area with contact information. Contact the FEB in your area to obtain a list of **ALL** federal offices in your area. This valuable resource gives the job seeker a total picture of potential employment options that are within commuting distance of their present location.

There are currently 29 FEBs located in cities that are major centers of federal activity. The boards are located in the following metropolitan areas: Albuquerque, Atlanta, Baltimore, Boston, Buffalo, Chicago, Cincinnati, Cleveland, Dallas-Fort Worth, Denver, Detroit, Honolulu, Houston, Kansas City, Los Angeles, Miami, Minneapolis-St. Paul, Newark, New Orleans, New York, Oklahoma City, Philadelphia, Pittsburgh, Portland Oregon, St. Louis, San Antonio, San Francisco, and Seattle. The boards are composed of the federal field office agency heads and military commanders in these cities.

In cities where FEBs do not exist, another organization of local principal federal agency officials often exists. These organizations are generally entitled Federal Executive Associations or Councils, and have purposes and objectives similar to FEBs. They do not, however, function within the same formal set of parameters (e.g., officially established by presidential memorandum, policy direction and guidance from the Office of Personnel Management, etc.) as do the FEBs.

Address all correspondence to the Federal Executive Board at the following listed addresses. Most FEBs have Internet Web sites. You may be surprised at the number of small local agency offices and facilities that may be located in your area. I originally started working for the Federal Aviation Administration in a small town of 3,056 residents in central Pennsylvania, and there were several small offices in the area. The FEBs compile lists of all offices, regardless of size, in their area of control, and that list can be a valuable networking resource that you can use to find potential employment in your area.

Use this list for networking purposes and to call or e-mail local offices for listings of agencies in your area:

FEDERAL EXECUTIVE BOARD LISTINGS

ALBUQUERQUE/SANTA FE, NM

David C. Iglesias, Co-Chairperson
John Kwait, Executive Director
P.O. Box 156
Albuquerque, NM 87103-1056
Phone: (505) 248-6415
FAX: (505) 248-6414
E-mail: John_Kwait@fws.gov

ATLANTA, GA

Cindy L. Brown, Chairperson
Gwendolyn Campbell, Executive Dir.
Richard B. Russell Federal Building
75 Spring St.SW, Room 1142
Atlanta, GA 30303
Phone: (404) 331-4400
FAX: (404) 331-4270
E-mail: gwenne.campbell@gsa.gov

BALTIMORE, MD

Felicita Sola-Carter, Chairperson
Richard Howell, Executive Director
Fallon Federal Building
31 Hopkins Plaza, Room 820A
Baltimore, MD 21201
Phone: (410) 962-4047
FAX: (410) 962-6198
E-mail: Baltimore.feb@verizon.net

BOSTON, MA

Diane P. LeBlanc, Chairperson
Kim Ainsworth, Executive Director
10 Causeway St. Room 178
Boston, MA 02222
Phone: (617) 565-6769
FAX: (617) 565-8178
E-mail: kim.ainsworth@gsa.gov

BUFFALO, NY

Philip C. Dissek, Chairperson
Paul Kendzierski, Executive Director
130 South Elmwood Ave., Suite 416
Buffalo, NY 14202
Phone: (716) 551-5655
FAX: (716) 551-3007
E-mail: director@buffalofeb.org

CHICAGO, IL

Jack G. Hetrick, Chairperson
Jan Stinson, Executive Director
230 S. Dearborn St., Room 3816
Chicago, IL 60604
Phone: (312) 353-6790
FAX: (312) 353-3058
E-mail: jan.stinson@gsa.gov

CINCINNATI, OH

James Cunningham, Chairperson
(Vacant), Executive Director
Cincinnati Federal Executive Board
1116 JWP Federal Office Building
550 Main St.
Cincinnati, OH 45202-3215
Phone: (513) 684-2102
FAX: (513) 684-2103
www.cincinnati.feb.gov
E-mail: tina@gcfeb.com

CLEVELAND, OH

Greg White, Chairperson
Michael Goin, Executive Director
A. J. Celebrezze Federal Building
1240 E. Ninth Street, Room 355
Cleveland, OH 44199-2002
Phone: (216) 433-6633
FAX: (216) 433-9463
www.cleveland.feb.gov
E-mail: Michael.w.goin@nasa.gov

DALLAS-FT. WORTH, TX

Peggy Moore-Swann, Chairperson
Gladean Butler, Executive Director
525 S. Griffin St., Suite 870-LB102
Dallas, TX 75202
Phone: (214) 767-5370
FAX: (214) 767-5380
E-mail: gbutler@dfwfeb.com

DENVER, CO

Darlene Barnes, Chairperson
Lawrence Grandison, Executive Dir.
6760 E. Irvington Place
Denver, CO 80279-8000
Phone: (303) 676-7009
FAX: (303) 676-6666
www.denver.feb.gov
E-mail: larry.grandison@dfas.mil

DETROIT, MI

Michael Jansen, Chairperson
Michelle Rhodes, Executive Director
477 Michigan Ave. Room M10
Detroit, MI 48226
Phone: (313) 226-3534
FAX: (313) 226-2155
E-mail: Rhodesm@tacom.army.mil

HONOLULU, HI

Edward H. Kubo Jr., Chairperson
Gloria Uyehara, Executive Director
300 Ala Moana Blvd, Rm 8-125
P.O. Box 50268
Honolulu, HI 96850
Phone: (808) 541-2637
FAX: (808) 541-3429
E-mail: guyehara@hpfeb.org

HOUSTON, TX

Captain Richard Kaser, Chairperson
Mike Mason, Executive Director
1919 Smith St. Suite 632
Houston, TX 77002
Phone: (713) 209-4524
FAX: (713) 209-3465
E-mail: Michael.mason@seabridge.net

KANSAS CITY, MO

Steven N. Tanner, Chairperson
Cindy Hillman, Executive Director
1500 E. Bannister Rd., Suite 1176
Kansas City, MO 64131
Phone: (816) 823-5100
FAX: (816) 823-5104
E-mail: feb.mail@gsa.gov

LOS ANGELES, CA

Tom Reid, Chairperson
Kathrene Hansen, Executive Director
501 W. Ocean, Suite 3200
Long Beach, CA 90802
Phone: (562) 980-3445
FAX: (562) 980-3448
www.losangeles.feb.gov
Kathrene.Hansen@dhs.gov

MIAMI, FL

Dorothy Johnson, Chairperson
Jaqueline Arroyo, Executive Director
440 Sawgrass Corp. Parkway, Suite 212
Sunrise, FL 33323
Phone: (954) 846-8248
FAX: (954) 846-9260
www.miami.feb.gov
E-mail: jarroyo@doc.gov

MINNEAPOLIS

Kenneth Kasprisin, Chairperson
Ray Morris, Executive Director
Bishop Henry Whipple Federal Building,
Room 510
St. Paul, MN 55111-4008
Phone: (612) 713-7201
FAX: (612) 713-7203
www.doi.gov/febtc/
E-mail: Ray_morris@os.doi.gov

NEWARK, NJ

Brian W. Tait, Chairperson
Angela A. Zaccardi, Executive Dir.
970 Broad St., Room 1434-B
Newark, NJ 07102
Phone: (973) 645-6217
FAX: (973) 645-6218
E-mail: Angela.zaccardi@gsa.gov

NEW ORLEANS, LA

William Gibson, Chairperson
Kathy Barre, Executive Director

P.O. Box 53206
New Orleans, LA 70153-3206
Phone: (504) 426-0106
FAX: (504) 426-8212
http://sig.nfc.usda.gov/feb
Email: kathy.barre@usda.gov

NEW YORK, NY

Clifford Kirsch, Chairperson
Cynthia Gable, Executive Director
26 Federal Plaza, Room 3016
New York, NY 10278
Phone: (212) 264-1890
FAX: (212) 264-1172
E-mail: cynthia.gable@gsa.gov

OKLAHOMA CITY, OK

Michael W. Roach, Chairperson
LeAnn Jenkins, Executive Director
215 Dean A. McGee Ave., Suite 320
Oklahoma City, OK 73102
Phone: (405) 231-4167
FAX: (405) 231-4165
www.oklahoma.feb.gov
E-mail: leannjenkins@juno.com

PORTLAND, OR

Anne Badgley, Chairperson
Ron Johnson, Executive Director
1220 SW Third Ave., Suite 1776
Portland, OR 97204-2823
Phone: (503) 326-2060
FAX: (503) 326-2070
E-mail: rjohnson@pcez.com

PHILADELPHIA, PA

V. Chapman-Smith, Chairperson
Jack Ratcliffe, Executive Director
William J. Green Jr. Federal Bldg.
600 Arch St., Room 4320
Philadelphia, PA 19106
Phone: (215) 861-3665
FAX: (215) 861-3667
E-mail: jack.ratcliffe@gsa.gov

PITTSBURGH, PA

John Pinto, Chairperson
George Buck, Executive Director
1000 Liberty Ave., Room 406
Pittsburgh, PA 15222
Phone: (412) 395-6223
FAX: (412) 395-6221
E-mail: GPB920@aol.com

ST. LOUIS, MO

Colonel Debra Cook, Chairperson
Susanne Valdez, Executive Director
1222 Spruce St., Room 2.202c
St. Louis, MO 63103
Phone: (314) 539-6312
FAX: (314) 539-6314
www.stlouis.feb.gov
E-mail: Susanne.valdez@gsa.gov

SAN ANTONIO, TX

Laurin Lee Jimenez, Chairperson
Rebecca Froboese, Executive Director
7411 John Smith, Suite 1210

San Antonio, TX 78229
Phone: (210) 616-8151
FAX: (210) 616-8155
E-mail: Rebecca.froboese@med.va.gov

SAN FRANCISCO, CA

Larry Eckerman, Chairperson
Dianna Louie, Executive Director
1301 Clay St., Room 1240N
Oakland, CA 94612-5209
Phone: (510) 637-6103
FAX: (510) 637-6253
E-mail: dianna.louie@gsa.gov

SEATTLE, WA

Carl L. Rabun, Chairperson
Anne Tiernan, Executive Director
Federal Executive Board
Jackson Federal Building, Room 2942
915 Second Av.
Seattle, WA 98174-1010
Phone: (206) 220-6171
FAX: (206) 220-6132
E-mail: anne.tiernan@gsa.gov

APPENDIX C
Federal Agency Contact List

This appendix provides a functional summary and general employment information for the three branches of the government and for 18 federal departments under the executive branch. Larger independent agencies are also listed.

The information and statistics provided in this appendix were extracted from the U.S. Government Manual 2006/2007, Federal Civilian Workforce Statistics Employment and Trends as of September 2006, the Federal Career Directory, and the Central Personnel Data File, Office of Workforce Information. The agency summaries include Internet Web site addresses and specific employment contact information when available. Many listings also include a summary of occupations employed by that organization. Use this Appendix in conjunction with Appendix D to target specific agencies that employ individuals in your occupational group. Also, explore related occupations that you may be qualified for. The more occupations and job series that you target, the better your chances are for employment.

Notice

If you're unable to reach an agency at the listed number, call directory assistance by dialing the area code plus 555-1212. For directory assistance in the metropolitan Washington, D.C., area call (202) 555-1212, for Virginia (703) 555-1212, and (301) 555-1212 for agencies located in Maryland in close proximity to the District of Columbia. You can also locate phone numbers at www.usbluepages.gov or www.info.gov/phone.htm.

LEGISLATIVE BRANCH

The Congress of the United States was created by Article 1, Section 1, of the Constitution. All legislative powers are vested in Congress, which consists of a Senate and House of Representatives. The Legislative branch has 29,486 employees.

The Senate is composed of 100 members, two from each state. Senators are elected for a six-year term. The House of Representatives is made up of 435 representatives. Each state elects representatives based on population distribution. The more populous the state the more representatives it has.

The vice president of the United States is the presiding officer of the Senate. The following offices are under the legislative branch (the number employed by each office is noted in parentheses):

Congress	(16,881)
Architect of the Capitol	(2,235)
United States Botanic Garden	(57)
General Accounting Office	(3,388)
Government Printing Office	(2,241)
Library of Congress	(3,994)
Congressional Budget Office	(233)

ARCHITECT OF THE CAPITOL
U.S. Capitol Building, Washington, DC 20515 (202)-228-1793, www.aoc.gov

The Architect of the Capitol is responsible for the care and maintenance of the Capitol building and nearby buildings and grounds.

UNITED STATES BOTANIC GARDEN
Office of The Director, 245 First St. SW., Washington, DC 20024
(202) 226-8333, www.usbg.gov

The United States Botanic Garden collects and grows various vegetable productions of this and other countries for exhibition and public display, student study, scientists, and garden clubs.

GOVERNMENT ACCOUNTABILITY OFFICE

441 G St. NW., Washington, DC 20548
(202) 512-3000, www.gao.gov

The General Accountability Office is the investigative arm of Congress and is charged with examining all matters related to the receipt and disbursement of public funds.

GOVERNMENT PRINTING OFFICE
732 North Capitol Street NW, Washington, DC 20401
(202) 512-0000, www.gpo.gov

This office prints, binds, and distributes the publications of Congress as well as the executive departments. Employment is primarily in administrative, clerical and technical fields.

LIBRARY OF CONGRESS
Recruitment & Placement Office
101 Independence Ave. SE,
Washington, DC 20540
(202) 707-5000, www.loc.gov

The Library of Congress is the national library of the United States, offering diverse materials for research including comprehensive historical collections.

CONGRESSIONAL BUDGET OFFICE
Second & D Streets SW,
Washington, DC 20515
(202) 226-2600, www.cbo.gov

Provides Congress with assessments of the economic impact of the congressional budget.

JUDICIAL BRANCH

Article III, Section 1, of the Constitution of the United States provides that "the judicial power of the United States shall be vested in one Supreme Court, and in such inferior courts as the Congress may from time to time ordain and establish." The Supreme Court was established on September 24, 1789. This branch employs 33,760 legal professionals, clerks, administrative personnel, secretaries, and other related specialties. The following offices are under this branch:

Supreme Court of the United States
Lower Courts
Special Courts
Administrative Office of the United States Courts
Federal Judicial Center
United States Sentencing Commission

THE SUPREME COURT
One First Street NE,
Washington, DC 20543
(202) 479-3000, www.supremecourtus.gov

Composed of the chief justice and eight associate justices, who are nominated by the president of the United States.

LOWER COURTS
Administrative Office of the U.S. Courts,
Thurgood Marshall Federal Judiciary Bldg.
One Columbus Circle NE,
Washington, DC 20544
(202) 502-2600

The 12 circuits include all states. There are 89 district offices located throughout the country. Consult your local telephone book for offices located near you. Includes Court of Appeals, U.S. District Courts, Territorial Courts, and the Judicial Panel on Multidistrict Litigation.

SPECIAL COURTS
Clerk's Office, U.S. Court of Federal Claims
717 Madison Place NW.,
Washington, DC 20005
(202) 357-6400

Consists of the U. S. Claims Court, Court of International Trade, Court of Military Appeals, United States Tax Court, Temporary Emergency Court of Appeals, Court of Veterans Appeals, and others.

ADMINISTRATIVE OFFICE OF U.S. COURTS
Human Resource Division
Thurgood Marshall Federal Judiciary Bldg.
One Columbus Circle NE,
Washington, DC 20544
(202) 502-2600, www.uscourts.gov

Charged with the nonjudicial, administrative business of U.S. courts. Includes the following divisions; Bankruptcy, Court Admin, Defender Services, Financial Management, General Counsel, Magistrates, Personnel, Probation, and Statistical Analysis.

FEDERAL JUDICIAL CENTER
Thurgood Marshall Federal Judiciary Bldg.
One Columbus Circle NE,
Washington DC 20002
(202) 502-4000, www.fjc.gov

The Federal Judiciary Center is the agency for policy research and continuing education.

U.S. SENTENCING COMMISSION
Suite 2-500, South Lobby,
One Columbus Circle NE,
Washington DC 20002
(202) 502-4500, www.ussc.gov

U.S. Sentencing Commission develops sentencing guidelines and policies for the federal courts.

EXECUTIVE BRANCH

The president is the administrative head of the executive branch and is responsible for numerous agencies as well as 14 executive departments. The administration of this vast bureaucracy is handled by the president's Cabinet, which includes the heads of the 15 executive departments. The executive branch consists of 1,879,679 employees distributed among the 15 departments and numerous independent agencies. The following offices, departments, and over 63 independent agencies are under the executive branch (The number employed by each office is noted in parentheses):

Executive Office of the President	(1,698)
The White House Office	(399)
Office of Management and Budget	(479)
Council of Economic Advisors	(24)
National Security Council	(60)
Office of Policy Development	(25)
U. S. Trade Representative	(226)
Council on Environmental Quality	(17)
Office of Science & Technology Policy	(26)
Office of Administration	(223)
Office of the Vice President	(19)
Office of National Drug Control Policy	(112)

THE WHITE HOUSE OFFICE
1600 Pennsylvania Avenue NW,
Washington, DC 20500
(202) 456-1414, www.whitehouse.gov

This office assists the president in the
performance of the many duties and
responsibilities of the office. The staff
facilitates and maintains communication
with Congress, agencies and the public.

**OFFICE OF MANAGEMENT &
BUDGET**
Executive Office Building
Washington, DC 20503
(202) 395-3080, www.whitehouse.gov/omb

Evaluates, formulates, and coordinates
management procedures and program
objectives among federal departments and
agencies. Employment inquiries: (202) 395-
1088.

NATIONAL SECURITY COUNCIL
Eisenhower Executive Building
Washington, DC 20504
(202) 456-1414

Advises the president with respect to the
integration of domestic, foreign, and
military policies relating to national
security.

OFFICE OF POLICY DEVELOPMENT
Eisenhower Executive Office Bldg.,
Room 469
Washington, DC 20502
(202) 456-5594

Advises the president in the formulation,
evaluation, and coordination of long-range
domestic and economic policy.

U.S. TRADE REPRESENTATIVE
600 17th Street NW,
Washington, DC 20508

(202) 395-3230, www.ustr.gov

Responsible for the direction of all trade
negotiations of the United States and for
the formulation of trade policy for the
United States.

**COUNCIL OF ECONOMIC
ADVISORS**
1800 G St. NW,
Washington DC 20502
(202) 395-5084, www.whitehouse.gov/cea

Analyzes the National Economy to provide
policy recommendations to the president.

**COUNCIL ON ENVIRONMENTAL
QUALITY**
722 Jackson Place NW,
Washington, DC 20503
(202) 395-5750, www.whitehouse.gov/ceq

Develops and recommends to the president
national environmental quality policies.

**OFFICE OF SCIENCE &
TECHNOLOGY**
Executive Office Bldg. 725 17th St. NW,
Washington, DC 20502
(202) 456-7116, www.ostp.gov

Provides scientific, engineering, and
technological analysis and judgment for the
president in major policy, plans, and
programs.

**OFFICE OF DRUG CONTROL
POLICY**

Executive Office of the President,
Washington, DC 20503
(202) 395-6700,
www.whitehousedrugpolicy.go

Assists the president in making policies
and objectives in national drug control

strategy. Employment Inquiries: (202) 395-6695

OFFICE OF ADMINISTRATION

Eisenhower Executive Building
725 17th St. NW,
Washington, DC 20503
(202) 456-2861

Provides administrative support to all units within the Executive Office of the President.

OFFICE OF THE VICE PRESIDENT

Eisenhower Executive Office Building
Washington, DC 20501
(202) 456-7549

The executive functions of the vice president include participation in Cabinet meetings and, by statute, membership on the National Security Council and the Board of Regents of the Smithsonian Institution.

THE 15 EXECUTIVE DEPARTMENTS

Agriculture	(105,047)
Commerce	(40,079)
Defense — nonmilitary	(675,744)
Education	(4,229)
Energy	(14,795)
Health & Human Services	(61,163)
Homeland Security	(154,100)
Housing & Urban Development	(9,935)
Interior	(72,274)
Justice	(106,781)
Labor	(16,199)
State	(34,160)
Transportation	(53,865)
Treasury	(106,925)
Veterans Affairs	(239,299)

DEPARTMENT OF AGRICULTURE

1400 Independence Ave. SW,
Washington, DC 20250
(202) 720-4623, www.usda.gov

This department works to maintain and improve farm income and develop and expand markets abroad for agricultural products. Helps curb and cure poverty, hunger, and malnutrition. Enhances the environment and maintains production capacity through efforts to protect the soil, water, forests, and other natural resources.

General employment inquiries may be sent to the Staffing & Personnel Information Systems Staff, Office of Personnel, Department of Agriculture, Washington, DC 20250.

EMPLOYMENT INFORMATION — Employment opportunities within the Food & Consumer Service can be researched by contacting the national headquarters in Washington, D.C., phone (703) 305-2286. Regional offices are located in Atlanta, Chicago, Dallas, San Francisco, Denver, Boston, and N.J. For these locations look up the Department of Agriculture, Food & Nutrition Services in the above cities' phone directory or obtain addresses from the headquarters in Washington, D.C.

Field meat and poultry inspector units are located throughout the country in hundreds of metropolitan areas. Employment opportunities exist at hundreds of locations that are administered from the central offices. Persons interested in employment in the Food Safety and Inspection Service should contact the USDA Office of Personnel, Washington, DC 20250. Phone (301) 504-9605, E-mail: mphotline.fsis@usda.gov. Internet Web site: www.fsis.usda.gov

DEPARTMENT OF COMMERCE (DOC)
Fourteenth Street and Constitution Ave. NW,
Washington, DC 20230
(202) 482-2000, employment: (202) 482-4807
Employment Web site: www.doc.gov/ohrm

This department promotes the nation's international trade, economic growth, and technological advancement. The Department of Commerce provides assistance and information to increase America's competitiveness in the world economy, administers programs to prevent unfair foreign trade competition, provides research and support for the increased use of scientific engineering and technological development. Other responsibilities include the granting of patents and registration of trademarks, development of policies, and conducting various research projects.

DOC OFFICES, AGENCIES AND BUREAUS

- **BUREAU OF THE CENSUS** — This bureau is a general-purpose statistical agency that collects, tabulates, and publishes a wide variety of statistical data about people and the economy of the nation. For additional information contact the Marketing Service Office, Bureau of the Census, Dept. of Commerce, Washington, DC 20233. Phone (301) 763-INFO.

- **ECONOMIC & STATISTICS ADMINISTRATION** — This bureau provides a picture of the U. S. economy. For additional information contact the Public Information Office, Bureau of Economic Analysis, Dept. of Commerce, Washington, DC 20230. Phone (202) 482-3727. .

- **ECONOMIC DEVELOPMENT ADMINISTRATION** — This agency was created to generate new jobs, to help protect existing jobs, and to stimulate commercial and industrial growth in economically distressed areas. For further information contact the Economic Development Administration, Department of Commerce, Washington, DC 20230. Phone, (202) 482-2900.

- **INTERNATIONAL TRADE ADMINISTRATION** — The International Trade Administration was established to strengthen the international trade and investment position of the United States. There are 47 district offices located throughout the country. A listing of district offices and specific employment information can be obtained through the International Trade Administration, Department of Commerce, Washington, DC 20230. Phone (202) 482-3917.

- **MINORITY BUSINESS DEVELOPMENT AGENCY** — This agency was created to assist minority enterprise in achieving effective and equitable participation in the American free enterprise system. Provides management and technical assistance to minority firms on request, primarily through a network of minority business development centers. For additional information contact the Office of the Director, Minority Business Development Agency, Department of Commerce, Washington, DC 20230. Phone (202) 482-5061, www.mbda.gov

- **NATIONAL OCEANIC AND ATMOSPHERIC ADMINISTRATION (NOAA)** — NOAA's mission is to explore, map, and chart the global ocean and its living resources and to manage, use, and conserve those resources. Predicts atmospheric conditions, ocean, sun, and space environment. Maintains weather stations including an electronic maintenance staff to service weather radar systems and other related weather equipment. Field employment offices:

  Northwest Region
  Bin C15700, Bldg. 1
  7600 Sand Point Way NE, Seattle, WA 98115
  206-526-6150

  Northeast Region
  1 Blackburn Dr., Gloucester, MA 02543
  978-281-9250

  Southwest Region
  Suite 4200, 501 W. Ocean Blvd., Long Beach CA 90802
  562-980-4001

  Southeast Region
  263 13th Ave., St. Petersburg, FL 33701
  727-824-5320

- **PATENT AND TRADEMARK OFFICE** — Examines hundreds of thousands of patents and trademarks each year. Sells copies of issued patents and trademark registrations, records and indexes documents transferring ownership, maintains a scientific library and searches over 30 million documents. Office of Public Affairs, Patent and Trademark Office, Washington, DC 22202. Phone (703)-305-8341, www.uspto.gov

- **NATIONAL INSTITUTE OF STANDARDS AND TECHNOLOGY-**
  Conducts research for the nation's physical and technical measurement systems as well as scientific and technological measurement systems. Phone, (301) 975-NIST, e-mail: inquiries@nist.gov, or visit their Web site at www.nist.gov

DEPARTMENT OF DEFENSE (DOD)

Office of the Secretary, The Pentagon,
Washington, DC 20301-1155
(703) 545-6700, www.defenselink.mil

Responsible for providing the military forces needed to deter war and protect the security of the United States. Major elements are the Army, Navy, Marine Corps, and Air Force, consisting of close to 1.5 million men and women on active duty. In case of emergency, they are backed up by 1 million reserve forces members. In addition, there are about 675,744 Defense Department civilian employees.

The DOD is composed of the Office of the Secretary of Defense; the military departments and the military services within those departments; the Organization of the Joint Chiefs of Staff; the unified and specified combatant commands; the Armed Forces Policy Council; the Defense agencies, and various DOD field facilities. This executive branch department is the largest civilian employer. The jobs are interspersed through the United States and at several hundred installations overseas.

For overseas locations and employment contacts see Chapter Seven. The jobs in the United States are distributed throughout every state plus the District of Columbia. The majority of military installations hire civilian personnel. Many are hired off of OPM's federal registers, and others are special appointments for hiring veterans, spouses and family members of military personnel, the handicapped, minorities and others.

Locate military installations in your area in the yellow pages of your phone directory under government. Also, the blue pages in the white page telephone directory provide comprehensive listings of government offices including military installations in your area.

> **EMPLOYMENT INFORMATION** - Additional employment information can be obtained by writing to the Human Resources Directorate, Washington Headquarters Services, 1155 Defense Pentagon, Washington, DC 20301-1155. Phone 866-205-4975, Web site: https://storm.psd.whs.mil/cgi-bin/apply.pl

DEPARTMENT OF EDUCATION

400 Maryland Ave. SW,
Washington, DC 20202
(800) USA-LEARN, www.ed.gov

The Department of Education is the Cabinet-level department that establishes policy for, administers, and coordinates most federal assistance to education. Total employment within this department is less than 5,000. There are 10 regional offices, located in Atlanta, Boston, Chicago, Dallas, Denver, Kansas City, New York, Philadelphia, San Francisco, and Seattle.

> **EMPLOYMENT INFORMATION -** Employment inquiries and applications should be directed to the Human Resources Group at the above address. Phone (202) 401-0553.

DEPARTMENT OF ENERGY

1000 Independence Ave. SW,
Washington, DC 20585
(202) 586-5000, www.energy.gov

The Department of Energy provides a balanced national energy plan through the coordination and administration of the energy functions of the federal government. The department is responsible for long-term, high-risk research and development of energy technology; the marketing of federal power, energy conservation; the nuclear weapons program, energy regulatory programs, and a central energy data collection and analysis program.

The majority of the department's energy research and development activities are carried out by contractors who operate government-owned facilities. Management and administration of these government-owned, contractor operated facilities are the major responsibility of this department.

> **EMPLOYMENT INFORMATION -** Employment inquiries and applications should be directed to the Office of Human Capital Management. Phone (202) 586-1234.

DEPARTMENT OF HEALTH AND HUMAN SERVICES (HHS)

200 Independence Ave. SW,
Washington, DC 20201
(202) 619-0257, www.hhs.gov

The Department of Health and Human Services employs 61,163 persons and touches the lives of more Americans than any other federal agency. This department advises the president on health, welfare, and income security plans, policies, and programs of the federal government. These programs are administered through five operating divisions: the Social Security Administration, the Health Care Financing Administration, the Office of Human Development Services, the Public Health Service, and the Family Support Administration.

ADMINISTRATION, SERVICES AND OTHER OFFICES

- **ADMINISTRATION FOR CHILDREN AND FAMILIES** - Provides national leadership and direction to plan, manage, and coordinate the nationwide administration of comprehensive and supportive programs for vulnerable children and families. Contact the Office of Human Resource Management, Administration for Children and Families, 370 L'Enfant Promenade SW, Washington, DC 20447. Phone 202-401-9261, www.acf.dhhs.gov

- **AGENCY FOR HEALTHCARE RESEARCH & QUALITY**- The research arm of the Public Health Service. They work with the private sector and other public organizations to help consumers make better informed choices. 540 Gaither Rd., Rockville, MD 20850. Contact the agency at 301-427-1889, Internet www.ahrq.gov

- **CENTER FOR DISEASE CONTROL AND PREVENTION -** CDC is the federal agency charged with protecting the public health of the nation by providing leadership and direction in the prevention and control of diseases and other conditions. Contact the CDC at 1600 Clifton Road NE, Atlanta, GA 30333. Phone 404-639-3286, www.cdc.gov

- **FOOD AND DRUG ADMINISTRATION (FDA) -** The FDA's programs are designed to achieve the objective of consumer protection. FDA, 5600 Fishers Lane, Rockville, MD 20857. Phone 888-463-6332. Schools interested in the college recruitment program should also contact 301-827-4120.

- **INDIAN HEALTH SERVICE -** Provides a comprehensive health services delivery system for American Indians and Alaska Natives. Contact the Management Policy Support Staff, Room 6-34, Suite 400, 801 Thompson Ave., Rockville, MD 20852. Phone 301-443-2650 www.ihs.gov

- **NATIONAL INSTITUTES OF HEALTH -** NIH seeks to expand fundamental knowledge about the nature and behavior of living systems, to apply that knowledge to extend the health of human lives, and to reduce the burdens resulting from disease and disability. Contact the Office of Human Resources at 301-496-4000 or visit www.nih.gov for employment information.

  EMPLOYMENT INFORMATION - General employment inquiries should be directed to 1 Center Lane, Bethesda,, MD 20892. Phone 301-496-4000, Employment Web site: www.jobs.nih.gov

DEPARTMENT OF HOMELAND SECURITY (DHS)
Washington, DC 20528
(202) 282-8000, www.dhs.gov

Homeland Security employs 154,100 federal workers, and the department's mission is to protect the United States using state-of-the-art intelligence information. DHS was established by the Homeland Security Act of 2002, (6 U.S.C. 101) to consolidate the functions of 22 agencies under one vast network to protect the United States.

The Department of Homeland Security transferred functions from the Department of the Treasury, Justice, HHS, Defense, FBI, Secret Service, GSA, Energy, Agriculture, Transportation, and the U.S. Coast Guard. The new organization is comprised of five major directorates:

Policy Directorate

U.S. Custom Service
US Citizenship & Immigration Service
Federal Protective Service
Transportation Security
Federal Law Enforcement Training Center
Animal & Plant Health Inspection Service
Office for Domestic Preparedness

Federal Emergency Management

Federal Emergency Management Agency (FEMA)
Strategic National Stockpile & National Disaster Medical System
Nuclear Incident Response Team
Domestic Emergency Support Team
National Domestic Preparedness Office

Preparedness Directorate

Federal Computer Incident Response Center
National Communications System
National Infrastructure Protection Center
Energy Security and Assurance Program

Science and Technology

CBRN Countermeasures Program
Environmental Measurement Laboratory
National BW Defense Analysis Center
Plum Island Animal Disease Center

Management

> **EMPLOYMENT INFORMATION -** Homeland Security advertises most jobs through OPM's Web site at http://usajobs.opm.gov. However, some online applications are accepted for specific jobs on their site at http://www.dhs.gov and they offer informative applicant study guides, career information, and videos. Their U.S. Immigration and Customs Enforcement (ICE) site at http://ice.gov provides career information for Federal Air Marshals, Office of Intelligence, Detention and Removal, Air and Marine Operations, and their Office of Investigations.

DEPARTMENT OF HOUSING AND URBAN DEVELOPMENT (HUD)
451 Seventh St. SW,
Washington, DC 20410
(202) 708-1422, www.hud.gov

This department employs 9,935 persons and is the federal agency responsible for programs concerned with the nation's housing needs, the development and preservation of the nation's communities, and the provisions of equal housing opportunity.

The department administers the Federal Housing Administration mortgage insurance programs, rental assistance programs for lower income families; the Government National Mortgage Association (GNMA) mortgage-backed securities programs and other programs. Regional offices are located in Boston, New York City, Philadelphia, Atlanta, Fort Worth, Kansas City, Denver, San Francisco, and Seattle.

> **EMPLOYMENT INFORMATION -** General employment inquiries should be directed to the Office of Human Resources, 202-708-0408; or visit the Web site at www.hud.gov/jobs.

DEPARTMENT OF THE INTERIOR
1849 C St. NW,
Washington, DC 20240
(202) 208-3100, www.doi.gov

The nation's principal conservation agency employs 72,274 persons. The Department of the Interior has responsibility for most of our nationally owned public lands and natural resources. This includes fostering the wisest use of our land and water resources, protecting our fish and wildlife, preserving the environmental and cultural values of our national parks and historical places, and providing for the enjoyment of life through outdoor recreation.

BUREAUS, SERVICES AND OTHER OFFICES

- **U.S. FISH, WILDLIFE & PARKS SERVICE** - This service is composed of a headquarters office in Washington, D.C., seven regional offices in the lower 48 states and Alaska, a regional research structure, and a variety of field units and installations. These include 540 national wildlife refuges and 63 fish and wildlife management assistance offices, 64 fishery resource offices, 69 national fish hatcheries, and a nationwide network of wildlife law enforcement agents. Office of Public Affairs, Fish and Wildlife Service, Department of the Interior, Washington, DC 20240. Phone (202) 208-5634, Headquarters Personnel Office: (703) 358-1743, www.fws.gov/jobs.

- **NATIONAL PARK SERVICE -** The National Park Service has a service center in Denver and a center for production of exhibits in Harpers Ferry, W.Va.. There are 390 units in the national parks, monuments, scenic parkways, riverways, seashores, lakeshores, recreation areas, reservoirs, and historic sites. This service develops and implements park plans and staffs the area offices. Phone (202) 208-4747. Internet, www.nps.gov.

    EMPLOYMENT INFORMATION - Direct inquiries to the Personnel Office, National Parks Service, Department of the Interior, Washington, DC 20240. **Applications for temporary employment** must be received between September 1 and January 15 and should be sent to the Division of Personnel Management, National Parks Service, 1849 C St. NW, Washington, DC 20240. Phone (202) 513-7280.

- **BUREAU OF LAND MANAGEMENT -** This service has responsibility for programs associated with public land management; operations management and leasing for minerals on public lands. Contact the bureau for employment information at Department of the Interior, LS-406, 1849 C St. NW, Washington DC 20240. Phone (202) 452-5125, Internet, www.blm.gov.

- **U.S. GEOLOGICAL SURVEY** - The primary responsibilities of this service are to identify the nation's land, water, energy, and mineral resources. U.S. Geological Survey, Dept. of the Interior, 12201 Sunrise Valley Drive, Reston, VA 20192. Phone 703-648-4000. E-mail: ask@usgs.gov, Visit USGS jobs at www.usgs.gov/ohr/oars.

- **OFFICE OF SURFACE MINING RECLAMATION & ENFORCEMENT -** Protects the environment from the detrimental effects of coal mining. Office of Surface Mining Reclamation and Enforcement, Dept. of the Interior, Washington, DC 20240. Phone (202) 208-2565. Internet, www.osmre.gov.

- **MINERALS MANAGEMENT SERVICE** - Assesses the nature and recoverability of minerals including environmental review for Outer Continental Shelf lands. Mineral Management Service, Dept. of the Interior, Room 4259, MS

4230, 1849 C St. NW., Washington, DC 20240. Phone (202) 208-3985. Internet, www.mms.gov.

- **BUREAU OF INDIAN AFFAIRS** - The principal objectives of the bureau are to actively encourage and train Indian and Alaska Native people to manage their own affairs under the trust relationship to the federal government. For information contact the Office of the Assistant Secretary, Bureau of Indian Affairs, Dept. of the Interior, 1848 C St. NW, Washington, DC 20240. Phone (202) 208-3710.

- **BUREAU OF RECLAMATION** - The largest water supplier and second largest hydroelectric power supplier in the US. Bureau of Reclamation, Dept. Of the Interior, Washington, DC 20240. Phone (202) 513-0575. Internet, www.usbr.gov.

DEPARTMENT OF JUSTICE
950 Pennsylvania Avenue NW,
Washington, DC 20530
(202) 514-2000, www.usdoj.gov
Agency Wide Employment HOTLINE: 202-514-3397

The Department of Justice employs 106,781. It is the largest law firm in the nation and serves as counsel for its citizens. It represents them in enforcing the law in the public interest. This department conducts all suits in the Supreme Court in which the United States is concerned. The attorney general supervises and directs these activities, as well as those of the U.S. attorney and U.S. marshals in the various districts around the country.

DIVISIONS — DEPARTMENT OF JUSTICE

ANTITRUST - Responsible for promoting and maintaining competitive markets by enforcing the federal antitrust laws. This division has field offices at the federal buildings in Atlanta, Chicago, Cleveland, Dallas, New York, Philadelphia, and San Francisco. Contact the FOIA Unit, Antitrust Division, Department of Justice, 325 Seventh St. NW, Washington DC 20530. Phone (202) 514-2692.

CIVIL - Litigation involves cases in federal district courts, the U.S. Courts of Appeals, the U.S. Claims Court, etc This division represents the United States, its departments and agencies, members of Congress, Cabinet officers, and other federal employees. There are three field office facilities. The Commercial Litigation Branch has two field offices. For employment information contact the Civil Division, Tenth Street & Pennsylvania Ave. NW, Washington, DC 20530. Phone, 202-514-3301.

CRIMINAL - Formulates criminal law enforcement policies, enforces and exercises general supervision over all federal criminal laws except those assigned to the other divisions. Contact Criminal Division, Dept. of Justice, Tenth St. & Pennsylvania Ave. NW, Washington DC 20530. Phone (202) 514-2601.

ENVIRONMENT AND NATURAL RESOURCES DIVISION - Enforces criminal and civil environmental laws to protect the U.S. and its environment. Environment and Natural Resources Division, Dept. of Justice, Tenth St. and Pennsylvania Ave. NW, Washington, DC 20530. Phone (202) 514-2701.

TAX DIVSION - Ensures fair tax enforcement of federal tax laws in both the state and federal court systems. Contact the Tax Division, Dept. of Justice, Tenth St. & Pennsylvania Ave. NW, Washington, DC 20530. Phone (202) 514-2001. Internet www.usdoj.gov/tax.

BUREAUS AND SERVICES

- **FEDERAL BUREAU OF INVESTIGATION (FBI)**
  935 Pennsylvania Ave, NW
  Washington, DC 20535
  (202) 324-3000, www.fbi.gov

  The FBI is the principal investigative arm of the U.S. Department of Justice. It is charged with gathering and reporting facts, locating witnesses, and compiling evidence in cases involving federal jurisdiction. The bureau's investigations are conducted through 58 field offices.

  > **EMPLOYMENT INFORMATION** - Direct inquiries to the Director, Federal Bureau of Investigation, Washington, DC 20535. You can also contact any of the 58 field offices. Consult your local telephone directory for the office nearest you.

- **BUREAU OF PRISONS**
  320 First St. NW,
  Washington, DC 20534
  (202) 307-3198, www.bop.gov

  Responsible for maintaining secure, safe, and humane correctional institutions for individuals placed in the care and custody of the attorney general. Maintains and staffs all federal penal and correctional institutions.

  > **EMPLOYMENT INFORMATION** - Direct inquiries to the Bureau of Prisons, Central Office, 320 First St. NW, Washington, DC 20534, 202-307-3082 or to any regional or field office.

- **UNITED STATES MARSHALS SERVICE**
  Washington, DC 20530
  (202) 307-9000, www.usmarshals.gov

The presidentially appointed marshals and their support staff of just over 4,300 deputy marshals and administrative personnel operate from 427 office locations in all 94 federal judicial districts nationwide, from Guam to Puerto Rico and from Alaska to Florida.

- **DRUG ENFORCEMENT ADMINISTRATION**
  600-700 Army Navy Drive
  Arlington, VA 22202
  (202) 307-1000

  The Drug Enforcement Administration is the lead federal agency in enforcing narcotics and controlled substances laws and regulations. The administration has offices throughout the United States and in 43 foreign countries. Special agents conduct criminal investigations and prepare for the prosecution of violators of the drug laws. Entry level is at the GS-7 or GS-9 grade with progression to GS-12 in three years.

  This administration uses accountants, engineers, computer scientists, language majors, chemists, history majors, mathematicians, and other specialties for special agents. Investigators, intelligence research and administrative positions are also filled.

  > **EMPLOYMENT INFORMATION -** Contact or direct inquiries to the Office of Personnel at the address listed above or call the job hotline at 202-514-3397.

DEPARTMENT OF LABOR
200 Constitution Ave. NW,
Washington, DC 20210
(202) 693-5000, www.dol.gov

The Department of Labor was created to foster, promote and develop the welfare of the wage earners of the United States, to improve their working conditions, and to advance their opportunities for profitable employment. The department administers a variety of federal labor laws guaranteeing workers the right to safe and healthful working conditions.

This department has 16,195 employees and ranks 12th out of the 15 departments in total number of employees. Yet the Department of Labor affects every worker in the United States through one of its many internal components: the Pension and Welfare Benefits Administration, Office of Labor-Management Standards, Office of Administrative Law Judges, Benefits Review Board, Bureau of International Labor Affairs, Bureau of Labor Statistics, Women's Bureau, Employment Standards Administration, Employment and Training Administration, Mine Safety and Health Administration, Veterans' Employment and Training Service, and Occupational Safety and Health Administration (OSHA).

EMPLOYMENT INFORMATION - Personnel offices use lists of eligibles from the clerical, scientific, technical, and general examinations of the Office of Personnel Management. Inquiries and applications may be directed to the address listed above or consult your telephone directory (under U.S. Government - Department of Labor) for field offices nearest you.

DEPARTMENT OF STATE
2201 C St. NW,
Washington, DC 20520
(202) 647-4000 (24-hour job vacancy hotline), www.state.gov

The Department of State advises the president in the formulation and execution of foreign policy. The department's primary objective is to promote the long-range security and well-being of the United States.

There are hundreds of staffed facilities internationally including U.S. embassies, missions, consulates general, U.S. Liaison offices and consular agencies throughout the world , manned by several thousand Foreign Service officers of the Department of State. The State Department's total employment exceeds 34,000 full time employees assigned stateside and overseas in administrative, personnel, management, engineering, communications electronics, security, and career Foreign Service officer positions.

EMPLOYMENT INFORMATION - **For Foreign Service Opportunities contact**: Foreign Service, Recruitment Division, HR/REE, Room H-518, 2401 E St. NW, Washington, DC 20522. Phone (202) 261-8888, www.careers.state.gov. **For Civil Service Opportunities**: Use the same Web site or phone (202) 663-2176.

DEPARTMENT OF TRANSPORTATION (DOT)
Central Employment Information Office
400 Seventh St. SW,
Washington, DC 20590
(202) 366-4000, www.dot.gov

The Department of Transportation employs 53,865 persons and establishes the nation's overall transportation policy. There are 11 administrations, whose jurisdiction includes highway planning, urban mass transit, railroads, aviation, and the safety of waterways, ports, highways, and pipelines. **For Employment opportunities:** Contact the Transportation Administrative Service Center (TASC), Room PL-402, 400 Seventh St. SW, Washington DC 20590. Phone (202) 366-9391 or (800) 525-2878.

ADMINISTRATIONS & OFFICES OF THE DOT

Federal Aviation Administration
Federal Highway Administration
Federal Railroad Administration
National Highway Traffic Safety Administration
Federal Transit Administration
St. Lawrence Seaway Development Corporation
Maritime Administration
Research and Innovative Technology Administration
Pipeline and Hazardous Materials Safety Administration
Federal Motor Carrier Safety Administration
Surface Transportation Board

- ## FEDERAL AVIATION ADMINISTRATION (FAA)
800 Independence Ave. SW,
Washington, DC 20591
(202) 366-4000, www.faa.gov

The administration is charged with regulating air commerce, controlling navigable airspace, promoting civil aeronautics, research and development, installing and operating air navigation facilities, air traffic control, and environmental impact of air navigation.

EMPLOYMENT INFORMATION: Entry level engineers start at the FV-5/7/9 grade depending on college grades and work experience. The FAA is now an excepted agency and their pay system is determined by a core compensation pay band system. Engineers progress to the FV-11 or 12 pay grade. Air traffic control specialists start at an equivalent FG-7 pay grade and can progress through an equivalent FV-14 grade and higher. Electronics technicians typically start in the F or G band (equivalent to the FV 9/11) and journeyman specialists are in the H band, which is greater than a typical GS-12 grade. A large number of administrative, clerical, and personnel specialists are also needed.

- ## FEDERAL HIGHWAY ADMINISTRATION
400 Seventh St. NW,
Washington, DC 20590
(202) 366-0650, www.fhwa.dot.gov

This agency is concerned with the total operation and environment of highway systems. Civil/highway engineers, motor carrier safety specialists, accountants, contract specialists, computer programmers, and administrative and clerical skills are needed.

EMPLOYMENT INFORMATION - Major occupations include Civil and Highway Engineer, Motor Carrier Safety Specialists, Accountants, Contract Specialists, Computer Programmers, Administrative, Clerical and Transportation Specialists.

- **FEDERAL RAILROAD ADMINISTRATION**
  Office of Personnel
  1120 Vermont Ave. NW,
  Washington, DC 20590
  (202) 493-6000, www.fra.dot.gov

  The Federal Railroad Administration enforces railroad safety, conducts research and development, provides passenger and freight services, and staffs and maintains the Transportation Test Center.

  EMPLOYMENT INFORMATION — Major occupations include economist, contract specialist, accountant, attorney, law clerk, administrative and clerical.

- **NATIONAL HIGHWAY TRAFFIC SAFETY ADMINISTRATION**
  Office of Personnel
  400 Seventh St. SW,
  Washington, DC 20590 (202) 366-9550, www.nhtsa.gov

  The National Highway Traffic Safety Administration was established to reduce the number of deaths, injuries, and economic losses resulting from traffic accidents on national highways.

  EMPLOYMENT INFORMATION — Major occupations include attorney advisor, law clerk, highway safety specialist, mathematical statistician, mechanical engineer, safety standard engineer, and administrative and clerical.

- **FEDERAL TRANSIT ADMINISTRATION**
  400 Seventh St. SW,
  Washington, DC 20590
  (202) 366-4043, www.fta.dot.gov

  Its mission is to assist in the development of improved mass transportation, to encourage the planning and establishment of area wide urban mass transit systems, and to provide assistance to state and local governments in financing such systems.

  EMPLOYMENT INFORMATION - Transportation specialist, civil engineer, general engineer, contract specialist, and administrative and clerical.

- **RESEARCH & INNOVATIVE TECHNOLOGY ADMINISTRATION**
  Personnel Office, Room 8401
  400 Seventh St. SW,
  Washington, DC 20590
  (202) 366-4433, www.rita.dot.gov

  This administration consists of the Office of Hazardous Materials Transportation, office of Pipeline Safety, Office of Civil Rights, Office of the Chief Counsel, the Transportation Systems Center in Cambridge, Massachusetts, Office of Emergency Transportation, Office of Aviation Information Management, and the Office of Administration.

  > **EMPLOYMENT INFORMATION -** Major occupations include transportation specialist, general engineer (pipeline), mechanical engineer, chemical engineer, writer/editor, and administrative and clerical.

DEPARTMENT OF THE TREASURY
1500 Pennsylvania Ave. NW,
Washington, DC 20220
(202) 622-2000, www.treas.gov

The Department of the Treasury employs 106,925 persons and performs four basic functions: formulating and recommending economic, financial, tax, and fiscal policies; serving as financial agent for the US Government; enforcing the law; and manufacturing coins and currency.

BUREAUS, SERVICES, and OFFICES OF THE TREASURY

Internal Revenue Service
Bureau of Alcohol, Tobacco, & Trade
Bureau of Engraving and Printing
Financial Management Service
U.S. Mint
Office of the Comptroller of the Currency
Bureau of the Public Debt

- **INTERNAL REVENUE SERVICE (IRS)**
  1111 Constitution Ave. NW,
  Washington, DC 20224
  (202) 622-5000, www.irs.gov

  The Internal Revenue Service has more than 100,000 employees and is the largest organization in the Department of the Treasury. Approximately 7,000 of these employees work in Washington, D.C. Others are employed in hundreds of offices throughout the U.S. There is an IRS office in or near every town.

EMPLOYMENT INFORMATION - Almost every major field of study has some application to the work of the IRS. A substantial number of positions are in accounting, business administration, finance, economics, criminology, and law. There are also a number of persons whose college major was political science, public administration, education, liberal arts, or other fields not directly related to business or law.

- **BUREAU OF ALCOHOL & TOBACCO TAX & TRADE BUREAU**
  1310 G St. NW.,
  Washington, DC 20220
  (202)927-5000, www.ttb.gov

  The bureau is responsible for enforcing and administering the existing federal laws and Tax Code provisions related to the production and taxation of alcohol and tobacco products. It also collects all excise taxes on the manufacture of firearms and ammunition.

- **BUREAU OF ENGRAVING & PRINTING**
  Office of External Relations
  14 and C Streets SW,
  Washington, DC 20228
  (202) 874-3019, www.moneyfactory.com

  The Bureau of Engraving & Printing designs, prints, and finishes a large variety of security products including Federal Reserve notes, U.S. postage stamps, Treasury securities, and certificates. The bureau is the largest printer of security documents in the world; over 40 billion documents are printed annually. The bureau's headquarters and most of its production operations are located in Washington, D.C. A second currency plant is in Fort Worth, Texas.

  EMPLOYMENT INFORMATION - Selections are highly competitive. Major occupations include police officer, computer specialist, engineer, con-tract specialist, engraver, production manager, security specialist, accountant, auditor, and administrative and clerical positions. Phone 202-874-2633 for information.

- **U.S. MINT**
  801 Ninth St. NW,
  Washington, DC 20220
  (202) 354-7200, www.usmint.gov

  The United States Mint employs some 2,300 employees at six locations including Washington, D.C. Field facilities are located in Philadelphia, Denver, San Francisco, West Point, N.Y., and Fort Knox, Ky. The U.S. Mint produces bullion and domestic and foreign coins, distributes gold and silver, and controls bullion.

- **BUREAU OF PUBLIC DEBT**
999 E St. NW,
Washington, DC 20239-0001
(202) 504-3500, www.publicdebt.treas.gov

The bureau administers the public debt by borrowing money through the sale of United States Treasury securities. The sale, service, and processing of Treasury securities involves the Federal Reserve Banks and their branches, which serve as fiscal agents of the Treasury. This bureau also manages the U.S. Savings Bond program.

> **EMPLOYMENT INFORMATION -** The major occupations include accountant, operating accountant, computer systems analyst, computer programmer, computer analyst. Employment inquiries: Bureau of the Public Debt, Division of Personnel Management, Employment and Classification Branch, Parkersburg, WV 26106. Phone (304) 480-6144.

DEPARTMENT OF VETERANS AFFAIRS

810 Vermont Ave. NW,
Washington, DC 20420
(202) 273-4900, www.va.gov

The Department of Veterans Affairs employs 239,299 persons and operates programs to benefit veterans and members of their families. Benefits include compensation payments for disabilities or death related to military service; pensions; education and rehabilitation; home loan guaranty; burial; and a medical care program incorporating nursing homes, clinics, and medical centers.

> **EMPLOYMENT INFORMATION -** The VA employs physicians, dentists, podiatrists, optometrists, nurses, nurse anesthetists, physician assistants, expanded function dental auxiliaries, registered respiratory therapists, certified respiratory therapists, licensed physical therapists, occupational therapists, pharmacists, and licensed practical or vocational nurses under the VA's excepted merit system. This does not require civil service eligibility.
>
> Other major occupations include accounting, all B.S. and B.A. majors, architecture, business, computer science, engineering, law, statistics, and numerous administrative and clerical positions. There are hundreds of national Veterans Affairs facilities within the United States. Consult your local telephone directory for the facility nearest you or search the VA Web site at www.va.gov/jobs.

INDEPENDENT AGENCIES (Partial List)

Central Intelligence Agency
Office of Personnel
Washington, DC 20505
(703) 482-0623, www.cia.gov

Commission on Civil Rights
624 Ninth St., NW,
Washington, DC 20425
(202) 376-7700, www.usccr.gov

Commodity Futures Trading Commission
1155 21st St. NW,
Washington, DC 20581
(202) 418-5000, www.cftc.gov

Consumer Product Safety Commission
Division of Personnel Management
4330 East West Hwy.
Bethesda, MD 20814
(301) 504-7908, www.cpsc.gov

Defense Nuclear Facilities Safety Board
Suite 700, 625 Indiana Ave. NW,
Washington, DC 20004
(202) 694-7000, www.dnfsb.gov

Environmental Protection Agency
1200 Pennsylvania Ave. NW,
Washington, DC 20460
(202) 272-0167, Employment 202-564-3300
www.epa.gov

Equal Opportunity Commission
1801 L Street NW,
Washington, DC 20507
202-663-4900, TTY, 202-663-4494
Employment, (202) 663-4306,
www.eeoc.gov

Farm Credit Administration
Human Resources Division
1501 Farm Credit Drive
McLean, VA 22102-5090
(703) 883-4000

Employment (703) 883-444, www.fca.gov

Federal Communications Commission
445 12th St. SW,
Washington, DC 20554
888-225-5322, Employment 202-418-0130
www.fcc.gov

Federal Deposit Insurance Corporation
Director of Personnel
550 17th St. NW,
Washington, DC 20429
(202) 736-6000, www.fdic.gov

Federal Election Commission
999 E. St. NW,
Washington, DC 20463
(202) 694-1100 or (800) 424-9530
www.fec.gov

Federal Housing Finance Board
1625 I Street NW,
Washington, DC 20006
(202) 408-2500, www.fhfb.gov

Federal Labor Relations Authority
1400 K Street NW.,
Washington, DC 20005
(202) 218-7770, Employment (202) 218-7963
www.flra.gov

Federal Maritime Commission
800 North Capital St. NW,
Washington, DC 20573-0001
(202) 523-5707, Employment (202) 523-5773
www.fmc.gov

Federal Mine Safety & Health Commission
601 New Jersey Ave. NW, Suite 9500
Washington, DC 20001-2021
202-434-9900, www.fmshrc.gov

Federal Reserve System
20th St. and Constitution Ave. NW,
Washington, DC 20551
202-452-3000, www.federalreserve.gov

Federal Retirement Thrift Investment Board
1250 H Street NW,
Washington, DC 20005
(202) 492-1600, www.tsp.gov

Federal Trade Commission
600 Pennsylvania Ave. NW,
Washington, DC 20580
(202) 326-2222, Employment 202-326-2021
www.ftc.gov

General Services Administration
1800 F Street NW,
Washington, DC 20405
(202) 708-5082,
Employment (202) 501-0370 www.gsa.gov

Government Printing Office
Chief Employment Branch
732 North Capitol Street NW,
Washington, DC 20401
(202) 512-1957, www.gpo.gov

Merit Systems Protection Board
Personnel Division
5th Floor, 1615 M St. NW,
Washington, DC 20419
(202) 653-7200, www.mspb.gov

NASA
NASA Headquarters
300 E St. SW,
Washington, DC 20546
(202) 358-0000, Employment 202-358-1543
www.nasa.gov

National Archives and Records Admin.
8601 Adelphi Rd.
College Park, MD 20740-6001
(866) 272-6272,

Employment (800) 827-4898
www.archives.gov

National Credit Union Administration
Office of Human Resources
1775 Duke St.
Alexandria, VA 22314-3428
(703) 518-6300, www.ncua.gov

National Endowment for the Humanities
1100 Pennsylvania Ave. NW,
Washington, DC 20506
(202) 606-8400, www.neh.gov

National Endowment for the Arts
1100 Pennsylvania Ave. NW,
Washington, DC 20506-0001
(202) 682-5400, www.arts.gov

National Labor Relations Board
Personnel Operations
1099 Fourteenth St. NW,
Washington, DC 20570
(202) 273-1000, www.nlrb.gov

National Mediation Board
1301 K Street NW, Suite 250 East,
Washington, DC 20572
(202) 692-5000, www.nmb.gov

National Railroad Passenger Corporation
60 Massachusetts Ave. NE,
Washington, DC 20002
(202) 906-3000, www.amtrak.com

National Science Foundation
Division of Personnel Management
4201 Wilson Blvd.
Arlington, VA 22230
(703) 292-5111, www.nsf.gov

National Transportation Safety Board
490 L'Enfant Plaza SW,
Washington, DC 20594
(202) 314-6000, www.ntsb.gov

Nuclear Regulatory Commission
Washington, DC 20555
(301) 415-7000, www.nrc.gov

Occupational Safety and Health Commission
1120 20th St. NW,
Washington, DC 20036-3419
(202) 606-5398, www.oshrc.gov

Office of Government Ethics
Suite 500, 1201 New York Ave. NW,
Washington, DC 20005-3917
(202) 482-9300, www.usoge.gov

Office of Personnel Management (OPM)
Recruitment/Employment, Room 1469
1900 E. St. NW,
Washington, DC 20415
(202) 606-1800,
Employment (202) 606-2400
www.opm.gov

Office of Special Counsel
1730 M St. NW,
Washington, DC 20036-4505
(800) 872-9855, www.osc.gov

Peace Corps
1111 20th St. NW,
Washington, DC 20526
(202) 692-2000, www.peacecorps.gov

Pension Benefit Guaranty Corporation
1200 K St. NW,
Washington, DC 20005
(202) 326-4000, www.pbgc.gov

Postal Rate Commission
901 New York Ave. NW,
Washington, DC 20268-0001
(202) 789-6800, www.prc.gov

Railroad Retirement Board
844 N Rush St.
Chicago, IL 60611-2092
(312) 751-4777, www.rrb.gov

Securities and Exchange Commission
100 F St. NE,
Washington, DC 20549
(202) 551-7500, Employment 202-942-7500
www.sec.gov

Selective Service System
Arlington, VA 22209-2425
(703) 605-4000, www.sss.gov

Small Business Administration
409 Third St. SW,
Washington, DC 20416
202-205-6600, www.sba.gov

Social Security Administration
6401 Security Blvd.
Baltimore, MD 21235
(410) 965-1234, www.ssa.gov

United States International Trade Commission
500 E St. SW
,
Washington, DC 20436
(202) 205-2000, www.usitc.gov

APPENDIX D
Federal Occupation List

The government's classification system includes an occupational structure which groups similar jobs together. There are 23 occupational groups comprising 441 different white-collar occupations under the General Schedule (GS): GS-000 through GS-2200. Each occupational group is further subdivided into specific numerical codes (for example: GS-856, Electronics Technician, GS-318, Secretary Series, etc.). The Wage Grade (WG) Trades and Labor Schedule offers an additional 36 occupational families: WG-2500 through WG-9000.

This Appendix presents a comprehensive listing of both GS and WG occupational groups, families and related series. First, locate the occupational group or groups in which you have specific knowledge, skill, and/or training. Then review each job series under the primary occupation group or family.[1]

More than a quarter of white-collar workers had an occupation in the General Administrative, Clerical and Office Services group. The other four large white-collar groups are: Medical, Hospital, Dental and Public Health; Engineering and Architecture; Accounting and Budget; and Business and Industry.

Certain white-collar occupations are concentrated in particular federal agencies. The Department of Agriculture employs the majority of Biological Science employees and almost all Veterinary Medical Science workers. The Department of Health and Human Services was the major employer of the Social Science, Psychology and Welfare group and the Legal and Kindred group.. The Veterans Administration employed almost three-quarters of the Medical, Hospital, Dental and Public Health group. The Department of Commerce employed the vast majority of the Copyright, Patent and Trademark group. The Department of Transportation employs most Transportation group employees. The Library of Congress and Department of Defense together employed over half of the Library and Archives group. The Departments of Homeland Security, Treasury and Justice together employed the majority of the Investigative group. The Department of Defense was the major employer in all the other white collar occupational groups.

---

[1] References for the General Schedule Occupational Groups and Series are the Handbook of Occupational Groups & Series, published by the U.S. Office of Personnel Management, and Pamphlet PB97-170591.

GENERAL SCHEDULE (GS) OCCUPATIONAL GROUPS

GS-000: MISCELLANEOUS — This group includes all classes of positions, the duties of which are to administer, supervise, or perform work which cannot be included in other occupational groups either because the duties are unique, or because they are complex and come in part under various groups.

GS-100: SOCIAL SCIENCE, PSYCHOLOGY, AND WELFARE GROUP — This group includes all classes of positions, the duties of which are to advise on, administer, supervise, or perform research or other professional and scientific work, subordinate technical or related clerical work in one or more of the social sciences; in psychology; in social work; in recreational activities; or in the administration of public welfare and insurance programs.

GS-200: PERSONNEL MANAGEMENT & INDUSTRIAL RELATIONS GROUP — This group includes all classes of positions, the duties of which are to advise on, administer, supervise, or perform work involved in the various phases of personnel management and industrial relations.

GS-300: GENERAL ADMIN, CLERICAL, & OFFICE SERVICES GROUP — This group includes all classes of positions the duties of which are to administer, supervise, or perform work involved in management analysis; stenography, typing, correspondence, and secretarial work; mail and file work; the operation of office appliances; the operation of communications equipment, use of codes and ciphers, and procurement of the most efficient communications services; the operation of microform equipment, peripheral equipment, duplicating equipment, mail processing equipment, and copier/duplicating equipment; and other work of a general clerical and administrative nature.

GS-400: BIOLOGICAL SCIENCE GROUP — This group includes all classes of positions, the duties of which are to advise on, administer, supervise, or perform research or other professional and scientific work or subordinate technical work in any of the fields of science concerned with living organisms, their distribution, characteristics, life processes, and adaptations and relations to the environment; the soil, its properties and distribution, and the living organisms growing in or on the soil; and the management, conservation, or utilization thereof for particular purposes or uses.

GS-500: ACCOUNTING AND BUDGET GROUP — This group includes all classes of positions, the duties of which are to advise on, administer, supervise, or perform professional, technical, or related clerical work of an accounting, budget administration, related financial management, or similar nature.

GS-600: MEDICAL, HOSPITAL, DENTAL, & PUBLIC HEALTH GROUP — This group includes all classes of positions, the duties of which are to advise on, administer, supervise, or perform research or other professional and scientific work, subordinate technical work, or related clerical work in the several branches of medicine, surgery, and dentistry or in related patient care services such as dietetics, nursing, occupational therapy, physical therapy, pharmacy, and others.

GS-700: VETERINARY MEDICAL SCIENCE GROUP — This group includes all classes of positions, the duties of which are to advise and consult on, administer, manage, supervise, or perform research or other professional and scientific work in the various branches of veterinary medical science.

GS-800: ENGINEERING AND ARCHITECTURE - This group includes all classes of positions, the duties of which are to advise on, administer, supervise, or perform professional, scientific, or technical work concerned with engineering or architectural projects, facilities, structures, systems, processes, equipment, devices, material or methods. Positions in this group require knowledge of the science or art, or both, by which materials, natural resources, and power are made useful.

GS-900: LEGAL AND KINDRED GROUP — This group includes all classes of positions, the duties of which are to advise on, administer, supervise, or perform professional legal work in the preparation for trial and the trial and argument of cases, the presiding at formal hearings afforded by a commission, board, or other body having quasi-judicial powers, as part of its administrative procedure, the administration of law entrusted to an agency, the preparation or rendering of authoritative or advisory legal opinions or decisions to other federal agencies or to administrative officials of own agency, the preparation of various legal documents; and the performance of other work requiring training equivalent to that represented by graduation from a recognized law school and in some instances requiring admission to the bar; or quasi-legal work which requires knowledge of particular laws, or of regulations, precedents, or departmental practice based thereon, but which does not require such legal training or admission to the bar.

GS-1000: INFORMATION AND ARTS GROUP — This group includes positions which involve professional, artistic, technical, or clerical work in (1) the communication of information and ideas through verbal, visual, or pictorial means, (2) the collection, custody, presentation, display, and interpretation of art works, cultural objects, and other artifacts, or (3) a branch of fine or applied arts such as industrial design, interior design, or musical composition. Positions in this group require writing, editing, and language ability; artistic skill and ability; knowledge of foreign languages; the ability to evaluate and interpret informational and cultural materials; the practical application of technical or aesthetic principles combined with manual skill and dexterity; or related clerical skills.

GS-1100: BUSINESS AND INDUSTRY GROUP — This group includes all classes of positions, the duties of which are to advise on, administer, supervise, or perform work pertaining to and requiring a knowledge of business and trade practices, characteristics and use of equipment, products, or property, or industrial production methods and processes, including the conduct of investigations and studies; the collection, analysis, and dissemination of information; the establishment and maintenance of contracts with industry and commerce; the provision of advisory services; the examination and appraisement of merchandise or property; and the administration of regulatory provisions and controls.

GS-1200: COPYRIGHT, PATENT, AND TRADEMARK GROUP — This group includes all classes of positions, the duties of which are to advise on, administer, supervise, or perform professional scientific, technical, and legal work involved in the cataloging and registration of copyright, in the classification and issuance of patents, in the registration of trade-marks, in the prosecution of applications for patents before the Patent Office, and in the giving of advice to government officials on patent matters.

GS-1300: PHYSICAL SCIENCE GROUP — This group includes all classes of positions, the duties of which are to advise on, administer, supervise, or perform research or other professional and scientific work or subordinate technical work in any of the fields of science concerned with matter, energy, physical space, time, nature of physical measurement, and fundamental structural particles; and the nature of the physical environment.

GS-1400: LIBRARY AND ARCHIVES GROUP — This group includes all classes of positions, the duties of which are to advise on, administer, supervise, or perform professional and scientific work or subordinate technical work in the various phases of library archival science.

GS-1500: MATHEMATICS AND STATISTICS GROUP — This group includes all classes of positions, the duties of which are to advise on, administer, supervise, or perform research or other professional and scientific work or related clerical work in basic mathematical principles, methods, procedures, or relationships, including the development and application of mathematical methods for the investigation and solution of problems; the development and application of statistical theory in the selection, collection, classification, adjustment, analysis, and interpretation of data; the development and application of mathematical, statistical, and financial principles to programs or problems involving life and property risks; and any other professional and scientific or related clerical work requiring primarily and mainly the understanding and use of mathematical theories, methods, and operations.

GS-1600: EQUIPMENT, FACILITIES, AND SERVICES GROUP — This group includes positions the duties of which are to advise on, manage, or provide instructions and information concerning the operation, maintenance, and use of equipment, shops, buildings, laundries, printing plants, power plants, cemeteries, or other government facilities, or other work involving services provided predominantly by persons in trades, crafts, or manual labor operations. Positions in this group require technical or managerial knowledge and ability, plus a practical knowledge of trades, crafts, or manual labor operations.

GS-1700: EDUCATION GROUP — This group includes positions which involve administering, managing, supervising, performing, or supporting education or training work when the paramount requirement of the position is knowledge of, or skill in, education, training, or instruction processes.

GS-1800: INVESTIGATION GROUP — This group includes all classes of positions, the duties of which are to advise on, administer, supervise, or perform investigation, inspection, or enforcement work primarily concerned with alleged or suspected offenses against the laws of the United States, or such work primarily concerned with determining compliance with laws and regulations.

GS-1900: QUALITY ASSURANCE, INSPECTION, & GRADING GROUP — This group includes all classes of positions, the duties of which are to advise on, supervise, or perform administrative or technical work primarily concerned with the quality assurance or inspection of material, facilities, and processes; or with the grading of commodities under official standards.

GS-2000: SUPPLY GROUP — This group includes positions which involve work concerned with finishing all types of supplies, equipment, material, property (except real estate), and certain services to components of the federal government, industrial, or other concerns under contract to the government, or receiving supplies from the federal government. Included are positions concerned with one or more aspects of supply activities from initial planning, including requirements analysis and determination, through acquisition, cataloging, storage, distribution, utilization to ultimate issue for consumption or disposal. The work requires a knowledge of one or more elements or parts of a supply system, and/or supply methods, policies, or procedures.

GS-2100: TRANSPORTATION GROUP — This group includes all classes of positions, the duties of which are to advise on, administer, supervise, or perform work which involves two or more specialized transportation functions or other transportation work not specifically included in other series of this group.

GS-2200: INFORMATION TECHNOLOGY GROUP — This group includes administrative positions in the information technology group covering only those positions for which the paramount requirement is knowledge of IT principles, concepts, and methods; e.g., data storage, software applications, and networking.

GENERAL SCHEDULE GROUPS & RELATED SERIES

GS-000-MISCELLANEOUS OCCUPATIONS GROUP (Not Elsewhere Classified)

Correctional Institution Administration Series	GS-006	Chaplain Series	GS-060
Correctional Officer	GS-007	Clothing Design Series	GS-062
Bond Sales Promotion Series	GS-011	Fingerprint Identification Series	GS-072
Safety and Occupational Health Mgmt Series	GS-018	Security Administration Series	GS-080
Safety Technician Series	GS-019	Fire Protection and Prevention Series	GS-081
Community Planning Series	GS-020	United States Marshal Series	GS-082
Community Planning Technician Series	GS-021	Police Series	GS-083
Outdoor Recreation Planning Series	GS-023	Nuclear Materials Courier Series	GS-084
Park Ranger Series	GS-025	Security Guard Series	GS-085
Environmental Protection Specialist Series	GS-028	Security Clerical Assistance Series	GS-086
Environmental Protection Assistant Series	GS-029	Guide Series	GS-090
Sports Specialist Series	GS-030	Foreign Law Specialist Series	GS-095
Funeral Directing Series	GS-050	General Student Trainee Series	GS-099

GS-100-SOCIAL SCIENCE, PSYCHOLOGY, AND WELFARE GROUP

Social Science Series	GS-101	Geography Series	GS-150
Social Science Aid and Technician Series	GS-102	Civil Rights Analysis Series	GS-160
Social Insurance Administration Series	GS-105	History Series	GS-170
Unemployment Insurance Series	GS-106	Psychology Series	GS-180
Economist Series	GS-110	Psychology Aide and Technician Series	GS-181
Economics Assistant Series	GS-119	Sociology Series	GS-184
Food Assistance Program Specialist Series	GS-120	Social Work Series	GS-185
Foreign Affairs Series	GS-130	Social Services Aide & Assistant Series	GS-186
International Relations Series	GS-131	Social Services Series	GS-187
Intelligence Series	GS-132	Recreation Specialist Series	GS-188
Intelligence Aide and Clerk Series	GS-134	Recreation Aide and Assistant Series	GS-189
Foreign Agricultural Affairs Series	GS-135	General Anthropology Series	GS-190
International Cooperation Series	GS-136	Archeology Series	GS-193
Manpower Research and Analysis Series	GS-140	Social Science Student Trainee Series	GS-199
Manpower Development Series	GS-142		

GS-200-PERSONNEL MANAGEMENT AND INDUSTRIAL RELATIONS GROUP

Personnel Management Series	GS-201	Employee Development Series	GS-235
Personnel Clerical and Assistance Series	GS-203	Mediation Series	GS-241
Military Personnel Clerical and Technician Series	GS-204	Apprenticeship and Training Series	GS-243
Military Personnel Management Series	GS-205	Labor Mgmt Relations Examining Series	GS-244
Personnel Staffing Series	GS-212	Contractor Industrial Relations Series	GS-246
Position Classification Series	GS-221	Wage and Hour Compliance Series	GS-249
Occupational Analysis Series	GS-222	Equal Employment Opportunity Series	GS-260
Salary and Wage Administration Series	GS-223	Federal Retirement Benefits Series	GS-270
Employee Relations Series	GS-230	Personnel Management Student Trainee Series	GS-299
Labor Relations Series	GS-233		

GS-300-GENERAL ADMINISTRATION, CLERICAL, AND OFFICE SERVICES GROUP

Miscellaneous Administration and Program Series	GS-301	Clerk-Typist Series	GS-322
Messenger Series	GS-302	Office Automation Clerical & Assist. Series	GS-326
Miscellaneous Clerk and Assistant Series	GS-303	Computer Operation Series	GS-332
Information Receptionist Series	GS-304	Computer Specialist Series	GS-334
Mail and File Series	GS-305	Computer Clerk and Assistant Series	GS-335
Correspondence Clerk Series	GS-309	Program Management Series	GS-340
Clerk-Stenographer and Reporter Series	GS-312	Administrative Officer Series	GS-341
Work Unit Supervising Series	GS-313	Support Services Administration Series	GS-342
Secretary Series	GS-318	Management and Program Analysis Series	GS-343
Closed Microphone Reporting Series	GS-319	Management Clerical and Assistance Series	GS-344
Logistics Management Series	GS-346	Electric Account. Machine Project Planning	GS-362
Equipment Operator Series	GS-350	Telephone Operating Series	GS-382

Printing Clerical Series	GS-351	Telecommunications Processing Series	GS-390
Data Transcriber Series	GS-356	Telecommunications Series	GS-391
Coding Series	GS-357	General Communications Series	GS-392
Electric Accounting Machine Operation Series	GS-359	Communications Clerical Series	GS-394
Equal Opportunity Compliance Series	GS-360	Admin/ Office Support Student Trainee Series	GS-399
Equal Opportunity Assistance Series	GS-361		

GS-400-BIOLOGICAL SCIENCES GROUP

General Biological Science Series	GS-401	Range Conservation Series	GS-454
Microbiology Series	GS-403	Range Technician Series	GS-455
Biological Science Technician Series	GS-404	Soil Conservation Series	GS-457
Pharmacology Series	GS-405	Soil Conservation Technician Series	GS-458
Agricultural Extension Series	GS-406	Irrigation System Operation Series	GS-459
Ecology Series	GS-408	Forestry Series	GS-460
Zoology Series	GS-410	Forestry Technician Series	GS-462
Physiology Series	GS-413	Soil Science Series	GS-470
Entomology Series	GS-414	Agronomy Series	GS-471
Toxicology Series	GS-415	Agricultural Management Series	GS-475
Plant Protection Technician Series	GS-421	General Fish and Wildlife Admin. Series	GS-480
Botany Series	GS-430	Fishery Biology Series	GS-482
Plant Pathology Series	GS-434	Wildlife Refuge Management Series	GS-485
Plant Physiology Series	GS-435	Wildlife Biology Series	GS-486
Plant Protection and Quarantine Series	GS-436	Animal Science Series	GS-487
Horticulture Series	GS-437	Home Economics Series	GS-493
Genetics Series	GS-440	Biological Science Student Trainee Series	GS-499

GS-500 ACCOUNTING AND BUDGET GROUP

Financial Administration and Program Series	GS-501	Voucher Examining Series	GS-540
Financial Clerical and Assistance Series	GS-503	Civilian Pay Series	GS-544
Financial Management Series	GS-505	Military Pay Series	GS-545
Accounting Series	GS-510	Budget Analysis Series	GS-560
Auditing Series	GS-511	Budget Clerical and Assistance Series	GS-561
Internal Revenue Agent Series	GS-512	Financial Institution Examining Series	GS-570
Accounting Technician Series	GS-525	Tax Examining Series	GS-592
Tax Technician Series	GS-526	Insurance Accounts Series	GS-593
Cash Processing Series	GS-530	Financial Management Student Trainee Series	GS-599

GS-600-MEDICAL, HOSPITAL, DENTAL, AND PUBLIC HEALTH GROUP

General Health Science Series	GS-601	Diagnostic Radiologic Technologist Series	GS-647
Medical Officer Series	GS-602	Therapeutic Radiologic Technologist Series	GS-648
Physician's Assistant Series	GS-603	Medical Instrument Technician Series	GS-649
Nurse Series	GS-610	Medical Technical Assistant Series	GS-650
Practical Nurse Series	GS-620	Respiratory Therapist Series	GS-651
Nursing Assistant Series	GS-621	Pharmacist Series	GS-660
Medical Supply Aide and Technician Series	GS-622	Pharmacy Technician Series	GS-661
Autopsy Assistant Series	GS-625	Optometrist Series	GS-662
Dietitian and Nutritionist Series	GS-630	Restoration Technician Series	GS-664
Occupational Therapist Series	GS-631	Speech Pathology and Audiology Series	GS-665
Physical Therapist Series	GS-633	Orthotist and Prosthetist Series	GS-667
Corrective Therapist Series	GS-635	Podiatrist Series	GS-668
Rehabilitation Therapy Assistant Series	GS-636	Medical Records Administration Series	GS-669
Manual Arts Therapist Series	GS-637	Health System Administration Series	GS-670
Recreation/Creative Arts Therapist Series	GS-638	Health System Specialist Series	GS-671
Educational Therapist Series	GS-639	Prosthetic Representative Series	GS-672
Health Aid and Technician Series	GS-640	Hospital Housekeeping Management Series	GS-673
Nuclear Medicine Technician Series	GS-642	Medical Records Technician Series	GS-675
Medical Technologist Series	GS-644	Medical Clerk Series	GS-679
Medical Technician Series	GS-645	Dental Officer Series	GS-680
Pathology Technician Series	GS-646	Dental Assistant Series	GS-681

Dental Hygiene Series	GS-682	Industrial Hygiene Series	GS-690
Dental Laboratory Aid and Technician Series	GS-683	Consumer Safety Series	GS-696
Public Health Program Specialist Series	GS-685	Environmental Health Technician Series	GS-698
Sanitarian Series	GS-688	Medical and Health Student Trainee Series	GS-699

GS-700-VETERINARY MEDICAL SCIENCE GROUP

Veterinary Medical Science Series	GS-701	Veterinary Student Trainee Series	GS-799
Animal Health Technician Series	GS-704		

GS-800-ENGINEERING AND ARCHITECTURE GROUP

General Engineering Series	GS-801	Computer Engineering Series	GS-854
Engineering Technician Series	GS-802	Electronics Engineering Series	GS-855
Safety Engineering Series	GS-803	Electronics Technician Series	GS-856
Fire Protection Engineering Series	GS-804	Biomedical Engineering Series	GS-858
Materials Engineering Series	GS-806	Aerospace Engineering Series	GS-861
Landscape Architecture Series	GS-807	Naval Architecture Series	GS-871
Architecture Series	GS-808	Ship Surveying Series	GS-873
Construction Control Series	GS-809	Mining Engineering Series	GS-880
Civil Engineering Series	GS-810	Petroleum Engineering Series	GS-881
Surveying Technician Series	GS-817	Agricultural Engineering Series	GS-890
Engineering Drafting Series	GS-818	Ceramic Engineering Series	GS-892
Environmental Engineering Series	GS-819	Chemical Engineering Series	GS-893
Construction Analyst Series	GS-828	Welding Engineering Series	GS-894
Mechanical Engineering Series	GS-830	Industrial Engineering Technician Series	GS-895
Nuclear Engineering Series	GS-840	Industrial Engineering Series	GS-896
Electrical Engineering Series	GS-850	Engineering/Architecture Student Series	GS-899

GS-900-LEGAL AND KINDRED GROUP

Law Clerk Series	GS-904	Legal Clerical and Assistance Series	GS-986
General Attorney Series	GS-905	Tax Law Specialist Series	GS-987
Estate Tax Examining Series	GS-920	General Claims Examining Series	GS-990
Hearings and Appeals Series	GS-930	Workers' Compensation Claims Examining	GS-991
Clerk of Court Series	GS-945	Loss and Damage Claims Examining Series	GS-992
Paralegal Specialist Series	GS-950	Social Insurance Claims Examining Series	GS-993
Pension Law Specialist Series	GS-958	Unemployment Comp. Examining Series	GS-994
Contact Representative Series	GS-962	Dependents and Estates Claims Examining	GS-995
Legal Instruments Examining Series	GS-963	Veterans Claims Examining Series	GS-996
Land Law Examining Series	GS-965	Claims Clerical Series	GS-998
Passport and Visa Examining Series	GS-967	Legal Occupations Student Trainee Series	GS-999

GS-1000-INFORMATION AND ARTS GROUP

General Arts and Information Series	GS-1001	Music Specialist Series	GS-1051
Interior Design Series	GS-1008	Theater Specialist Series	GS-1054
Exhibits Specialist Series	GS-1010	Art Specialist Series	GS-1056
Museum Curator Series	GS-1015	Photography Series	GS-1060
Museum Specialist and Technician Series	GS-1016	Audiovisual Production Series	GS-1071
Illustrating Series	GS-1020	Writing and Editing Series	GS-1082
Office Drafting Series	GS-1021	Technical Writing and Editing Series	GS-1083
Public Affairs Series	GS-1035	Visual Information Series	GS-1084
Language Specialist Series	GS-1040	Editorial Assistance Series	GS-1087
Language Clerical Series	GS-1046	Information and Arts Student Trainee Series	GS-1099

GS-1100-BUSINESS AND INDUSTRY GROUP

General Business and Industry Series	GS-1101	Property Disposal Series	GS-1104
Contracting Series	GS-1102	Purchasing Series	GS-1105
Industrial Property Management Series	GS-1103	Procurement Clerical and Technician Series	GS-1106
Property Disposal Clerical and Technician Series	GS-1107	Crop Insurance Administration Series	GS-1161

Public Utilities Specialist Series	GS-1130
Trade Specialist Series	GS-1140
Commissary Store Management Series	GS-1144
Agricultural Program Specialist Series	GS-1145
Agricultural Marketing Series	GS-1146
Agricultural Market Reporting Series	GS-1147
Industrial Specialist Series	GS-1150
Production Control Series	GS-1152
Financial Analysis Series	GS-1160

Crop Insurance Underwriting Series	GS-1162
Insurance Examining Series	GS-1163
Loan Specialist Series	GS-1165
Internal Revenue Officer Series	GS-1169
Realty Series	GS-1170
Appraising and Assessing Series	GS-1171
Housing Management Series	GS-1173
Building Management Series	GS-1176
Business/Industry Student Trainee Series	GS-1199

GS-1200-COPYRIGHT, PATENT, AND TRADE-MARK GROUP

Patent Technician Series	GS-1202
Copyright Series	GS-1210
Copyright Technician Series	GS-1211
Patent Administration Series	GS-1220
Patent Advisor Series	GS-1221

Patent Attorney Series	GS-1222
Patent Classifying Series	GS-1223
Patent Examining Series	GS-1224
Design Patent Examining Series	GS-1226
Copyright and Patent Student Trainee Series	GS-1299

GS-1300-PHYSICAL SCIENCES GROUP

General Physical Science Series	GS-1301
Health Physics Series	GS-1306
Physics Series	GS-1310
Physical Science Technician Series	GS-1311
Geophysics Series	GS-1313
Hydrology Series	GS-1315
Hydrologic Technician Series	GS-1316
Chemistry Series	GS-1320
Metallurgy Series	GS-1321
Astronomy and Space Science Series	GS-1330
Meteorology Series	GS-1340
Meteorological Technician Series	GS-1341
Geology Series	GS-1350

Oceanography Series	GS-1360
Navigational Information Series	GS-1361
Cartography Series	GS-1370
Cartographic Technician Series	GS-1371
Geodesy Series	GS-1372
Land Surveying Series	GS-1373
Geodetic Technician Series	GS-1374
Forest Products Technology Series	GS-1380
Food Technology Series	GS-1382
Textile Technology Series	GS-1384
Photographic Technology Series	GS-1386
Document Analysis Series	GS-1397
Physical Science Student Trainee Series	GS-1399

GS-1400-LIBRARY AND ARCHIVES GROUP

Librarian Series	GS-1410
Library Technician Series	GS-1411
Technical Information Services Series	GS-1412

Archivist Series	GS-1420
Archives Technician Series	GS-1421
Library and Archives Student Trainee	GS-1499

GS-1500-MATHEMATICS AND STATISTICS GROUP

Actuary Series	GS-1510
Operations Research Series	GS-1515
Mathematics Series	GS-1520
Mathematics Technician Series	GS-1521
Mathematical Statistician Series	GS-1529
Statistician Series	GS-1530

Statistical Assistant Series	GS-1531
Cryptography Series	GS-1540
Cryptanalysis Series	GS-1541
Computer Science Series	GS-1550
Math/Statistics Student Trainee Series	GS-1599

GS-1600-EQUIPMENT, FACILITIES, AND SERVICES GROUP

General Facilities and Equipment Series	GS-1601
Cemetery Administration Series	GS-1630
Facility Management Series	GS-1640
Printing Management Series	GS-1654
Laundry and Dry Cleaning Plant Mgmt.	GS-1658

Steward Series	GS-1667
Equipment Specialist Series	GS-1670
Equipment/ Facilities Mgmt Student Series	GS-1699

GS-1700-EDUCATION GROUP

General Education and Training Series	GS-1701	Training Instruction Series	GS-1712
Education and Training Technician Series	GS-1702	Vocational Rehabilitation Series	GS-1715
Educational and Vocational Training Series	GS-1710	Education Program Series	GS-1720
Public Health Educator Series	GS-1725	Instructional Systems Series	GS-1750
Education Research Series	GS-1730	Education Student Trainee Series	GS-1799
Education Services Series	GS-1740		

GS-1800-INVESTIGATION GROUP

General Insp. Investigation & Compliance Series	GS-1801	Consumer Safety Inspection Series	GS-1862
Compliance Inspection and Support Series	GS-1802	Food Inspection Series	GS-1863
General Investigating Series	GS-1810	Public Health Quarantine Inspection Series	GS-1864
Criminal Investigating Series	GS-1811	Customs Patrol Officer Series	GS-1884
Game Law Enforcement Series	GS-1812	Import Specialist Series	GS-1889
Air Safety Investigating Series	GS-1815	Customs Inspection Series	GS-1890
Immigration Inspection Series	GS-1816	Customs Entry and Liquidating Series	GS-1894
Mine Safety and Health Series	GS-1822	Customs Warehouse Officer Series	GS-1895
Aviation Safety Series	GS-1825	Border Patrol Agent Series	GS-1896
Securities Compliance Examining Series	GS-1831	Customs Aid Series	GS-1897
Agri. Commodity Warehouse Examining Series	GS-1850	Admeasurement Series	GS-1898
Alcohol, Tobacco and Firearms Inspection Series	GS-1854	Investigation Student Trainee Series	GS-1899

GS-QUALITY ASSURANCE, INSPECTION, AND GRADING GROUP

Quality Assurance Series	GS-1910	Agricultural Commodity Aide Series	GS-1981
Agricultural Commodity Grading Series	GS-1980	Quality Inspection Student Trainee Series	GS-1999

GS-2000-SUPPLY GROUP

General Supply Series	GS-2001	Packaging Series	GS-2032
Supply Program Management Series	GS-2003	Supply Cataloging Series	GS-2050
Supply Clerical and Technician Series	GS-2005	Sales Store Clerical Series	GS-2091
Inventory Management Series	GS-2010	Supply Student Trainee Series	GS-2099
Distribution Facilities / Storage Mgmt Series	GS-2030		

GS-2100-TRANSPORTATION GROUP

Transportation Specialist Series	GS-2101	Transportation Loss and Damage Claims	GS-3135
Transportation Clerk and Assistant Series	GS-2102	Examining Series	GS-2136
Transportation Industry Analysis Series	GS-2110	Cargo Scheduling Series	GS-2144
Transportation Rate and Tariff Examining Series	GS-2111	Transportation Operations Series	GS-2150
Railroad Safety Series	GS-2121	Dispatching Series	GS-2151
Motor Carrier Safety Series	GS-2123	Air Traffic Control Series	GS-2152
Highway Safety Series	GS-2125	Air Traffic Assistance Series	GS-2154
Traffic Management Series	GS-2130	Marine Cargo Series	GS-2161
Freight Rate Series	GS-2131	Aircraft Operation Series	GS-2181
Travel Series	GS-2132	Air Navigation Series	GS-2183
Passenger Rate Series	GS-2133	Aircrew Technician Series	GS-2185
Shipment Clerical and Assistance Series	GS-2134	Transportation Student Trainee Series	GS-2199

GS-2200 - INFORMATION TECHNOLOGY GROUP

Information Technology Specialist	GS-2210

WAGE GRADE TRADES AND LABOR JOB FAMILIES AND OCCUPATIONS

The government's Personnel Classification System includes Wage Grade occupations grouped into families of like jobs. The 36 occupational families range from WG-2500 to WG-9000. Each occupational family has its own group number and title which makes it distinctive from every other family grouping. The following is a list of the Wage Grade families.[2]

Each occupational family has a three part identifier: the Pay System, Occupational Group Number, and Title. In the example WG-2500, Wire Communications Equipment Installation and Maintenance Family, WG means the job is in the Wage Grade Schedule (or blue collar) pay system; 2500 is the Occupational Family Number; and Wire Communications Equipment Installation and Maintenance is the Occupational Family Title. Each occupational family lists the individual jobs that comprise the family with their corresponding Job Series Numbers and Titles. A brief description is provided for each of the occupational Wage Grade families and the jobs within that family. There were 201,988 Wage Grade workers in 2007.

WG-2500   Wire Communications Equipment Installation and Maintenance Family

This job family includes occupations involved in the construction, installation, maintenance, repair and testing of all types of wire communications systems and associated equipment which are predominantly electrical-mechanical. Work involved in the installation and repair of communications equipment which requires in-depth knowledge of operating electronic principles should be coded to electronic equipment installation and maintenance family, 2600.

WG-2502   Telephone Mechanic
WG-2504   Wire Communications Cable Splicing
WG-2508   Communications Line Installing and Repairing
WG-2511   Wire Communications Equip. Install/Repair

WG-2600   Electronic Equipment Installation and Maintenance Family

This job family includes occupations involved in the installation, repair, overhaul, fabrication, tuning, alignment, modification, calibration, and testing of electronic equipment and related devices, such as radio, radar, loran, sonar, television, and other communications equipment; industrial controls; fire control, flight/landing control, bombing-navigation, and other integrated systems; and electronic computer systems and equipment.

WG-2602   Electronic Measurement Equip. Mechanic
WG-2604   Electronics Mechanic
WG-2606   Electronic Industrial Controls Mechanic
WG-2698   Electronic Digital Computer Mechanic
WG-2610   Electronic Integrated Systems Mechanic

[2]The Wage Grade listing is taken from the Government Printing Office publication TS-PB97-170591.

WG-280   Electrical Installation & Maintenance Family

This job family includes occupations involved in the fabrication, installation, alteration, maintenance, repair, and testing of electrical systems, instruments, apparatus, and equipment.

WG-2800   Electrician
WG-2810   Electrician (High Voltage)
WG-2854   Electrical Equipment Repairing
WG-2892   Aircraft Electrician

WG-3100   Fabric & Leather Work Family

This job family includes occupations involving the fabrication, modification, and repair of clothing and equipment made of (a) woven textile fabrics of animal, vegetable, or synthetic origin; (b) plastic film and filaments; (c) natural and simulated leather; (d) natural and synthetic fabrics; and (e) paper. Work involves use of hand tools and mechanical devices and machines to lay out, cut, sew, rivet, mold, fit, assemble, and attach bindings to articles such as uniforms, rain gear, hats, belts, shoes, briefcases, holsters, equipage articles, tents, gun covers, bags, parachutes, upholstery, mattresses, brushes, etc.

WG-3103   Shoe Repairing
WG-3105   Fabric Working
WG-3106   Upholstering
WG-3111   Sewing Machine Operating
WG-3119   Broom & Brush Making

WG-3300   Instrument Work Family

This job family includes occupations that involve fabricating, assembling, calibrating, testing, installing, repairing, modifying, and maintaining instruments and instrumentation systems for measuring, regulating, and computing physical quantities such as movement, force, acceleration, displacement, stress, strain, vibration or oscillation frequency, phase and amplitude, linear or angular velocity, voltage, current, power, impedance, etc. Examples of such instruments and equipment are: gyro, optical, photographic, timekeeping, electrical, metered, pressure, and geared instruments, test equipment, and navigation, flight control, and fuel totalizing systems. The work requires knowledge of electrical, electronic, mechanical, optical, pneumatic, and/or hydraulic principles. Work that primarily involves fabricating and repairing electronic instruments should be coded to the electronic equipment installation and maintenance family, 2600.

WG-3306   Optical Instrument Repairing
WG-3314   Instrument Making
WG-3341   Scale Building, Install/Repair
WG-3359   Instrument Mechanic
WG-3364   Projection Equipment Repairing

WG-3400   Machine Tool Work Family

This job family includes occupations that involve setting up and operating machine tools and using hand tools to make or repair (shape, fit, finish, assemble) metal parts, tools, gages, models, patterns, mechanisms, and machines; and machining explosives and synthetic materials.

WG-3414   Machining
WG-3416   Toolmaking
WG-3417   Tool Grinding
WG-3422   Power Saw Operator
WG-3428   Die Sinker
WG-3431   Machine Tool Operating

WG-3500 General Services & Support Work Family

This job family includes occupations not specifically covered by another family that require little or no specialized training or work experience to enter. These occupations usually involve work such as moving and handling material (e.g., loading, unloading, digging, hauling, hoisting, carrying, wrapping, mixing, pouring, spreading); washing and cleaning laboratory apparatus, cars, and trucks, etc.; cleaning and maintaining living quarters, hospital rooms and wards, office buildings, grounds, and other areas; and doing other general maintenance work, by hand or using common hand tools and power equipment. They may involve heavy or light physical work and various skill levels. Skills are generally learned through job experience and instruction from supervisors or, in some instances, formal training programs lasting a few days or weeks or longer.

WG-3502	Laboring	WG-3515	Laboratory Support Working
WG-3506	Summer Aide/Student Aide	WG-3543	Stevedoring
WG-3508	Pipeline Working	WG-3546	Railroad Repairing
WG-3511	Laboratory Working	WG-3566	Custodial Working
WG-3513	Coin/Currency Checking		

WG-3600 Structural & Finishing Work Family

This job family includes occupations not specifically covered by another family that involve doing structural and finishing work in construction, maintenance, and repair of surfaces and structures, e.g., laying brick, block, and stone; setting tile; finishing cement and concrete; plastering; installing, maintaining, and repairing asphalt, tar, and gravel; roofing; insulating and glazing.

WG-3602	Cement Finishing	WG-3609	Floor Covering Installing
WG-3603	Masonry	WG-3610	Insulating
WG-3604	Tile Setting	WG-3611	Glazing
WG-3605	Plastering	WG-3653	Asphalt Working
WG-3604	Roofing		

WG-3700 Metal Processing Family

This job family includes occupations which involve processing or treating metals to alter their properties or produce desirable qualities such as hardness or workability, using processes such as welding, plating, melting, alloying, annealing, heat treating, and refining.

WG-3702	Flame/Arc Cutting	WG-3720	Brazing & Soldering
WG-3703	Welding	WG-3722	Cold Working
WG-3705	Nondestructive Testing	WG-3725	Battery Repairing
WG-3707	Metalizing	WG-3727	Buffing & Polishing
WG-3708	Metal Process Working	WG-3735	Metal Phototransferring
WG-3711	Electroplating	WG-3736	Circuit Board Making
WG-3712	Heat Treating	WG-3741	Furnace Operating
WG-3716	Leadburning	WG-3769	Shot Peening Machine

WG-3800 Metal Working Family

This job family includes occupations involved in shaping and forming metal and making and repairing metal parts or equipment. Includes such work as the fabrication and assembly of sheet metal parts and equipment; forging and press operations; structural iron working, stamping, etc. Doesn't include machine tool work.

WG-3802	Metal Forging	WG-3819	Airframe Jig Fitting
WG-3804	Coppersmithing	WG-3820	Shipfitting
WG-3806	Sheet Metal Mechanic	WG-3830	Blacksmithing
WG-3807	Iron Working	WG-3832	Metal Making
WG-3808	Boilermaking	WG-3833	Transfer Engraving
WG-3809	Mobile Equip. Metal Mech.	WG-3858	Metal Tank & Radiator Repair
WG-3815	Pneumatic Tool Operating	WG-3869	Metal Forming Mach. Operating
WG-3816	Engraving	WG-3872	Metal Tube Making & Installing
WG-3818	Springmaking		

WG-3900 Motion Picture, Radio, Television, and Sound Equipment Operation Family

This job family includes occupations involved in setting up, testing, operating, and making minor repairs to equipment such as microphones, sound and radio controls, sound recording equipment, lighting and sound effect devices, television cameras, magnetic videotape recorders, motion picture projectors, and broadcast transmitters used in the production of motion pictures and radio and television programs. Also includes occupations that involve related work.

WG-3910	Motion Picture Projection	WG-3940	Broadcasting Equip. Operating
WG-3911	Sound Recording Equip. Operating	WG-3941	Public Address Equip. Operating
WG-3919	Television Equip. Operating		

WG-4000 Lens and Crystal Work Family

This job family includes occupations involved in making precision optical elements, crystal blanks or wafers, or other items of glass, polished metals, or similar materials, using such methods as cutting, polishing, etc.

WG-4005	Optical Element Working	WG-4015	Quartz Crystal Working
WG-4010	Prescription Eyeglass Making		

WG-4100 Painting & Paperhanging Family

This job family includes occupations which involve hand or spray painting and decorating interiors and exteriors of buildings, structures, aircraft, vessels, mobile equipment, fixtures, furnishings, machinery, and other surfaces; finishing hardwoods, furniture, and cabinetry; painting signs; covering interiors of rooms with strips of wallpaper or fabric, etc.

WG-4102	Painting	WG-4104	Sign Painting
WG-4103	Paperhanging	WG-4157	Instrument Dial Painting

WG-4200 Plumbing & Pipefitting Family

This job family includes occupations that involve the installation, maintenance, and repair of water, air, steam, gas, sewer, and other pipelines and systems, and related fixtures, apparatus, and accessories.

WG-4204 Pipefitting
WG-4206 Plumbing

WG-4255 Fuel Distribution Systems Mechanic

WG-4300 Pliable Materials Work Family

This job family includes occupations involved in shaping, forming, and repairing items and parts from non-metallic moldable materials such as plastic, rubber, clay, wax, plaster, glass, sand, or other similar material.

WG-4351 Plastic Molding Equip. Operating
WG-4352 Plastic Fabricating
WG-4360 Rubber Products Molding
WG-4361 Rubber Equipment Repairing

WG-4370 Glassblowing
WG-4371 Plaster Pattern Casting
WG-4373 Molding
WG-4374 Core Making

WG-4400 Printing Family

This job family includes occupations involved in letterpress (relief), offset-lithographic, gravure (intaglio), or screen printing; including layout, hand composition, typesetting from hot metal type, platemaking, printing, and finishing operations.

WG-4402 Bindery Work
WG-4403 Hand Composing
WG-4405 Film Assembly-Stripping
WG-4406 Letterpress Operating
WG-4407 Linotype Machine Operating
WG-4413 Negative Engraving
WG-4414 Offset Photography
WG-4416 Platemaking
WG-4417 Offset Press Operating
WG-4419 Silk Screen Making & Printing

WG-4422 Dot Etching
WG-4425 Photoengraving
WG-4441 Bookbinding
WG-4445 Bank Note Designing
WG-4446 Bank Note Engraving
WG-4447 Sculptural Engraving
WG-4448 Siderographic Transferring
WG-4449 Electrolytic Intaglio Platemaking
WG-4450 Intaglio Die & Plate Finishing
WG-4454 Intaglio Press Operating

WG-4600 Wood Work Family

This occupation includes jobs involved in blocking, bracing, staying, and securing cargo for shipment by land, sea, or air. It requires skill in construction, placing, and installing wooden blocks, wedges, bracing, structures, and other staying devices, as well as skill in securing items using wires, ropes, chains, cables, plates, and other hardware.

WG-4602 Blocking & Bracing
WG-4604 Wood Working
WG-4605 Wood Crafting
WG-4607 Carpentry
WG-4616 Patternmaking

WG-4618 Woodworking Mach. Operating
WG-4620 Shoe Lasting Repairing
WG-4639 Timber Working
WG-4654 Form Block Making

WG-4700 General Maintenance & Operations Work Family

This job family includes occupations which (1) consist of various combinations of work such as are involved in constructing, maintaining and repairing buildings, roads, grounds, and related facilities; manufacturing, modifying, and repairing items or apparatus made from a variety of materials or types of components; or repairing and operating equipment or utilities; and (2) require the application of a variety of trade practices associated with occupations in more than one job family (unless otherwise indicated), and the performance of the highest level of work in at least two of the trades involved.

WG-4714	Model Making	WG-4741	General Equipment Operating
WG-4715	Exhibits Making/Modeling	WG-4742	Utility System Repair/Operating
WG-4716	Railroad Car Repairing	WG-4745	Research Laboratory Mechanic
WG-4717	Boat Building and Repairing	WG-4749	Maintenance Mechanic
WG-4737	General Equipment Mechanic	WG-4754	Cemetery Caretaking

WG-4800 General Equipment Maintenance Family

This job family includes occupations involved in the maintenance or repair of equipment, machines, or instruments which are not coded to other job families because the equipment is not characteristically related to one of the established subject-matter areas such as electronics, electrical, industrial, transportation, instruments, engines, aircraft, ordnance, etc., or because the nature of the work calls for limited knowledge/skill in a variety of crafts or trades as they relate to the repair of such equipment, but not a predominant knowledge of any one trade or craft.

WG-4802	Musical Instrument Repairing	WG-4839	Film Processing Equip. Repair
WG-4804	Locksmithing	WG-4840	Tool & Equipment Repairing
WG-4805	Medical Equipment Repairing	WG-4841	Window Shade Assembling, Repairing
WG-4806	Office Appliance Repairing		
WG-4807	Chemical Equipment Repairing	WG-4843	Navigation Aids Repairing
WG-4808	Custodial Equipment Servicing	WG-4844	Bicycle Repairing
WG-4812	Saw Reconditioning	WG-4845	Orthopedic Appliance Repairing
WG-4816	Protective/Safety Equip. Fab.	WG-4848	Mechanical Parts Repairing
WG-4818	Aircraft Survival/Flight Equip.	WG-4850	Bearing Reconditioning
WG-4819	Bowling Equipment Repairing	WG-4851	Reclamation Working
WG-4820	Vending Machine Repairing	WG-4855	Domestic Appliance Repairing

WG-5000 Plant and Animal Work Family

This job family includes occupations involved in general or specialized farming operations; gardening, including the general care of grounds, roadways, nurseries, greenhouses, etc.; trimming and felling trees; and propagating, caring for, handling, and controlling animals and insects, including pest species.

WG-5002	Farming	WG-5034	Dairy Farming
WG-5003	Gardening	WG-5035	Livestock Ranching/Wrangling
WG-5026	Pest Controlling	WG-5042	Tree Trimming and Removing
WG-5031	Insects Production Working	WG-5048	Animal Caretaking

WG-5200 Miscellaneous Occupations Family

This job family includes occupations which are not covered by the definition of any other job family or which are of such a general or miscellaneous character as to preclude placing them within another job family.

WG-5205	Gas and Radiation Detecting	WG-5221	Lofting
WG-5210	Rigging	WG-5222	Diving
WG-5220	Shipwright	WG-5235	Test Range Tracking

WG-5300 Industrial Equipment Maintenance Family

This job family includes occupations involved in the general maintenance, installation, and repair of portable and stationary industrial machinery, tools, and equipment such as sewing machines, machine tools, woodworking and metal working machines, printing equipment, processing equipment, driving machinery, power generating equipment, air conditioning equipment, heating and boiler plant equipment, and other types of machines and equipment used in the production of goods and services.

WG-5306	Air Conditioning Equip. Mech.	WG-5334	Marine Machinery Mechanic
WG-5309	Heating and Boiler Plant Mech.	WG-5335	Wind Tunnel Mechanic
WG-5310	Kitchen/Bakery Equip. Repairing	WG-5341	Industrial Furnace Building & Repairing
WG-5312	Sewing Machine Repairing	WG-5350	Production Machinery Mechanic
WG-5313	Elevator Mechanic	WG-5352	Industrial Equipment Mechanic
WG-5317	Laundry/Dry Cleaning Equip. Repairing	WG-5364	Door Systems Mechanic
WG-5318	Lock & Dam Repairing	WG-5365	Physiological Trainer Mechanic
WG-5323	Oiling & Greasing	WG-5378	Powered Support Systems Mech.
WG-5324	Powerhouse Equipment Repairing	WG-5384	Gas Dynamic Facility Installing/Repairing
WG-5326	Drawbridge Repairing		
WG-5330	Printing Equipment Repairing		

WG-5400 Industrial Equipment Operation Family

This job family includes occupations involved in the operation of portable and stationary industrial equipment, tools, and machines to generate and distribute utilities such as electricity, steam, and gas for heat or power; treat and distribute water; collect, treat, and dispose of waste; open and close bridges, locks and dams; lift and move workers, materials, and equipment; manufacture and process materials and products; etc.

WG-5402	Boiler Plant Operating	WG-5423	Sandblasting
WG-5403	Incinerator Operating	WG-5424	Weighing Machine Operating
WG-5406	Utility Systems Operating	WG-5426	Lock and Dam Operating
WG-5407	Electric Power Controlling	WG-5427	Chemical Plant Operating
WG-5408	Sewage Disposal Plant Operating	WG-5430	Drawbridge Operating
WG-5409	Water Treatment Plant Operating	WG-5433	Gas Generating Plant Operating
WG-5413	Fuel Distribution System Operating	WG-5435	Carton/Bag Making Machine Operating
WG-5414	Baling Machine Operating	WG-5438	Elevator Operating
WG-5415	Air Cond. Equip. Operating	WG-5439	Testing Equipment Operating
WG-5419	Stationary-Engine Operating	WG-5440	Packaging Machine Operating

WG-5444	Food/Feed Processing Equip. Operating	WG-5478	Portable Equipment Operating
WG-5446	Textile Equipment Operating	WG-5479	Dredging Equipment Operating
WG-5450	Conveyor Operating	WG-5484	Counting Machine Operating
WG-5454	Solvent Still Operating	WG-5485	Aircraft Weight & Balance Operating
WG-5455	Paper Pulping Machine Operating	WG-5486	Swimming Pool Operating
WG-5473	Oil Reclamation Equip.Operating		

WG-5700 Transportation/Mobile Equipment Operation Family

This job family includes occupations involved in the operation and operational maintenance of self-propelled transportation and other mobile equipment (except aircraft) used to move materials or passengers, including motor vehicles, engineering and construction equipment, tractors, etc. some of which may be equipped with power takeoff and controls to operate special purpose equipment; ocean-going and inland waterway vessels, harbor craft, and floating plants; and trains, locomotives, and train cars.

WG-5703	Motor Vehicle Operating	WG-5736	Braking-Switching & Conducting
WG-5704	Fork Lift Operating	WG-5737	Locomotive Engineering
WG-5705	Tractor Operating	WG-5738	Railroad Maint. Vehicle Ops.
WG-5706	Road Sweeper Operating	WG-5767	Airfield Clearing Equip. Ops.
WG-5707	Tank Driver	WG-5782	Ship Operating
WG-5716	Engineering Equip. Operating	WG-5784	Riverboat Operating
WG-5725	Crane Operating	WG-5786	Small Craft Operating
WG-5729	Drill Rig Operating	WG-5788	Deckhand
WG-5731	Mining/Tunneling Mach. Operating		

WG-5800 Heavy Mobile Equipment Mechanic

This job family includes occupations involved in repairing, adjusting, and maintaining self-propelled transportation and other mobile equipment (except aircraft), including any special-purpose features with which they may be equipped.

| WG-5803 | Heavy Mobile Equip. Mechanic | WG-5823 | Automotive Mechanic |
| WG-5806 | Mobile Equip. Servicing | WG-5876 | Electromotive Equip. Mechanic |

WG-6500 Ammunition, Explosives, & Toxic Materials Work Family

This job family includes occupations involved in the manufacturing, assembling, disassembling, renovating, loading, deactivating, modifying, destroying, testing, handling, placing, and discharging of ammunition, propellants, chemicals and toxic materials, and other conventional and special munitions and explosives.

| WG-6502 | Explosives Operating | WG-6511 | Missile/Toxic Materials Handling |
| WG-6505 | Munitions Destroying | WG-6517 | Explosives Test Operating |

WG-6600 Armament Work Family

This job family includes occupations involved in the installation, repair, rebuilding, adjusting, modification, and testing of small arms and artillery weapons and allied accessories. Artillery includes, but is not limited to, field artillery, antitank artillery, antiaircraft weapons, aircraft and shipboard weapons, recoilless rifles, rocket launchers, mortars, cannon, and allied accessories. Small arms includes, but is not limited to, rifles, carbines, pistols, revolvers, helmets, body armor, shoulder-type rocket launchers, machine guns, and automatic rifles.

WG-6605	Artillery Repairing	WG-6641	Ordnance Equipment Mechanic
WG-6606	Artillery Testing	WG-6652	Aircraft Ordnance Systems Mech.
WG-6610	Small Arms Repairing	WG-6656	Special Weapons Systems Mech.

WG-6900 Warehousing & Stock Handling Family

This family includes occupations involved in physically receiving, storing, handling, and issuing supplies, materials, and equipment; handling, marking, and displaying goods for customer selection; identifying and condition classifying materials and equipment; and routing and expediting movement of parts, supplies, and materials in production and repair facilities.

WG-6902	Lumber Handling	WG-6912	Materials Examining & Identifying
WG-6903	Coal Handling	WG-6915	Store Working
WG-6904	Tools and Parts Attending	WG-6941	Bulk Money Handling
WG-6907	Materials Handling	WG-6968	Aircraft Freight Loading
WG-6910	Materials Expediting		

WG-7000 Packing and Processing Family

This job family includes occupations involved in determining the measures required to protect items against damage during movement or storage; selecting proper method of packing, including type and size of container; cleaning, drying, and applying preservatives to materials, parts, or mechanical equipment; and packing, equipment, parts, and materials.

WG-7002	Packing	WG-7009	Equipment Cleaning
WG-7004	Preservation Packaging	WG-7010	Parachute Packing
WG-7006	Preservation Servicing		

WG-7300 Laundry, Dry Cleaning, & Pressing Family

This job family includes occupations involved in receiving, sorting, washing, drying, dry cleaning, dyeing, pressing, and preparing for delivery clothes, linens, and other articles requiring laundering, dry cleaning, or pressing.

WG-7304	Laundry Working	WG-7306	Pressing
WG-7305	Laundry Machine Operating	WG-7307	Dry Cleaning

WG-7400 Food Preparation & Servicing Family

This job family includes occupations involved in the preparation and serving of food.

WG-7402	Baking	WG-7407	Meatcutting
WG-7404	Cooking	WG-7408	Food Service Working
WG-7405	Bartending	WG-7420	Waiter

WG-7600 Personal Services Family

This job family includes occupations concerned with providing grooming, beauty, or other personal services to individuals, patrons, guests, passengers, entertainers, etc., or attending to their personal effects.

WG-7603	Barbering	WG-7641	Beautician
WG-7640	Bus Attending		

WG-8200 Fluid Systems Maintenance Family

Includes occupations involving repair, assembly, and testing of fluid systems and components of aircraft, aircraft engines, missiles, and mobile and support equipment. These fluid systems store, supply, distribute, and move gases or liquids to produce power, transmit force, and pressurize, cool, and condition cabins.

WG-8255	Pneudraulic Systems Mechanic	WG-8268	Aircraft Pneudraulic Systems Mechanic

WG-8600 Engine Overhaul Family

This job family includes occupations concerned primarily with the manufacture, repair, modification, and major overhaul of engines (except where covered by another job family) including the disassembly, reassembly, and test phases of engine overhaul programs.

WG-8602	Aircraft Engine Mechanic	WG-8675	Liquid Fuel Rocket Engine Mech.
WG-8610	Small Engine Mechanic		

WG-8800 Aircraft Overhaul Family

This job family includes occupations concerned primarily with the overhaul of aircraft, including the disassembly, reassembly, and test phases of aircraft overhaul programs.

WG-8810	Aircraft Propeller Mechanic	WG-8862	Aircraft Attending
WG-8840	Aircraft Mech. Parts Repairing	WG-8863	Aircraft Tire Mounting
WG-8852	Aircraft Mechanic	WG-8882	Airframe Test Operating

WG-9000 Film Processing Family

This job family includes occupations that involve processing film, for example, operating motion picture developers and printers; cleaning, repairing, matching, cutting, splicing, and assembling films; and mixing developing solutions. Does not include processing work that requires specialized subject-matter knowledge or artistic ability.

WG-9003	Film Assembling and Repairing	WG-9055	Photographic Solution Mixing
WG-9004	Motion Picture Mach. Operating		

Appendix E
Agency Skills Index

Individuals interested in government employment seldom know where to begin their job search. Larger agencies offer employment in a wide range of occupations and many smaller agencies use a diverse cross section of skills and trades.

This index captures 28 departments and agencies plus various independent government organizations. After locating the organizations that utilize your skills, education, and background, review the earlier chapters for specific guidance on how to complete your federal style resume and apply for jobs.

Skills and occupations are listed alphabetically and agencies or departments that utilize these skills follow each listing. An asterisk precedes the agency that is the largest employer for a skill. The total number of federal employees within each occupation is identified in parentheses following each entry.

This list is not complete. A broad cross-section of occupations is presented to steer you in the right direction. If a related occupation is identified it is highly probable that your skills will also be required by that agency. Agencies other than those identified for each skill or occupation may offer employment in small numbers for a specific occupation. Many agencies hire small numbers of employees within a series or group. These agencies are not on this list.

The purpose of this list is to steer you to the agencies that offer the greatest opportunities and chance of employment. However, don't overlook any agency in your job search, especially those within your commuting area. Identify local agencies in your phone book under "U.S. Government" in the blue pages of the regular phone directory and contact your local Federal Executive Board, see Appendix B, to request a list of agencies in your area.

Use this index to locate federal agencies and departments that are seeking your skills, academic major, or related field of study for entry level jobs.

323

ABBREVIATIONS LIST

ALL	All Agencies	FAA	Federal Aviation Administration
ATC	Architect of the Capitol	FBI	Federal Bureau of Investigation
CIA	Central Intelligence Agency	FCC	Federal Communications Commission
DOA	Dept. of Agriculture		
DOC	Dept. of Commerce	GSA	General Services Administration
DOD	Dept. of Defense	HHS	Health & Human Services
DOE	Dept. of Energy	HUD	Health & Urban Development
EDU	Dept. of Education	NAS	NASA
DHS	Dept. of Homeland Security	OPM	Office of Personnel Management
DOI	Dept. of the Interior	SBA	Small Business Administration
DOJ	Dept. of Justice	SMI	Smithsonian Institution
DOL	Dept. of Labor	TRE	Dept. of the Treasury
DOS	Dept. of State	USI	U.S. Information Agency
DOT	Dept. of Transportation	VA	Veterans Administration
EPA	Environmental Protection Agency		

*   The largest employing agency

( )   The number in parentheses represents the total number employed.

The total employment number may represent a WG Family or GS Group. For example, Family 5300 has 23 individual occupations listed in Appendix D. The total employment is distributed among all 23 occupations.[1]

SKILLS / OCCUPATIONS

ACCOUNTING / AUDITING ACCOUNTING TECHNICIAN - GROUP GS-500
* DOT, ALL (103,292)

ADMINISTRATIVE / CLERK TYPIST / CLERICAL / SECRETARY GROUP GS-300
* DOT, (278,191)

AGRICULTURAL GS-1145/46/47/48
*DOA (1,040)

ADVERTISING
DOL

AERONAUTICAL ENGINEERING SERIES GS-861
NASA, *DOD, DOT, DOC (4,184)

AIR CONDITIONING/HEATING REPAIR FAMILY WG-5300

TRE, *DOD, DOA, DOJ, DOI, DOC, HHS, DOT, ATC, GSA, DHS, SMI, VA (9,338)

AIR TRAFFIC CONTOLLERS GS-2152
*DOT-FAA, DOD (20,594)

AIRCRAFT OPERATIONS (PILOTS) GS-2181 INCLUDES COPILOTS
*DOD, DOT-FAA, DHS, DOJ, DOI, DOA, DOE, NASA (2,218)

AIRCRAFT OVERHAUL FAMILY WG-8800
*DOD, NASA, DOJ, DOI, DOA, DHS (13,475)

---

[1] Excerpted from *Occupations of Federal White-Color & Blue-Collar Workers* & OPM's September 2006 Employment Cubes on http://www.opm.gov.

AMMUNITION, EXPLOSIVES WORK FAMILY WG-6600
*DOD, GSA, DOJ, DHS (3,057)

AMERICAN HISTORY
National Archives & Records Administration

ANIMAL SCIENCE GS-487/700
DOA (103)

ARCHEOLOGY GS-193
*DOA, DOD (1,112)

ARCHITECTURE ENGINEERING GS-808
*DOD, DOJ, DOI, DOA, HHS, HUD, DOT, DOE, GSA, TVA, DHS, VA (1,351)

ART SPECIALIST GS-1056
*DOD, DHS, HHS (32)

ASTRONOMY & SPACE SCIENCE GS-1330 *NASA, DOD (105)

AUDITING GS-0511
*DOD, ALL AGENCIES (9,820)

AUTOMOTIVE MECHANIC WG-5823
*DOD, ALL (2,688)

BAKING WG-7402
*DOD, DOI (60)

BANKING
DOA, Farm Credit Administration
DOT, Office of the Comptroller
Federal Reserve

BARBERING WG-7603
*VA, DOD (45)

BIOLOGICAL SCIENCES GS-400 GROUP
*DOA, DOI, DOD, HHS, DOC, EPA, NASA, VA, DHS (68,990)

BOILERMAKER WG-3808
*DOD (155)

BORDER PATROL AGENT GS-1896
*DHS, (12,278)

BOTANY
*DOA, DOD, DOI (416)

BUDGET CLERICAL & ASSISTANCE GS-561 *DOD, ALL (2,195)

BUILDING MANAGEMENT GS-1176
*GSA, DOD, DOJ, DOC, HHS, DOL (336)

BUSINESS & INDUSTRY GROUP GS-1100 *DOD, ALL (78,284)

CARPENTRY WG-4607
*DOD, ALL BUT DOS & DOL (1,429)

CEMENT FINISHING WG-3602
*DOD, DOI (43)

CEMETERY CARETAKING WG-4754
*VA, DOD (612)

CHEMICAL ENGINEERING GS-893
*DOD, DOI, DOA, DOC, DHS, DOJ, DOI, NASA (945)

CIVIL ENGINEERING GS-810
*DOD. MOST AGENCIES (10,494)

CLERK TYPIST GS-322
ALL (390)

CLERK-STENOGRAPHER & REPORTER GS-312 *DOD (19)

CLINICAL PSYCHOLOGY
DOJ - Bureau of Prisons

COMPUTER GROUP GS-332/5 and GS-2210 ALL (64,505)

CONTRACTING GS-1102
*DOD, ALL (25,069)

COOK WG-7404
*DOD, DOJ, DOI, DOA, HHS, VA (4,110)

COPYRIGHT GROUP GS-1200
*DOC, DOA, DHS, DOD, DOJ, DOI, DOE, NASA (5,750)

CORRECTIONS OFFICER GS-007
*DOJ, DOI (16,273)

CRIMINAL INVESTIGATION SERIES GS-1811 *DOJ, ALL (39,821)

CRYPTANALYSIS SERIES GS-1541
DOJ (20)

CUSTODIAL WORKING WG-3566
*VA, ALL (10,649)

DECKHAND WG-5788
*DOD, DOJ, (218)

DENTAL SERIES GS 680/1/2/3
*DOD, HHS, VA (5,536)

DIETITIAN & NUTRITION GS-630
*VA, HHS, DOD, DOA, DOJ, DHS (1,803)

DISPATCHING GS-2151
*DOD, DOI, DOA, VA, GSA (777)

EARTH SCIENCE
DOD - Defense Intelligence Agency, Defense
Mapping Agency

ECOLOGY GS-408
*DOI, DOA, DOD, DOC, DOE, EPA (1,092)

ECONOMICS GS-110/119
*DOL, ALL AGENCIES (4,150)

EDUCATION/TRAINING GS-1700
*DOD, ALL AGENCIES (39,984)

ELECTRICAL ENGINEERING GS-850
*DOD, ALL BUT HUD, OPM, USI & SBA
(3,383)

ELECTRICIAN WG-2805
*DOD, ALL BUT DOE, DHS (4,180)

**ELECTRONIC EQUIPMENT
INSTALLATION & MAINTENANCE
FAMILY WG-2600** *DOD, DOT, HHS, DOI,
DOE, DOA, DOC, TVA (12,821)

ELECTRONICS TECHNICIAN GS-856
*DOD, DOT-FAA, DOS, DOT, DOJ, DOI, DOA,
DOC, HHS, DOE, EPA, GSA, USI, NASA, VA
(8,274)

ELEVATOR MECHANIC WG-5313
*Architect of the capitol, DOD,
HHS, VA, DOC, DOJ, DOI, DOT, VA (51)

ENGINE OVERHAUL FAMILY WG-8600
*DOD, DOI, DHS, VA (3,484)

ENGINEERING PSYCHOLOGY
Consumer Product Safety Commission

ENGLISH
Federal Trade Commission
*DOL, DOD, DOT, USI

ENTOMOLOGY GS-414
*DOA, DOD, HHS, EPA, DOI (599)

ENVIRONMENTAL ENGINEERING GS-819
*DOD, TVA, DOE, HHS, DHS, DOT, DOI, DOJ,
DOA (2,692)

**EQUAL EMPLOYMENT OPPORTUNITY
GS-0260** *DOD, ALL AGENCIES (2,298)

EQUIPMENT OPERATOR GS-350
*DOD, MOST AGENCIES (493)

EXPLOSIVES OPERATING WG-6502
DOD, DOA (819)

FARMING WG-5002
*DOA, DOJ, DOI (31)

FACILITY MANAGEMENT GS-1640
*DOD, TVA, DOJ, DOI, DOC, NASA, HH, DHS
(1,592)

FINANCIAL ADMINISTRATION GS-501
*DOD, ALL AGENCIES (13,810)

FINGERPRINT IDENTIFICATION GS-072
*DOJ, DHS, DOD (434)

FIRE PROTECTION GS-081
*DOD, VA, DOE, NASA, GSA, HHS, DOS,
DOT, DHS, DOC (9,121)

FISH BIOLOGY GS-0482
*DOI, DOC, DOA, DOD, DOE (2,466)

FOOD INSPECTION GS-1863
*DOA (3,929)

FOOD TECHNOLOGY GS-1382
*DOA, DOC, HHS, DOD (158)

FOREIGN AFFAIRS GS-130
*DOS, DHS, DOS, DOE, DOD, DOC (3,823)

FORK LIFT OPERATOR WG-5704
*DOD, DOC, GSA,DOT, VA (325)

FORESTRY GS-460
*DOA, DOD, TRE, TVA (2,841)

FUEL DISTRIBUTION WG-5413
*DOD, DOI (895)

GENERAL ADMINISTRATION, CLERICAL, & OFFICE SERVICES GS-300 ALL (286,894)

GARDENING WG-5003
*VA, DOD, DOJ, DOI, DHS, DOA, DOC, HHS, DOT, GSA, VA (543)

GENERAL MAINTENANCE & OPERATION WG-4700 *DOD, ALL (15,678)

GENETICS GS-440
DOA, HHS, DOI, DOC (458)

GEOCHEMICAL ENGINEERING
Nuclear Regulatory Commission

GEODETIC TECHNICIAN GS-1374
*DOC, DOD (44)

GEOGRAPHY GS-150
*DOI, DOC, DOD, DOA, DOE, DOT (635)

GEOLOGY GS-1350
*DOI, DOD, DOT, DOA, EPA, DOE, DOL, TVA (1,518)

GUARD GS-085
*DOD, TRE, DOJ, DOI, DOC, HHS, DOT, TVA, VA, GSA, USI (3,363)

GUIDE GS-090
*DOI, DOD, DOA (857)

HEALTH GROUP GS-600
*VA, HHS, DOT, DOJ, DOA, DOS, NASA, DOD (189,526)

HISTORY GS-170
*DOD, DOJ, DOI, DOA, DOT, TRE (714)

HORTICULTURE GS-437
*DOA, DOI, DOD, VA (100)

HOUSING MANAGEMENT GS-1173
*DOD, DOI, HHS, DHS, HUD, VA (1,630)

HUMAN RESOURCE MANAGEMENT GS-0201 *DOD, ALL AGENCIES (20,586)

HYDROLOGY GS-1315
*DOI, DOD, EPA, DOA, DOC, DHS (2,451)

ILLUSTRATING GS-1020
*DOD, DOI, DOJ, DOA, DOC, VA, DOT, DOE (283)

IMPORT SPECIALIST GS-1889
* DHS (990)

INDUSTRIAL EQUIPMENT MECHANIC WG-5352
*DOD, TRE, DOI, DOA, VA, HHS, TRE, DOT, GSA (1,172)

INDUSTRIAL HYGIENE GS-690
*DOD, DOL, DHS, DOI, DOA, HHS, DOE, EPA, GSA, TVA, VA (1,370)

INSURANCE EXAMINING GS-1163
*DHS, DOD, DOT, DOE (36)

INTELLIGENCE GS-132
*DOD, DHS, DOS, TRE, DOJ, DOI, DOC, DOT, DOE (4,732)

INTERNAL REVENUE AGENT GS-512
TRE (13, 581)

INTERNATIONAL RELATIONS GS-131
*DOD, DOT, DOE, DOS, DOA, DOC (221)

INVENTORY MANAGEMENT GS-2010
*DOD, ALL (4,895)

INVESTIGATION GROUP GS-1800
*DHS, ALL AGENCIES (162,158)

LABORING WG-3502
*DOD, ALL (3,632)

LANDSCAPE ARCHITECTURE GS-807
*DOA, DOI, DOD, VA, TVA (454)

LAND SURVEYING GS-1373
*DOI, DOD, DOA, DOE (409)

LANGUAGE SPECIALIST GS-1040
*DOJ, DOD, DOC, DOS, TRV, HHS, USI, NASA (917)

LAUNDRY WORK WG-7300
*VA, DOD, DOJ, DOI, DOS, HHS (1,221)

LEGAL GS-900
*TRE, ALL (59,622)

LIBRARIAN GS-1410
*DOD, ALL (1,226)

LITERATURE
DOL

LOAN SPECIALIST GS-1165
*DOA, HUD, DOI, DOA, DOC, VA, SBA (4,646)

LOCK AND DAM REPAIR WG-5318
*DOD, DOI, DOT (427)

LOCKSMITHING WG-4804
*DOD, VA, DOI, DOC, DOJ, HHS (258)

LOGISTICS MANAGEMENT GS-346
*DOD, ALL AGENCIES (3,933)

MACHINE TOOL WORK FAMILY WG-3400
*DOD, ALL BUT DOL & DOS (4,722)

MAIL & FILE GS-305
*TRE, ALL (6211)

MAINTENANCE MECHANIC WG-4749
*DOD, ALL AGENCIES (10,207)

MANUAL ARTS THERAPIST GS-637
VA (32)

MARINE CARGO GS-2161
DOD (71)

MARKETING
DOC, DOD, TRE

MATERIALS ENGINEERING GS-806
*DOD, NASA, DOI, DOA, DOC, TRE, TVA,
GSA, DOE, DHS (850)

MASONRY WG-3603
*DOD, VA, NASA, GSA, DOT, HHS, DHS, DOJ,
DOI, DOE (336)

MATERIALS HANDLING WG-6907
*DOD, ALL AGENCIES (8,479)

MATHEMATICS GROUP GS-1500
*DOD, ALL (15,404)

MEATCUTTING WG-7407
*DOD, DOA (1,254)

MEDICAL GROUP GS-600
*VA, ALL (189,526)

**MEDICAL EQUIPMENT REPAIR
WG-4805** *VA, HHS, DHS, DOD, DOJ (175)

MEDICAL OFFICER GS-0602
*VA, MOST AGENCIES (23,691)

MEDICAL TECHNICIAN GS-0645
*VA, DOD, HHS, DHS (2,050)

MESSENGER GS-302
*HHS, DOD, DHS, VA, TVA (22)

METAL PROCESSING FAMILY WG-3700
*DOD, DOA, DOJ, DHS, DOI, DOT, VA (4,360)

METALLURGY GS-1321
*DOD, TRE, DOI, DOC, TVA, DOE (71)

MICROBIOLOGY GS-403
*HHS, VA, DOD, EPA, DOI, DOA, DOC DOJ,
DHS, DOJ, DOE (2,290)

MINE SAFETY & HEALTH GS-1822
*DOL (1,218)

MOBILE EQUIP. SERVICING WG-5806
*DOD, DOJ, DOI, DOA, GSA, VA, TVA, DOE,
DHS (379)

**MOTION PICTURE, RADIO, TV WORK
WG-3900** *DOD, DOI, HHS (41)

MOTOR VEHICLE OPERATING WG-5703
*DOD, ALL 5,740)

MUNITIONS WORK WG-6500
*DOD, DOA (1,831)

MUSEUM CURATOR GS-1015
*DOI, DOD, Smithsonian, DHS, HHS, DOT,
DOC, DOA (319)

MUSEUM SPECIALIST GS-1016
*DOD, DOI TRE, DOS, DOC, DOJ, HHS, DHS,
Smithsonian (383)

MUSIC SPECIALIST GS-1051
*DOD, DOT (13)

NAVAL ARCHITECTURE GS-871
*DOD, DOC, DOT, DHS (749)

NUCLEAR ENGINEERING GS-840
*DOD, TVA, DOE, DOC, DOI, DOS (2,014)

NUTRITION
DOA, VA

NURSE GS-610
*VA, HHS, DOD, TRE, DOS, DOJ, DOI, DOC,
DOA, DOT, DOL, DHS, NASA (51,714)

OCCUPATIONAL THERAPIST GS-631
*VA, HHS, DOD, DOI (849)

OFFSET PHOTOGRAPHY WG-4414
*DOJ, DOD, DOI, DOT (19)

OPTOMETRIST GS-662
*VA, DOD, DOT (681)

OUTDOOR RECREATION PLANNING
GS-023 *DOI, DOA, DOD (606)

PACKAGING GS-2032
*DOD, DOS, DOT (167)

PAINTING & PAPERHANGING GROUP
WG-4100 *DOD, ALL (4,147)

PACKING & PROCESSING GROUP WG-
7000 *DOD, DHS, DOJ, DOC, DOT, HHS, GSA,
VA (1,238)

PARALEGAL SPECIALIST GS-950
*DOJ, ALL (4,225)

PARK RANGER GS-025
*DOI, DOD (6009)

PATENT ADMINISTRATION GS-1220
*DOC (138)

PATHOLOGY TECHNICIAN GS-646
*VA, HHS, DOD (443)

PERSONNEL MANAGEMENT GROUP
GS-200 *DOD, ALL (37,309)

PEST CONTROL WG-5026
*DOD, VA, DOA, DOI, GSA (279)

PHARMACOLOGY GS-0405
*HHS, DOD, DOA, DOJ, VA (430)

PHOTOGRAPHY GS-1060
*DOD, ALL (627)

PHYSICAL SCIENCE GROUP GS-1300
*DOD, ALL but DOE, OPM USI (28,001)

PHYSICS GS-1310
*DOD, HHS, DOE, DOC VA, (2,302)

PIPEFITTING WG-4204
*DOD, DOJ, HHS, DHS, VA, DOT (2,633)

PLUMBING WG-4206
*DOD, MOST AGENCIES (904)

POLICE GS-083
*DOD, DOC, DHS, DOT, DOJ, VA, TRE, DOI,
HHS, GSA (12,291)

PROCUREMENT GS-1106
*DOD, ALL (1,935)

PSYCHOLOGY AIDE & TECHNICIAN
GS-181 *VA, DOD, HHS, DOT (596)

PSYCHOLOGY GS-180
*VA, ALL (4,382)

PUBLIC AFFAIRS GS-1035
*DOD, ALL (4,101)

PURCHASING GS-1105
*DOD, ALL (2,905)

QUALITY ASSURANCE, INSPECTION,
& GRADING GROUP GS-1900
*DOD (11,743)

RAILROAD SAFETY GS-2121
*DOT (466)

RAILROAD REPAIRING WG-3546
*DOD, DOI (45)

RECREATION AIDE & ASSISTANT GS-189
*DOD, DOI, DOA, VA, (1,543)

REHABILITATION THERAPY ASSISTANT
GS-636 *VA, HHS, DOD (752)

RESPIRATORY THERAPIST GS-651
*DOD, VA, HHS, DHS, DOJ (512)

ROOFING WG-3606
*DOD (59)

SAFETY ENGINEERING GS-803
*DOD, DOI, VA, TVA, DOL, HHS, DOT, DOE,
DOC, GSA, NASA (465)

SALES STORE CLERICAL GS-2091
*DOD, VA (5,010)

SECURITY GUARD GS-085
*DOD, MOST AGENCIES (3,636)

SEWAGE DISPOSAL PLANT OPERATION WG-5408 *DOD, DOJ, DOA, VA, DOI (317)

SHEETMETAL MECHANIC WG-3806 *DOD, DOA, DOJ, HHS, DHS, VA DOE, TRE (6,795)

SHIPWRIGHT WG-5220 *DOD (853)

SIGN PAINTING WG-4104 *DOD, DOI, VA (114)

SMALL ARMS REPAIR WG-6610 *DOD, DOJ, GSA (478)

SMALL ENGINE MECHANIC WG-8610 *DOD, DOI, (68)

SOCIAL SERVICES GS-187 *DOD, VA, DOI, HHS, DHS, DOA (647)

SOCIAL WORK GS-185 *VA, DOD, HHS, DOJ, DOI, DOT, DHS (6,116)

SOIL CONSERVATION GS-457 *DOA, DOD, DOI, DOE (4,517)

SPEECH PATHOLOGY & AUDIOLOGY GS-665 *VA, HHS, DOD, DOI (1,257)

SPORTS SPECIALIST GS-030 *DOD, DOJ, DHS, DOI, VA (492)

STATISTICIAN GS-1530 *DOC, ALL (2,915)

SUPPLY GROUP GS-2000 *DOD, ALL (30,494)

SURVEYING TECHNICIAN GS-817 *DOI, DOD, DOA, DOC (376)

TAX EXAMINING GS-592 TRE (11,677)

TECHNICAL WRITING & EDITING GS-1083 *DOD, ALL (969)

TELEPHONE MECHANIC WG-2502 *DOD, VA (414)

TELEPHONE OPERATING GS-382 *VA, DOD, DOJ, DOI, DOA, DOC, DOL, HHS, GSA (782)

TOOLMAKING WG-3416 *DOD, DOJ, DOE, NASA (464)

TOXICOLOGY GS-0415 *HHS, DOD, DOA, DOI, VA, DOC, DOE (203)

TRANSPORTATION GROUP GS-2100 *DOT, ALL (42,248)

TRANSPORTATION MOBILE EQUIPMENT MAINTENANCE FAMILY WG-5800 *DOD, ALL EXCEPT DOS & DOL (16,581)

UNITED STATES MARSHAL GS-082 DOJ (839)

UTILITY SYSTEMS REPAIR WG-4742 *DOD, MOST AGENCIES (1,729)

VAETERINARY SCIENCE GS-700 *DOA, HHS, DHS, VA (2,768

VOCATIONAL REHABILITATION GS-1715 *VA, TVA, DOL, DOI, DOJ (530)

WELDING GS-3703 *DOD, DOA, DOJ, DOE, DOI, DHS, VA, (2,444)

WILDLIFE BIOLOGY GS-0486 *DOA, DOI, DOD, DOE (2,471)

WILDLIFE MANAGEMENT GS-485 DOI (669)

WOOD WORK GROUP WG-4600 *DOD, MOST AGENCIES (2,411)

WRITING GS-1082 *DOD, ALL (1,173)

ZOOLOGY GS-410 *DOI, DOD, DOA, DOC, HHS (58)

Index

THE BOOK OF U.S. GOVERNMENT JOBS: *Where They Are, What's Available, and How to Get One*, *10th Edition*, by Dennis V. Damp.
$22.95, 2008, 352 pages, paperback, ISBN: 978-0-943641-26-3

There are over 2,700,000 federal civilian employees, of whom half are now eligible for regular or early retirement. Over a million jobs must be filled as baby boomers retire. The average annual federal worker's compensation, pay plus benefits, was **$106,871** compared to **$53,288** in 2005 for the private sector. Job seekers will learn about student loan payoff programs, and relocation and cash incentives for hard to fill positions, and the benefits package is exceptional. This **ALL NEW** and expanded 10th edition helps readers write dynamic federal résumés, prepare for tests, and tells about professional and entry level jobs, student hiring, overseas jobs, postal jobs, interviewing techniques, and over 1,000 job resources.

"An updated, comprehensive how-to-guide. Written in a clear, readable style, this book is Recommended."
— LIBRARY JOURNAL

POST OFFICE JOBS: *How to Get a Job With the U.S. Postal Service*
by Dennis V. Damp. **$19.95, 256 pages**, ISBN: 0-943641-22-5, *Fourth Edition*

Anyone interested in a challenging career, with job security and excellent pay, needs to explore the lucrative Postal Service job market. The average annual salary, including benefits, overtime and premiums, exceeds $62,348 a year. There are 757,000 workers in 300 job categories at 38,000 post offices, branches, and stations throughout the United States so opportunities are abundant. The new 4th Edition features the most up-to-date information available for those interested in working for the Postal Service, including a comprehensive study guide for the new **473** and **473-C Postal Exams.** It covers ALL occupations including professional, administrative, mail carrier, maintenance, and clerical.

"This popular book has been expanded and updated...Over a third of this book is devoted to testing, with realistic sample exams as well as tips and answer keys. Recommended."
— LIBRARY JOURNAL

HEALTH CARE JOB EXPLOSION!: *High Growth Health Care Careers and Job Locator*, *Fourth Edition*, 2006, by Dennis V. Damp. **$19.95, 320 pages**, ISBN: 0-943641-25-X

The health services job market is **EXPLODING!** Employment in health care is projected to increase 30% through 2014. Thirteen of the 20 fastest-growing occupations are concentrated in health services, and the Bureau of Labor Statistics projects the healthcare field will generate **4,700,000 JOB OPENINGS** through 2014. Nineteen percent of all job growth to 2014 will be in health care services. Explore high growth health care occupations with this book's 1,400-plus resources and find job vacancies and networking contacts.

"...This book will be a boon to those seeking jobs. Well rounded... Recommended for general collections; this book will be in demand."
— LIBRARY JOURNAL

FEDERAL RÉSUMÉ GUIDEBOOK: *Strategies for Writing a Winning Federal Electronic Résumé, KSAs, and Essays,* **Fourth Edition**, 2007, by Kathryn Kraemer Troutman, **$21.95**

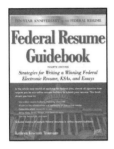

You'll find all of the latest information, résumé and KSA examples, and job hunting tips in this comprehensive guide. Most agencies require job applicants to use online résumé builders and you have to know how to write and format your résumés to get the highest rating possible. Kathryn takes job hunters through the entire process so that you too can land a high paying government job. This updated edition includes 30 sample online formatted résumés, tips for completing KSAs, and detailed information on security clearance requirements.

MILITARY TO FEDERAL CAREER GUIDE: *Ten Steps to Transforming Your Military Experience into a Competitive Federal Résumé,* by Kathryn Kraemer Troutman, 237 pages, **$38.95** *with CD*

A comprehensive guide to federal jobs and the Military federal résumé for enlisted personnel and officers. This book shows you where you can work, how to find and apply for jobs, how much you can earn and includes interview preparation. The CD-ROM includes 150 pages of ready-to-use sample résumé templates. Each of the 10 steps is fully covered in a separate chapter that includes networking, federal hiring benefits for veterans, writing your basic military federal résumé, understanding vacancy announcements, and much more. A valuable and indispensable guide for all military personnel.

TAKE CHARGE OF YOUR FEDERAL CAREER: *A Practical, Action-Oriented Career Management Workbook for Federal Employees,* by Dennis V. Damp, 202 pages, **$17.95**.

Do you dream of a better life, more pay, a challenging position? You can turn your dreams into reality and be one of the hundreds of thousands of federal employees each year who are promoted or obtain higher-level jobs. Packed with proven tips and valuable assessment and evaluation tools, this unique workbook provides federal workers with the individualized know-how and guidance they need to identify, obtain, and successfully demonstrate the skills and experience required to qualify for federal jobs.

QUICK & EASY Version 6.1 FEDERAL JOBS KIT, Software
WINDOWS 95, 98, 2000, NT, ME, XP & VISTA COMPATIBLE

$49.95   **(Personal Version)** Unlimited applications & résumés for 1 person
$59.95   **(Family Version)** Unlimited applications & résumés for 2 people
$129.95   **(Office Pack)** Unlimited applications & résumés for 8 people
$499.95   **(Professional Version)** Unlimited applications/résumés for 1 computer

Use DataTech's Quick & Easy Federal Jobs Kit to get the federal job you want. The complete software package for getting a federal job and completing your application.
Contains everything you need including the SF 171, OF 612, OF-306, KSAOs, and eight Federal résumé formats including RESUMIX. Also includes many forms including the SF-15 Veterans' Preference, IRS-9686, VA 10-2850, AID 1420-17, OPM 1170/17, SSF-181, DA 3433, AD 770 USDA and the SF-172.

ORDER FORM (Please Print)

❑ ____ copies of *The Book of U.S. Government Jobs* - 10th ed at **$22.95** each.   _____
❑ ____ copies of *Post Office Jobs* - 4th ed. at **$19.95** each.   _____
❑ ____ copies of *Health Care Job Explosion* - 4th ed at **$19.95** each.   _____
❑ ____ copies of *Federal Resume Guide Book* - 4th ed. **$21.95** each.   _____
❑ ____ copies of Military to Federal Career Guide at **$38.95** each.   _____
❑ ____ copies of *Take Charge of Your Federal Career* at **$17.95** each.   _____
❑ ____ *Quick & Easy* Federal Jobs Kit Software:
   Personal ❑ $49.95, Family ❑ $59.95 ❑ Office $129.95, ❑ Pro $499.95   _____

❑ Add shipping, $4.95 for first book + $1.75 x __ (# of additional books ordered)   _____
   Note: Quick & Easy Software shipping is $5.95 for Priority mail.
❑ Pennsylvania residents add 7% sales tax.   _____
                                                                TOTAL: _____

Name: _____

Title: _____

Address: _____

Company Name: _____

City: _____ State: _____ ZIP: _____

Phone: _____ Ext: _____

E-mail Address: _____

Make checks payable to: **Bookhaven Press LLC**

1-800-782-7424 (Credit Card Phone Orders Only)

Mail Orders to:
Bookhaven Press LLC
249 Field Club Circle
McKees Rocks, PA 15136-1034
412-494-6926, FAX: 412-494-5749

(Purchase Orders Accepted from Agencies or Institutions)
http://bookhavenpress.com — E-mail: bookhaven@aol.com